A·N·N·U·A·L E·D·I·T·I·O·N·S

Educating Exceptional Children

00/01

Twelfth Edition

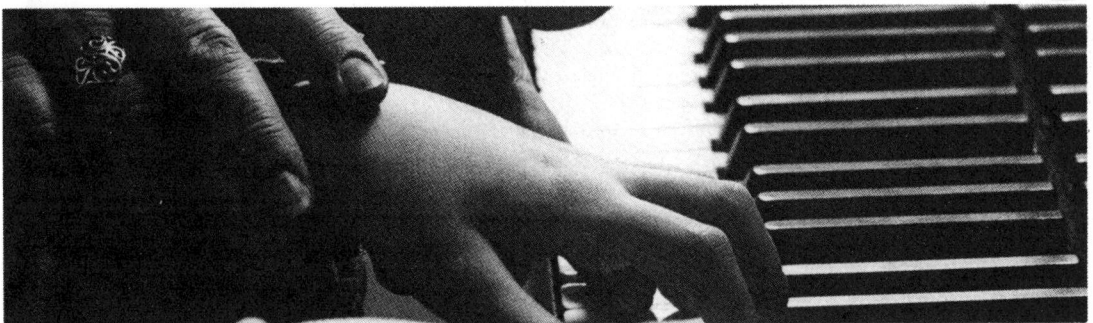

EDITOR

Karen L. Freiberg
University of Maryland, Baltimore County

Dr. Karen Freiberg has an interdisciplinary educational and employment background in nursing, education, and developmental psychology. She received her B.S. from the State University of New York at Plattsburgh, her M.S. from Cornell University, and her Ph.D. from Syracuse University. She has worked as a school nurse, a pediatric nurse, a public health nurse for the Navajo Indians, an associate project director for a child development clinic, a researcher in several areas of child development, and a university professor. Dr. Freiberg is the author of an award-winning textbook, *Human Development: A Life-Span Approach*, which is now in its fourth edition. She is currently on the faculty at the University of Maryland, Baltimore County.

CALLAHAN LIBRARY
ST. JOSEPH'S COLLEGE
25 Audubon Avenue
Patchogue, NY 11772-2399

Dushkin/McGraw-Hill
Sluice Dock, Guilford, Connecticut 06437

Visit us on the Internet
http://www.dushkin.com/annualeditions/

Credits

1. Inclusive Education
Unit photo—courtesy Rio Grande, Colo., City High School.
2. Early Childhood
Unit photo—© 1999 by PhotoDisc, Inc.
3. Learning Disabilities
Unit photo—Therese Frare/New York Times Pictures.
4. Speech and Language Impairments
Unit photo—United Nations photo by Marta Pinter.
5. Developmental Disabilities and Traumatic Brain Injuries
Unit photo—United Nations photo by O. Monsen.
6. Emotional and Behavioral Disorders
Unit photo—courtesy of EPA Documerica.
7. Vision and Hearing Impairments
Unit photo—United Nations photo by L. Solmssen.
8. Multiple Disabilities
Unit photo—United Nations photo by Jan Corash.
9. Orthopedic and Health Impairments
Unit photo—United Nations photo by W. A. Graham.
10. Giftedness
Unit photo—Dushkin/McGraw-Hill photo by Pamela Carley.
11. Transition
Unit photo—United Nations photo by John Isaac.

Copyright

Cataloging in Publication Data
Main entry under title: Annual Editions: Educating exceptional children. 2000/2001.
    1. Exceptional children—Education—United States—Periodicals. 2. Educational innovations—United States—Periodicals. I. Freiberg, Karen, comp. II. Title: Educating exceptional children.
ISBN 0-07-236511-0   371.9'05   76-644171   ISSN 0198-7518

© 2000 by Dushkin/McGraw-Hill, Guilford, CT 06437, A Division of The McGraw-Hill Companies.

Copyright law prohibits the reproduction, storage, or transmission in any form by any means of any portion of this publication without the express written permission of Dushkin/McGraw-Hill, and of the copyright holder (if different) of the part of the publication to be reproduced. The Guidelines for Classroom Copying endorsed by Congress explicitly state that unauthorized copying may not be used to create, to replace, or to substitute for anthologies, compilations, or collective works.

Annual Editions® is a Registered Trademark of Dushkin/McGraw-Hill, A Division of The McGraw-Hill Companies.

Twelfth Edition

Cover image © 2000 PhotoDisc, Inc.

Printed in the United States of America   1234567890BAHBAH543210   Printed on Recycled Paper

Editors/Advisory Board

Members of the Advisory Board are instrumental in the final selection of articles for each edition of ANNUAL EDITIONS. Their review of articles for content, level, currentness, and appropriateness provides critical direction to the editor and staff. We think that you will find their careful consideration well reflected in this volume.

EDITOR

Karen L. Freiberg
University of Maryland
Baltimore County

ADVISORY BOARD

Elizabeth Begley
Ithaca College

Erin Brumbaugh
Marietta College

Lorna Catford
Sonoma State University

Jozi De Leon
New Mexico State University

Sheila Drake
Mid America Nazarene college

Colleen Finegan-Stoll
Wright State University

Mark B. Goor
George Mason University

Robin Herman
Central State University

Donna L. Jacobs
Essex Community College

Thomas J. Long
Catholic University of America

Roberta Lubinsky
Monroe Community College

Mack McCoulskey
Angelo State University

Sharon A. Merrill
Xavier University

Susan M. Munson
Duquesne University

Gael L. Ragle
Arizona State University
West Campus

Christina C. Ramirez-Smith
Christopher Newport University

Marcia J. Reinholtz
Greensboro College

Louise Sherman
University of Colorado

Joyce M. Smith
SUNY College
Oswego

Faith M. Stayer
Augusta State University

Linda A. Svobodny
Moorhead State University

Ruth Thompson
Edinboro University

Kathleen S. Whittier
SUNY at Plattsburgh

Steve L. Williams
California State University
Hayward

Staff

EDITORIAL STAFF

Ian A. Nielsen, Publisher
Roberta Monaco, Senior Developmental Editor
Dorothy Fink, Associate Developmental Editor
Addie Raucci, Senior Administrative Editor
Cheryl Greenleaf, Permissions Editor
Joseph Offredi, Permissions/Editorial Assistant
Diane Barker, Proofreader
Lisa Holmes-Doebrick, Program Coordinator

PRODUCTION STAFF

Brenda S. Filley, Production Manager
Charles Vitelli, Designer
Lara M. Johnson, Design/Advertising Coordinator
Laura Levine, Graphics
Mike Campbell, Graphics
Tom Goddard, Graphics
Eldis Lima, Graphics
Juliana Arbo, Typesetting Supervisor
Marie Lazauskas, Typesetter
Kathleen D'Amico, Typesetter
Larry Killian, Copier Coordinator

To the Reader

In publishing ANNUAL EDITIONS we recognize the enormous role played by the magazines, newspapers, and journals of the public press in providing current, first-rate educational information in a broad spectrum of interest areas. Many of these articles are appropriate for students, researchers, and professionals seeking accurate, current material to help bridge the gap between principles and theories and the real world. These articles, however, become more useful for study when those of lasting value are carefully collected, organized, indexed, and reproduced in a low-cost format, which provides easy and permanent access when the material is needed. That is the role played by ANNUAL EDITIONS.

New to ANNUAL EDITIONS is the inclusion of related World Wide Web sites. These sites have been selected by our editorial staff to represent some of the best resources found on the World Wide Web today. Through our carefully developed topic guide, we have linked these Web resources to the articles covered in this ANNUAL EDITIONS reader. We think that you will find this volume useful, and we hope that you will take a moment to visit us on the Web at *http://www.dushkin.com* to tell us what you think.

The Education for All Handicapped Children Act of 1975 revolutionized educational practices in the United States. It required that all children with disabilities receive free and appropriate public school education in the least restrictive environment with fair assessment procedures and clear management plans. In 1997 it was reauthorized by Congress as the Individuals with Disabilities Education Act (IDEA). IDEA retained the major provisions of the earlier act but greatly strengthened the regular education initiative. The reauthorized law threatened to withhold federal funding from states that did not support inclusive education in regular education classes. Most special education classes have been discontinued in compliance with IDEA's call for the "least restrictive environment."

Assessment of individuals with disabilities must begin as soon as a disability is suspected and must be conducted fairly, without regard to race, sex, or socioeconomic status. Assessment, as mandated by IDEA, should also be conducted with standardized, objective procedures and instruments with clearly stated criteria for defining exceptional conditions. Assessments should be repeated at frequent intervals to keep all service providers apprised of the changing conditions of the disability over time.

This twelfth edition of *Annual Editions: Educating Exceptional Children 00/01* includes 11 articles that deal directly with the important topic of assessment of individuals with disabilities. The newer, stronger language of IDEA requires schools to work with parents as partners in the education of individuals with disabilities. The 1997 reauthorization expanded educational services to persons with special needs from time of diagnosis (birth, if applicable) through age 21. Educators, in collaboration with parents and other service providers, are required to provide individualized family service plans (IFSPs) to infants and young children who are at risk of developing disabilities, or who acquire disabilities before they enter public school. The IFSP describes how the young child and his or her family will be given special services prior to entrance into public school. Working with parents is vital to the success of special education. For this reason, one-quarter of all the articles in this edition deal with family involvement.

Every child with a disability who is enrolled in public school has an annually updated individualized education plan (IEP). This describes how the child will receive special services, and where, when, why, and what services will be provided. It is written in collaboration with parents and all applicable service providers. IDEA directs IEPs to be outcomes-oriented. IDEA also requires that older children and adolescents concurrently have an annually updated individualized transition plan (ITP). This describes what services will be provided to help the student move into higher education, the community, and/or the workforce, and to attain a more independent lifestyle.

Is the education of exceptional children best carried out in regular education classes? Proponents of inclusion cite benefits such as socialization of both the special needs children and their nondisabled peers. Tolerance and acceptance begin with exposure and are taught by egalitarian teachers who focus on positive interaction and differential abilities. Opponents of inclusive education cite lack of preparation of regular education teachers, crowded and ill-equipped classrooms, and the negative effects of competition. They fear that children with disabilities will be ridiculed and marginalized in integrated classes.

Annual Editions: Education Exceptional Children 00/01 includes articles explaining how the IDEA provisions are being implemented in all areas of special education. Selections have been made with an eye to conveying information, some personal experiences, and many practical suggestions for implementation.

To improve future editions of this anthology, please complete and return the postage-paid article rating form on the last page. Your suggestions are valued and appreciated.

Good luck in using this anthology to make your own and others' lives easier and more rewarding.

Karen Freiberg

Karen Freiberg, Ph.D.
Editor

Contents

To the Reader iv
Topic Guide 2
○ Selected World Wide Web Sites 4

Overview 6

1. **Inclusion of Children with Disabilities: Seeking the Appropriate Balance,** Martha M. McCarthy, *Educational Horizons,* Spring 1998. 8
   This article reviews recent **legal processes** involving **inclusive education.** The courts today are placing the burden on parents or schools to prove that a segregated placement might be better for an individual student. The regular education classroom is usually considered best because of the benefits of role models, socialization, and language stimulation.

2. **The Parent Panel: Supporting Children with Special Needs,** Susanna V. Duckworth and Patricia H. Kostell, *Childhood Education,* Summer 1999. 12
   Legal processes mandate **family involvement** in the **inclusive education** of children with disabilities. This article suggests a parent panel to build better communication, help with **conflict resolution,** and increase educators' awareness of **cultural diversity** and different perspectives on child care.

3. **What Do I Do Now? A Teacher's Guide to Including Students with Disabilities,** Michael F. Giangreco, *Educational Leadership,* February 1996. 16
   Michael Giangreco puts forth 10 strategies to help teachers successfully integrate students with disabilities into **inclusive education** programs. Some suggestions pertain to **individualized education programs (IEPs).** Others discuss ways to help change the attitudes of students without disabilities toward their new peers.

4. **Four Inclusion Models That Work,** Dori Elliott and Merry McKenney, *Teaching Exceptional Children,* March/April 1998. 19
   The authors argue that 20 years of segregated instruction for students with special needs has not been superior to regular classrooms. They support **inclusive education** and make a strong case for **collaboration** between special education and regular education with consultation, team teaching, aide services, and limited pullouts.

5. **Promoting a Safe School Environment through a Schoolwide Wellness Program,** Patricia A. Gallagher and Linda S. Satter, *Focus on Exceptional Children,* October 1998. 23
   This article describes IMPACT, a **collaborative** program that teaches students with and without disabilies in **inclusive education** to recognize trouble and **resolve conflicts** quickly. It suggests methods of conflict **assessment,** problem-solving steps, and effective ways to involve **peers** in the mediation of disputes.

UNIT 1

Inclusive Education

Five articles present strategies for establishing positive interactions between students with and without special needs.

UNIT 2

Early Childhood

Four unit articles discuss the implementation of special services to preschoolers with disabilities.

Overview 34

6. **From Philosophy to Practice in Inclusive Early Childhood Programs,** Tom Udell, Joyce Peters, and Torry Piazza Templeman, *Teaching Exceptional Children*, January/February 1998. 36

   Developmentally appropriate **early childhood education** should be **inclusive education** with functional, hands-on goals, multidisciplinary **collaboration, family involvement,** monitoring and adjustment of services, and plans for **transition** to elementary school, according to the authors.

7. **Together Is Better: Specific Tips on How to Include Children with Various Types of Disabilities,** Jane Russell-Fox, *Young Children*, May 1997. 41

   A strong supporter of **inclusive education,** Jane Russell-Fox gives readers easy approaches to **early childhood** integration of children with recognized disabilities. Specific strategies are given for children with **hearing and visual impairments, learning and physical disabilities,** and **speech and language needs.**

8. **Wellness Programming for Preschoolers with Disabilities,** Carol Huettig and John O'Connor, *Teaching Exceptional Children*, January/February 1999. 44

   Early childhood special education, which helps preschoolers identify and understand human emotions, can prevent later **emotional and behavioral disorders.** Play between children with and without disabilities paves the way for **inclusive education.** Occupational and vocational play helps develop interests that may make the **transition** to eventual adult independence easier.

9. **Is Everyone Included? Using Children's Literature to Facilitate the Understanding of Disabilities,** Joan K. Blaska and Evelyn C. Lynch, *Young Children*, March 1998. 50

   This article discusses children's books that celebrate different abilities, **cultural diversity,** and **inclusion.** The authors contend that **early childhood** education programs are a most appropriate place to portray children from all walks of life in the most positive light to help build positive attitudes for future interactions.

UNIT 3

Learning Disabilities

The assessment and special needs of students with learning disabilities are addressed in this unit's three selections.

Overview 54

10. **Learning Disabilities,** G. Reid Lyon, *The Future of Children*, Spring 1996. 56

    Learning disabilities are defined and their **prevalence rates** discussed with emphases on **legal processes,** co-occurring disorders (attention deficit disorder, social maladjustment), and methods of **assessment.** In this essay, G. Reid Lyon suggests possible biological causative factors and includes a summary of treatment methods that work.

11. **Cognitive Credit Cards: Acquiring Learning Strategies,** Alan L. Edmunds, *Teaching Exceptional Children*, March/April 1999. 76

    A cognitive credit card (CCC) is a card-sized laminated set of cues for students with **learning disabilities** (LDs) that reminds them to think about their thinking. Well-designed CCCs can be used during tests without unfair advantage. Each student's uniqueness is **assessed** and the CCC addresses specific LDs. **Computers** can be used to create CCCs with ease.

12. **Dropout Prevention: A Case for Enhanced Early Literacy Efforts,** Louis G. Denti and Gilbert Guerin, *The Clearing House,* March/April 1999. — 81

The high drop-out rates for students with **learning disabilities** and **emotional behavioral disorders** can be reduced with earlier intervention. Better **assessment,** use of **computer reading games,** increased **family involvement,** sensitivity to **cultural diversity, peer tutoring,** and explicit instruction in **conflict resolution** should be basic elements of school programs.

Overview — 86

13. **Distinguishing Language Differences from Language Disorders in Linguistically and Culturally Diverse Students,** Celeste Roseberry-McKibbin, *Multicultural Education,* Summer 1995. — 88

In this essay, a diagnostic pie chart illustrates four groups of children with problems of **communication.** Language differences versus language disorders and normal learning ability versus learning disability are considered. Methods of **assessment** are enumerated. A consideration of **cultural diversity** can prevent false negative and false positive identifications.

14. **Language Interaction Techniques for Stimulating the Development of At Risk Children in Infant and Preschool Day Care,** William Fowler, *Early Child Development and Care,* Volume 3, 1995. — 92

William Fowler explains the principles of language stimulation in **early childhood** and discusses methods of helping at-risk children who have **communication disorders.** The personal experiences and successes of several at-risk children help illustrate the usefulness of Dr. Fowler's techniques in preschool programs.

15. **Family and Cultural Alert! Considerations in Assistive Technology Assessment,** Jack J. Hourcade, Howard P. Parette Jr., and Mary Blake Huer, *Teaching Exceptional Children,* September/October 1997. — 100

Individualized education plans (IEPs) for students with **speech and language impairments** must involve careful **assessment** of need, **family involvement, cultural sensitivity,** and **technological acceptability.** Refusals to use assistive devices result when **collaboration** with parents and cultural norms are ignored.

Overview — 104

16. **Collaborative Planning for Inclusion of a Student with Developmental Disabilities,** Jane E. Doelling, Suzanne Bryde, Judy Brunner, and Barbara Martin, *Middle School Journal,* January 1998. — 106

This article describes the **transition** into a middle school **inclusive classroom** of a student who has **mental retardation** and **language impairment. Collaboration, family involvement, individualized education programs,** writing, and **peer** networks were essential ingredients of success.

UNIT 4
Speech and Language Impairments

In this unit, three selections examine communication disorders and suggest ways in which students can develop their speech and language.

UNIT 5
Developmental Disabilities and Traumatic Brain Injuries

Four articles in this section discuss concerns and strategies for providing optimal educational programs for students with developmental disabilities, Down Syndrome, and traumatic brain injuries.

17. **Children with Down Syndrome: Implications for Adult-Child Interactions in Inclusive Settings,** Dolores J. Appl, *Childhood Education,* Fall 1998. 112

The ***developmental disability*** Down Syndrome (DS) affects each child who has DS differently. ***Individualized education plans (IEPs)*** need to be tailored to unique needs. This article reviews research on better ways to ***collaborate,*** get ***family involvement,*** and teach children with DS in ***inclusive educational*** settings.

18. **Getting the Student with Head Injuries Back in School: Strategies for the Classroom,** Mary Steensma, *Intervention in School and Clinic,* March 1992. 117

Students with ***traumatic brain injuries*** have difficulty reentering school. A majority are placed in education programs for ***mental retardation, physical impairments,*** or ***emotional disturbances.*** Mary Steensma argues that because their disabilities are acquired suddenly, their IEPs (individualized education programs) should address their special needs in ***transitional*** programs.

19. **Identifying Depression in Students with Mental Retardation,** Laura M. Stough and Lynn Baker, *Teaching Exceptional Children,* March/April 1999. 120

Students with ***developmental disabilities*** have a higher rate of depression and ***emotional disorders*** than students without disabilities. The ***assessment*** of their symptoms is difficult because of their co-occurring problems, and it must be performed frequently. ***Legal processes*** mandate psychological treatment when such problems are diagnosed.

UNIT 6

Emotional and Behavioral Disorders

Ways to teach emotionally and behaviorally disordered students are discussed in the unit's three articles.

Overview 124

20. **Teaching Students to Regulate Their Own Behavior,** Lewis R. Johnson and Christine E. Johnson, *Teaching Exceptional Children,* March/April 1999. 126

Students with ***emotional and behavioral disorders*** are frequently co-diagnosed with attention deficit hyperactive disorders. This article suggests ways for such students to practice ***self-assessment*** and self-regulation of their behaviors. Graphing and self-recording of behavior reduces teacher monitoring time and increases student's self-esteem.

21. **"Look! I'm on TV!" Using Videotaped Self-Modeling to Change Behavior,** Tom Buggey, *Teaching Exceptional Children,* March/April 1999. 130

Computers and videotape technology allow students with ***emotional and behavioral disorders*** to see themselves self-modeling appropriate behavior. It increases their motivation to behave correctly and enhances their self-esteem. Video self-modeling can be used in ***conflict resolution,*** and in ***transition*** programs to reinforce job and parenting skills.

22. **How to Defuse Defiance, Threats, Challenges, Confrontations . . . ,** Geoff Colvin, David Ainge, and Ron Nelson, *Teaching Exceptional Children,* July/August 1997. 134

The authors of this essay advise teachers in ***inclusive education*** classrooms how to manage the behavior of students who have ***emotional and behavioral disorders.*** Use of these ***defusing strategies*** can minimize confrontations and maximize learning opportunities.

| Overview | 138 |

23. **Schools for the Visually Disabled: Dinosaurs or Mainstays?** Michael J. Bina, *Educational Leadership*, March 1999. — 140

    Students with **visual impairments** and **multiple disabilities** plus low vision thrive in settings with more services to meet their special needs. **Legal processes** do not mandate **inclusive education** but, rather, the most appropriate education in the least restrictive environment. Special schools may be the most credible placements to meet the educational and real-world **transition** needs of such students.

24. **A Child with Severe Hearing Loss Joins Our Learning Community,** Mary Jane Blasi and Lori Priestley, *Young Children*, March 1998. — 143

    This story of a school child with both a **hearing** and **language impairment,** who was placed in an **inclusive** classroom, has much to teach about **family involvement, collaboration,** and the use of special **technology** such as a phonic ear and cued speech.

25. **Multimedia Stories for Deaf Children,** Jean F. Andrews and Donald L. Jordan, *Teaching Exceptional Children*, May/June 1998. — 149

    Multimedia **computers** make it much easier to teach children with **hearing** and/or **speech and langauge impairments,** as well as children from **diverse cultures** whose first language is not English. Print can be positively augmented with sound, graphics, animation, and movies.

UNIT 7

Vision and Hearing Impairments

Three selections discuss the special needs of visually and hearing impaired children from infancy through secondary school.

| Overview | 154 |

26. **Training Basic Teaching Skills to Paraeducators of Students with Severe Disabilities,** Marsha B. Parsons and Dennis H. Reid, *Teaching Exceptional Children*, March/April 1999. — 156

    Students with **multiple severe disabilities** often require a great deal of individual instruction. **Collaboration** between teachers and paraeducators in **inclusive education** settings can help meet their needs. This article describes a **one-day** teaching-skills training program (TSTP) to prepare teaching aides in appropriate strategies to use.

27. **The Unexpected Benefits of High School Peer Tutoring,** Amy Wildman Longwill and Harold L. Kleinert, *Teaching Exceptional Children*, March/April 1998. — 162

    Students with **multiple disabilities** need performance-based **assessment. The use of peer tutors** in **inclusive education** programs is especially beneficial in assisting with special areas of performance such as the development of career interests and making the **transition** into community living. Tutors receive benefits as well.

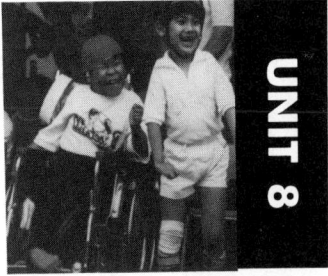

UNIT 8

Multiple Disabilities

The implications of educational programs for children with multiple impairments are examined in this unit's three articles.

28. **Perspectives on Technology in Special Education,** 168
A. Edward Blackhurst, *Teaching Exceptional Children,* May/June 1997.
Computers and technology are tools that can be used to assist in the education of students with ***multiple disabilities. Collaboration*** between teams of educators and/or other professionals can make technological assistance less complicated and more effective.

Overview 174

29. **"Can I Play Too?" Adapting Common Classroom Activities for Young Children with Limited Motor Abilities,** Kristyn Sheldon, *Early Childhood Education Journal,* Winter 1996. 176
Kristyn Sheldon offers suggestions for ***inclusive education*** of ***students with orthopedic impairments. Computers,*** dramatic play, art, sensory play, circle time, and other activities can be adapted to increase the participation of children with limited motor abilities.

30. **Listening to Parents of Children with Disabilities,** Linda Davern, *Educational Leadership,* April 1996. 181
Changing teachers' and classmates' attitudes toward children with ***physical and health impairments*** by building alliances with parents is Linda Davern's focus in this essay. She helps unravel concerns about ***cultural diversity,*** the ***impact on the family*** of having a child with a disability, and effective ***individualized education plan*** (IEP) problem solving.

31. **Accessible Web Site Design,** Stacy Peters-Walters, *Teaching Exceptional Children,* May/June 1998. 184
Three ***orthopedically impaired*** quadriplegic students give testimony on how ***technology*** has broken down barriers for them. Access to the Web also benefits students with ***visual, auditory, mental,*** and ***learning disabilities.*** The author gives suggestions on how to overcome barriers to using the Web.

Overview 190

32. **Meeting the Needs of Gifted Learners in the Early Childhood Classroom,** Brooke Walker, Norma Lu Hafenstein, and Linda Crow-Enslow, *Young Children,* January 1999. 192
Early childhood inclusive educational settings have a legal obligation to meet the needs of students with exceptionalities. To meet the needs of ***gifted learners*** also, the authors suggest ways to ***assess*** gifted and talented preschoolers, and they present an in-depth integrated unit for meeting the needs of gifted young children in an inclusive classroom environment.

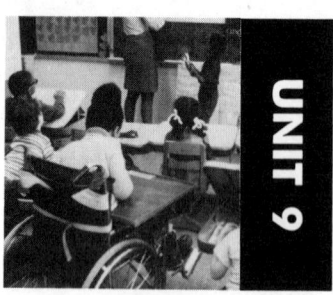

UNIT 9
Orthopedic and Health Impairments

In this unit, three articles discuss how health problems and mobility impairments have an impact on a child's education.

UNIT 10
Giftedness

Three articles examine the need for special services for gifted and talented students, assessment of giftedness, and ways to teach these students.

The concepts in bold italics are developed in the article. For further expansion please refer to the Topic Guide and the Index.

33. **Gifted Students Suggest Reforms for Education: Listening to Gifted Students' Ideas,** Lugene Polzella, *Gifted Child Today,* July/August 1997.   **198**
Fifty **gifted and talented** students completed a survey about what would best meet their educational needs. Many of their suggestions are easy to implement. **Family involvement** with administrators and teachers can help make their dreams a reality.

34. **Accountability for Gifted Students,** James J. Gallagher, *Phi Delta Kappan,* June 1998.   **202**
As the twenty-first century begins, educators must justify their requests for resources and most document their good works. James Gallagher presents arguments for providing differentiated programs for **gifted and talented** students. **Assessment** evaluation of the success of such programs will profoundly add to the important process of accountability.

Overview   **206**

35. **Making Comprehensive Inclusion of Special Needs Students Work in a Middle School,** Paul D. Deering, *Middle School Journal,* January 1998.   **208**
Results of a 2-year study are presented that offer insights on how to help students with special needs to make the **transition** from elementary to middle school **inclusive education. Collaboration** of special and regular education teachers and **peer tutoring** are stressed.

36. **Competitions and Exceptional Children: A Great Combination,** Tracy L. Riley and Frances A. Karnes, *Teaching Exceptional Children,* May/June 1999.   **216**
Students with **developmental disabilities** and **orthopedic and health impairments** can benefit from competitions. Contests can lead to lifelong interests and aid **transitions** from school to community. This article suggests competitions that can be incorporated into **individualized education plans (IEPs)** and **individualized transition plans (ITPs).**

37. **School-to-Work: A Model for Learning a Living,** Michael Hartoonian and Richard Van Scotter, *Phi Delta Kappan,* April 1996.   **220**
The authors discuss the need for education to promote self-development, citizenship, and employment (artisanship). Our attitudes about **individualized transition plans** (ITPs) need to acknowledge all three characteristics. **Transition** requires learning cultural and civic virtues as well as how to earn a living.

Index   **225**
Article Review Form   **228**
Article Rating Form   **229**

Transition

The three articles in this section examine the problems and issues regarding transitions within school or from school to the community and workforce.

Topic Guide

This topic guide suggests how the selections and World Wide Web sites found in the next section of this book relate to topics of traditional concern to students and professionals involved with educating exceptional children. It is useful for locating interrelated articles and Web sites for reading and research. The guide is arranged alphabetically according to topic.

The relevant Web sites, which are numbered and annotated on pages 4 and 5, are easily identified by the Web icon (◉) under the topic articles. By linking the articles and the Web sites by topic, this ANNUAL EDITIONS reader becomes a powerful learning and research tool.

TOPIC AREA	KNOWLEDGE	ATTITUDES	TEACHING
	(These articles provide information about a handicap or a special education concept.)	(These articles contain personal experiences of exceptional persons or discussions about changing children's attitudes toward a handicap.)	(These articles contain practical suggestions about how to apply special education principles to teaching of exceptional children.)
Assessment ◉ (1, 2, 5, 8, 13, 16, 17)	10. Learning Disabilities 13. Distinguishing Language Differences 19. Identifying Depression 32. Meeting the Needs of Gifted Learners 34. Accountability for Gifted Students	15. Family and Cultural Alert! 27. Unexpected Benefits of High School Peer Tutoring	5. Promoting a Safe School Environment 11. Cognitive Credit Cards 12. Dropout Prevention 20. Teaching Students to Regulate Their Own Behavior
Collaboration ◉ (8, 9, 16, 20, 22)	6. From Philosophy to Practice 16. Collaborative Planning 17. Children with Down Syndrome 28. Perspectives on Technology	4. Four Inclusion Models 15. Family and Cultural Alert! 24. Child with Severe Hearing Loss	5. Promoting a Safe School Environment 26. Training Basic Teaching Skills 35. Making Comprehensive Inclusion of Special Needs Students Work
Computers and Technology ◉ (5, 6, 24, 25)	28. Perspectives on Technology 31. Accessible Web Site Design	15. Family and Cultural Alert! 21. "Look! I'm on TV!" 24. Child with Severe Hearing Loss	11. Cognitive Credit Cards 12. Dropout Prevention 25. Multimedia Stories for Deaf Children 29. "Can I Play Too?"
Conflict Resolution	2. Parent Panel 22. Defuse Defiance, Threats	21. "Look! I'm on TV!"	5. Promoting a Safe School Environment 12. Dropout Prevention
Cultural Diversity ◉ (4, 8, 9, 10, 12, 13)	13. Distinguishing Language Differences	9. Is Everyone Included? 15. Family and Cultural Alert! 30. Listening to Parents	2. Parent Panel 12. Dropout Prevention 25. Multimedia Stories for Deaf Children
Developmental Disabilities and Traumatic Brain Injuries ◉ (20, 21)	16. Collaborative Planning 17. Children with Down Syndrome 19. Identifying Depression	30. Listening to Parents 31. Accessible Web Site Design	8. Wellness Programming 14. Language Interaction Techniques 18. Getting the Student with Head Injuries Back in School 36. Competitions and Exceptional Children
Early Childhood ◉ (4, 10, 11, 12, 13)	6. From Philosophy to Practice 7. Together Is Better 32. Meeting the Needs of Gifted Learners	9. Is Everyone Included?	8. Wellness Programming 14. Language Interaction Techniques
Emotional and Behavioral Disorders ◉ (17, 23, 27)	19. Identifying Depression 22. Defuse Defiance, Threats	8. Wellness Programming 21. "Look! I'm on TV!"	12. Dropout Prevention 18. Getting the Student with Head Injuries Back in School 20. Teaching Students to Regulate Their Own Behavior
Family Involvement ◉ (3, 7, 11, 13, 20, 24, 31)	6. From Philosophy to Practice 16. Collaborative Planning 17. Children with Down Syndrome	15. Family and Cultural Alert! 24. Child with Severe Hearing Loss 30. Listening to Parents 33. Gifted Students Suggest Reforms	2. Parent Panel 12. Dropout Prevention

TOPIC AREA	KNOWLEDGE	ATTITUDES	TEACHING
Gifted and Talented (31)	34. Accountability for Gifted Students	33. Gifted Students Suggest Reforms	32. Meeting the Needs of Gifted Learners
Hearing Impairments (19, 24, 27)	7. Together Is Better	24. Child with Severe Hearing Loss 31. Accessible Web Site Design	
Inclusive Education (8, 9, 10, 12, 20, 22, 24, 25, 28, 30)	1. Inclusion of Children with Disabilities 6. From Philosophy to Practice 7. Together Is Better 16. Collaborative Planning 17. Children with Down Syndrome 22. Defuse Defiance, Threats 32. Meeting the Needs of Gifted Learners	3. What Do I Do Now? 9. Is Everyone Included? 24. Child with Severe Hearing Loss 27. Unexpected Benefits of High School Peer Tutoring	2. Parent Panel 4. Four Inclusion Models 5. Promoting a Safe School Environment 8. Wellness Programming 23. Schools for the Visually Disabled 26. Training Basic Teaching Skills 29. "Can I Play Too?" 35. Making Comprehensive Inclusion of Special Needs Students Work
Individualized Plans (IEP, IFSP, ITP) (11, 13, 15, 18, 20, 22, 23, 27)	16. Collaborative Planning 17. Children with Down Syndrome	3. What Do I Do Now? 30. Listening to Parents 37. School-to-Work	15. Family and Cultural Alert! 36. Competitions and Exceptional Children
Learning Disabilities (13, 15, 16, 17)	7. Together Is Better 10. Learning Disabilities	30. Listening to Parents 31. Accessible Web Site Design	11. Cognitive Credit Cards 12. Dropout Prevention
Legal Processes (2, 4, 6, 8, 9)	10. Learning Disabilities 19. Identifying Depression	1. Inclusion of Children with Disabilities	2. Parent Panel 23. Schools for the Visually Disabled
Multiple Disabilities (26, 27)	28. Perspectives on Technology	27. Unexpected Benefits of High School Peer Tutoring	23. Schools for the Visually Disabled 26. Training Basic Teaching Skills
Orthopedic and Health Impairments (28, 29, 30)	7. Together Is Better 36. Competitions and Exceptional Children	30. Listening to Parents 31. Accessible Web Site Design	18. Getting the Student with Head Injuries Back in School 29. "Can I Play Too?"
Peer Tutoring (13, 31)	16. Collaborative Planning	27. Unexpected Benefits of High School Peer Tutoring	5. Promoting a Safe School Environment 12. Dropout Prevention 35. Making Comprehensive Inclusion of Special Needs Students Work
Speech and Language Impairments (18, 19)	7. Together Is Better 13. Distinguishing Language Differences 16. Collaborative Planning	15. Family and Cultural Alert! 24. Child with Severe Hearing Loss	14. Language Interaction Techniques 25. Multimedia Stories for Deaf Children
Transition (32)	6. From Philosophy to Practice 16. Collaborative Planning 36. Competitions and Exceptional Children	21. "Look! I'm on TV!" 27. Unexpected Benefits of High School Peer Tutoring 37. School-to-Work	8. Wellness Programming 18. Getting the Student with Head Injuries Back in School 23. Schools for the Visually Disabled 35. Making Comprehensive Inclusion of Special Needs Students Work
Visual Impairments (25)	7. Together Is Better	21. "Look! I'm on TV!"	5. Promoting a Safe School Environment 12. Dropout Prevention

AE: Educating Exceptional Children

The following World Wide Web sites have been carefully researched and selected to support the articles found in this reader. If you are interested in learning more about specific topics found in this book, these Web sites are a good place to start. The sites are cross-referenced by number and appear in the topic guide on the previous two pages. Also, you can link to these Web sites through our DUSHKIN ONLINE support site at http://www.dushkin.com/online/.

The following sites were available at the time of publication. Visit our Web site—we update DUSHKIN ONLINE regularly to reflect any changes.

General Sources

1. The Big Pages of Special Education Links
http://www.mts.net/~jgreenco/special.html
This site leads to links that deal with disabilities related to special education.

2. Council for Exceptional Children
http://www.cec.sped.org
The Council for Exceptional Children is a large professional organization that is dedicated to improving education for children with exceptionalities, students with disabilities, and/or the gifted child. Its home page leads to the ERIC Clearinghouse on disabilities and gifted education and the National Clearinghouse for Professions in Special Education.

3. Family Village
http://www.familyvillage.wisc.edu/index.htmlx
Here is a global community of disability-related resources that is set up under such headings as library, shopping mall, school, community center, and others. This wide-ranging site includes What's New, Search, Discussion, and Chat.

4. National Information Center for Children and Youth with Disabilities (NICHCY)
http://www.nichcy.org/index.html
NICHCY provides information and makes referrals in areas related to specific disabilities, early intervention, special education and related services, individualized education programs, and much more. The site also connects to a listing of Parent's Guides to resources for children and youth with disabilities.

5. National Rehabilitation Information Center
http://www.naric.com
A series of databases that can be keyword-searched on subjects that include physical, mental, and psychiatric disabilities, vocational rehabilitation, special education, assistive technology, and more can be found on this site.

6. Other Disability-Related Sites
http://www.ici.coled.umn.edu/ici/othersites.html
A wide-ranging list of disability-related Internet sites is available here.

7. Special Education Exchange
http://www.spedex.com/main_graphics.htm
SpEdEx, as this site is more commonly known, offers a wealth of information, links, and resources to everyone interested in special education, whether an educator, parent, student or professional.

Inclusive Education

8. Inclusive Education: Cooperative Teaching
http://www.uni.edu/coe/inclusion/cooperative.html
How regular education and special education teachers can work together to promote and implement inclusive education is covered here.

9. One Size Doesn't Fit All: Full Inclusion Inhibits Academic Progress of Special Education Students
http://141.218.70.183/SPED603/paperHewitt.html
Michele Hewitt discusses the decline of academic progress of special education students in an inclusive classroom.

Early Childhood

10. Early Childhood Care and Development
http://www.ecdgroup.com
Dedicated to the improvement of conditions of young children at risk, the Consultative Group provides an International Resources site on Early Childhood Care and Development. Child development theory, programming data, parenting data, research, and other related areas that support young children (ages 0–8) and their families can be found on this site.

11. I Am Your Child
http://www.iamyourchild.org/start.html
Resources for parents and caregivers regarding early childhood development are provided here.

12. Institute on Community Integration Projects
http://www.ici.coled.umn.edu/ici/overview/projects.html#1
Research projects related to Early Childhood and early intervention services for special education are described here.

13. SERI: Special Education Resources on the Internet
http://www.hood.edu/seri/serihome.htm
This excellent resource offers helpful sites in all phases of special education in early childhood, including disabilities, mental retardation, behavior disorders, autism, gifted and talented, and other problem areas.

Learning Disabilities

14. The Instant Access Treasure Chest
http://www.fln.vcu.edu/ld/ld.html
Billed as the Foreign Language Teacher's Guide to Learning Disabilities, this site contains a very thorough list of resources for anyone interested in LD education issues.

15. Learning Disabilities and Disorders
http://fly.hiwaay.net/~garson/learnd.htm
This is a good source for information about all kinds of learning disabilities with links to other related material.

16. Learning Disabilities Association of America
http://www.ldanatl.org
The purpose of the LDA is to advance the education and general welfare of children of normal and potentially normal intelligence who show handicaps of a perceptual, conceptual, or coordinative nature. Its home page contains What's New, Fact Sheets, Resources, Publications, and more.

17. Teaching Children with Attention Deficit Disorder
http://www.kidsource.com/kidsource/content2/add.html
This in-depth site defines both types of ADDs and discusses establishing the proper learning environment.

Speech and Language Impairments

18. Speech and Language Impairment
http://www.socialnet.lu/handitel/wwwlinks/dumb.html
A thorough collection of Web sites, plus an article on the relationship between form and function in the speech of specifically language-impaired children, may be accessed here.

19. YaacK
http://www.mrtc.org/~duffy/yaack/toc.html
The purpose of AAC (Augmentive and Alternative Communication) is to increase the ability of a child with a communication impairment to achieve the functions necessary to communicate with others.

Developmental Disabilities and Traumatic Brain Injuries

20. Autism Society Early Interventions Package
http://www.autism-society.org/packages/early_intervention.html
Answers to FAQs about early intervention in cases of autism as well as online help with obtaining early intervention services, reading lists, and organizations to contact for further information are located on this Web site. Go to *http://www/autism-society.org/packages/educating_children.html* for the Society's Educating Children Information Package.

21. Disability-Related Sources on the Web
http://www.arcofarizona.org/dislnkin.html
This resource's many links include grant resources, federally funded projects and federal agencies, assistive technology, national and international organizations, and educational resources and directories.

22. Gentle Teaching
http://utopia.knoware.nl/users/gentle/
Maintained by the foundation for Gentle Teaching in the Netherlands, this page explains a nonviolent approach for helping children and adults with special needs.

Emotional and Behavioral Disorders

23. Resources in Emotional or Behavioral Disorders (EBD)
http://www.gwu.edu/~ebdweb/index.html
At this page, link to a collection of Web resources for teachers of students with serious emotional disturbances.

Vision and Hearing Impairments

24. British Columbia Education, Skills, and Training: Special Education Branch
http://www.bced.gov.bc.ca/specialed/hearimpair/toc.htm
A complete resource guide to support classroom teachers of hard of hearing and deaf students is available here.

25. The New York Institute for Special Education
http://www.nyise.org/index.html
This school is an educational facility that serves children who are blind or visually impaired. The site includes program descriptions and resources for the blind.

Multiple Disabilities

26. Activity Ideas for Students with Severe, Profound, or Multiple Disabilities
http://www.palaestra.com/featurestory.html
The Fall 1997 issue of the *Palaestra* contains this interesting article on teaching students who have multiple disabilities. The complete text is offered here on line.

27. Related Services Research Project: Abstract
http://www.uvm.edu/~mgiangre/RSRPab1.html
This is an abstract from "Severe and Multiple Disabilities," by Michael Giangreco of the University of Vermont, which describes the problems that students with multiple disabilities have and offers actions that can be taken.

Orthopedic and Health Impairments

28. Association to Benefit Children (ABC)
http://www.a-b-c.org
ABC presents a network of programs that includes child advocacy, education for disabled children, care for HIV-positive children, employment, housing, foster care, and day care.

29. Introduction: Community Travel
http://isd.saginaw.k12.mi.us/~mobility/ctpintro.htm
The purpose of community-based education is to help students in special education to become more independent. Here is an excellent description of how it is being done in at least one community.

30. Resources for VE Teachers
http://cpt.fsu.edu/tree/ve/tofc.html
Effective practices for teachers of varying exceptionalities (VE) classes of physically and health-impaired students are listed here.

Giftedness

31. Kenny Anthony's Gifted and Talented and General Educational Resources
http://www2.tsixroads.com/~kva/
In addition to definitions and characteristics of giftedness and needs of the gifted, an excellent list of education resources for the gifted can be found at this site.

Transition

32. National Transition Alliance (NTA) Home Page
http://www.dssc.org/nta/index.html
This NTA site provides state transition resources, searchable databases for keyword searching on transition, school to work, model programs in interactive format, links to other on-line databases, and includes a database of model transition programs.

We highly recommend that you review our Web site for expanded information and our other product lines. We are continually updating and adding links to our Web site in order to offer you the most usable and useful information that will support and expand the value of your Annual Editions. You can reach us at: *http://www.dushkin.com/annualeditions/.*

www.dushkin.com/online/

Unit 1

Unit Selections

1. **Inclusion of Children with Disabilities: Seeking the Appropriate Balance,** Martha M. McCarthy
2. **The Parent Panel: Supporting Children with Special Needs,** Susanna V. Duckworth and Patricia H. Kostell
3. **What Do I Do Now? A Teacher's Guide to Including Students with Disabilities,** Michael F. Giangreco
4. **Four Inclusion Models That Work,** Dori Elliott and Merry McKenney
5. **Promoting a Safe School Environment through a Schoolwide Wellness Program,** Patricia A. Gallagher and Linda S. Satter

Key Points to Consider

❖ What does the 1997 reauthorization of IDEA require of states who fail to include children with disabilities in regular education classes?

❖ How does the parent panel approach to parental/educator collaboration work?

❖ How can Michael Giangreco's 10 recommendations (see "What Do I Do Now? A Teacher's Guide to Including Students with Disabilities") improve a regular education teacher's abilities to work with special needs children in an inclusive classroom?

❖ How do children learn best? Does specialized instruction really help? What are the three biggest challenges facing inclusive education?

❖ Explain how educators can promote a safe inclusive school environment and advance conflict resolution through IMPACT, a specialized schoolwide wellness program.

 **Links**   www.dushkin.com/online/

8. **Inclusive Education: Cooperative Teaching**
   http://www.uni.edu/coe/inclusion/cooperative.html
9. **One Size Doesn't Fit All: Full Inclusion Inhibits Academic Progress of Special Education Students**
   http://141.218.70.183/SPED603/paperHewitt.html

These sites are annotated on pages 4 and 5.

Inclusive Education

The reauthorization of IDEA (Individuals with Disabilities Education Act) in 1997 called for more diagnoses of exceptional children to be made and more special needs to be met. The number of children who qualify for special educational services has risen to about 5½ million children in the United States. Over 40 percent of these children are in inclusive, general education classrooms.

Public schools have an obligation to provide free educational services in the least restrictive environment possible to all children with diagnosed conditions of exceptionality. Although laws in Canada and the United States differ slightly, and laws in each state of the United States recognize different diagnostic criteria, public schools have an obligation to serve children with exceptional conditions in as normal an educational environment as possible. Inclusive education is difficult. It works very well for some students with exceptionalities in some situations, and, to the contrary, it works marginally or not at all for other students with exceptionalities in other situations.

For inclusion to succeed within a school, everyone must be committed to be part of the solution: superintendent, principal, teachers, coaches, aides, ancillary staff, students, parents, and families. High-quality education for students, regardless of abilities, requires good communication and collaboration. It is complicated to achieve. One or two persons who oppose it strongly and vocally can dramatically alter its implementation. Everyone must be educated about its philosophical antecedents and goals. Likewise, open ledgers, financial account- ability, and projections of future benefits should be set out. Inclusion requires sufficient monetary support as well as extraordinary human effort.

The term "least restrictive environment" is often mistakenly understood as the need for all children to be educated in a regular education classroom. Terms such as *normalization* and *inclusion* are used to describe the education of children with exceptional conditions in the regular or general education classroom. If students can learn and achieve better in inclusive programs, then the programs are well worth the effort. If students can succeed only marginally in inclusive education classrooms, some alternate solutions are necessary. Current laws do not require that every child be placed in a regular education classroom, but rather that every child be educated in the least restrictive environment possible. A continuum of placement options exists to maximize the goal of educating every child. For some children, a separate class, or even a separate school, is still optimal.

Special education and regular education teachers are becoming more and more intertwined. Collaboration between teachers is increasing as separate special education classes are serving fewer students. Every child with an exceptional condition is different from every other child; in symptoms, needs, and teachability. Each child is, therefore, provided with an individualized education plan (IEP). This plan consists of both long- and short-term goals for education, specially designed instructional procedures with related services, and methods to evaluate the child's progress. The IEP is updated and revised annually. Special education teachers, parents, and all applicable service providers make recommendations for goals and teaching strategies on IEPs. The IEPs should always be outcomes-oriented.

The first article included in this anthology is a legal update written by Martha McCarthy for all persons involved in the care and/or education of children with disabilities. It discusses the impact that the 1997 reauthorization of IDEA is having and will continue to have on our students, their teachers, and our society. Courts of law must consider the social as well as the educational benefits of including children with disabilities in the least restrictive environment possible, and the relative costs of regular classes versus special classes when adjudicating any educational placement dispute. Several 1990s cases that were resolved in favor of regular education placement are contrasted with some court decisions that were rendered in favor of more segregated placements. McCarthy summarizes her presentation with a discussion of the controversial "sticky wickets" of education, which remain unresolved.

In the second article, Susanna Duckworth and Patricia Kostell suggest setting up parent panels to involve families more fully in their children's education, especially when children have special needs. Parent panels include diverse parents, who represent a broad array of opinions, in collaboration with education specialists. Meetings are held at least twice a year in neutral settings and with guaranteed confidentiality. Everyone benefits from these collaborative efforts.

The third essay addresses how to make inclusion work. Drawing on two recent books on inclusion (*Inclusion: A Guide for Educators* [1996] by W. Stainback and S. Stainback, and *Creativity and Collaborative Learning: A Practical Guide to Empowering Students and Teachers* [1994] by J. Thousand, R. Villa, and A. Nevin), Michael Giangreco presents 10 practical recommendations for teachers. All educators who find themselves faced with the task of making their classrooms good learning environments for included children with varying abilities will benefit from these 10 suggestions. The article will also initiate discussions of a hypothetical nature, such as "If I have this student, then . . . " Such exercises can generate more creative solutions to the questions about how to include unique students with very individualized abilities in regular education classrooms.

The fourth selection in unit 1 is a discussion of the implementation of four different types of inclusion: consultation, team teaching, aide services, and limited pullout services. Dori Elliott, a regular education teacher, and Merry McKenney, a special education teacher, give many realistic and practical suggestions for success with each of these models. They expect positive outcomes and help the reader understand how they can be achieved.

The last article included in this unit describes the experiences of a midwestern school whose collaborative program, called IMPACT, was successful in changing its students' attitudes and behaviors toward each other. The program, which emphasizes cooperation, tolerance, and empathy, has tremendous potential for making inclusive classrooms safer and more successful educational environments for students with special needs.

Inclusion of Children with Disabilities:
Seeking the Appropriate Balance

by Martha M. McCarthy

In the 1990s courts have interpreted the Individuals with Disabilities Education Act (IDEA) as entailing a strong preference for inclusion.

The fastest-growing area of school law pertains to special education services and the rights of children with disabilities. Most of the controversies involve interpretations of the Individuals with Disabilities Education Act (IDEA), a federal funding law that guarantees all children with disabilities a free appropriate education at public expense.[1] A volatile topic is the IDEA requirement that children with disabilities must be placed in the "least restrictive environment" (LRE).

This LRE mandate means that each state education agency must ensure that "to the maximum extent appropriate, children with disabilities, including children in public or private institutions or other care facilities, are educated with children who are not disabled."[2] Under IDEA regulations, children may be placed in special classes or separate facilities "only when the nature or severity of the disability is such that education in regular classes with the use of supplementary aids and services cannot be achieved satisfactorily."[3] In addition, the 1997 reauthorization of the IDEA requires states to revise their special-education funding formulas if they discourage placing children with disabilities in the regular education environment.[4]

The term "inclusion" is not mentioned in the federal law. It is a popular term that refers to placing students with disabilities in the regular classrooms of their home schools *with their age and grade peers* to the maximum extent possible. In short, inclusion means bringing support services to the child rather than moving the child to a segregated setting to receive special services.[5] This concept has been extremely controversial, especially in connection with children who have *severe* mental, emotional, or physical disabilities.

IDEA's Preference for Inclusion

In the 1990s courts have interpreted the IDEA as entailing a strong preference for inclusion. Accordingly, they have placed the burden on school authorities to establish that a regular education placement is not appropriate for a given child with disabilities. Although various criteria have been proposed for making this determination, in general courts consider at least the following: the educational benefits of the inclusive versus segregated settings; the noneducational (e.g., social) benefits of both placements; the impact of the inclusive placement on other children in the class; and the costs of the respective placements.[6]

MARTHA M. MCCARTHY is a chancellor professor at Indiana University in Bloomington, Indiana.

The Eleventh Circuit Court of Appeals in 1991 held that a school district had not given adequate consideration to educating a child with Down syndrome in the regular class with supplementary aids and services.[7] The court recognized that academic benefits are not the only advantages of a regular education placement; there are social, language, and role-modeling benefits as well. Assessing inclusive versus segregated placements in terms of educational and noneducational effects on the child, costs, and impact on other students, the court required placement of the child in a general education program at her neighborhood school rather than in a separate special education class.

In a significant 1993 decision, *Oberti v. Board of Education of the Borough of Clementon School District*, the Third Circuit Court of Appeals ruled that school districts have an affirmative obligation to consider placing students with disabilities in general education and supplementary aids and services before they explore other alternatives.[8] The court stated that the law's strong presumption that children should be educated in the regular classroom may be rebutted only with evidence that (a) the student's disabilities are so severe he or she will receive little or no benefit from inclusion; (b) the child is so disruptive that others' education is impaired; or (c) costs are so significant that they will have a negative effect on other students. The court declared that inclusion is a right, not a privilege for a select few.

In a subsequent California case, the Ninth Circuit Court of Appeals assessed the educational and noneducational benefits, costs, and impact on other children of an inclusive placement for a moderately mentally handicapped child.[9] The court concluded that the IDEA favors inclusion if the child can receive a satisfactory education, even if it is not the best setting for the student.[10] Because the school district had proposed a segregated placement for the child, her parents enrolled her in a private school, where she attended kindergarten through second grade in regular classes with support services. Relying on testimony of her teachers and parents, the court found that the child had made substantial progress in regular education and that there had been no detrimental effect on the regular education program. Thus, the court ordered the child placed in an inclusive environment in the public school.

It should not be assumed that school authorities generally support the more restrictive environment. In several cases parents have contested the school district's proposed inclusive placement, requesting instead residential or other segregated settings for their children. In 1996, the Seventh Circuit Court of Appeals affirmed a federal district court's conclusion that a private school for disabled students was not the LRE for a student with attention deficit hyperactivity disorder (ADHD). The court agreed with school authorities that the student could receive an appropriate education at the public high school.[11] Also, the Fifth Circuit Court of Appeals found that a school district's proposed inclusive placement for a child with learning and emotional difficulties that entailed some individualized instruction and counseling as well as some regular classes was the LRE, notwithstanding parents' request for a residential placement.[12]

The same court in 1997 affirmed a federal district court's decision that reversed a hearing officer's award of reimbursement to parents for costs of a residential placement for their child with ADHD and Tourette's syndrome.[13] The school district had attempted various placements for the child, who was quite disruptive and abusive toward other students. Noting that the individually designed education program need not be the best possible program,[14] the court found that placing the child in adaptive-behavior classes for part of the day and in the regular education program for the remainder of the day was appropriate. Thus, the parents were not entitled to reimbursement for the more restrictive residential placement.

Appropriate Noninclusive Placements

Although courts are interpreting the IDEA as entailing a presumption that children with disabilities should be placed in regular education, they are not requiring inclusive placements under all circumstances. Courts will review the specific circumstances of each case, and it is not impossible for school authorities to substantiate that the welfare of the child or classmates would be jeopardized in the regular classroom. To illustrate, the Eighth Circuit Court of Appeals upheld a centralized program for a wheelchair-bound student with spina bifida.[15] The court reasoned that school authorities satisfied the IDEA by making an appropriate program available for the student even though it was not at his home school.

In several cases dealing with hearing-impaired students, courts have upheld centralized programs, some in segregated settings, because the language needs of these children would be served more appropriately.[16] Other courts also have ruled that when more restrictive placements are superior and comparable services cannot feasibly be provided in the regular classroom, placements in segregated settings—including those away from students' home schools—are appropriate for specific children.[17]

For example, the Ninth Circuit Court of Appeals ruled that a child with Tourette's syndrome and ADHD should be placed in a special school for learning-disabled children rather than in the regular classroom.[18] The court reasoned that this child's disruptive classroom behavior, including sexual harassment of female students, prevented him from learning in the regular classroom and posed a threat to others.

Thus, placement in the special school proposed by school authorities was appropriate for this child.

In a subsequent case, the same court held that inclusion was not appropriate for a high school student who suffered from attention deficit disorder. The court noted that prior attempts to educate the child in the regular classroom had resulted in total failure, while instruction in a segregated setting produced superior results.[19]

The Third Circuit Court of Appeals held that a full-time residential facility was the least-restrictive educationally appropriate setting for a severely mentally retarded student; such a residential program was necessary for the student to make meaningful educational progress.[20] Earlier, the Seventh Circuit Court of Appeals had held that a segregated placement was appropriate for a child who was not benefiting from interaction with nonhandicapped students and who needed a more structured program with additional support services. Although the parents wanted the child placed in an integrated setting, the court noted that prior efforts at mainstreaming had proven unsuccessful: the student's behavior had regressed and he had substantially disrupted classmates.[21] In most cases upholding more restrictive placements, efforts had been made to educate the children in the regular classroom, and these efforts had not been successful.

The Continuing Controversy

Judging from the litigation to date, it appears that courts will place the burden on the party seeking a more restrictive placement. That party will have to establish that the regular education classroom with support services is not an appropriate environment for a specific child. The merits and mechanics of inclusion are likely to remain controversial among special and regular educators, school leaders, and parent advocacy groups. Teachers unions, which are skeptical at best about full inclusion, contend that students with disabilities should not be placed in regular education unless class size is reduced and all teachers receive appropriate preparation in dealing with such children.[22] There are also fiscal concerns that inclusion might result in a reduction in funds targeted for children with disabilities. Such children, it is feared, will be placed in regular education *without* appropriate support services.

Several other issues remain unresolved. For example, how superior

> *The merits and mechanics of inclusion are likely to remain controversial among special and regular educators, school leaders, and parent advocacy groups.*

must a segregated program be to justify placing a child there instead of in the regular classroom? Unless an inclusive placement has been tried and its impact assessed, will school authorities or parents ever be able to argue that inclusion is not appropriate for a given child? How should students with severe cognitive disabilities be integrated into the regular classroom at the high school level, where students often are tracked by ability in academic classes? If the curriculum for such children is modified beyond recognition, is this still inclusion? These and related issues seem destined to generate a steady stream of litigation and perhaps ultimately a Supreme Court ruling to clarify the parameters of the LRE mandate.

---

1. 20 U.S.C. § 1401 (1997).
2. 20 U.S.C. 1412(5)(B) (1997); 34 CFR 300.550 (1997).
3. 34 CFR 300.550 (1997).
4. 20 U.S.C.A. § 1413 (1997).
5. See National Association of State Boards of Education, *Winners All: A Call For Inclusive Schools* (Alexandria, Va.: 1992); Joy Rogers, "The Inclusion Revolution," *Research Bulletin* No. 11, Phi Delta Kappa Center for Evaluation, Development and Research, May 1993; "Inclusion: What Does It Mean?" *SEAS Cable*, vol. 14, no. 7, July 1993, 1–3.
6. For a discussion of these criteria, see *Sacramento City Unified Sch. Dist. Bd. of Educ. v. Rachel H. ex rel. Holland*, 14 F.3d 1398 (9th Cir. 1994), cert. denied, 512 U.S. 1207 (1994). In earlier cases, two federal appeals courts articulated slightly different standards, but both entailed some consideration of these criteria. The Fifth Circuit Court of Appeals suggested that courts must first determine whether the child can be educated in the general classroom satisfactorily with supplementary aids and services. If not, special education must be provided and the school district must mainstream the student to the maximum extent appropriate. *Daniel R.R. v. State Bd. of Educ.*, 874 F.2d 1036, 1048 (5th Cir. 1989). The Sixth Circuit Court of Appeals noted that "where the segregated facility is considered superior, the court should determine whether the services which make that placement superior could be feasibly provided in a non-segregated setting." If so, the segregated placement would not be appropriate under the IDEA. *Roncker v. Walter*, 700 F.2d 1058, 1063 (6th Cir. 1983), cert. denied, 464 U.S. 864 (1983).
7. *Greer v. Rome City Sch. Dist.*, 950 F.2d 688 (11th Cir. 1991), opinion withdrawn, 956 F.2d 1025 (11th Cir. 1992), opinion reinstated in part, 967 F.2d 470 (11th Cir. 1992).
8. 995 F.2d 1204 (3d Cir. 1993). See also *Mavis v. Sobol*, 839 F.Supp. 968 (N.D.N.Y. 1994) (holding that school districts have the burden of proving that the LRE requirement is satisfied.)
9. *Sacramento City Unified Sch. Dist. Bd. of Educ. v. Rachel H. ex rel. Holland*, 14 F.3d 1398 (9th Cir. 1994), cert. denied, 114 S.Ct. 2679 (1994).
10. See also *Kerkam v. Superintendent, D.C. Pub. Schs.*, 931 F.2d 84 (D.C. Cir. 1991) (holding that local extended-day program conferred education benefit on severely retarded student in the LRE and thus satisfied the IDEA even if student could have made more progress in a residential placement); *Schreiber v. Ridgewood Bd. of Educ.*, 952 F.Supp. 205 (D.N.J. 1997) (holding that day program in alternative middle school was the LRE that provided educational benefit to neurologically impaired student, even though residential program might be more intense); *P. J. v.*

Connecticut Bd. of Educ., 788 F.Supp. 673 (D.C. Conn. 1992) (ruling that a Down syndrome child with mild to moderate mental impairment was entitled to a fully integrated setting with appropriate special education services or the individualized program must detail a strong justification for any segregation).

11. *Monticello Sch. Dist. No. 125 v. Illinois State Bd. of Educ.*, 910 F.Supp. 446 (C.D. Ill. 1995), aff'd, 102 F.3d 895 (7th Cir. 1996). See also *School Dist. of Kettle Moraine v. Grover*, 755 F.Supp. 243 (E.D. Wis. 1990) (holding that despite parents' desire to have student placed in segregated program, student's educational and socialization needs would be met in an integrated program at the neighborhood high school).

12. *Salley v. St. Tammany Parish Sch. Bd.*, 57 F.3d 458 (5th Cir. 1995). See also *Doe v. Board of Educ. of Tullahoma City Schs.*, 9 F.3d 455 (6th Cir. 1993), cert. denied, 511 U.S. 1108 (1994) (denying parents reimbursement for the private placement of a child with learning disabilities; the proposed public regular education program with support services was appropriate); *Jonathan G. v. Lower Merion Sch. Dist.*, 955 F.Supp. 413 (E.D. Pa. 1997) (upholding inclusive placement for a child with learning disabilities despite parental objections); *Mather v. Hartford Sch. Dist.*, 928 F.Supp. 437 (D. Vt. 1996) (rejecting reimbursement to parents for private education of a learning disabled child; placement in regular education with intensive instruction in a resource room was appropriate, even though the private program might be better).

13. *Cypress-Fairbanks Indep. Sch. Dist. v. Michael F.*, 118 F.3d 245 (5th Cir. 1997) (also assessing the school district's costs incurred in the litigation against the parents). The Supreme Court has ruled that parents who unilaterally enroll their children with disabilities in private programs may be entitled to reimbursement if the proposed public school placements are challenged through proper procedures and found to be inappropriate. See *Florence County Sch. Dist. v. Carter*, 510 U.S. 7 (1993); *Burlington Sch. Committee v. Department of Educ.*, 471 U.S. 359 (1985).

14. See *Board of Educ. of the Hendrick Hudson Cent. Sch. Dist. v. Rowley*, 458 U.S. 176 (1982).

15. *Schuldt v. Mankato Indep. Sch. Dist.*, 937 F.2d 1357 (8th Cir. 1991), cert. denied, 502 U.S. 1059 (1992).

16. Upholding placements of hearing-impaired students in centralized programs rather than in schools closer to the students' homes, see, e.g., *Flour Bluff Indep. Sch. Dist. v. Katherine M.*, 91 F.3d 689 (5th Cir. 1996), cert. denied, 117 S.Ct. 948 (1997); *Poolaw v. Bishop*, 67 F.3d 830 (9th Cir. 1995); *Barnett v. Fairfax County Sch. Bd.*, 927 F.2d 146 (4th Cir. 1991), cert. denied, 502 U.S. 859 (1991); *Briggs v. Board of Educ. of Conn.*, 882 F.2d 688 (2d Cir. 1989); *Lachman v. Illinois State Bd. of Educ.*, 852 F.2d 290 (7th Cir. 1988), cert. denied, 488 U.S. 925 (1988).

17. See, e.g., *Murray v. Montrose County Sch. Dist. RE-1J*, 51 F.3d 921 (10th Cir. 1995) (upholding removal of child from neighborhood school and placement in school with program for children with severe disabilities); *Devries v. Fairfax County School Bd.*, 882 F.2d 876 (4th Cir. 1989) (holding that county vocational center thirteen miles away was the appropriate LRE for a severely autistic child); *A.W. v. Northwest R-1 Sch. Dist.*, 813 F.2d 158 (8th Cir. 1987), cert. denied, 484 U.S. 847 (1987) (upholding segregated school for a severely mentally retarded child); *Wilson v. Marana Unified School Dist. No. 6 of Pima County*, 735 F.2d 1178 (9th Cir. 1984) (upholding placement of a severely physically disabled child thirty minutes away where instruction by a teacher specially certified to address physical disabilities was available); *Thornock by Baugh v. Boise Indep. Sch. Dist. No. 1*, 767 P.2d 1241 (Idaho 1988), cert. denied, 490 U.S. 1068 (1989) (holding that inclusion may be inappropriate where educational experience would not or could not be productive or enriching to the student or where it would disrupt the classroom).

18. *Clyde K. and Sheila K. v. Puyallup School Dist.*, 35 F.3d 1396 (9th Cir. 1994).

19. *Capistrano Unified Sch. Dist. v. Wartenberg*, 59 F.3d 884 (9th Cir. 1995).

20. *M. C. v. Central Regional Sch. Dist.*, 81 F.3d 389 (3rd Cir. 1996), cert. denied, 117 S.Ct. 176 (1996).

21. *Rheinstrom v. Lincolnwood Bd. of Educ., Dist. 74*, 56 F.3d 67 (7th Cir. 1995). See also *D.F., M.F. and D.J.F. v. Western Sch. Corp. and Kokomo Area Special Educ. Coop.*, 921 F.Supp. 559 (S.D. Ind. 1996) (holding that a child with severe mental disabilities could not meet his individualized education program goals in the general education classroom and did not model or imitate other students so as to attain nonacademic benefits from inclusion).

22. See David Hoff, "NEA Policy Sets Parameters for Special Ed Inclusion," *Education Daily*, 7 July 1994, 1–2; Joanna Richardson, "A.F.T. Says Poll Shows Many Oppose 'Inclusion,'" *Education Week*, 3 August 1994, 14.

The Parent Panel

Supporting Children With Special Needs

Parents and teachers can collaborate and cooperate to meet children's specific needs. By working together, everyone—parents, teachers, and children—benefits.

Susanna V. Duckworth & Patricia H. Kostell

Susanna V. Duckworth is Professor, Special Education, Winthrop University, Rock Hill, South Carolina. Patricia H. Kostell is an Educational Consultant, Rock Hill, South Carolina.

The 1997 reauthorization of P.L. 105–17 (The Individuals With Disabilities Education Act, or IDEA) requires educators to work with parents of children with disabilities as partners in the process of education (Bailey et al., 1998). One means for satisfying IDEA's legal mandate is the parent panel approach to parental/educator collaboration. As parents gain confidence in using their communication and advocacy skills with professionals from early intervention programs (Rockwell, Andre, & Hawley, 1995), they will be ready to take an active role in providing school personnel with necessary information about their children.

Parents, of course, are a key source of vital information about their children because they have firsthand knowledge of their children's physical, social, emotional, and cognitive traits (Hedrick,1997). Parental involvement, therefore, is indispensable to early intervention, and teachers should focus on strengthening such involvement.

Parents and teachers can collaborate and cooperate to meet children's specific needs. By working together, everyone—parents, teachers, and children—benefits. Useful collaborative strategies include one-on-one conferences, team meetings, and home visits. The success of the interactions depends upon, in part, appropriate communication, resolution of conflicts, and mutual respect (Bathshaw, 1991), and it may also be contingent upon a teacher's awareness of different cultural perspectives on communication and child rearing practices (Washington, 1996). Although it is impossible to understand all cultural viewpoints, teachers can at least analyze their personal reactions to information shared by parents. When teachers and parents are discussing methods of behavior management, for example, teachers must be aware of their own opinions about personal discipline methods. By exchanging opinions about management strategies, teachers and parents can reach a better understanding of how to discipline specific children (Sturm, 1997). In order for parents to consider themselves to be trusted, valued, and equal partners in the education process, a teacher must listen objectively and respond appropriately. Parents benefit most when provided with encouragement and precise feedback (Brinkerhoff & Vincent, 1987).

The Parent Panel

The parent panel is one approach to building appropriate communication, resolving conflicts, and creating mutual respect between teachers and parents of children with disabilities. The parent panel typically consists of three to six parents, providing them a forum for candid discussion about what it is like to have a child with a disability. Research documents the advantages of this approach (Payne, Robinson, & Todd, 1997). The approach provides different benefits to parents and teachers. These include:

Advantages to Parents

- *Strength and safety in numbers.* Parents feel comfortable getting support from fellow panel members (Smith, 1997).
- *Invited views.* Parents' ideas are valued precisely because their views are solicited. Parents who serve as panel members can provide useful information, including personal anecdotes related to the unique experiences of their children, as well as their desires and wishes for their children's development (Hedrick, 1997).
- *Trusted team members.* Parent participants become trusted as team members once they display a willingness to listen, an ability to empathize, and a proficiency in the teaming process (Hedrick, 1997).

Advantages to Teachers

- *A broader cultural perspective.* Through the parent panel approach, parents can share cultural information that teachers would not typically request. Such information is valuable because it enables teachers to respond and adapt to a variety of cultural styles (Sturm, 1997).
- *Help with conflict resolution.* Having people interact in a large group setting can help reduce one-on-one conflicts. Focusing on children with disabilities in general, rather than on specific children with special needs, may prevent such conflicts. This is advantageous to parents, as well (Bailey & Wolery, 1992).
- *Increased open-mindedness.* Teachers learn to listen objectively, without the pressure of responding or defending their position.
- *Historical benefits.* By sharing their children's past experiences with teachers, parents can provide valuable and beneficial chronological information, which gives teachers a comprehensive view of each child.

Setting Up the Parent Panel

When setting up the parent panel, several factors must be considered, including parent and teacher schedules and the presentation site. It is important when planning a parent panel to accommodate both parents' and teachers' schedules. Such panels may be held during faculty meetings, inservice training, or special conferences. The parent panel should convene at least twice during the school year. Site locations could include school areas such as classrooms or more neutral settings (e.g., a small community center). A small, intimate site is best, to help create a comfortable, nonthreatening atmosphere.

Another variable to consider when planning for a parent panel is the room arrangement, including the proximity of the panel members to the audience. Having the panel sit behind tables provides parents a buffer from the audience. The table also can be used to display such items as photographs of children, posters, and audio- or videotapes. Such items provide a glimpse into family culture.

Still another consideration is the panel's cultural makeup. The panel should be diverse, representing the community in which the panel members reside. A diverse panel will allow for a broad array of parents' opinions.

Guidelines for Panel Content

When asked to participate in a forum such as the parent panel, parents often need guidelines to help them sift through and focus on relevant aspects of their children's lives. Such guidelines will help frame parents' issues and concerns, and will help them communicate concerns to teachers and other professionals. For these reasons, the content of the parents' presentation should focus on the following:

- Their children and families
- Background and historical information concerning the child with special needs
- Personal anecdotes.

For example, parents may relate details about a child's physical, emotional, social, and cognitive growth and development, starting from birth. They could describe their interactions with medical personnel, including what information they first learned about the child's disability, and how the pediatrician (or other professional) shared the information. Bluntly? With sensitivity? Parents also may recount stories of educators' reactions to their child's enrollment in school or child care. Stories about transitions from one program setting to another also may be informative and revealing. Guidelines provide parents with a structure for delivering specific information about their children with special needs, and they can take professionals on a "tour" of the children's past and present experiences. Parents must be fully assured that information shared as part of the panel presentation will remain confidential. As a safeguard, all persons present at the panel meetings should be required to sign forms prohibiting use of material addressed by panel members.

One Example of the Parent Panel in Action

One sultry July morning, three mothers met with 26 teachers and two college professors to share their views of having young children with disabilities (Payne, Robinson, & Todd, 1997). The following comments showcase the parents' presentations that day, and they provide a glimpse into their lives.

Comments from Parent #1

Sometimes the shaky voice means I'm emotional, but sometimes my voice is shaky just because I never speak in front of a lot of people.

Boy, Adam has come a long way. The neurologist did not know if he would walk or talk.

The pediatrician laughed when I related that I had seen 13 doctors. I didn't think it was funny. I was [the one] paying the bills.

I feel guilty when I medicate my child.

[The] preschool director's response to me about the initial placement of my child [was], "Don't call us. We'll call you."

Comments from Parent # 2

I said, He can't walk and he can't . . . and he can't . . . but please listen to me about what he *can* do!

The hardest is when you sit down for that IEP. I dread to hear what they may say.

Teachers, always have hope. Parents of special needs children have to have hope.

Parents, you are not a pain. What you do for your child, you are also doing for others who come after him.

Comments from Parent # 3

It was going so smoothly until October. Samuel brought home his first negative report. The next day he cried before going to school.

We loved the teacher. The teacher loved our child. [We were] just trying to bring the teacher in touch with where we have been and where we are now.

I was the driver on a field trip and had Samuel and three of his friends in the car. A comment by Samuel's friend was, "You're going to get a fine. You are parking in a handicapped parking place." I replied that I had a card to park in the handicapped parking place. He replied, "Well, who do you know that is handicapped?"

Some of the teachers' responses to the parent panel presentation follow:

Comments from Teachers

Thank goodness these were tough parents.

I will be so much more understanding. This is not something I could have learned from reading my textbook.

I will be careful when I am responding to a child with special needs. The way I treat him can make his life miserable or happy.

Even though doctors are highly trained and are supposed to have the answers, they are often limited in their knowledge of specific disabilities.

Conclusion

The parents of a child with a disability can play an integral role in their child's education as full partners in the education process. By sharing information through the parent panel approach, the participants—including parents, teachers, and other professionals—will be complying with the spirit of federal law, and, more important, enhancing the life of the child with special needs.

References

Bailey, D. B., Jr., McWilliam, R. A., Darkes, L. A., Hebbeler, K., Simeonsson, R. J., Spiker, D., & Wagner, M. (1998). Family outcomes in early intervention: A framework for program evaluation and efficacy research. *Exceptional Children, 64*(3), 314.

Bailey, D. B., & Wolery, M. (1992). *Teaching infants and preschoolers with disabilities.* (2nd ed.). Englewood Cliffs, NJ: Merrill.

Bathshaw, M. L. (1991). *Your child has a disability: A complete source book of daily and medical care.* Boston: Little, Brown.

Brinkerhoff, J., & Vincent, L. (1987). Increasing parental decision-making at the individualized program meeting. *Journal of the Division of Early Childhood, 11,* 46–58.

Hedrick, L. (1997). Parents and professionals working together. In L. L. Dunlap (Ed.), *An introduction to early childhood special education* (pp. 118–136). Boston: Allyn and Bacon.

Payne, J., Robinson, R., & Todd, N. (1997, July). Parents and teachers working together: The parent panel. In S. V. Duckworth & P. H. Kostell (Co-chairs), *Teaching young children with disabilities: Curriculum development and implementation.* Presentation delivered at the meeting of South Carolina State Department of Education, Office of Programs for Exceptional Children, grant funded course, Winthrop University, Rock Hill, SC.

Rockwell, R. E., Andre, L. C., & Hawley, M. K. (1995). *Parents and teachers as partners: Issues and challenges.* Fort Worth, TX: Harcourt Brace College Publishers.

Smith, P. M. (1997). You are not alone: For parents when they learn that their child has a disability. *NICHCY (National Information Center for Children and Youth with Disabilities) News Digest, 20*(2), 3.

Sturm, C. (1997). Creating parent-teacher dialogue: Intercultural communication in child care. *Young Children, 52*(5), 34–38.

Washington, V. (1996). Valuing diversity: A key to grassroots success. *Journal of Early Intervention, 20*(2),179–182.

What Do I Do Now?
A Teacher's Guide to Including Students with Disabilities

Michael F. Giangreco

Michael F. Giangreco is Research Assistant Professor, The University of Vermont, College of Education and Social Services, 499C Waterman Building, Burlington, VT 05405-0160.

Teachers who successfully teach students without disabilities have the skills to successfully teach students with disabilities. Here are 10 recommendations to guide you.

As students with disabilities are increasingly being placed in general education classrooms, teachers are asking many legitimate questions about what to do about their instruction and how to do it. For the past seven years, I've consulted with teachers, administrators, support personnel, and families who are grappling with these concerns. I've also joined with colleagues in conducting 12 research studies at some of these schools. The following suggestions are concrete actions to consider as you pursue success for both students with disabilities and their classmates.

1. Get a Little Help from Your Friends

No one expects teachers to know all the specialized information about every disability, or to do everything that may be necessary for a student with disabilities.

Thus, in schools where students with disabilities are successful in general education classes, teams usually collaborate on individualized educational programs. Team members often include the student and his or her parents, general educators, special educators, para-educators, and support staff, such as speech and language pathologists, and physical therapists. And don't forget: each classroom includes some 20–30 students who are creative and energetic sources of ideas, inspiration, and assistance.

Although teamwork is crucial, look out for some common problems. When groups become unnecessarily large and schedule too many meetings without clear purposes or outcomes, communication and decision making get complicated and may overwhelm families. Further, a group is not necessarily a team, particularly if each specialist has his or her own goals. The real team shares a single set of goals that team members pursue in a coordinated way.

2. Welcome the Student in Your Classroom

Welcoming the student with disabilities may seem like a simple thing to do, and it is. But you'd be surprised how often it doesn't happen. It can be devastating for such a student (or any student) to feel as if he or she must earn the right to belong by meeting an arbitrary standard that invariably differs from school to school.

Remember, too, that your students look to you as their primary adult model during the school day. What do you want to model for them about similarities and differences, change, diversity, individuality, and caring?

So when children with disabilities come to your classroom, talk with them, walk with them, encourage them, joke with them, and teach them. By your actions, show all your students that the child with disabilities is an important member of your class and, by extension, of society.

3. Be the Teacher of All the Students

When a student with disabilities is placed in a general education class, a common practice is for the teacher to function primarily as a host rather than a teacher. Many busy teachers actually embrace this notion because it means someone else is responsible for that student. Many teachers, in fact, think of these students as the responsibility of the special education teacher or para-educator.

Merely hosting a student with disabilities, however, doesn't work very well (Giangreco et al. 1992). Inevitably, these other professionals will work with the student, and the "host" will end up knowing very little about the student's educational program or progress. This perpetuates a lack of responsibility for the student's education and often places important curricular and instructional decisions in the hands of hardworking, but possibly underqualified, paraprofessionals.

Be flexible, but don't allow yourself to be relegated to the role of an outsider in your own classroom. Remember that teachers who successfully teach students without disabilities have the skills to successfully teach students with disabilities (Giangreco et al. 1995).

4. Make Sure Everyone Belongs to the Classroom Community

How, where, when, and with whom students spend their time is a major determinant of their affiliations and status in the classroom (Stainback and Stainback 1996). Too often, students with disabilities are placed with mainstream students, but take part in different activities and have different schedules from their peers. These practices inhibit learning with and from classmates, and may contribute to social isolation.

To ensure that students with disabilities are part of what's happening in class, seat them with their classmates, and at the same kind of desk, not on the fringe of the class.

Make sure, too, that the student participates in the same activities as the rest of the class, even though his or her goals may be different. If the class is writing a journal, the student with a disability should be creating a journal, even if it's in a nonwritten form. If you assign students homework, assign it to this student at an appropriate level. In like manner, if the class does a science experiment, so should this student. Although individualization and supports may be necessary, the student's daily schedule should allow ample opportunities to learn, socialize, and work with classmates.

THE PRESENCE OF A student with disabilities may simply highlight the need to use more active and participatory approaches.

5. Clarify Shared Expectations with Team Members

One of the most common sources of anxiety for classroom teachers is not understanding what other team members expect them to teach. "Do I teach this student most of or all of what I'm teaching the other students?" Sometimes the answer will be yes, sometimes no. In either case, team members must agree on what the student should learn and who will teach it.

To do this, the team should identify a few of the student's learning priorities, as well as a larger set of learning outcomes as part of a broad educational program. Doing so will clarify which parts of the general curriculum the student will be expected to pursue and may include learning outcomes that are not typically part of the general program.

Many students with disabilities also need supports to participate in class. These supports should be distinguished from learning outcomes. If the supports are inadvertently identified as learning outcomes, the educational program may be unnecessarily passive.

Finally, on a one- or two-page program-at-a-glance, summarize the educational program, including, for example, priority learning outcomes, additional learning outcomes, and necessary supports (Giangreco et al. 1993). This concise list will help the team plan and schedule, serve as a reminder of the student's individual needs, and help you communicate those needs to teachers in special areas, such as art, music, and physical education. By clarifying what the team expects the student to learn, you set the stage for a productive school year.

6. Adapt Activities to the Student's Needs

When the educational needs of a student with disabilities differ from those of the majority of the class, teachers often question the appropriateness of the placement. It's fair to ask, for example, why an 11-year-old functioning at a 2nd grade level is placed in a 6th grade class.

The answer is that such a student can still have a successful educational experience. In fact, many schools are purposely developing multigrade classrooms, where teachers accommodate students with a wide range of abilities.

When a student's needs differ from other members of the class, it is important to have options for including that student in activities with classmates. In some cases, the student requires instructional accommodations to achieve learning outcomes within the same curriculum area as his or her classmates, but at a different level.

The student might need to learn, for example, different vocabulary words, math problems, or science concepts. Or the student may be pursuing learning outcomes from different curriculum areas. For example, during a science activity, the student could be learning communication, literacy, or socialization skills, while the rest of the class focuses on science.

7. Provide Active and Participatory Learning Experiences

TEACHERS CAN BECOME BETTER ADVOCATES for their students and themselves by becoming informed consumers of support services.

I've heard teachers of students with disabilities say, "He wouldn't get much out of being in that class because the teacher does a lot of lecturing, and uses worksheets and paper-and-pencil tests." My first reaction is, "You're right, that situation doesn't seem to match the student's needs." But then I wonder, Is this educational approach also a mismatch for students without disability labels?

Considering the diversity of learning styles, educators are increasingly questioning whether passive, didactic approaches meet their students' needs. Activity-based learning, on the other hand, is well suited to a wide range of students. The presence of a student with disabilities may simply highlight the need to use more active and participatory approaches, such as individual or cooperative projects and use of art media, drama, experiments, field study, computers, research, educational games, multimedia projects, or choral responding (Thousand et al. 1994). Interesting, motivating activities carry an added bonus—they encourage positive social behaviors, and can diminish behavior problems.

8. Adapt Classroom Arrangements, Materials, and Strategies
Alternate teaching methods or other adaptations may be necessary. For example, if a group lecture isn't working, try cooperative groups, computer-assisted instruction, or peer tutoring. Or make your instruction more precise and deliberate.

Adaptations may be as basic as considering a different way for a student to respond if he or she has difficulty speaking or writing, or rearranging the chairs for more proximity to peers or access to competent modeling.

You may also have to adapt materials. A student with visual impairments may need tactile or auditory cues. A student with physical disabilities may require materials that are larger or easier to manipulate. And a student who is easily bored or distracted may do better with materials that are in line with his or her interests.

Rely on the whole team and the class to assist with adaptation ideas.

9. Make Sure Support Services Help
Having many support service personnel involved with students can be a help or a hindrance. Ideally, the support staff will be competent and collaborative, making sure that what they do prevents disruptions and negative effects on students' social relationships and educational programs. They will get to know the students and classroom routines, and also understand the teacher's ideas and concerns.

Teachers can become better advocates for their students and themselves by becoming informed consumers of support services. Learn to ask good questions. Be assertive if you are being asked to do something that doesn't make sense to you. Be as explicit as you can be about what type of support you need. Sometimes you may need particular information, materials, or someone to demonstrate a technique. Other times, you may need someone with whom to exchange ideas or just validate that you are headed in the right direction.

10. Evaluate Your Teaching
We commonly judge our teaching by our students' achievements. Although you may evaluate students with disabilities in some of the same ways as you do other students (for example, through written tests, reports, or projects), some students will need alternative assessment, such as portfolios adapted to their needs.

Often it is erroneously assumed that if students get good grades, that will translate into future educational, professional, and personal success. This is a dangerous assumption for any student, but particularly for those with disabilities. Although traditional tests and evaluations may provide certain types of information, they won't predict the impact of your teaching on the student's post-school life. Unfortunately, far too many graduates with disabilities are plagued by unemployment, health problems, loneliness, or isolation—despite their glowing school progress reports.

We need to continually evaluate whether students are applying their achievements to real life, by looking at the effects on their physical and emotional health, personal growth, and positive social relationships; and at their ability to communicate, advocate for themselves, make informed choices, contribute to the community,

UNFORTUNATELY, FAR TOO MANY GRADUATES with disabilities are plagued by unemployment, despite their glowing school progress reports.

and increasingly access places and activities that are personally meaningful. The aim is to ensure that our teaching will make a real difference in our students' lives.

References
Giangreco, M., D. Baumgart, and M. B. Doyle. (1995). "How Inclusion Can Facilitate Teaching and Learning." *Intervention in School and Clinic* 30, 5: 273–278.
Giangreco, M., C. J. Cloninger, and V. Iverson. (1993). *Choosing Options and Accommodations for Children: A Guide to Planning Inclusive Education.* Baltimore: Brookes.
Giangreco, M., R. Dennis, C. Cloninger, S. Edelman, and R. Schattman. (1992). "'I've Counted Jon': Transformational Experiences of Teachers Educating Students with Disabilities." *Exceptional Children* 59: 359–372.
Stainback, W., and S. Stainback. (1996). *Inclusion: A Guide for Educators.* Baltimore: Brookes.
Thousand, J., R. Villa, and A. Nevin. (1994). *Creativity and Collaborative Learning: A Practical Guide to Empowering Students and Teachers.* Baltimore: Brookes.

Promoting A Safe School Environment Through A Schoolwide Wellness Program

Patricia A. Gallagher and Linda S. Satter

When school officials have metal detectors at school entrances for weapon checks, conduct random drug testing of athletes, use breathalyzers to detect alcohol, inspect lockers, forbid pagers and cell telephones, and install video cameras in buses, they are doing so to protect youth from injury and tragedy. "Although some safety measures may need to be in place, this approach cannot be at the forefront of safe school plans (Lantieri, 1997, p. 157).

A balance can be created between promoting safe school environments through inspection practices and surveillance equipment and presenting a comprehensive wellness program that promotes a positive and supportive environment. School curricula should be taught by competent and caring teachers who provide students with experiences in problem solving and decision making strategies and opportunities to practice responsibility and respect. Teachers need to involve students as active participants and collaborators in program activities and extracurricular experiences to help them undertake commitments that encourage and reinforce kinder and gentler relationships.

IMPACT is such a program. It is a comprehensive high school program that promotes a positive and supportive environment by involving students, faculty, and the community in a variety of prevention, collaboration, and intervention activities in response to students' needs.

Patricia Gallagher is a Professor in the Special Education Department, University of Kansas, Medical Center. Linda Satter is IMPACT Coordinator, North Kansas City High School, North Kansas City, Missouri.

The long-range goal of the program is to equip students with essential skills to be healthy adults.

ORIGIN OF THE TOTAL WELLNESS PROGRAM

The program at North Kansas City High School (NKCHS), a small community adjacent to Kansas City, Missouri, grew out of an incentive grant written by the building principal to secure funding for safe-school training. The grant enabled eight of her teachers and some from area high schools to complete 36 hours of professional training through the Baptist Medical Center in Kansas City, Missouri.

The training is referred to as a student assistance program. Student assistance programs became prominent in the middle 1970s as an approach to addressing the growing problems related to adolescents' use and abuse of alcohol and other drugs. Over the years, advocates of student assistance programs realized that substance abuse is the result of, and is accompanied by, many problems. These include parental drinking or substance abuse, family frustrations with rearing children in today's culture, teenage depression and suicide, teen pregnancy, sexually transmitted diseases, divorce, and nicotine addictions.

As a result, the original training expanded to address the many and varied issues affecting adolescents today. It taught the adult learners the roles they can play to improve the school climate, promote students' self-image, and provide a home base where students can go to get help. As such, the program emphasized a comprehensive program designed to meet adolescents' needs. It also encouraged participants to find and network with human and community resources to assist the youth and their families. Essentially, the program teaches the value of enabling.

From it's "humble" beginning, which focused on keeping kids in and drugs out of school, IMPACT expanded each year with the addition of innovative programs to meet the needs of safety in the school and community. Currently, IMPACT is a total wellness and awareness program that provides students with a support network of peers, teachers, parents, and school and community programs. It is designed to recognize troubling trends and respond to societal changes that can consume the lives of youth and drive some from the education system. The ultimate outcome is to provide students with the necessary skills to be healthy adults.

When the initial group of North Kansas City High School teachers returned from their student assistance training, they reported their experiences at a faculty meeting. Their enthusiasm for what could be done at the school was contagious and encouraged other colleagues to become part of this new wellness program. Now when new faculty members arrive at the school, they are encouraged to take the training offered at Baptist Medical Center.

Students learn about the program's activities during registration and the freshmen orientation session. Throughout the school year posters and announcements are made inviting students to join.

Block-scheduling arrangements give students and staff members interested in the IMPACT program opportunities for participation. This scheduling allows students to meet their seven classes on Monday and four 85-minute classes from Tuesday to Friday. Two of these classes are designated as seminar times encompassing a variety of activities. For example, students can use seminar time to plan skits, organize events, and present lessons to children in nearby elementary and middle schools. Teachers are assigned to five classes, two planning periods, and three extra-duty assignments. Teachers can fulfill their extra-duty requirements by acting as sponsors for an IMPACT program.

THE CURRENT WELLNESS PROGRAM

IMPACT consists of two major components: a "participation" and a "helping" component. The *participation component* is composed of a variety of student activities that include SAVE, peer mediation, Impact Improv, SADD, Hi-Step, PAL, high school heroes, and TRY. The *helping component* includes PATHS, a student's resource officer services, individual counseling, community counseling services, conflict-resolution meetings, support groups, ethical decision-making and problem-solving workshops, teen institute, and referral services to outside agencies. The following descriptions will reveal an interconnection between these two major components of the wellness program.

In addition, there is a complementary relationship between IMPACT and the school discipline policies and procedures. For example, peer mediation may be an alternative to suspension or arrest. If word reaches IMPACT that a potential fight may erupt, the likely violators can be offered a mediation session that potentially can prevent a suspension or arrest. Peer mediation also has been used after an incident that resulted in disciplinary action. In this case, mediation assists the violators to think ahead to acceptable responses if a similar incident, temptation, or problem should arise.

Participation Component

SAVE

Students Against Violence Everywhere is a group of concerned students who work closely with local police departments and community agencies to find ways to decrease violence in the schools and communities. The program was designed to address violence in the high schools and to carry the message that school is a safe environment. At first it was concerned with six topics: gangs, cliques, weapons, students feeling like outcasts, racial problems, and drugs.

SAVE began in 1991 when the Kansas City, Missouri, Police Department decided that a comprehensive program was needed to make the school environment safer. Faculty members at the four high schools within two school districts in the North Patrol Division of Kansas City, Missouri, were asked to provide a group of students that the police could talk to about violence in their schools. The students gave their perceptions of violence in the schools, and recommendations on how to combat it.

Students from each grade level in each high school were brought together to discuss the problem of violence in the area's high schools and to design a program that would address the problem. They suggested that the following three committees be formed to help carry out a series of activities as outlined below:

- a Student Steering Committee, composed of three students from each of the four high schools;
- an Administration Committee made up of representatives from law enforcement, the school administration, social service agencies; IMPACT coordinators from the four high schools who represented the teachers, and juvenile justice officers;
- an Advisory Committee composed of community leaders.

Once the committees had been established, the following 10 activities were recommended as a means to address violence in the schools.

1. *Mediation.* Students were to be trained to serve as mediators to handle disputes between fellow students.

2. Police. Uniformed police were to be present in the school to interact with the students and to enforce the laws. The officer would instruct, counsel, and arrest.
3. *Disciplinary procedures.* The police would be called and appropriate action taken when students commit acts of violence in schools. Students would be disciplined by assigning them jobs at the school, such as assisting the custodians in cleaning the school or in the community, such as working at the city's recycling center. Suspension from school was not seen as punitive. Therefore, detention periods were recommended during the offender's free time, such as Friday nights and Saturday mornings.
4. Family counseling. Services were to be made available to families needing counseling assistance. This would include problem counseling for the students and assistance for parents who were having difficulty with parenting skills.
5. *Awareness.* As an initial effort to change some destructive attitudes of students and adults, it was recommended that publicity be generated about SAVE and the causes of violence in the schools.
6. *Teen hotline.* A hotline was to be established. Through the hotline, individuals could notify school administrators and the police about illegal activity, such as students carrying weapons and engaging in gang activity.
7. *Legislation.* Legislation was recommended for holding parents accountable for the weapons they have in their homes.
8. Student body. A cross-section of the student body was to give suggestions to students with disciplinary problems.
9. Activity night. Occasional nights were to be designated for dances at a neutral place for all high school students.
10. Questionnaire. A questionnaire was to be developed and distributed to all students to secure their perceptions of violence in their school and to solicit suggestions on how to combat violence. This was to be the basis for further program development.

As an initial step, the Student Steering Committee developed a questionnaire and gave it to each student in the four high schools. More than 4,000 students responded. The questionnaire and responses are shown in Figure 1.

After the responses to the questionnaire were analyzed, the Student Steering Committee, faculty, school administrators, IMPACT coordinators, law enforcement personnel, and social service agencies proceeded to implement their safe school programs. North Kansas City High School implemented the following:

- A faculty member teaches students to mediate disputes between peers. This peer mediation enables students to negotiate differences before they escalate. The training also covers information on racial and cultural differences.
- A uniformed police officer is present. The officer is available to teach in the classrooms; assists in counseling sessions with students, and serves as a liaison between the school and outside agencies, such as the county juvenile justice personnel. In addition, the officer takes reports and makes necessary arrests.
- A disciplinary procedure requires parent involvement and alternative solutions to after-school detention periods. Detentions are on Friday from 2:40 p.m. to 5 p.m. Parents or guardians are asked to check their child into the detention period.
- A process enables students to work out personal problems and directs students and their parents to family counseling. A youth and family service agency provides services including counseling, a place for runaways, and a girl's home. The program offers a 24-hour hotline for personal problems. The telephone number is displayed on a SAVE poster.
- Displays of SAVE posters and SAVE certificates for participating classrooms endorse the SAVE concept. The poster, designed by a student, contains two telephone numbers: one number for personal problem counseling and the other for reporting illegal activity.
- A method has been established to report illegal activity. Students call to report illegal activity anonymously. The Kansas City Crime Commission staffs the telephone number, and contacts the appropriate school administrator to report the information. When necessary, the school administrator works with the police to address the activity.
- Mandatory reporting of violent activities is required. Missouri Code, Chapter 12.3, requires that certain crimes be reported to the police; therefore every school has to report violent crimes to the police who would handle each case on its merit. During a meeting, representatives from the juvenile justice system informed the students, police, IMPACT coordinators, and administrators about prosecution for juvenile crimes.
- A curriculum that addresses violence is in place. The material promotes a decrease of dating/domestic violence and abuse of children and their families. In addition, it advocates prevention in educational videos and during lectures and discussions. The program is designed to promote (a) effective interpersonal communication skills, (b) conflict resolution in a peaceful manner, (c) self-awareness and appropriate identification and expression of feelings, and (d) awareness and understanding of the dynamics of abusive relationships. The program is taught by classroom teachers who have been trained at a facility for abused children and adults.

The SAVE program is reviewed annually. When the first year ended, new Steering Committee members were selected to replace graduated seniors. In addition, a bro-

```
            Students Against Violence Everywhere
1. Do you think violence is a problem in your school?
   Total Responses = 2386     Yes = 654 (27%)        No = 1732 (73%)
2. Do you think your safety is threatened at your school?
   Total Responses = 2380     Yes = 308 (13%)        No = 2072 (87%)
3. Do you think the administration takes proper measures in handling violence?
   Total Responses = 2322     Yes = 1441 (62%)       No = 881 (38%)
4. Would you rather discuss your problem with trained peers than the administration?
   Total Responses = 2272     Yes = 1450 (64%)       No = 822 (36%)
5. Have you personally experienced a violent confrontation while in school?
   Total Responses = 2326     Yes = 651 (28%)        No = 1675 (72%)
6. Do you think weapons are a problem at your school?
   Total Responses = 2302     Yes = 438 (19%)        No = 1864 (81%)
7. Do you think a lot of violence starts with racism?
   Total Responses = 2311     Yes = 1522 (66%)       No = 789 (34%)
8. What do you think is a leading cause of violence in your school?
   A. Broken Relationships         = 684 (17%)
   B. Sports Competition           = 482 (12%)
   C. Drugs and Alcohol            = 669 (17%)     Total Responses = 4054
   D. Racism                       =1526 (38%)
   E. Sexual Harassment/Date Rape  = 357 (9%)
   F. Other                        = 336 (7%)
9. How do you think violence can be prevented in your school?
   A. Harsher Punishments          = 949 (45%)
   B. Uniformed Police Officers    = 539 (26%)     Total Responses = 2093
   C. Other                        = 605 (29%)
10. Where do you think violence originates?
    A. Home                        =1347 (41%)
    B. School                      = 941 (28%)
    C. Work                        = 203 ( 6%)    Total Responses = 3315
    D. Television                  = 565 (17%)
    E. Other                       = 259 ( 8%)
```

FIGURE 1
Results of Questionnaire

chure was designed to describe the SAVE programs. Funding was secured from an advertising agency and a printing company to have a brochure printed for every student in the four high schools.

Among the comments of SAVE students is the following from a junior who plays varsity football and plays golf. He said the program had a direct effect upon him by helping curb his tendency to get involved in fights.

> I had a short quick temper. I've learned to control it and realize there is no point giving into violent behavior. I have other solutions and ways out. I will back off.

Another student shared his experiences:

> SAVE has given me the opportunity to voice my opinion of how we should deal with the growing amount of violence. Not only have I told my ideas, but I see them going into effect.

Peer Mediation

Peer mediators are students who, with adult supervision, help resolve disputes between students. Issues that create disputes include rumors, threats, name-calling, fighting and loss of property. Peer mediators are selected for their abilities of fairness, reliability, and good communication. In addition to training in effective communication techniques, problem solving, and critical thinking skills, they are taught a conflict resolution approach wherein disputants have the chance to sit face-to-face and talk uninterrupted so each side of the dispute is heard.

As the outside persons who lead the discussion, peer mediators do not take sides, and they keep all information confidential. After the disputants relate their versions of the incident the mediators define the problem. Then the mediators and disputants brainstorm options to resolve the conflicts and write them on the **Brainstorming Worksheet** form (Figure 2). They discuss what could have been done differently, what they can do to solve the immediate dispute, and what options they could choose if a similar problem should arise again in the future. When a solution is reached and agreed upon, it is written on the **Peer Mediation Agreement Form** (Figure 3), which the disputants and the mediators sign.

After the conflict resolution session, the peer mediators are responsible for completing *a self-evaluation form* designed to encourage the student's mastery of the mediation skills (Figure 4). Mediators receive feedback and support throughout their work with peers.

A peer mediator, who was the senior class president, wrestler, and down lineman for the football team, said he believes that involvement in athletics is a healthy outlet for potentially aggressive behavior:

> I'm not a fighter. When I see a fight, I think there are other ways out. I like to help people and look for reasonable solutions for problems. There are a lot of things we can do through peer mediation.

Impact IMPROV Impact IMPROV is a group of students who perform skits with wellness themes to preschool, elementary, middle, and high school students. IMPROV students receive education in drug and alcohol abuse, family dysfunction, peer pressure, dating issues, eating disorders, and other social skills. Then they and a teacher work together to plan skits on requested topics. After the students give a performance, they ask questions of the audience to initiate dialogue. For example, at a day care center where the students performed *Stranger Danger*, the 4-year-olds were asked to identify the stranger in the performance. They were asked why they should not go with strangers and were asked what they would do if a stranger were to approach them.

IMPROV activities have been effective in that they not only keep everyone's attention but also elicit great conversations. One of the actresses said,

> We enjoy performing for our audiences. It makes us feel that we're helping them solve their problems. In return it makes us feel better.

IMPROV activities are described in a brochure circulated to the elementary schools and in verbal communications with civic groups. Requests for performances come from elementary counselors, teachers, day care centers, civic groups such as the Rotary, church groups, and PTAs. During the past year, IMPROV performed at four elementary schools during each of five lunchtimes. In addition, the group does after-school, breakfast, evening, and weekend performances. Requests are now coming in from other cities and school districts.

Thank-you notes have come from preschool children, parents, teachers and community members. The group has become very popular. Demands for after-school performance have become so extensive that IMPROV has been included in the school's Drama II class.

SADD

Students Against Destructive Decisions (formerly known as students against drunk drivers) is a program designed to raise students' awareness of the dangers of drinking and driving. To reinforce its message, the group engages in a number of activities throughout the academic year. For example, in May SADD presents a skit to demonstrate the risks of drinking and driving. During a mock scene, SADDs members wear "fatal vision" goggles that simulate the effects of alcohol by impairing their ability to walk a straight line.

In a docudrama held outdoors, police, medical technicians, squad cars, and ambulances join the SADD group for a DWI mock car accident. The emergency personnel attend to the accident victims, and the police question the witnesses to highlight the consequences of drinking. After the audience has watched the scene, they wear "fatal vision" goggles to learn firsthand how vision, coordination, driving skills, and mental judgment become impaired after drinking. Thus, the potential for fatal consequences becomes very real. The goggles give students the opportunity to understand the dangers of alcohol and drug ingestion without actually experimenting with them.

SADDs also send birthday cards, with a quarter enclosed, to sophomores when they turn 16. Students are encouraged to use the money to call home for a ride if

Peer Mediation Agreement

Peer mediator ____________________ Date __________

Briefly describe the conflict: ____________________

____

____

____

____

____

Type of conflict (check one) ☐ Rumor ☐ Threat ☐ Name-calling ☐ Fighting

☐ Loss of property ☐ Other (specify) ____________________

The students whose signatures appear below met with a peer mediator and with the assistance of the mediator reached the following agreement.

Disputant ____________________

Agrees to ____________________

____

____

Disputant ____________________

Agrees to ____________________

____

____

We have made and signed this agreement because we believe it resolves the issue(s) between us.

____________________ ____________________

Disputant signature Disputant signature

____________________ ____________________

Peer mediator signature Length of mediation (minutes)

FIGURE 3
Peer Mediation Form

Brainstorming Worksheet

List all the possible options.

▲ What could be done to resolve this dispute?

▲ What other possibilities can you think of?

▲ In the future, what could you do differently?

1. ____________________
2. ____________________
3. ____________________
4. ____________________
5. ____________________
6. ____________________
7. ____________________
8. ____________________
9. ____________________
10. ____________________

FIGURE 2
Brainstorming Worksheet

Peer Mediator Self-Evaluation

Peer mediator ____________________ Date __________

Directions: Place a checkmark (✓) by each step where you did quality work. Place an asterisk (*) by each step where you think the quality could improve.

☐ Step 1: Open the session

☐ Step 2: Gather information

☐ Step 3: Focus on common interests

☐ Step 4: Create options

☐ Step 5: Evaluate options and choose a solution

☐ Step 6: Write the agreement and close

1. What did you do well?

2. If you could do this mediation again, what might you do differently?

3. Were certain steps more difficult for you than others? If so, what could you do to strengthen these steps?

4. Do you have any other concerns or questions?

Staff supervisor ____________________ Date __________

Comments:

FIGURE 4
Peer Mediation Self-Evaluation

they have been drinking. A week in the fall is designated Red Ribbon Week. This is a time when students are asked to wear red ribbons to remind everybody of the dangers of drinking and driving. During this week SADD also places small white crosses on the school grounds to demonstrate how many teenagers die daily in alcohol-related deaths. During Christmas week the student body is encouraged to stay safe over the holidays.

Hi-Step

High School-Taught Elementary Program is a cross-age teaching program in which high school students teach fourth graders about peer pressure, conflict mediation, drug and alcohol abuse, and relationships. Two faculty members sponsor the program.

Because Hi-Steppers are viewed as role models for the younger students candidates are carefully screened. They are chosen for good academic records and having an interest in helping fourth grade students grow emotionally and socially.

Hi-Step students receive their training during late winter and early spring. They attend an 8-hour training session to become familiar with the characteristics of fourth graders, learn to investigate topics, plan activities, and learn to write lesson plans. After their training, Hi-Step participants develop six lessons. Students meet with one of the sponsors weekly during seminar time to review their lessons, receive feedback, and practice with the other students in their group.

After the six lessons are ready, the group is assigned to an elementary school. Hi-Steppers are responsible for meeting with the fourth grade teachers and setting up times to meet with their classes. For this purpose, the Hi-Steppers have permission to leave high school during the seminar times. They have time to arrive at their assigned elementary school and teach the hour-long lessons with their accompanying activities, and returning before their own academic periods begin.

Although publicity for the program is done in the classrooms through the school's television channel and posted flyers, the most compelling publicity comes from the enthusiastic Hi-Steppers. Telephone calls start coming in October of the year preceding the performance.

Hi-Step experiences are great for the high school students who have a career interest in teaching or social services and for the fourth graders who have met teenage models. Hi-Step students tell how important they feel when they meet the fourth graders at the mall and are introduced to the parents.

The president of the Hi-Steppers summarized the group's intentions:

> If we reach one child, giving them the courage to do what is right, then we've met our goal. We want kids to know that their high school years can be a great time in their lives if they make the right decisions, and we help them to realize what those good decisions are. Most of all, we want them to know that we care.

PAL

Peers Always Listen (PAL) provides a group of students to whom other students can talk. PALs make a commitment to do what they can to encourage a positive and supportive atmosphere at the school. PALS do not give advice but, instead, listen and try to help their peers sort out their feelings. Consequently, all PALS receive training in assertive listening skills. They learn that emotion can be "energy" in motion and that the best way to defuse an emotional moment is to give the excited student an opportunity to "let the air out." They accomplished this by listening attentively. A student who is "highly charged" may talk only in syllables or phrases. A PAL listens until the peer is able to express himself or herself coherently. PALs are committed to the positive action of listening with care.

PALs also take part in other IMPACT programs such as SADD and IMPROVS. They tutor, distribute, and hang red ribbons for Red Ribbon Week and participate in activities that have the potential to improve the school atmosphere. They welcome new students and help them adjust to school.

One of the latest activities to be included in PAL is to spend some seminar time in a special day school for students who have behavior disorders. PALs engage in non-academic tasks such as playing board games, shooting baskets, and making crafts. They have been well received by the students and teachers alike.

A PALs participant stated,

> The group teaches students how to be more aware of their peers' feelings and about themselves. It introduced me to many new students like myself who are interested in the well-being of their classmates. The training teaches great people skills.

High School Heroes

High School Heroes is a group of students who teach a tobacco prevention program to fourth, fifth and sixth graders, sponsored by the American Lung Association. This organization prepares the students to be peer educators regarding the forces that influence children's decisions to smoke or not to smoke. In preparation for their roles, the High School Heroes learn about the immediate effects of smoking, how to reinforce positive attitudes about being a nonsmoker, how to make specific decisions, and how to use the refusal skills necessary to resist pressures to smoke. They also learn how to lead a discussion about the respiratory system that includes a demonstration of the effects of smoking.

The American Lung Association recommends that the Heroes program be used as part of a health curriculum to enhance the existing substance abuse program. The Association provides a guide with activities for tobacco education. After the Heroes complete their training, they work in groups of five to prepare a 1-hour tobacco education lesson. After completing their lesson work, they contact fourth-, fifth-, and sixth-grade teachers to set up times for delivering their lesson.

The Lung Association suggests that peer education can have a significant influence on students' knowledge and attitudes about smoking. They believe their training can have an impact on high school students' leadership skills and can reinforce positive attitudes about being a nonsmoker.

TRY

Teaching and Reaching Youth (TRY) is composed of parents and community members from business, police, the service agencies, and education. Its main purpose is to engage the community in focusing on developing knowledge, attitudes, and skills concerning tobacco, alcohol and other drug abuse, and related wellness issues. Specific efforts familiarize the community with state laws, school district policy, and local ordinances relating to these topics. The group's mission is to promote physical and mental wellness in young people through community involvement.

TRY recognizes that youth can be at risk when drugs and alcohol are present during social events. It knows that some students will be pressured by peers to participate. Therefore, one of its programs is Safe Homes for Teens, in which information is sent to parents to secure their support in providing safe homes for student parties. Safe Homes provides homes free of drugs and alcohol. Safe Home parents have access to other committed parents who have pledged to support this cause. TRY has also met with hotel and motel managers requesting that they deny room reservations to prom students who seek accommodations for their parties.

TRY has provided some of the financial support for a popular annual youth activity, school lock-in, in which the SAVE group is also involved. A lock-in provides a safe environment, such as a community center, for a night of social activities that include music, dancing, basketball, swimming, gameroom fun, food, and nonalcoholic beverages.

Some of TRY's other activities include sponsorship of Red Ribbon Week with a community kick-off rally. The group purchases ribbons to tie on utility poles and trees, and yard signs caring the message Drug Free and Proud throughout the city. TRY also sponsors community PIE (Parent Informational Evenings) nights. Here, speakers from the community share information about current topics—for example, the issue of methadone laboratories and what to do about their accessibility to the youth. Methadone labs, for some reason, are prevalent in the surrounding area; hence the need to address the situation.

Helping Component

PATHS

Practical and Academic Transitions to High School (PATHS) is a 3-week summer course designed to prepare eighth graders for a smooth transition to high school. During this course incoming students receive an orientation to the school and community and participate in a special curriculum that promotes student bonding and thematic learning.

For the development phase of PATHS, the building principal recruited a group of teachers interested in the PATHS concept. They developed the summer program, an environment in which students making the transition from middle school to high school could feel more secure and successful. The principal presented the idea to the central office and received funding for the 3-week program.

Two faculty members became co-directors of PATHS. They were joined by four teachers, an instructional assistant, and an attendance secretary to develop the summer program's activities. Peer helpers representing a diverse student population were also selected to give special presentations to middle school students, the potential participants for the summer program.

Peer helpers serve as tutors, conflict mediators, teacher assistants, and hall monitors. They operate the school store during the breaks, are group leaders in the homerooms, and run errands.

In the first PATHS program in 1994 four middle schools enrolled 91 students. They received one-half elective credit for attending all the sessions and completing assignments. The five peer helpers received credit also. The 3-week program began with student bonding activities that continued into week two and week three, which focused on thematic learning.

Week 1. The main objective of the first week was to encourage the students to bond as a team and to become oriented to the school and community. The activities were as follows:

- *The Challenge* consisted of high and low rope courses designed to teach cooperation, communication, peer support, team building, and self-confidence through a series of well-supervised physical challenges. Students spent a full day off campus at an adventure site in the woods.
- *Being Successful* focused on characteristics that successful people have in common. These include being responsible, hard-working, and team players, as well as going the extra mile. Students became acquainted with successful peers and guest speakers who taught the school's expectations for its students. They were asked to reflect and write about someone whom they considered successful. In addition, they were instructed in the components of peer mediation leading to win/win situations.
- *Community Orientation* involved students in a picture-taking walking tour of North Kansas City. Students learned about aspects of the city including its history, architecture, and culture. The mayor welcomed the students and discussed city government. When the students returned from the day's adven-

tures, they worked together to develop a travel brochure of the city.
- *School Orientation* familiarized the students with traditions of the high school. The students went on a walking tour of the campus and learned the buildings and locations of departments. Course offerings, transcripts, school rules, and expectations were discussed. Students became acquainted with the school planner, which they are responsible to keep during their freshmen year.
- *Diversity Training* was presented by Anytown USA, a program sponsored by the Council of Christians and Jews. It begins with participatory situations for students to experience being different, such as having the disability of blindness, deafness, or confinement in a wheelchair. These are followed by decision-making activities that promote an understanding of and appreciations for diversity of people in the community and school. The experiences encourages positive self-image, communication skills, leadership ability, male/female perceptions, police/youth relations, racial understanding, cultural awareness, and family and peer relationships.

Week 2 and Week 3. A thematic learning experience focused on the music industry and provided continuity throughout the second and third weeks. A music theme was selected because of its appeal to the adolescents. Students attended three classes per day. At the end of each day, students assembled in the auditorium to participate in musical enrichment. A variety of musical groups performed, and students responded to and critiqued the performances. Three specific academic areas were imbedded in the learning: mathematics, communication, and study skills and are described as follows:

- *The Mathematical Skill Program* invited the students to use their skills to manage a band. They were responsible for scheduling performance events, figuring time cards, using charts and graphs to record number of performances and the time schedules, mapping travel routes, and writing paychecks. Students were scheduled individually to work in the Computer Curriculum Corporation, a programmed learning of computer use for the development of math skills.
- *The Communication Skills Program* prepared students to read, discuss, and analyze music reviews. Students wrote critiques of the musical performances they heard in the afternoon. They practiced proofreading skills and oral presentation of their work. They engaged in an art activity by making a collage around the theme of music.
- *The Study Skills Program* familiarized the students with teacher expectations. Students were taught techniques for previewing lessons and learning the value of understanding each section. Techniques for oral and written reviews also were taught and applied to the materials they were using in the thematic unit. Test-taking skills were presented. Instruction included the teaching of skills required to pass verbal, multiple-choice, and essay tests successfully. Students also were exposed to the assignment procedures the faculty used for grading assignments.

PATHS participants get together several times during the academic year. They have plays, speakers, and casual conversation periods to talk about how school life is going. The Peer Helpers have initiated many informal one-on-one meetings with the freshmen.

School Resource Officer

The School Resource Officer is available to assist students with various legal concerns. These concerns have been about abusive parents, abusive boyfriends, DUI arrests, traffic tickets, and probation contingencies.

The School Resource Officer program, begun in Phoenix, Arizona, in the mid-1980s, has been adopted by some police departments throughout the United States. The duties of the School Resource Officer in the IMPACT program are as follows:

1. To be a resource to instructional units to students on issues related to a basic understanding of the law and the role of law enforcement.
2. To be a resource for instruction to students on issues related to violence, prevention of violence, and personal safety.
3. To facilitate individual and small-group discussions based on material presented in class, or other topics such as date rape, driving while intoxicated, and automobile accidents relevant to student/officer interests. These groups take place during school time or outside of school time.
4. To hold conferences with students to assist them with problems regarding alcohol, other drugs, law enforcement, crime prevention, or personal safety.
5. To meet with students and make referrals to community agencies that offer assistance to youth and their families.
6. To provide informational services to the staff on issues related to alcohol and other drugs, the law, violence, gangs, safety and security.
7. To provide faculty training on skills related to violence prevention, violence diffusion, creation and maintenance of a safe environment.
8. To meet and interact with the Student Steering and Administrative Committees to assist them in any of the programs or legislative issues that SAVE is pursuing.

The SRO commented at the conclusion of his 4 years in the school:

> My job as an SRO has been a very rewarding period of my law enforcement career. I've been able to interact with, educate, and positively influence more kids over time than many officers do throughout a career. Since the inception of my role, the number of fights, gang activity, thefts, and drug-related cases has consistently de-

clined. An SRO should be mandatory for every middle school and high school. The value of a safe school environment and the positive law enforcement presence cannot be overstated. SROs are a necessity in schools today. They not only assist in maintaining a safe school environment but also help in building responsible adults.

Operation Drug Dog

In 1997 the entire community took a proactive position on the drug issue by purchasing Twiko, a black Belgian Malinois dog, born and trained in the Netherlands for police work. His specialty is sniffing for drugs, especially marijuana, cocaine, heroin, and methamphetamines. Twiko became part of the community as a result of a campaign spearheaded by a trio of adults—the School Resource Officer, the IMPACT coordinator, and a mathematics teacher.

Although drug reduction efforts had been established in the school and community, not all drugs are found because they are concealed so easily. Teachers had been concerned about the prevalence of drugs in the community and how it was reflected in the school. Some students were returning "high" from open lunch and some were passing drugs on school grounds. At a faculty meeting the teachers said, "We're sick of losing students to drugs." The School Resource Officer, dedicated to the students' welfare, was adamant about finding ways, in addition to his work, to eliminate drugs from the school. The SRO, the IMPACT coordinator, and a mathematics teacher approached the school administration, police chief, community organizations, and city council regarding a plan, "Operation Drug Dog." They received approval, but not financial support, for the plan.

The School Resource Officer searched for other communities that had raised $20,000 required to cover the cost of the dog, his training, travel, kennel and cage, the travel lodging and training of the officer (who is not the SRO) assigned to Twiko. After finding a community that issued stock to raise funds, the trio decided to use that approach for fund raising. Stock was sold to individuals, including students and senior citizens, civil organizations, and corporations, for $10, $25, and $100, respectively. Within 4 months the funds had been raised. The dog was purchased and trained with the officer. Then Twiko arrived to live in the community that owns him.

After his arrival each contributor was presented with a stock certificate and a photograph of Twiko with his officer. Their duties include night patrols, searching for drugs at sporting events, and random visits to the high school. There Twiko is treated to plenty of petting and attention. He is successful in sniffing out drugs, even minute amounts.

Counseling Services

Counseling services are available for individuals and groups during school hours and with a variety of community agencies. Students are referred by parents, teachers, friends, and self-referrals to the IMPACT coordinator, who devotes all her time to the role. Reasons for referrals include suspected drug and alcohol abuse, poor or failing grades, eating disorders, pregnancy, abuse, depression, and suicidal tendencies. When a student discusses a problem with the IMPACT coordinator, it is followed by an appraisal relevant to the type of support that will be needed. This may include school support, a community referral, a support group, or professional counseling.

The IMPACT coordinator contacts others, such as the parents, teachers, or community personnel, to gather pertinent information that will be useful in an intervention and treatment plan. If a student receives services outside the school, the coordinator is in contact with the agency to facilitate communications and coordinate everyone's efforts. In addition, if the student spends time in a treatment facility, the coordinator notifies the student's teacher, collects homework, and maintains communication between the agencies.

One student commented,

> Being sent for treatment saved my life because it helped me realize that I did have things to live for and look forward to when I'm older.

A parent noted,

> I rally appreciate your efforts, your compassion, and your understanding during all of this with my daughter. We have been down a long, rocky road, and without the support of others like you, I don't think the ending of this story would have turned out nearly so well.

The IMPACT coordinator has seen a change in students' attitudes about getting help with their problems.

> It's no longer "un-cool" to talk about having problems. In fact, I can see where students have become more comfortable about dealing with their issues. I can't think of anything more important than the emotional well-being of our youth. If students aren't ready emotionally, they are never going to get it together academically.

Grief Counseling

Grief counseling became prominent in 1995, when the staff at NKCHS and other high schools throughout the United States recognized changes in the emotional health of students after traumatic events. Fatal and near-fatal injuries from accidents and acts of violence, as well as serious illness, were touching students' lives. When adolescents suffer grief from the loss, injury, or illness of someone they love, the emotional experience affects their behavior and can affect academic performance. They are particularly vulnerable to loss. "Grief is a keen and complex emotional experience that includes fear, anger, relief, despair, peace, guilt, numbness, agitation and sorrow" (Naierman, 1997, p. 62). As students go through the stages of bereavement, they do not always know that others are having similar experiences. In an effort to reach out to the students, NKCHS established guidelines to help the students heal. A plan was written describing an organized way to respond to a crisis.

During the time when the committee was working on the plan, a tragedy occurred: Four students were killed in an automobile accident. The developing guidelines were immediately put into operations, subsequently reviewed, and changes made. The IMPACT coordinator contacts community agencies for their support and obtains trained teachers to lead support groups. The guidelines delineate duties between the administrative team and the counseling team, and the lines of communication to students, staff, parents, community agencies, and the media. The teams provide crisis counseling and crisis rooms as long as they are needed. All activities are documented on a checklist for the management of a traumatic event.

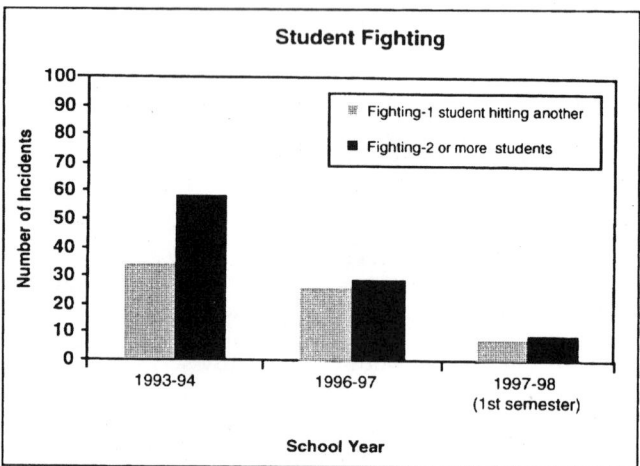

FIGURE 5
Number of Student Fights

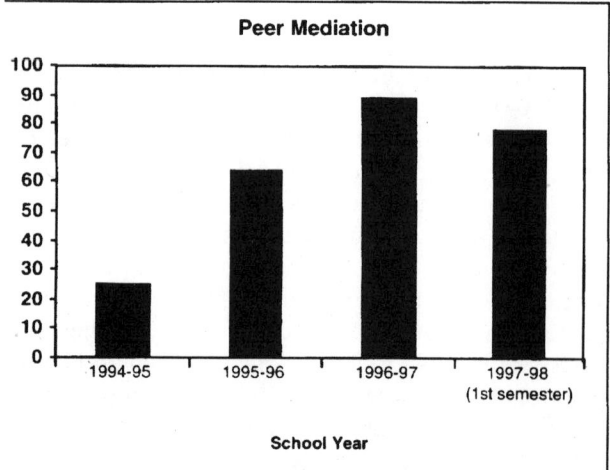

FIGURE 6
Number of Peer Mediation Sessions

DATA AND RESULTS OF IMPACT

The success of IMPACT is revealed informally by the participants in their comments cited throughout this article. In addition to these statements, data records for the number of student fights and student conflicts reveal a decline in student to student confrontations. Data on peer mediation illustrate an increase in the number of sessions. Figures 5 and 6 present these data. It is reasonable to assume that the following variables contributed to the decline of fighting: (a) the SAVE program had been initiated in the 1993–94 school year: (b) the peer mediation program was initiated in 1994–95; (c) a school resource officer was assigned to the school; and (d) a zero-tolerance policy relevant to fighting was implemented in the 1995–96 school year.

SUMMARY

One midwestern high school is taking proactive, constructive steps to protect students and strengthen their relationships with their peers, the faculty, and the community. The IMPACT program focuses on the importance of improving the entire school environment as a significant way to enhance students' wellness and safety. When students, faculty, and community members nourish inviting relationships, caring communities develop. Schools that implement only measures such as metal dectectors, student identification badges, and locker inspections have confined themselves to solutions that are problematic. If, on the other hand, schools include practices that promote cooperation, teach conflict resolution, highlight the value of service to others, encourage empathy, and promote belonging and trust, they truly create safe schools.

REFERENCES

Lantieri, L. (1997). From punishment to prevention: Educating the heart. *Reclaiming Children and Youth.* 6(3).

Naierman, N. (1997). Reaching out to grieving students. *Educational Leadership.* 55(2).

We thank the many persons who have contributed to the success of IMPACT, the schoolwide wellness program, especially Evelyn Matthys, IMPACT coordinator for North Kansas City School District; Dr. Vicki Baker, Associate Superintendent of North Kansas City School District; Debbie Burns, Special Education Teacher; Rob Russell, School Resource Officer; IMPACT Care Team; IMPACT Student Participants; Bob Kelly and John Admire, Baptist Medical Center, Kansas City, Missouri.

APPENDIX

Demographics of KNCHS

North Kansas City High School (NKCHS) is one of three high schools serving the North Kansas City School District, which includes 20 elementary schools and four middle schools. The school is located in the small town of North Kansas City; therefore, most of the students are residents of the surrounding areas. The school district is north of the business and financial nucleus of metropolitan Kansas City, Missouri. It is a campus-style facility composed of five separate buildings, the oldest of which was constructed in 1925.

The population represents nearly a complete cross-section of socioeconomic groups. Primary employers of the parents include the major airport, federal and state government agencies, automobile, electronic, paint, and agriculture industries.

The school has 1,400 students. The ethnic make-up of the school is 90% Caucasian; the minority populations are represented equally by African American, Asian American, and Latin/Hispanic American cultures.

The school is a Missouri A+ school. A major benefit of this designation is that students who plan to attend a Missouri 2-year community college or vocational school after graduation may be eligible for State-reimbursed fees, books, and tuition. To be eligible, a student must complete the standards for graduation set by the school. In addition, the student must (a) have attended an A+ school for at least 3 years, (b) maintain 95% attendance, (c) have a 2.5 grade-point average on a 4.0 scale, (d) complete 50 house of unpaid tutoring or mentoring, and (e) maintain good citizenship.

Unit 2

Unit Selections

6. **From Philosophy to Practice in Inclusive Early Childhood Programs,** Tom Udell, Joyce Peters, and Torry Piazza Templeman
7. **Together Is Better: Specific Tips on How to Include Children with Various Types of Disabilities,** Jane Russell-Fox
8. **Wellness Programming for Preschoolers with Disabilities,** Carol Huettig and John O'Connor
9. **Is Everyone Included? Using Children's Literature to Facilitate the Understanding of Disabilities,** Joan K. Blaska and Evelyn C. Lynch

Key Points to Consider

❖ How can early childhood educators merge developmentally appropriate practices with special education strategies in inclusive preschool programs?

❖ How can a preschool teacher set up a classroom and offer choices to children with a variety of types of disabilities so that all students can learn together?

❖ Why is wellness programming important for preschoolers with disabilities? How does it effect quality of life and, perhaps, longevity?

❖ Why should books that include representations of children with disabilities be read to all preschoolers? Give examples of some possible books.

 Links www.dushkin.com/online/

10. **Early Childhood Care and Development**
    http://www.ecdgroup.com
11. **I Am Your Child**
    http://www.iamyourchild.org/start.html
12. **Institute on Community Integration Projects**
    http://www.ici.coled.umn.edu/ici/overview/projects.html#1
13. **SERI: Special Education Resources on the Internet**
    http://www.hood.edu/seri/serihome.htm

These sites are annotated on pages 4 and 5.

Early childhood

The 1986 amendment to the Individuals with Disabilities Education Act (IDEA) provided for intervention for young children with disabilities much earlier than elementary school. The 1997 reauthorization of IDEA supported and augmented the mandate for early childhood special education and especially for family-child intervention at home. All services to be provided for any infant, toddler, or preschooler with a disability, and for his or her family, are to be articulated in an individualized family service plan (IFSP). The IFSP is to be written and implemented as soon as the infant or young child is determined to be at risk for a developmental delay. At-risk conditions may be problems associated with prematurity, low birth weight, birth injuries, and early environmental trauma. IFSPs specify what services will be provided for the parents, for the diagnosed child, for siblings, and for all significant caregivers. Children with autism, traumatic brain injuries, blindness, deafness, orthopedic impairments, health impairments, or multiple disabilities may require extensive and very expensive early childhood interventions. Today, a great deal of educational money is being spent on early diagnosis and treatment of conditions of disability.

IFSPs are written in collaboration with parents, experts in the area of the child's exceptional condition, teachers, home-service providers, and other significant providers. They are updated every 6 months until the child enters public school and receives an individualized education plan (IEP). A case manager is assigned to oversee each individual child with an IFSP to ensure high quality and continuous intervention services.

In the United States, an association called Child Find has the responsibility for locating and identifying infants, toddlers, and young children who qualify for early childhood special education and family services. Infants and children are viewed as qualifying for special services if they are at risk for delayed development. An actual diagnosis, or label of condition of exceptionality, is not required. Assessment is usually accomplished in a multidisciplinary fashion. It can be very difficult. As much as possible, it is conducted in the child's home in a nonthreatening fashion. Diagnosis of exceptionalities in children who cannot yet answer questions is complicated. Personal observations are used as well as parent reports. Most of the experts involved in the multidisciplinary assessment want to see the child more than once to help compensate for the fact that all children have good days and bad days. Despite the care taken, many children who qualify for, and would benefit from, early intervention services are missed.

A challenge to all professionals providing early childhood special services is how to work with diverse parents. Some parents welcome any and all intervention, even if it is not merited. Other parents resist any labeling of their child as "disabled" and refuse services. Professionals must make allowances for cultural, economic, and educational diversity, multiple caregivers, and single parents. Regardless of the situation, parental participation is the sine qua non of early childhood intervention.

At-home services may include instruction in the use of any aids (wheelchair, hearing aid, cane), ways of meeting the educational goals of the IFSP, and basic skills such as discipline, behavior management, nutritional goals, and health maintenance. At-home services usually also include counseling for parents, siblings, and significant others to help them deal with their fears, anger, and anxiety and to help them understand how to accept, love, and challenge their special child to become all he or she is capable of being. The case manager helps ensure that there is cooperation and coordination of services by all team and family members.

Most children receiving early childhood services have some center-based or combined center- and home-based special education. Center care introduces children to peers and introduces the family to other families with similar concerns. It is easier to ensure quality education and evaluate progress when a child spends at least a part of his or her time in a well-equipped educational setting.

The first selection for this unit on early childhood takes the reader on a journey from the philosophical roots of programs for young children to the practice of special education in early childhood education inclusion programs for children with disabilities. The authors believe that research-supported special education practices should not be excluded from inclusive preschool curricula. Rather there should be a merging of developmentally appropriate practices for serving young children with intervention practices focused on special education goals and services.

The second article in this unit provides specific tips on how to include children with various types of disabilities in a preschool program. Jane Russell-Fox, a preschool teacher, has had success working in inclusive classrooms and writes about her tried-and-true techniques enthusiastically. She gives lists of specific suggestions for children with a variety of needs: communication, health, hearing, learning, physical, vision. She pays particular attention to the facilitation of social skills in all children.

Wellness programming is the subject matter of the third article in this early childhood section. The notion that health and well-being is multifaceted and complex should be introduced very early in life. Young children benefit most from lessons on emotions, environmental concerns, ethics, intellectual aspects of life, nutrition, physical fitness, and vocational considerations when they are embraced on a daily basis through preschool play.

The last article in unit 2 presents books that explain how to facilitate young children's understanding of disabilities. The recommended readings can be powerful tools that enable IDEA and integrated classrooms to achieve more successful education of all children in the future.

From Philosophy to Practice in Inclusive Early Childhood Programs

Tom Udell
Joyce Peters
Torry Piazza Templeman

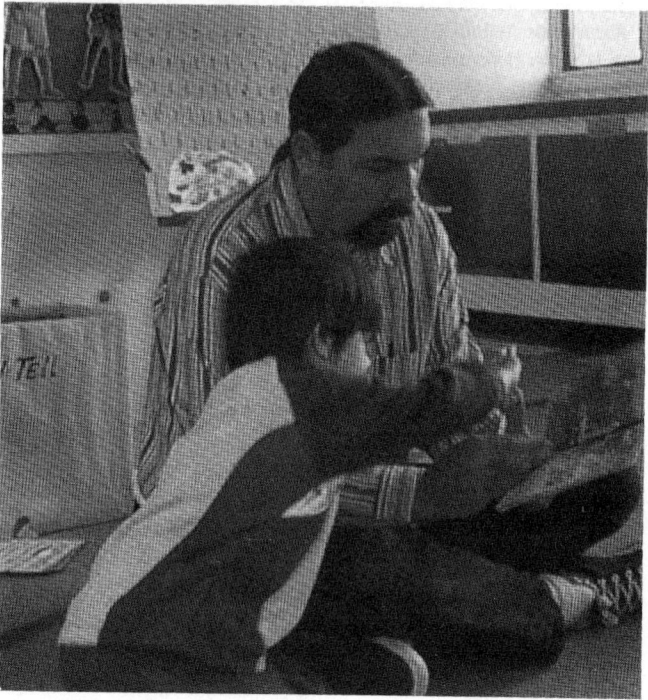

Two 4-year-olds are playing at the water table. Their teacher observes that Michelle splashes her hand on the surface repeatedly, chortling with delight. Carlos is busy pouring water from a large container into several smaller ones and then arranging them in a pattern to his liking.

These children of the same age are at different developmental points in their lives. How can a teacher or a child care provider allow Michelle to do all the splashing she needs to do, teach her social skills in water play, and also encourage Carlos to continue his absorption in measuring and artistic design—as well as learn the social skills of playing with Michelle? A simple water table activity is more complicated than it seems. Why is this play activity important? How can an inclusive program meet the needs of both children?

The Individuals with Disabilities Education Act has challenged all providers of service to young children with disabilities to provide services in natural community settings where young children without disabilities participate. Educators are looking for ways to merge developmentally appropriate practices with practices found effective in the field of early childhood special education. Although these two sets of practices converge at certain points, professionals agree that differences remain (Bredekamp & Rosegrant, 1992).

The Teaching Research Early Childhood Program has developed a conceptual framework to meet the challenge of blending developmentally appropriate practices with early childhood special education recommended practices. This blended approach has resulted in the delivery of quality services within an inclusive preschool/child care setting.

Elements of an Inclusive Program

In the context of early childhood education, what are the differences among practices known as *mainstreaming*, *reverse mainstreaming*, *integration*, and *inclusion*? All these terms denote the introduction of children with disabilities into a "typical" environment for some portion of the day, or in the case of reverse mainstreaming, the introduction of some typically developing peers into what is essentially a special education program.

Inclusion goes further in that no one is introduced into anyone else's program. All children attend the same program, all of the time. Each child is given the support he or she needs to be successful in the setting. For children age 3 to school age, these settings are most often public and private community preschool and child care programs.

The most comprehensive and widely disseminated guidelines defining quality services in these settings are *developmentally appropriate practices*, as defined by the National Association for the Education of Young Children (NAEYC).

Research in early childhood special education indicates that those using these developmental guidelines as the *sole* principles for providing services to young children with disabilities would fall short of providing the full range of services these children need. Carta, Schwartz, Atwater, and McConnell (1991) warned against the adoption of these guidelines to the potential exclusion of principles and practices that we know are effective for children with disabilities, but also suggest that educators not overlook developmentally appropriate practices in providing inclusive services for these children. Indeed, Bredekamp and Rosegrant stated in a 1992 NAEYC publication:

> Experiences with mainstreaming over the past two decades suggest a conclusion that probably will be made concerning the guidelines... and children with special needs 20 years from now: The guidelines are the context in which appropriate early education of children with spe-

Principles of Early Childhood Special Education

- Intervention focused on functional goals
- Family-centered services
- Regular monitoring and adjustment of intervention
- Transition planning
- Multidisciplinary services

cial needs should occur; however, a program based on the guidelines alone is not likely to be sufficient for many children with special needs. (p. 106)

Let's look at both recommended practices—developmentally appropriate practices and early childhood special education practices—and find points where educators, children, families, and communities can work together to make inclusive programs successful.

Developmentally Appropriate Practice

NAEYC published a widely used position statement about developmentally appropriate practices for serving young children from birth to age 8 in early childhood programs (Bredekamp, 1987). The association compiled and published this statement in reaction to the concern of early childhood educators with the increasing academic demands made of young children in early childhood programs and general misconceptions about how teachers should provide instruction to young children.

This position statement became the most widely recognized guideline in the field of early childhood education. In 1997 NAEYC published the revised *Developmentally Appropriate Practice in Early Childhood Programs* (Bredekamp & Copple, 1997), clarifying the misunderstandings and misinterpretations that arose from a decade of extensive dissemination of the original position statement.

Based on the developmental theories of Piaget and Vygotsky, the NAEYC guidelines convey the primary message that *learning occurs through exploratory play activities* and that formal instruction beyond the child's current developmental level will result in nonfunctional, rote learning at best. Developmentally appropriate practice suggests that teachers should not attempt to direct or tightly structure learning experiences and that formal academic instruction at the preschool level should not occur.

These guidelines have three dimensions, as follows:

1. *Age appropriateness*. According to child development knowledge and research, all children grow and change in a universal, predictable sequence during the first 9 years of life. This knowledge about typical child development allows teachers to plan appropriate environments and experiences.
2. *Individual appropriateness*. Each child has his or her own unique pattern of growth, strengths, interests, experiences, and backgrounds. Both the curriculum and adults' interactions with children should be responsive to these individual differences.
3. *Cultural appropriateness*. To truly understand each child, teachers and child care providers must recognize and respect the social and cultural context in which the child lives. When teachers understand the cultural context in which children live, they can better plan meaningful experiences that are relevant for each child (Bredekamp & Copple, 1997).

Teachers should use knowledge of child development to identify the range of appropriate behaviors, activities, and materials for a specific age group. As well, they should use this knowledge in conjunction with an understanding of each child in the classroom and his or her unique personalities, backgrounds, and abilities to design the most appropriate learning environment.

NAEYC recommends that instructional practices emphasize child-initiated, child-directed play activities, based on the assumption that young children are intrinsically motivated to learn by their desire to understand their environment. Teaching strategies include hands-on exploratory activities with emphases on the use of concrete, real, and relevant activities.

Rationale of Early Childhood Special Education

Early childhood special education is based on the premise that early and comprehensive intervention maximizes the developmental potential of infants and children with disabilities. Such intervention produces child outcomes that would likely not occur in the absence of such intervention (McDonnell & Hardman, 1988).

Since the initiation of publicly supported services for preschool children with disabilities in the mid-1970s, professionals in early childhood special education have developed a body of practices. This body of practice has evolved from research, model demonstration, and evaluation efforts and is currently referred to as *early childhood special education recommended practices*. Researchers have documented syntheses of desired characteristics, or recommended practices, of exemplary, early childhood special education models (DEC, 1993; McDonnell & Hardman, 1988; Wolery, Strain & Bailey, 1992; Wolery & Wilbers, 1994). We have selected components of these models and practices that researchers have shown to be essential, effective, and compatible with the NAEYC guidelines (see Carta et al., 1991, for evaluation criteria). These components include setting functional goals and monitoring children's progress toward these goals, planning for transitions, and working closely with families.

Intervention Focused on Functional Goals

Intervention for children with disabilities should focus on producing specific and measurable child goals. To make meaningful changes in children's behavior, these goals need to be functional for each child and for the environments in which the child participates. A *functional* skill is one that is essential to participation within a variety of integrated environments. In early childhood settings, functional skills are those that assist children to interact more independently and positively with their physical and social environments.

For example, it is probably more functional for a child to be able to carry out his or her own toileting functions independently than to be able to name 10 farm animals. Shouldn't we give preference to skills that will enable the child to participate more fully in an integrated setting, as

---

Effective early childhood instructional practices emphasize child-initiated, child-directed play activities, based on the assumption that young children are intrinsically motivated to learn by their desire to understand their environment.

opposed to those skills that would be indicated in the developmental hierarchy or sequence? If our answer is yes, these goals then become the focus for providing individualized intervention. Teachers or care providers design services and instruction to produce a specific outcome—like independent toileting—and this outcome becomes the standard against which the success of an intervention is measured.

Family-Centered Services

The family is the heart of all early childhood programs. Families participate in planning and decision making in all aspects of their children's program.

A good school-family partnership includes a system for a child's family to have regular communication with the classroom staff and have frequent opportunities to participate in their child's program. Quality programs also include procedures for helping families link into existing community resources.

Regular Monitoring and Adjustment of Intervention

Educators and care providers should systematically monitor the effects of specific interventions. Researchers have shown the effectiveness of using *formative* assessment data to monitor children's progress toward their individual goals and objectives. (McDonnell & Hardman, 1988).

We know that such data must be gathered frequently enough to monitor the subtleties of progress or failure. Data-collection systems must measure child progress toward the acquisition of predetermined goals, including the application of skills in a variety of settings.

Transition Planning

Educators and care providers of all children—and particularly children with disabilities—must plan for transition from one school or child care setting to the next one. Early childhood special educators are particularly concerned with transition from preschool to kindergarten because this move signals a major change for the child and the family from familiar and secure surroundings to a new, unknown setting.

This is a time of considerable stress, and teachers and child care providers must engage in careful, timely planning to smooth the process. Many people are involved in the transition planning process: the child's family, the sending teacher, the early intervention specialist, support personnel, and the future receiving teacher. An effective transition plan often begins 1–2 years before the actual move. This preliminary planning enables the sending teachers to identify skills needed in the future environment. These skills are included in the child's curriculum during the last preschool years.

Key Aspects of Developmentally Appropriate Practices

- **Developmental evaluation of children for program planning and implementation**
- **High staff qualifications**
- **High ratio of adults to children**
- **Strong relationship between home and program**

Multidisciplinary Services

Professionals from many disciplines need to participate in the planning of comprehensive services for children with disabilities and their families. Because many of these children and their families have complex needs, no single professional and no one discipline can provide a full range of services.

The specific needs of each child and family determine what disciplines should be involved in assessing, planning, implementing, and monitoring services. The following disciplines are commonly involved in early childhood special education:

- Speech and language therapy.
- Occupational and physical therapy.
- Health and medical services.
- Audiology.
- Disability-specific specialists, such as a vision specialist or autism specialist.

Professionals in these disciplines provide services in an integrated manner: They share knowledge and methods across disciplines, and the entire team develops and implements one comprehensive plan. Following this plan, team members provide consultation services within the early childhood environment.

Merging Programs Through Developmentally Appropriate Practices

The first step to merging these approaches is to recognize the advantages a program adhering to developmentally appropriate practices offers for the successful inclusion of children with disabilities. Such a program will have high-quality components, many of which facilitate the inclusion process.

Facilitating Inclusion

The nature of developmentally appropriate practices allows for the inclusion of children with great variation in development within the same setting. Even in a group of young children without disabilities, of the same age, children can be as much as 2 years apart developmentally.

Thus, planning developmentally appropriate activities and providing equipment and materials for the preschool setting already accommodates children in a wide development range. This allowance in planning and material selection makes it possible to include children with mild and moderate disabilities without additional adaptation.

This developmental approach to planning creates an ideal environment for embedding instruction on individually targeted skills. The developmental emphasis on learning as a process rather than a product also facilitates targeting a variety of individualized objectives. To illustrate the process-versus-product approach, let's look at ways teachers might provide art experiences—and individualized instruction—for children.

The *process* approach to art allows children to explore available materials, experiment, and create individual designs with little regard for the end product. This approach also allows for intervention on a variety of instructional objectives for children with disabilities while all children are involved in the same activity. For example, all children are involved in a finger-painting activity; one child may be working on requesting objects, another on identifying colors, and yet another on staying with the group.

Providing Quality Indicators

Developmentally appropriate practices are not a curriculum, nor do they dictate a rigid set of standards. Developmental programs will not all look the same, but they will have a similar framework that pays careful attention to child development knowledge and will assist educators in providing quality services for children. The use of developmentally appropriate practices ensures quality in programs in many ways, such as developmental evaluation of children for program planning and implementation, high staff qualifications, a high ratio of adults to children, and strong relationship between home and program.

- *Developmental evaluation.* Decisions about enrollment and placement have a major effect on children. Educators and care providers base these decisions on multiple assessment data emphasizing observations by teachers and parents. Teachers use developmental assessment of child progress and achievement to adapt curriculum, communicate with families, and evaluate program effectiveness. Developmental evaluations of children use valid instruments developed for use with young children; these assessment tools are gender, culture, and socioeconomically appropriate (Bredekamp, 1987).

6. From Philosophy to Practice

Children of the same age can be as much as 2 years apart developmentally.

- *Staff qualifications.* The NAEYC guidelines for developmentally appropriate practice emphasize the need for staff with preparation and supervised experiences specific to working with young children. Early childhood teachers should have college-level preparation in early childhood education and child development.
- *High adult/student ratios.* A key to implementing developmentally appropriate practices is to have a small number of children per classroom and a high ratio of adults to children. Ratios suggested in the NAEYC position statement are higher than those required for licensing in most states. NAEYC recommended standards describe a ratio of 2 adults to 20 children ages 4–5, with younger children requiring smaller groups with higher adult-to-child ratios.
- *Home-to-program relationship.* NAEYC guidelines recommend parent involvement in all decision making, regular communication between parents and teacher, and encouragement of parent involvement in the day-to-day happenings of the program. These practices help in building a strong relationship between home and the child's community program.

Developing a Conceptual Base

We have developed a conceptual base, recognizing the two sets of practice, that will allow both developmentally appropriate practices and special education principles to exist within the same setting. The Teaching Research Early Childhood Program has developed a philosophy that views developmentally appropriate practices as the foundation on which individualized programs are built, adding special education instruction when needed for individual children. We believe that the two approaches to early childhood are not mutually exclusive.

Figure 1 illustrates this dilemma. The builder has two sets of clearly different materials and cannot decide which to use. The key to moving beyond this dilemma is to recognize that these practices serve distinctively different purposes—and we can view them as different types of resources.

- *Developmentally appropriate practices* are used to design an age-appropriate, stimulating environment supportive of all children's needs. These practices, however, were not developed to reflect or address specific individual needs of children with disabilities and offer little information about specific intervention strategies needed to serve these children.
- *Early childhood special education* practices are used to complement the basic program for children with exceptional developmental needs and to emphasize individualized strategies to maximize children's learning opportunities. These practices, however, do not provide guidelines for designing a quality early childhood learning environment.

When educators recognize these practices as being different, but compatible, they can then plan a single comprehensive program, as shown in Figure 2. The completed school uses developmentally appropriate practices as the material from which the foundation is built and special education practices as the material that completes the structure.

Implementing Both Practices Within the Same Setting

Let's look more closely at how this merger might work. A well-designed early childhood education program, following developmentally appropriate practices, uses a planned, well-organized environment where children interact with materials, other children, and adults. Here the NAEYC guidelines are apparent: Young children are intrinsically motivated to learn by their desire to understand their environment; the program is set up to allow children to self-select activities from a variety of interest centers.

When children show they need further support, educators use special education strategies that are made available in the program. These strategies include the following:

- *Directly prompting practice* on individually targeted skills, based on functional behavioral outcomes.
- *Reinforcing* children's responses.
- *Collecting data* to monitor children's progress and make intervention changes.

Some educators view these strategies as conflicting with developmentally appropriate practices. Some people liken this direct prompting to the formal instruction that NAEYC deplored for use with young children. We believe that this view is a misinterpretation of NAEYC's position statement and the guidelines for developmentally appropriate practices.

As we mentioned earlier, however, NAEYC guidelines do not exclude intervention strategies for children with identified special needs (Bredekamp & Rosegrant 1993). We hope that by clarifying this misinterpretation, we might encourage teach-

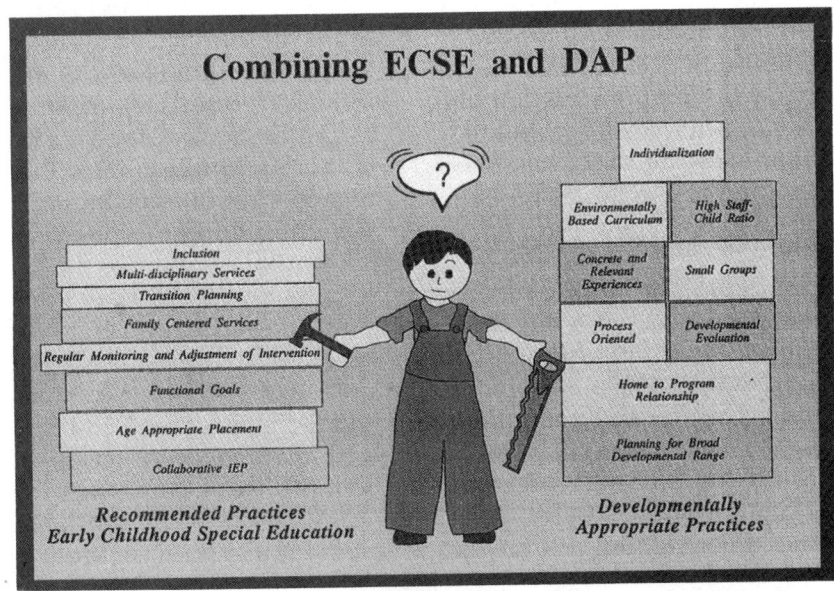

Figure 1

ers to view these intervention strategies as individually appropriate for some children.

As educators begin to merge these two approaches to early childhood education, we will find all children participating in the same well-organized, systematically planned environment—with direct instruction being provided to children who need this type of intervention. This direct instruction is blended into naturally occurring opportunities throughout the ongoing daily routine, such as play at the water table or learning independent toileting. An early childhood program adhering to developmentally appropriate practices provides a strong foundation for the provision of consultation services from professionals across different disciplines.

Consider transition services—an area of special education services that some educators believe conflicts with a child-centered developmental program. The transition planning process has an apparent conflict with developmentally appropriate practice because it presumes that the needs of some future environment should drive the child's curriculum at present. Guidelines for developmentally appropriate practices reject the idea of current curriculums being driven by the needs of a future environment.

To resolve this conflict we can look to the *foundation* concept. In developmentally appropriate practice, we find children participating in an environment planned to fit their current developmental demands and individual backgrounds and interests. Within this environment, children with special needs receive instruction on specific skills that will assist them to be successful in their next setting. Teachers have selected these specific skills or objectives with direct regard to the child's current needs and level of functioning, with some, but not predominant, focus on transition skills needs as dictated by future environments. Skills selected because of the demands of a future environment are ones that can be facilitated without disruption in the current environment. These skills are also within the boundaries of being developmentally appropriate in the future environment.

Mutually Beneficial, Not Mutually Exclusive

In inclusive early childhood education programs, we must caution against adopting developmentally appropriate practices to the exclusion of research-supported special education practices. Similarly, we must not fail to recognize the benefits offered by placing children with disabilities in developmentally appropriate programs. We need to develop an understanding of both sets of practices and to develop a program, from philosophy to practice, that merges practices.

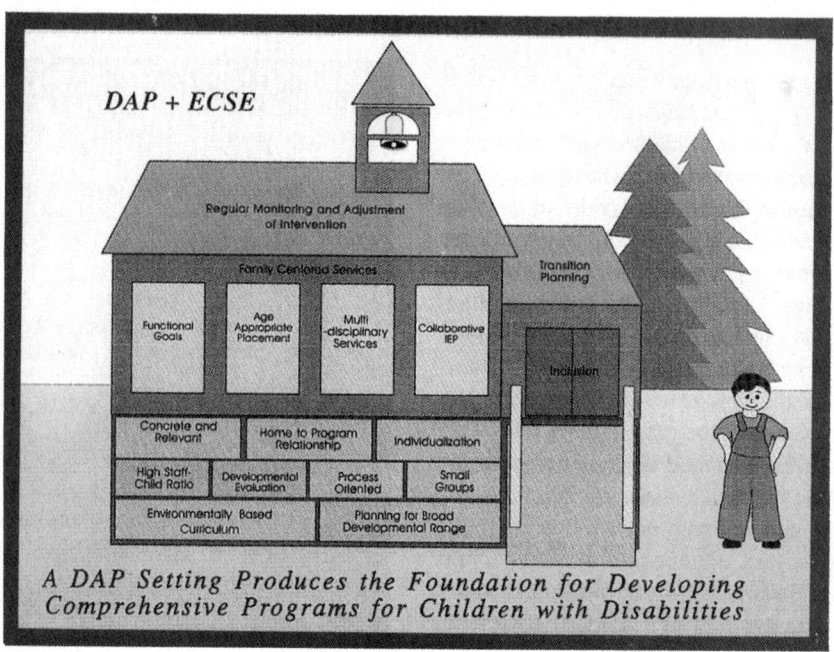

Figure 2

A DAP Setting Produces the Foundation for Developing Comprehensive Programs for Children with Disabilities

References

Bredekamp, S. (Ed.). (1987). *Developmentally Appropriate Practices in Early Childhood Programs Serving Children from Birth Through Age 8* (Exp. ed.). Washington, DC: National Association for the Education of Young Children.

Bredekamp, S., & Copple, C. (Eds.). (1997). *Developmentally Appropriate Practices in Early Childhood Programs* (Rev. ed.) Washington, DC: National Association for the Education of Young Children.*

Bredekamp, S., & Rosegrant, T. (Eds.). (1992). *Reaching potentials: Appropriate curriculum and assessment for young children* (Vol. 1, pp. 92–112). Washington, DC: National Association for the Education of Young Children.

Carta, J. J., Schwartz, I. S., Atwater, J. B., & McConnell, S. R. (1991). Developmentally appropriate practice: Appraising its usefulness for young children with disabilities. *Topics In Early Childhood Special Education 11*(1), 1–20.

DEC Task Force on Recommended Practices. (1993). *DEC recommended practices: Indicators of quality in programs for infants and young children with special needs and their families.* Reston, VA: The Council for Exceptional Children, Division of Early Childhood Education. (ERIC Document Reproduction Service No. ED 370 253)

McDonnell, A., & Hardman, M. (1988). A synthesis of "best practice" guidelines for early childhood services. *Journal of the Division of Early Childhood, 12,* 328–337.

Wolery, M., Strain, P. S., & Bailey, D. B. (1992). Reaching potentials of children with special needs. In S. Bredekamp & T. Rosegrant (Eds.), *Reaching potentials: Appropriate curriculum and assessment for young children* (Vol. 1, pp. 92–112). Washington, DC: National Association for the Education of Young Children.*

Wolery, M., & Wilbers, J. S. (Eds.). (1994). *Including children with special needs in early childhood programs.* Washington, DC: National Association for the Education of Young Children.*

Books Now

*To order books marked by an asterisk (*), please call 24 hrs/365 days: 1–800–BOOKS–NOW (266–5766) or (702) 258-3338 ask for ext. 1212 or visit them on the web at http://www.BooksNow.com/TeachingExceptional.htm. Use Visa, M/C, or AMEX or send check or money order + $4.95 S&H ($2.50 each add'l item) to: Books Now, 660 W. Charleston Blvd., Las Vegas, NV 89102.

Tom Udell, *Assistant Research Professor;* **Joyce Peters**, *(CEC Oregon Federation), Associate Research Professor;* **Torry Piazza Templeman**, *(CEC Oregon Federation), Associate Director, Teaching Research Division, Western Oregon University, Monmouth.*

Address correspondence to Tom Udell, Teaching Research Division, Western Oregon University, 345 N. Monmouth Ave., Monmouth, OR 97361 (e-mail:udellt@wou.edu).

We would like to thank Kathy Haydon for her illustrations.

Together Is Better:
Specific Tips on How to Include Children with Various Types of Disabilities

Jane Russell-Fox

Develop a professional relationship with the child's parents. Keep communication lines open among all involved—parents, physicians, special education teachers, and other relevant people.

Jane Russell-Fox, M.Ed., is a preschool teacher for the inclusive "Wee Wildcat" program for the Eastmont School District in East Wenatchee, Washington.

Photographs © The Growth Program.

My experiences with both inclusive and noninclusive environments has led me to conclude that "together is better." I believe that early childhood professionals who are including children with special needs in their classrooms can set up the environment so that it accommodates these children as well as typically developing children. In doing this the professional takes the first steps toward successful inclusion.

While working in several different self-contained settings, I spent most of my time negotiating with my peers and administrators to plan for inclusion of the special needs children in my group. Usually my plan was for inclusion that would operate 15 to 20 minutes of the school day to give my children a chance at least to hear others model language, involve themselves in cooperative play, and establish friendships.

Staff members who knew I was a strong supporter of inclusive classrooms tended continually to say to me, "That sounds like a good idea; we should try that next week." Next week always came, and we were no closer to the beginning of an inclusive environment than we were the week before.

After my experiences in inclusive environments, I know now that everyone has to be sold on inclusion before it can work successfully. After one is sold on inclusion, it's the job of the team to set up the environment and offer choices to all children at a variety of levels so that all can learn together in the same room.

It is also the job of the team to continue updating skills and working to improve the effectiveness of the program. Children with special needs do need specialized services based on individual needs, including predictable routines, accurate record keeping of goals, effective teaching strategies, all performed in a developmentally appropriate environment. There is no blueprint to follow—each person is an individual.

The following ideas are only a way to get you started. A range of services needs to be provided to most children with special needs. You can't do it all by yourself. Expect your team members to be there for you. Team members can include everyone from a child care provider to an occupational therapist.

The following processes are adaptations that are easy and use many commonsense ideas and readily available materials. For example, Jennifer has a vision impairment and is not able to see some of the books you read during circle time. What can you do? Try storytelling, enlarging the books, using flannel-board characters, or giving Jennifer a designated spot toward the front during circle time.

Working with a child who has exceptional health needs

• Develop a professional relationship with the child's parents and physician, and in some cases with other care providers who may come in contact with the child.
• Keep communication lines open among all.
• Get informed about the child's health needs, including medicine and diet.
• Invite the school nurse to become a part of the team.
• Develop a program plan for the child who may be out of the classroom for long periods of time. Home visits, telephone calls, classmate phone lists, and care packages from classmates or activity packets from the teacher can assist the child and his or her family in continuing to be a part of the classroom.*

Working with a child who has exceptional hearing needs

• Develop a professional relationship with the child's parents, audiologist, hearing specialist, sign language interpreter, and speech and language therapist.
• Keep communication lines open with them.
• Learn to change a hearing aid battery and cord.

Facilitating social skills is an essential part of facilitating true inclusion. Teachers will want to keep groups relatively small so children can interact as children typically do.

• Use visual and tactile aids as much as you can.
• Use the child's name when seeking the child's attention.
• Make sure you have the child's attention before beginning the activity, giving directions, or introducing additional material.
• Speak at normal speed and volume without exaggerating lip movements.
• Make certain the child sits up close for good visibility of the teacher, activity, and other children.
• Encourage language in group activities by allowing time for the child to start and finish speaking.*

Working with a child who has exceptional learning needs

• Concentrate on the child's strengths, not weaknesses.
• Present content in short segments using a multisensory approach (audio, visual, manipulative).

Provide for as much overlearning or repeated practice as necessary.
• Praise the child's progress.
• Use task analysis.
• Be patient when it is necessary to show a child how to do something many times.
• Give directions one at a time until a child can handle more than one.
• Help parents to recognize their children's small successes.
• Plan for modeling and imitation.
• Provide clear transitions; try to avoid abrupt changes in activities.
• Present developmental-level challenges.
• Allow time and opportunity to practice new skills needed for activities.

Specific intervention strategies for working with a child with visual impairments

• Consult with the child's parents and vision specialists to determine what the child can see and what play materials would be most appropriate.
• Orient the child to the classroom layout and locations of materials. Give a new orientation whenever changes are made.
• Provide the child with a rich variety of tactile, manipulative, and auditory experiences.
• Encourage independence both by your actions and in the way the room is arranged.
• Be alert to the need for physical prompts.
• Before beginning a new activity explain what is going to happen.*

Working with a child who has exceptional communication needs

• Be a good listener.
• Use parallel talk. Broadcasting play-by-play action of the child's activity helps to stimulate the acquisi-

---

*Source: Adapted by permission from R. E. Cook, A. Tessier, and M. D. Klein, *Adapting Early Childhood Curricula for Children with Special Needs,* 3d ed. New York: Merrill/Macmillan, 1992, 206–07, 209.

tion of language (e.g., "You're putting the ball in the basket").
• Use alternative communications as needed (e.g., sign language, augmentative communication).
• Have everyone in the classroom model good language by talking about and labeling what they are doing.
• Promote specific reasons for expressing language (i.e., giving information, requesting and getting attention, protesting, and commenting).

Working with a child who has exceptional physical needs

• Get input from the physical therapist on the proper handling and positioning of the child. Get specific directions on the length of time the child should be in a given position. Seek suggestions from the occupational therapist on adapting fine-motor materials so that the child participates in all of the classroom projects. (Of course parents must be included in all planning for the child.)
• Make sure materials and toys are accessible to the child.
• Remember that physical delays don't always have an accompanying mental disability.
• Become familiar with adaptive equipment and know how to use and care for it.
• Arrange the environment to accommodate adaptive equipment.
• Allow extra time for making transitions.
• Support and encourage that which the child can do physically.
• Foster independence by focusing on the child's nonphysical abilities.

Facilitating social skills is an essential part of facilitating true inclusion. Teachers will want to keep groups relatively small so children can interact as children typically do. Rewarding remarks reinforce specific desired behaviors. Materials appropriate to the skills of interaction desired need to be provided. For example, if your desired outcome is cooperation, set up situations in the classroom to encourage teamwork—"After we pick up the blocks, then we can get ready for snack." Making sufficient materials available helps promote cooperation and imitation.

With each new child with special needs, a few accommodations can be made to a classroom environment and the instruction to allow these children to be included. Placing children with special needs in a learning environment with their typical peers offers many challenges for families and staff, but the rewards reaped and the teamwork accomplished are well worth the effort.

Coming into a work environment that is already sold on inclusion and is *practicing* it has been one of the greatest rewards of my professional career. I strongly urge you to develop inclusive classrooms in *your* setting!

For further reading

Allen, K.E. 1980. *Mainstreaming in early childhood education.* Albany, NY: Delmar.

Barnes, E., C. Berrigan, & D. Biklen. 1978. *What's the difference: Teaching positive attitudes toward people with disabilities.* Syracuse, NY: Human Policy Press.

Buscaglia, L. 1983. *The disabled and their parents: A counseling challenge.* New York: Holt, Rinehart, & Winston.

Chandler, P.A. 1994. *A place for me: Including children with special needs in early care and education settings.* Washington, DC: NAEYC.

Cook, R.E., A. Tessier, & M.D. Klein. 1987. *Adapting early childhood curricula for children with special needs.* 3d ed. New York: Harcourt Brace Jovanovich.

Deiner, P.L. 1983. *Resources for teaching young children with special needs.* New York: Harcourt Brace Jovanovich.

Debelak, M., J. Herr, & M. Jacobson. 1981. *Creative innovative classroom materials for teaching young children.* New York: Harcourt Brace Jovanovich.

Froschl, M., L. Colon, E. Rubin, & B. Sprung. 1984. *Including all of us—An early childhood curriculum about disabilities.* New York: Project Educational Equity Concepts.

Fullwood, D. 1990. *Chances and choices: Making integration work.* Baltimore: Paul H. Brookes.

Trainer, M. 1991. *Differences in common. Straight talk on mental retardation, Down syndrome and life.* Bethesda, MD: Woodbine House.

Wellness Programming

For Preschoolers with Disabilities

Carol Huettig
John O'Connor

Children play like they are puppies. Others are kittens, and still others are turtles and clapping seals. What's this, a play-zoo nursery? No, it's a class full of young children using their imagination—happily exercising their muscles and getting fit.

The student moves on rocks to develop equilibrium.

This scenario is just one of many that educators can employ to promote wellness in young children. This article presents wellness as an approach to healthful living that emphasizes the integration of body, mind, and spirit. We describe activities to promote wellness for young children, with and without disabilities, that can be used in a carefully designed, coordinated effort by educators, caregivers, and parents.

> Wellness is an appreciation of the notion that everything a child does, thinks, feels, and believes has an effect on the quality of life and, perhaps, on longevity.

A Holistic Approach to Wellness

A holistic approach to educating young children in early childhood education programs is central to laying a lifetime foundation of wellness. Wellness is an appreciation of the notion that everything a child does, thinks, feels, and believes has an effect on the quality of life and, perhaps, on longevity. Wellness is a global term that reinforces the notion that human health and well-being is multifaceted and complex. Hettler (1979) defined wellness as a concept that includes the following dimensions:

- Physical fitness and nutrition.
- Spiritual values and ethics.
- Emotional health.
- Social, family, community, and environmental concerns.
- Intellectual aspects.
- Occupational and vocational considerations.

This multifaceted model is of use in the design and development of wellness programs for young children with and without disabilities. A wellness program, however, as a vital and integral part of the early childhood curriculum, must reflect recommended practices; that is, the program must be value based, family centered, multicultural, cross disciplinary, and developmentally and chronologically appropriate and must encourage normalization (McLean & Odom, 1996; see box, "Wellness Programming in Early Childhood Education").

Physical Fitness and Nutrition

The focus in physical fitness and nutrition programs for young children needs to be on *play choices* and *food preferences*. Educators, caregivers, and parents should help the child choose play that is vigorous and active, rather than passive, because it is crucial the young child has at least 30 minutes, if not several hours, of vigorous physical activity every day (American Association of Health, Physical Education, Recreation and Dance, 1998). We need to create an environment that provides the young child ample opportunity for play that involves vigorous gross motor activity. We must also reinforce the child if he or she chooses to participate in play that elevates heart rate, promotes flexibility, serves as the basis for the development of appropriate body composition, and fosters the development of muscular strength and endurance.

Physical fitness can be described in terms of health-related components: cardiorespiratory endurance, flexibility, body composition, and muscular fitness. Physical fitness programs for young children should begin with an assessment to determine current functional capacities. An "adapted" physical educator or a physical therapist can develop a specific program of exercise that addresses the child's unique needs (American College of Sports Medicine, ACSM, 1995). Our suggestions for activities are of use for most children, both with and without disabilities, but are not an exercise *prescription*.

A physical fitness program should include activities that address each of the components of health-related physical fitness.

Cardiorespiratory Endurance

Cardiorespiratory endurance involves the ability to move using large muscles in a rhythmic manner for long periods of time (ACSM, 1995) and may be enhanced through nature walks, running games, swimming, riding a tricycle, or dancing. Young children who use wheelchairs can participate in aerobic activities by rolling the chair or performing in-seat activities. The seated position may also be appropriate for students who have difficulty moving or who are overstimulated by vigorous locomotor activities. Examples of activities include punching the air or pumping the arms (above the head, in front of the chest, or to the side), twisting the upper body, doing arm circles, and touching toes (Huettig, Pyfer, & Auxter, 1993). While children are performing these activities, we should encourage them to move with smooth, large, rhythmical motions. Children should select their favorite music, particularly music that reflects their culture and heritage.

Flexibility

Flexibility is the maintenance of adequate range of motion in the body's joints (ACSM, 1995). Flexibility can be developed in static positions and rhythmic activities that encourage slow, smooth movements. Young children may imitate static stretching positions demonstrated by a "Gumby" or a "Raggedy Ann/Andy" doll. A child with a severe/profound physical disability may require a passive stretch in which the adult moves the young child through the movement or holds the child in a given position (Rimmer, 1994). Children with less severe disabilities may move through the stretching movement independently. Examples of simple rhythmic activities that encourage flexibility are "Preschool Favorites" and "Swing, Shake, Twist, & Stretch."

Body Composition

Body composition refers to the amount of body fat in relation to total body weight (ACSM, 1995). The Children's Defense Fund (1996) noted that 13.6 million American children, primarily from families with low socioeconomic status, suffer from malnutrition. Endres and Rockwall (1994) noted that 25%–29% of American children between the ages of 6 and 11 are overweight. Data from Women, Infants and Children of Dallas indicate that 30% of children between the ages of 3 and 5 years are obese (C. Wachtler, Nutritionist, personal communication, 1998). These figures are frightening.

Either excess or insufficient body fat can be harmful to health. Teachers, caregivers, and parents can help young children develop a healthy understanding of the need for a balance between diet and activity.

Muscular Fitness

The term *muscular fitness* has been adopted to describe the close relationship between the strength and endurance of muscles (ACSM, 1995). Muscular strength is the maximum amount of work that a muscle can perform, and muscular endurance is the ability to perform a task repeatedly (ACSM, 1995). Activities to develop muscular fitness in young children should address shoulder girdle/arm and abdominal muscles (see box, "Puppies, Kittens, and Turtles: Muscular Fitness Activities for Preschoolers").

Wellness Programming in Early Childhood Education

McLean and Odom (1996) discussed the six philosophical criteria for recommended practices in early childhood special education. How do these six criteria apply to wellness education?

Value Based. What could possibly be of more value to preschoolers, both with and without disabilities, and their parents, than the preschooler's health and wellness?

Family Centered. Parents must be respected as the child's primary educator, and as such, given every opportunity to plan, implement, and evaluate instruction. The specific activities and strategies designed to enhance the preschooler's wellness should be an integral part of programming in the preschool and in the home; the parents should help plan, implement, and evaluate instruction regarding wellness.

Multicultural. Suggestions for enhancing wellness attempt to be sensitive and respect a child's cultural, socioeconomic, and ethnic heritage. For example, books and music reflect diversity.

Cross-Disciplinary. Activities for promoting wellness are basic and could be easily implemented by direct and related services professionals, caregivers, and parents. For example, a speech and language therapist might use one of the nutrition activities as part of an integrated speech and language lesson. A physical therapist might help a preschooler navigate in his wheelchair on a nature walk. A special educator or a parent might use selected readings to address emotional wellness during storytime or reading before naptime. An assistive technologist might help a child with an expressive language deficit use a computer to express feelings and emotions. An adapted physical education teacher might help preschoolers with disabilities develop skills necessary to play on a playground.

Developmentally and Chronologically Appropriate. Each of the activities suggested has been specially designed for and used with preschoolers and their families.

Encourage Normalization. The wellness activities suggested can be used effectively in an inclusive preschool environment. The following groups of children have used and enjoyed each activity suggested: children in a preschool program for children with disabilities, children in Head Start, children attending prekindergarten, and kindergarten students.

Wellness programming should not be compartmentalized. The six dimensions of wellness must be considered every day as part of the total educational process.

EARLY CHILDHOOD

Fitness and Play

A child must have the opportunity to play in an environment with opportunities for active interaction with materials, other children, and adults. As adults, we must encourage children to choose *vigorous* activity, rather than passivity. We must create a learning environment for active play—indoors and outdoors—so that active, vigorous play is the most attractive choice for the child. Here are components of such an environment:

- Play materials are brightly colored (particularly important for the child with a visual impairment).
- Play equipment, indoors and outdoors, is child-sized.
- Carefully chosen objects and equipment (koosch balls, yarn balls, utility balls, bean bags, beach balls, covered balloons, and scoops) are in child-friendly sizes (large for catching and small, hand-sized for throwing) and vary in texture and shape.
- Transportation equipment (wheelbarrows, wagons, tricycles) is in a variety of child-appropriate sizes so the equipment can be used for individual play, partner play, or play with several children.
- Sandboxes have large shovels and pails, rather than spoons and small containers, so there is an emphasis on gross motor rather than fine motor skills.
- Children using wheelchairs, walkers, and crutches can access every part of the play area.

Most important, ensure that the play area has sufficient materials, equipment, and props to allow each child to play without sharing or wasting valuable movement time waiting turns to use a piece of equipment (Auxter, Pyfer, & Huettig, 1997).

Fitness Through Song and Dance

Educators and parents should address the physical fitness component of wellness in the daily classroom and home routine and must not limit children's fitness activities to the outdoor/indoor active learning centers, or worse yet, confined to "recess" time. Teachers can include active songs/dances in circle time; parents can sing/dance with children at home. Here are some simple songs/dances that foster the development of physical fitness (see Resources):

- "Swing, Shake, Twist and Bend," *Walter the Waltzing Worm*
- "Bean Bag Boogie I and II," *Kids in Motion*
- "Warm-Up Time," *Get a Good Start*

This student plays puppy on a leash, another muscular fitness activity for preschoolers.

- "Run, Run, Run in Place," *Preschool Aerobic Fun*

During story time at school and reading time at home, the teacher/caregiver and the parent should physically act out the story with the children. An adult who "huffs and puffs to blow the house down" makes the story of the "Three Little Pigs" come alive and encourages activity. When the class is making a transition from one room to another, let the children practice a locomotor skill. For example, ask the children to "march backward" to the cafeteria; the child using crutches can march, too.

Fitness Through Fun Nutrition

Nutritional awareness in preschoolers with disabilities is as basic as beginning to help the child make wise food choices. Several fun activities can help a preschooler with a disability begin to make good choices. For example, children can look through magazines to find pictures of food in the "Food Pyramid," cut and paste the pictures on cards, and play sorting and choosing games. Use a parachute to play "Tossed Salad": Ask some children to sit around the outside of the parachute. Ask a few children to be salad "stuff"—lettuce, tomatoes, peppers, celery, and other vegetables—and sit on the parachute, close to the center. Add dressing and croutons—balloons and beachballs. Then "toss the salad" by shaking the parachute.

Parents can play a great role in nutrition awareness by contributing healthy recipes for a class cookbook or by volunteering to cook nutritious foods, reflecting their culture and heritage, in the cooking center. They can then eat with their children at snacktime.

Spiritual Values and Ethics

Carefully designed play experiences give the preschooler the opportunity to explore and test limits in interaction with other children and with adults (Davis, Langon, & Malone, 1996). As teachers, caregivers, or parents, we can support the evolution of play in young children with disabilities by reinforcing kinds of behavior that help children move toward cooperative play.

For example, note if a child is beginning to watch another child at play: "Lashundra, I see that you are watching Ivy go down the slide." Ask another child if you can join him or her in sandbox play, or suggest that another child be allowed to join in: "Beth, can Jean grab a ride on the back of your tricycle?" If Beth answers, "No," honor her feelings and try again another time.

Preschoolers are definitely beginning to develop their values and ethics, and they test those values and ethics in and through play.

> **Children should select their favorite music for aerobic activities, particularly music that reflects their culture and heritage.**

Young children who use wheelchairs can participate in aerobic activities by rolling the chair or performing in-seat activities.

A consistently applied, fair set of simple classroom and home rules can also help a young child develop a sense of right and wrong.

Emotional Health

A substantial body of evidence suggests that a high "emotional quotient" may be infinitely more important to a child than a high "intelligence quotient" (Goleman, 1995). Certainly, a child's ability to interact effectively with peers and with adults is basic to success in life. Lieberman (1994) reflected on the healthy development about toddlers and young children:

> How do we know whether a toddler is growing well or not? Toddlers who are growing well seek approval but are not obsessed with it. They can tolerate reasonable amounts of frustration, and they can go back and forth flexibly between asserting their will and complying with the will of others. The healthy child also feels comfortable with a full range of emotions. A three-year-old boy I know was asked by his solicitous mother if he was happy. After thinking for a minute, he answered: "I am happy and sad and angry and bitey and clingy." (p. 4)

In this instance, the child was infinitely more wise than his mother. He acknowledged the whole realm of human emotion as a possibility. Recognizing that young children with disabilities need to be able to identify and understand human emotion, Furman (1995) stated:

> I would love to see as a part of every early childhood education program's evaluation a section covering the child's ability to identify appropriately his basic feelings of sadness, anger, fear, excitement, and happiness.
>
> Next could come the more shaded subtleties of feelings, such as lonely as well as sad, cross or annoyed, as well as excited, loving, as well as happy.... Can the child not only identify the basic feelings and their more subtle variations as he experienced them but also effectively and properly put them into words [or gestures]? This is often the first step toward mastery and control of feelings. (p. 37)

Furman (1995) suggested preschoolers begin to develop emotional wellness as they begin to identify their emotions and understand their meaning. Strategies for developing an understanding of emotions in preschoolers with disabilities needs to be simple and basic. Here again, songs, dance, and reading activities are important. For example, a wealth of books for preschoolers addresses emotions and feelings (see Resources). Here are a few:

- *A Book of Hugs*
- *Alexander and the Terrible, Horrible, No Good, Very Bad Day*
- *Because I Am Human*
- *Oonga Boonga*

Addressing emotional wellness also includes focusing on stress management and relaxation. Educators and parents can teach children simple skills to help them deal with stress. This is increasingly important as more and more of our children struggle with emotions due to post-traumatic stress syndrome (Demaree, 1995).

Kittens to the rescue here again: After active play, ask the children to play "Kitty Sleeping in Front of a Fire." Ask the children to lie down on a rug, stretch, and then curl in a ball. Encourage the children to breathe slowly; it works really well if you ask them to make purring noises. Relaxing music or cassettes of nature sounds during naptime can also help alleviate stress.

Social, Family, Community, and Environmental Concerns

The ability to play is the single most important variable in a well child. Vygotsky (translated work, 1978) emphasized the role of representational play, or fantasy play, or "make believe," as a crucial factor in child development. Young children with disabilities, as human beings who need to interact with members of their families and the community, may need help acquiring the play skills necessary to function as an integral part of their families and communities. The teacher, caregiver, parents—and other children—can help create an educational environment rich in opportunities to learn play

Puppies, Kittens, and Turtles: Muscular Fitness Activities for Preschoolers

According to Huettig, Pyfer, and Auxter (1993), the following activities are beneficial—and enjoyable—for preschoolers:

Clapping Seal. The child pulls his lower body along the floor, while supporting his body in a push-up position. Occasional stops to rock and "clap fins" make this a great deal more fun. If the child is unable to support his body in this position, the child's chest could be supported by a bolster or pillow.

Grazing Cow. Ask the child to move on all fours, while pushing a bean bag with her nose. The child may pretend to stop, every once in a while, and "chew her cud."

Bucking Horse. Ask the child to "stand" on all fours on a mat or quilt. Put bean bags or koosch balls on the child's back and ask the child to "buck."

Puppy. The child creeps on all fours, contralaterally. That is, the child moves the right hand and left knee forward together; then, the child moves the left hand and the right knee forward together (which is actually the natural way to creep). "Barking" is an absolute necessity!

Puppy with a Sore Paw. The "puppy" moves using both hands and *one* foot, or *one* hand and both feet.

Turtle Stuck on His Back. Ask the child to lie on his back and pretend to struggle to roll over, alternately flexing/extending her arms and legs. Throughout, the head should be tucked to the chest. When the child "struggles" hard enough, the teacher can help roll the "turtle" onto her stomach.

Individual or Group Balloon Bobble. Ask the child to lie on his back on a rug or mat and try to keep a balloon up in the air, using hands, knees, or feet.

Puppy on a Leash. Ask a child to lie on her back on a scooterboard, holding the end of a rope. Another child can take the "puppy" for a walk.

Mad Kitty. The child gets on all fours on the floor. Then, hissing loudly, the child presses his back up to form an arch. Ask the child to hold the position for several seconds, while hissing. This is more fun if some children are "kittens" and some are "puppies."

Resources: Games, Stories, Songs, and Other Wellness Resources

Fitness Games

"Bean Bag Boogie I and II," *Kids in Motion*, Greg and Steve, Youngheart, 1998.

"Run, Run, Run in Place," *Preschool Aerobic Fun*, Kimbo, 1998.

Preschool Favorites, Georgiana Stewart, Kimbo, 1990.

"Swing, Shake, Twist, and Bend," *Walter the Waltzing Worm*, Hap Palmer, Educational Activities, 1982.

"Warm-Up Time," *Preschool Favorites*, Georgiana Stewart, Kimbo, 1990.

Books

Alexander and the Terrible, Horrible, No Good, Very Bad Day, Judith Viorst, Aladdin Paperbacks.

Because I Am Human, Leo Buscaglia, Slack Inc. 1982.

A Book of Hugs, David Ross, Harper Collins, 1991.

Franklin in the Dark, Bourgeoois/Clark, Kids Can Press, 1987.

The Geranium on the Window Sill Just Died But Teacher You Went Right On, Albert Cullum, Harlan Quist, 1976.

The Grouchy Ladybug, Eric Carle, Harper Collins Juvenile Books, 1996.

Nana Upstairs and Nana Downstairs, Tomie de Paola, Putnam Pub Group, 1998.

I Like Me, Nancy Carlson, Viking Children's Books, 1997.

Oonga Boonga, Frieda Wishinsky, Little, Brown, 1998.

Songs

"Free to Be You and Me," *Free to Be You and Me*, Marlo Thomas, Arista, 1972.

"Ugly Duckling," *We All Live Together* (Vol. 4). Greg and Steve, Youngheart, 1998

"What a Miracle," *Walter the Waltzing Worm*, Hap Palmer, Educational Activities, 1982.

Sounds and Music

Dream Catcher, Toekeya Inajin, Earthbeat, 1993. Native American flute music and nature sounds.

Seagulls for Rest and Relaxation, Hap Palmer, Educational Activities, 1982.

Voices of the Earth, The Relaxation Company, Church, 1997. Four cassettes of actual nature sounds—the rain forest, the ocean, whales and dolphins, and a thunderstorm.

---

behaviors that are the very crux of the child's growth.

Perhaps the most important strategy is providing carefully designed, educational opportunities for young children with disabilities to play with other children, with and without disabilities, so they can learn from each other (Davis, Langon, & Malone, 1996). Here, as in the cooperative play mentioned earlier, the teacher or parent can comment positively on children's play, encouraging and facilitating "make-believe" with the time-honored preschool blocks, toy animals and dolls, and housekeeping items.

The development of complex play is the very foundation of the child's ability to develop complex relationships within a family and a community. Vygotsky (1978) and Berk and Winsler (1995) noted that in make-believe play children test their roles and explore those of others in a safe, nurturing environment.

Environmental wellness addresses the preschooler's ability to appreciate nature and the environment. One of the simplest ways that preschoolers can be introduced to the wonders of nature is in and through gardening (Clemens, 1996). Keeping and raising pets in the classroom can also help children address their role in nature and in the environment. Tomich (1996) stated:

> Anyone who has spent even a short amount of time with children recognizes the natural curiosity that children have for their environment. Young children's propensity for touching, tasting, and manipulating objects in their world is one of the challenging aspects of working with them. We want children to explore and to construct knowledge about their world, but sometimes we stifle this curiosity by trying to keep them safe—and clean. We, as parents and caregivers, can remember the wonder of our world when we allow children to pursue their investigations without our being too preoccupied with concerns for order and cleanliness or the touching of small crawling and wriggling creatures. (p. 28)

Intellectual Aspects

Intellectual wellness in a young child with disabilities is directly related to the child's ability to learn and show interest in the environment. Fostering intellectual wellness in a young child is linked directly to the process of engineering the environment to maximize the child's interest in interacting with the environment and with others in the environment. Perhaps most important, intellectual wellness can best occur when educators, caregivers, and parents acknowledge Gardner's (1983) assertion that there are at least seven types of intelligence—with an eighth added recently: linguistic, logical-mathematical, musical, spatial, bodily-kinesthetic, interpersonal, intrapersonal, and spiritual/naturalistic.

Children need to be respected for demonstrating one or all of the types of intelligence (Gardner, 1983). Using different ways to teach and to assess intelligence is at the crux of reenvisioning the process of developing wellness in young children with disabilities. If educators, caregivers, and parents focus on what children can do, rather than on what they cannot, the children will grow more confident in their interaction with the environment.

Occupational and Vocational Considerations

Preschoolers are very interested in occupations and vocations, particularly in what their mommy or daddy or grandma does. Typically, this interest is supported in a "community helpers" unit and in the dramatic play or housekeeping center. For a preschooler, that is a more than adequate exploration of that facet of wellness.

Final Thoughts

Creating an environment in which preschoolers with disabilities become "well" and develop early skills tied to a lifelong understanding and practice of wellness requires the educator/caregiver and parent to address physical fitness, nutrition, emotional health, and the other dimensions of wellness on a daily basis. Most important, we must remember and recognize the fact that *play* is the vehicle and the process in and through which a child can embrace wellness.

References

American Association of Health, Physical Education, Recreation and Dance (AAHPERD). (1998). *AAHPERD update*. Reston, VA: Author.

American College of Sports Medicine (ACSM). (1995). *ACSM's guidelines for exercise testing and prescription* (5th ed.). Baltimore: Williams & Wilkins.*

Auxter, D., Pyfer, J., & Huettig, C. (1997). *Principles and methods of adapted physical education*. St. Louis: Mosby. Note: Now available from W. C. Brown/McGraw Hill.*

Berk, L. E., & Winsler, A. (1995). *Scaffolding children's learning: Vygotsky and early childhood education*. Washington, DC: National Association for the Education of Young Children.

Children's Defense Fund. (1996). *The state of America's children yearbook: 1996*. Washington, DC: Author.

Clemens, J. B. (1996). Gardening with children. *Young Children, 51,* 22–27.

Davis, M. T., Langon, J., & Malone, D. M. (1996). Promoting prosocial behaviors among preschool children with and without disabilities. *International Journal of Disability, Development and Education, 43*(3), 219–246.

Demaree, M. (1995). Creating safe environments for children with post-traumatic stress disorder. *Dimensions of Early Childhood, 22*(3), 31–34.

Endres, J., & Rockwall, R. (1994). *Food, nutrition and the young child.* New York: Merrill.*

Furman, R. A. (1995). Helping children cope with stress and deal with feelings. *Young Children, 50,* 33–41.

Gardner, H. (1983). *Frames of mind: The theory of multiple intelligences.* New York: Basic Books.*

Goleman, D. (1995). *Emotional intelligence: Why it can matter more than IQ.* New York: Bantam.

Hettler, W. (1979). *The six dimensions of wellness.* Stevens Point, WI: University of Wisconsin-Stevens Point Health Center.*

Huettig, C., Pyfer, J., & Auxter, D. (1993). *Gross motor activities for young children with disabilities.* St. Louis: Mosby.*

Lieberman, A. F. (1994). The emotional life of the toddler. *The Signal: Newsletter of the World Association for Infant Mental Health, 51,* 1–6.*

McLean, M. E., & Odom, S. L. (1996). Establishing recommended practices in early intervention/early childhood special education. In S. L. Odom & M. E. McLean (Eds.), *Early intervention/early childhood special education: Recommended practices* (pp. 1–22). Austin, TX: Pro-Ed.*

Rimmer, J. H. (1994). *Fitness and rehabilitation programs for special populations.* Madison, WI: WC Brown & Benchmark.*

Tomich, K. (1996). Hundreds of ladybugs, thousands of ladybugs, millions and billions and trillions of ladybugs—and a couple of roaches. *Young Children, 51,* 28–30.

Vygotsky, L. (1978). The role of play in development. In R. Cole, et al. (Eds.), *Mind in society* (pp. 92–104). Cambridge, MA: Harvard University Press.*

Books Now

*To order books marked by an asterisk (*), please call 24 hrs/365 days: 1–800–BOOKS–NOW (266–5766) or (801) 261–1187 and ask for ext. 1212; or visit them on the Web at http://www.BooksNow.com/TeachingExceptional.htm. Use VISA, M/C, or AMEX or send check or money order + $4.95 S&H ($2.50 each add'l item) to: Books Now, Suite 125, 448 East 6400 South, Salt Lake City, UT 84107.

Carol Huettig, Visiting Professor, Project Inspire, Doctoral Grant Coordinator, Department of Kinesiology; **John O'Connor,** Doctoral Student, Department of Kinesiology, Texas Woman's University, Denton.

Address correspondence to Carol Huettig, Department of Kinesiology, Texas Woman's University. P.O. Box 425647, Denton, TX 76204 (e-mail: f_huettig@twu.edu).

Is Everyone Included? Using Children's Literature to Facilitate the Understanding of Disabilities

Joan K. Blaska and Evelyn C. Lynch

Joan K. Blaska, Ph.D., is a professor in the Department of Child and Family Studies of St. Cloud State University in Minnesota. She wrote Using Children's Literature to Learn about Disabilities and Illness, *based on her research on children's literature.*

Evelyn C. Lynch, Ed.D., is dean of the College of Education, Arkansas State University in Jonesboro. Evelyn has collaborated with school systems and community agencies in community-based, integrated preschool programs and researched early literacy experiences and families of young children with and without disabilities.

Photograph courtesy of Joan K. Blaska.

Books serve as mirrors for children, reflecting their appearances, relationships, and feelings in their immediate environment. Books also act as windows on the world, inviting young children to look beyond the immediate and encounter new characters and circumstances (Rudman & Pearce 1988). The images of characters and circumstances that children form from their earliest and emergent literacy experiences are important for overall development. This fact highlights the need for the presence of similar feelings, experiences, emotions (Hall 1987), and characters with whom they can identify (Rudman & Pearce 1988).

No group has been as overlooked and as inadequately presented in children's books, young readers' books, adult books, and the popular press as individuals with disabilities. Prior to 1980 few people with disabilities were protagonists in books, and even when included in stories, they were often depicted with extreme characteristics (i.e., as people of evil or godliness [Rudman

& Pearce 1988]). Difference or deviance—not a balance of strengths and weaknesses—was often the main personality or behavioral trait held up for the reader. Now, in this time of heightened awareness and sensitivity to differences and to portraying people with mental and physical disabilities in more positive roles, it is distressing that the depiction of people with disabilities remains generally negative in the mass media (Keller et al. 1990), although the situation is improving.

Can books and reading change attitudes and values and help shape a child's character? Research findings on guided reading demonstrate the effectiveness of changing attitudes by reading or by being read stories (Sawyer & Comer 1991). In their review of the effects of bibliotherapy or guided reading on attitude change in young readers, Schrank and Engles (1981) concluded that guided reading can bring about attitudinal change toward disabilities and exceptionalities. The conclusion of the Carnegie Corporation (1974) regarding the influences of books and reading remains relevant today:

> Books, perhaps children's books most of all, are powerful tools by which a civilization perpetuates its values—both its proudest achievements and its most crippling prejudices. In books children find characters with whom they identify and whose aspirations and actions they might one day try to emulate; they discover, too, a way of perceiving those who are of a different color, who speak a different language or live a different life. (p. 1)

All young children must be routinely represented in the children's fiction and nonfiction we select for our classrooms. We need to incorporate books that include people with disabilities into every program, just as we include books with people representing racial and cultural diversity.

Books about disabling conditions or with characters with disabilities can help children understand and accept people with varying abilities. Their use should not be limited to classes in which children with disabilities are mainstreamed (Blaska 1996).

While many children's books with characters portraying disabilities inform the reader about a disability, there is another group of books where the intent is not to inform. This group of books is inclusionary literature—that is, a person with a disability is included in the story much like a person with a disability might be a neighbor, a classmate, or a friend. Quality children's books are available in both groups. A resource for locating these books is *Using Children's Literature to Learn about Disabilities and Illness* (Blaska 1996). In the following 10 books, people with disabilities are portrayed in a respectful yet realistic manner. The first two books inform about a disability while the remaining eight are examples of inclusionary literature.

✦

I'm the Big Sister Now by Michelle Emmert, with illustrations by Gail Owens. 1989. Morton Grove, IL: Albert Whitman. Kindergarten—Grade 3. Disability: Multiple (cerebral palsy, severe brain damage).

Amy has cerebral palsy and multiple disabilities, and her story is told by her little sister. While Amy is unable to do many things, she is included by her family in many activities such as swimming, sending Christmas cards, and riding on the merry-go-round. As her sister grows bigger and taller and can help Amy to be happy and safe, she feels like she has become the big sister. The story is very sensitively written, with softly colored illustrations. The story promotes a positive image by showing how Amy is loved and included by her family. Children can gain a clearer understanding of what it is like to have multiple disabilities.

Just Like Emma: How She Has Fun in God's World by Christine Wright, with illustrations by Biz Hull. 1993. Minneapolis, MN: Augsburg Fortress. Kindergarten—Grade 3. Disability: Physical (spina bifida).

Emma has spina bifida and lives with her father and younger brother. She takes part in household tasks such as making the grocery list and drying the dishes. One day she and

---

All young children must be routinely represented in the children's fiction and nonfiction we select for our classrooms. We need to incorporate books that include people with disabilities into every program, just as we include books with people representing racial and cultural diversity.

her brother put crushed potato chips into the cereal box for their dad's breakfast! The emphasis of the story is on what Emma can do for herself and with her family. It is a very positive, yet realistic story. The color illustrations are very lifelike and capture the feelings of the characters.

Friends in the Park *by Rochelle Bunnett, with photographs by Carl Sahlhoff. 1992. Bellingham, WA: Our Kids Press. Preschool—Grade 2. Disability: Physical and Down syndrome.*

This delightful story illustrates a typical day at the neighborhood park with children with varying abilities and from diverse cultures. In all, 20 children are photographed as they participate in activities such as blowing bubbles, going down the slide, crawling through a tunnel, and drinking juice. Children with physical disabilities and others with Down syndrome are integrated in a very natural setting with children without disabilities. The wonderful photographs depict what the children can do and promote the feeling of being "one of us." The sequel to this book is *Friends at School* written by the same author and showing children of differing abilities together at school.

Lester's Dog *by Karen Hesse, with illustrations by Nancy Carpenter. 1993. New York: Crown. Preschool—Grade 3. Disability: Hearing loss.*

Corey wants to go up the hill, but his friend is afraid of Lester's dog, which lives up there. Corey is unable to hear his friend's complaints because he is deaf. Up the hill they go, and the boy overcomes his fears as he confronts the dog. The words and beautiful illustrations capture the extraordinary friendship between these two boys. This story demonstrates natural inclusion and is an excellent way to promote acceptance.

Mamma Zooms *by Jane Cowen-Fletcher, with illustrations by author. 1993. New York: Scholastic. Preschool—Grade 2. Disability: Physical (in wheelchair).*

This story is about a mother who takes her son everywhere in her wheelchair, which he calls her "zooming machine." The son imagines he's riding a racehorse, driving a race car, and going on other adventures. The mother is able to do many things and rarely needs help, which negates the old stereotype of being "confined" to a wheelchair. The son sees his mother as a "regular mom." Wonderful illustrations help tell this very positive story.

Mandy Sue's Day *by Roberta Karim, with illustrations by Karen Ritz. 1994. New York: Clarion Books. Preschool—Grade 3. Disability: Visual impairment.*

Mandy Sue lives on a farm, and each child is given a day free from chores. On Mandy Sue's Day she chooses to spend the entire day with her horse, grooming and riding him. At the end of the day Mandy Sue asks if she can spend the night in the hayloft so she can sleep near her horse. Her mom and dad agree that it would be OK. When her brother brings her a flashlight, Mandy Sue reminds him she doesn't need one because she can't see anyway. This story shows children the many things that Mandy Sue can do even though she is blind and that she is more like them than different. Full-page illustrations capture the beauty of this story.

Naomi Knows It's Springtime *by Jill Kastner, with illustrations by the author. 1993. Honesville, PA: Boyds Mills. Preschool—Grade 2. Disability: Visual impairment.*

Naomi knows it's springtime because she hears familiar sounds such as the chirps of baby birds. She smells the lilies and lilacs that bloom in her yard; they serve as annual signs that winter is over and spring has arrived. On the last page of the story, the reader discovers that Naomi is blind. This very positive story shows Naomi enjoying a new season in her own way. Exquisite oil paintings are part of the wonderful story.

Seal Surfer *by Michael Foreman, with illustrations by the author. 1996. San Diego, CA: Harcourt Brace & Company. Kindergarten—Grade 5. Disability: Physical (in wheelchair and with walking sticks).*

Ben loves the ocean and witnesses the actual birth of a seal. Each season he and his grandfather visit the ocean to watch the young seal. When Ben learns to surf, he discovers that seals can ride the waves too. One day Ben has to rely on his ocean friend for survival. An entertaining story about Ben and his love for the ocean and seals. No mention is made of a disability. The only way the reader is aware of a disability is through the realistic illustrations. Whenever Ben watches the ocean, near him is either a wheelchair or a pair of walking sticks. A wonderful story that shows the reader that Ben is more like other children than different.

Where's Chimpy? *by Berniece Rabe, with photographs by Diane Schmidt. 1988. Morton Grove, Il: Albert Whitman. Preschool—Grade 2. Disability: Down Syndrome.*

Misty is in bed, ready for Dad to read a story, when she realizes that she doesn't have Chimpy, her bedtime monkey. Misty and her father look in the car, on the swing set, in the sandbox, on the couch—everywhere. They find lots of things that Misty has left behind, but no monkey. Finally, Chimpy is found. Before she goes to bed, Misty and her father count all the toys they have found. The story is about a special relationship between a young child and her father. It is not about a disability—the child just happens to have Down syndrome.

With the Wind *by Liz Damrell, with illustrations by Stephen Marschesi. 1991. New York: Orchid Books. Pre-*

school—Grade 2. Disability: Physical (in leg braces and wheelchair).

A young boy is brought by his parents to a horseback riding session. He feels the strength of the horse beneath him and enjoys the freedom, joy, and power of riding. When he returns to the stable, his parents are waiting for him, and his father helps him off the horse and into his wheelchair. The text is a poem that reflects the sense of freedom the boy has when he rides. The story is not about a disability; it's about a boy who rides and just happens to have a disability. The illustrations are captivating.

References

Blaska, J. K. 1996. *Using children's literature to learn about disabilities and illness.* Moorhead, MN: Practical Press.

Carnegie Corporation. 1974. Racism and sexism and children's books. *Carnegie Quarterly* 22 (4): 1–8.

Hall, N. 1987. *The emergence of literacy.* Portsmouth, NH: Heinemann.

Keller, C., D. Hallahan, E. McShane, E. P. Cowley, & B. Blandford. 1990. The coverage of persons with disabilities in American newspapers. *Journal of Special Education* 24 (3): 271–82.

Rudman, M. K., & A. M. Pearce. 1988. *For the love of reading: A parent's guide to encouraging young readers from infancy through age 5.* Mount Vernon, NY: Consumer Reports.

Sawyer, S., & D. E. Comer. 1991. *Growing up with literature.* New York: Delmar.

Schrank, F. A., & D. W. Engels. 1981. Bibliotherapy as counseling adjunct: Research findings. *Personnel and Guidance Journal* 60 (3): 143–47.

NAEYC

Editor's note: *We hope that this article, and articles like it, will encourage you to choose an assortment of books that include children with various backgrounds and special circumstances.*

We urge you to look at all books before using them to ensure that the language, art, and message meet your standards of excellence. Not all books are equal. We want to use books which make children feel that they are equal.

Unit 3

Unit Selections

10. **Learning Disabilities,** G. Reid Lyon
11. **Cognitive Credit Cards: Acquiring Learning Strategies,** Alan L. Edmunds
12. **Dropout Prevention: A Case for Enhanced Early Literacy Efforts,** Louis G. Denti and Gilbert Guerin

Key Points to Consider

❖ How prevalent are LDs? How early can they be assessed? When can intervention begin? What intervention programs are most effective?

❖ Can students with learning disabilities acquire different learning strategies for different tasks? Is there a way to keep these strategies separate, organized, and efficient to use?

❖ What intervention programs are most effective for preventing students with LDs from giving up and dropping out of school before graduation?

 **Links**   **www.dushkin.com/online/**

14. **The Instant Access Treasure Chest**
    http://www.fln.vcu.edu/ld/ld.html
15. **Learning Disabilities and Disorders**
    http://fly.hiwaay.net/~garson/learnd.htm
16. **Learning Disabilities Association of America**
    http://www.ldanatl.org
17. **Teaching Children with Attention Deficit Disorder**
    http://www.kidsource.com/kidsource/content2/add.html

These sites are annotated on pages 4 and 5.

Learning Disabilities

Since the passage of PL 94-142 in 1975 and its reauthorization as PL 105-17 in 1997, the ways in which students with learning disabilities (LDs) are identified and educated has been radically transformed. Today it is the largest and most controversial area of exceptionality served by IDEA (Individuals with Disabilities Education Act). New assessment methods have made the identification of students with LDs easier and far more common. However, many educators feel that students who have behavior disorders, students with poor learning histories, and students from dysfunctional families are erroneously being diagnosed with LDs. The amendments to PL 94-142 in 1986 and 1990 mandated earlier diagnoses and provision of services (birth to public school admission), and later provision of education and transitional services (public school through age 21). The reauthorization of IDEA in 1997 required states to place students with disabilities in regular classrooms as much as possible or lose their federal funding. A landmark U.S. Supreme Court case in 1993 (*Carter v. Florence Co., SC*) ruled that public schools must give appropriate educational services to students with LDs or pay the tuition for private schools to do so.

Learning disabilities encompass a wide range of difficulties. There is no one accepted definition of an LD. To a large extent, exclusionary definitions help clarify the nature of LDs. They are not developmental disabilities. They are not deficiencies in any of the sensory systems (vision, hearing, taste, touch, smell, kinesthetics, vestibular sensation). They are not problems associated with health or physical mobility. They are not emotional or behavioral disorders. They are not disabilities of speech or language. They can be assessed as true LDs if there is a discrepancy between the child's ability to learn and his or her actual learning.

IDEA's strong emphasis on a free and appropriate educational placement for every child with a disability has forced schools to be more cautious about all assessments and labeling. Increasing numbers of children are now being assessed as LD who once might have been labeled developmentally disabled or disabled by speech, language, emotions, behavior, or one of the senses. A child with an LD may concurrently have a disability in any of these other areas, but if this occurs, both the LD and the other disability/ies must be addressed in an individualized education plan (IEP) designed especially for that unique child with multiple disabilities.

The 1990s saw a persistent annual increase in the number of children assessed as LD. They now account for about one-half of all children with exceptionalities, or about 5 percent of the total school enrollment. Recent research suggests that reading disabilities may affect about 15 percent of elementary school-aged children. If this is accurate, many LD children are not yet being identified and serviced. The question about where to draw the line in assessing LDs, especially reading disabilities, is currently problematic.

Learning disabilities are identified in many diverse disciplines outside of education, adding to the diagnostic difficulties. The American Psychiatric Association's *Diagnostic and Statistical Manual of Mental Disorders* (4th edition) divides LDs into academic skills disorders (reading, mathematics, written expression) and attention deficit hyperactive disorder (ADHD). The National Joint Committee for Learning Disabilities (NJCLD) stresses that LDs are heterogeneous. It separates LDs into specific problems related to the acquisition and use of listening, speaking, reading, writing, reasoning, or mathematical abilities. Attention deficit hyperactive disorder, if not accompanied by any specific learning problem or any specific behavioral/emotional disorder, is assessed as a health disability, especially when it can be ameliorated with medication.

The causes of LDs are unknown. Usually some central nervous system dysfunctions are believed to underlie the disabilities, even if their existence cannot be demonstrated with current diagnostic equipment. Other suspected causes include genetic inheritance and environmental factors such as poor nutrition or exposure to toxic agents. The NJCLD definition of LD states a presumption of biological causation and lifetime chronicity.

The education of students with LDs remains controversial. About two out of every five students assessed as having a learning disability leaves school before graduation. Frequently the school failure begins early, with delayed reading. Special education directed at reading frequently chooses either a phonic or a whole language strategy. Phonics seems to work better for children who do not automatically grasp what reading is about, while whole language seems to work better for students who grasp reading and writing but have difficulty accomplishing them. The need for individualized strategies for individual LD students is paramount.

This unit on learning disabilities addresses both the successes and the frustrations of educating children with LDs. The first article in the section is an overview of LDs. It especially speaks about the remediation of reading disorders, both because reading is critically important to academic success and because more is known about dyslexia (difficulty with words). G. Reid Lyon states that about 80 percent of children with LDs have their primary difficulties in learning to read. Reading difficulties further affect approximately 17 percent of school-age children to some degree. Teachers are not as well prepared as they should be to intervene when students have reading disabilities.

In the second article, Alan Edmunds suggests a method of helping teachers assess the individual differences of students with diverse manifestations of learning disabilities. It further suggests the use of unique strategies for helping students deal with their LDs. Each student can be helped to create a cognitive credit card to remind him or her of how to deal with learning each difficult subject. The cognitive aides focus on how the student is to learn rather than what, and can be used in test situations without unfair advantage.

The third article gives information about the high dropout rates of students with LDs. It suggests that explicit instructions in reading and writing in early intervention programs can reduce the dropout rates of these students. Active parental involvement in early programs is very important, as are one-on-one tutorials and ongoing assessments.

Article 10

Learning Disabilities

G. Reid Lyon

> *G. Reid Lyon, Ph.D., is a psychologist and director of extramural research in learning disabilities, language disorders, and disorders of attention at the National Institute of Child Health and Human Development at the National Institutes of Health, Bethesda, MD.*

Abstract

Approximately 5% of all public school students are identified as having a learning disability (LD). LD is not a single disorder, but includes disabilities in any of seven areas related to reading, language, and mathematics. These separate types of learning disabilities frequently co-occur with one another and with social skill deficits and emotional or behavioral disorders. Most of the available information concerning learning disabilities relates to reading disabilities, and the majority of children with learning disabilities have their primary deficits in basic reading skills.

An important part of the definition of LD is its exclusions: learning disabilities cannot be attributed primarily to mental retardation, emotional disturbance, cultural difference, or disadvantage. Thus, the concept of LD focuses on the notion of a *discrepancy* between a child's academic achievement and his or her apparent capacity to learn.

Recent research indicates, however, that disability in basic reading skills is primarily caused by deficits in phonological awareness, which is independent of any achievement-capacity discrepancy. Deficits in phonological awareness can be identified in late kindergarten and first grade using inexpensive, straightforward testing protocol. Interventions have varying effectiveness, depending largely on the severity of the individual child's disability.

The prevalence of learning disability identification has increased dramatically in the past 20 years. The "real" prevalence of LD is subject to much dispute because of the lack of an agreed-upon definition of LD with objective identification criteria. Some researchers have argued that the currently recognized 5% prevalence rate is inflated; others argue that LD is still underidentified. In fact, it appears that there are both sound and unsound reasons for the increase in identification rates.

Sound reasons for the increase include better research, a broader definition of disability in reading, focusing on phonological awareness, and greater identification of girls with learning disabilities. Unsound reasons for the increase include broad and vague definitions of learning disability, financial incentives to identify students for special education, and inadequate preparation of teachers by colleges of education, leading to overreferral of students with any type of special need.

There is no clear demarcation between students with normal reading abilities and those with mild reading disability. The majority of children with reading disabilities have relatively mild reading disabilities, with a smaller number having extreme reading disabilities. The longer children with disability in basic reading skills, at any level of severity, go without identification and intervention, the more difficult the task of remediation and the lower the rate of success.

Children with extreme deficits in basic reading skills are much more difficult to remediate than children with mild or moderate deficits. It is unclear whether children in the most severe range can achieve age- and grade-approximate reading skills, even with normal intelligence and with intense, informed intervention provided over a protracted period of time. Children with severe learning disabilities are likely to manifest an increased number of and increased severity of social and behavioral deficits. When children with disabilities in reading also manifest attention deficit disorder, their reading deficits are typically exacerbated, more severe, and more resistant to intervention.

While severe reading disorders are clearly a major concern, even mild deficits in reading skills are likely to portend significant difficulties in academic learning. These deficits, too, are worthy of early identification and intervention. Even children with relatively subtle linguistic and reading deficits require the expertise of a teacher who is well trained and informed about the relationships between language development and reading development. Unfortunately, such teachers are in short supply, primarily because of a lack of professional certification programs providing this training.

This article focuses primarily on deficits in basic reading skills, both because of their critical importance to academic success and because relatively more is known about these deficiencies. However, other academic, social, and behavioral manifestations of learning disability are also important and cannot be assumed to be adequately addressed by programs to improve basic reading skills. While early intervention is necessary, it should not be assumed to be sufficient to address the multiple manifestations of learning disability.

Approximately one-half of all children receiving special education services nationally, or about 5% of the total public school population, are identified as having a learning disability (LD) when the federal definition of LD is used by schools to formulate identification criteria.[1] At the same time, LD remains one of the least understood and most debated disabling conditions that affect children. Indeed, the field continues to be beset by pervasive, and occasionally contentious, disagreements about the definition of the disorder, diagnostic criteria, assessment practices, treatment procedures, and educational policies.[2-6]

Learning disability is not a single disorder, but is a general category of special education composed of disabilities in any of seven specific areas: (1) receptive language (listening), (2) expressive language (speaking), (3) basic reading skills, (4) reading comprehension, (5) written expression, (6) mathematics calculation, and (7) mathematical reasoning. These separate types of learning disabilities frequently co-occur with one another and also with certain social skill deficits and emotional or behavioral disorders such as attention deficit disorder. LD is not synonymous with reading disability or dyslexia although it is frequently misinterpreted as such.[7,8] However, most of the available information concerning learning disabilities relates to reading disabilities, and the majority of children with LD have their primary deficits in reading.[2]

Box 1 shows the statutory definition of learning disabilities contained in the Individuals with Disabilities Education Act (IDEA). An important part of the definition of learning disabilities under the IDEA is the exclusionary language: learning disabilities cannot be attributed primarily to mental retardation, emotional disturbance, cultural difference, or environmental or economic disadvantage. Thus, the concept of learning disabilities embedded in federal law focuses on the notion of a discrepancy between a child's academic achievement and his or her apparent capacity and opportunity to learn. More succinctly, Zigmond notes that "learning disabilities reflect unexpected learning problems in a seemingly capable child."[9]

Although poverty and disability are often found together and each tends to exacerbate the other (*see the article* by Wagner and Blackorby in *The Future of Children,* Spring 1996), Congress has established separate programs to serve children with disabilities (the IDEA) and children in poverty (Title 1). Title 1 of the Elementary and Secondary Education Act provides funding for supplemental programs in schools serving large numbers of economically disadvantaged children. Because individual children with disabilities have strong entitlements to services under the IDEA, Congress's intent was that the IDEA serve only children with "true disabilities" and that the IDEA specifically exclude those students whose underperformance is primarily attributable to poverty. However, in the category of learning disability, and perhaps also in the category of mental retardation, this distinction is difficult or impossible to draw, and no empirical data exist to support this exclusionary practice.

While there is some agreement about these general concepts, there is continued disagreement in the field about diagnostic criteria, assessment

> **Definition of Learning Disability Under the Individuals with Disabilities Education Act**
>
> "Specific learning disability" means a disorder in one or more basic psychological processes involved in understanding or in using language, spoken or written, that may manifest itself in an imperfect ability to listen, speak, read, write, spell, or to do mathematical calculations. The term includes such conditions as perceptual disabilities, brain injury, minimal brain dysfunction, dyslexia, and developmental aphasia. The term does not apply to children who have learning problems that are primarily the result of visual, hearing, or motor disabilities, of mental retardation, of emotional disturbance, or of environmental, cultural, or economic disadvantage.
>
> Source: Code of Federal Regulations, Title 34, Subtitle B, Chapter III, Section 300.7(b)(10).

Box 1

practices, treatment procedures, and educational policies for learning disabilities. A number of influences have contributed to these disagreements which, in turn, have made it difficult to build a generalizable body of scientific and clinical knowledge about learning disabilities and to establish reliable and valid diagnostic criteria.[4,5] While some progress has been made during the past decade in establishing more precise definitions and a theoretically based classification system for LD,[8-10] it is useful to understand these historical influences because of their continuing impact on diagnostic and treatment practices for children with learning disabilities.

The next section of this article reviews briefly the historical events that have molded the field of learning disabilities into its present form. Subsequent sections address issues related to the prevalence of learning disabilities, the validity of current prevalence estimates, impediments to the identification and teaching of the child with LD, advances in identification, classification, intervention practices in the area of reading disability, comorbidity of types of learning disabilities (reading, written expression, mathematics disabilities) with disorders of attention and social skills deficits, outcomes for individuals with learning disabilities, and the implications for teacher preparation and school policies.

Historical Influences

The study of learning disabilities was initiated in response to the need (1) to understand individual differences among children and adults who displayed *specific* deficits in spoken or written language while maintaining integrity in *general* intellectual functioning and (2) to provide services to these students who were not being adequately served by the general educational system.[6,9,10] Overall, the field of learning disabilities emerged primarily from a social and educational need and currently remains a diagnostic practice that is more rooted in clinical practice, law, and policy than in science. Advocates for children with learning disabilities have successfully negotiated a special education category as a means to educational protection at the same time that the schools have seen an increase in the identification of LD.[6]

The unexpected pattern of *general* strengths and *specific* weaknesses in learning was first noted and studied by physicians during the early twentieth century, thus giving the field its historical biomedical orientation.[10] Doctors noted that children with learning disabilities were similar to adults and children with focal brain damage in that specific impairments in some areas of learning could occur without diminishing strengths in general cognitive ability.

Although the clinical work conducted during the first half of the twentieth century recognized the existence of learning disabilities, such information had little influence on public school policies until the mid-1960s. At this time, behavioral scientists, educators,[11] and parents expressed concern that some children had learning handicaps that were not being served effectively by general educational practices.[9] At the same time, these children were ineligible for special education services because their characteristics did not correspond to any recognized categories of disability. This disenfranchisement stimulated an advocacy movement to provide special educational services to students with learning disabilities,[4,6,9] leading many states to establish a special education category for LD during the late 1960s and 1970s.

Prevalence

The influence of advocacy has, in turn, contributed to a substantial proliferation in the number of children who have been identified with learning disabilities relative to other handicapping conditions (see Figure 1). Clearly, the prevalence of LD identification has increased dramatically.

The "real" prevalence of learning disabilities is subject to much dispute because of the lack of an agreed-upon definition of LD and objective diagnostic criteria.[4,8,12] Some have argued that the currently recognized 5% prevalence rate is excessive and is based on vague definitions, leading to inaccurate identification. On the other hand, research efforts to identify objective early indicators of LD in basic reading skills have concluded that virtually all children scoring below the 25th percentile on standardized reading tests can meet the criteria for having a reading disorder.[12] While less is known about LD in written expression, researchers estimate its true prevalence at between 8% and 15% of the school population.[13] Research also indicates that approximately 6% of the school population has difficulties in mathematics which cannot be attributed to low intelligence, sensory deficits, or economic deprivation.[14]

Increase in Identification

The substantial increase in the identification of children with learning disabilities shown in Figure 1 has led many to question the validity and reliability of LD as a diagnostic category or its "realness" as a handicapping condition.[15] In fact, it appears likely that there are both sound and unsound reasons for the increase, as is discussed later.

It should be made clear that difficulties in the identification of children with learning disabilities do not make the disabilities any less "real" to the student who cannot learn to read, write, or understand mathematics despite good intelligence, an adequate opportunity to learn, and ostensibly good teaching. However, such an anecdotal understanding of learning disability and its prevalence seems inadequate now, given the increase in diagnoses of LD, the consequences of learning failure in children, and the tremendous financial resources that are applied to the identification and teaching of children with learning disabilities. Given what is at stake, it is critical that the construct of learning disability and procedures for identifying children and adults with LD be valid and accepted by the scientific and clinical communities.

The question remains, however, of how to go about increasing the ability to identify individuals with LD accurately. Valid prevalence estimates depend upon a set of criteria for identification that are clear, observable, measurable, and agreed upon.

The Discrepancy Standard

There is currently no universally accepted test, test battery, or standard for identifying children with LD. While a discrepancy between intelligence quotient (IQ) and achievement has been a widely accepted criterion for the identification of LD and still serves as the driving clinical force in the diagnosis of LD, there is considerable variation in how the discrepancy is derived and quantified.[9,16] Federal regulations and extant clinical criteria[17] do not specify particular formulas or numerical values to assess discrepancy objectively. The effect of this lack of specification on both clinical and research practices is substantial. From a clinical standpoint, a child can be identified as having a learning disability in one school district but not in a neighboring district because of differences in the measure of discrepancy used. From a research perspective, different approaches to the discrepancy measurement lead to substantially different sample characteristics and different prevalence estimates, which undermine the ability to replicate and generalize findings.[5,6,8,9]

For the individual child, use of the discrepancy standard clearly promotes a wait-to-fail policy because a significant discrepancy between IQ and achievement generally cannot be detected until about age eight or nine. In fact, most school districts do not identify children with learning disabilities until a child is reading well below grade level, generally in third or fourth grade.[18] By this time the child has already experienced at least a few years of school failure and probably has experienced the common attendant problems of low self-esteem, diminished motivation, and inadequate acquisition of the academic material covered by his classmates during the previous few years.

It is clear that the longer children with learning disabilities, at any level of severity, go without identification and intervention, the more difficult the task of remediation becomes and the harder it is for the children to respond. Specifically, the data strongly suggest that children at risk for reading failure should be identified before the age of nine if successful intervention results are to be anticipated.[13] For example, a longitudinal investigation of 407 students[19] found that 74% of the children whose disability in reading was first identified at nine years of age or older continued to read in the lowest quintile throughout their middle and high school years. In addition, the longer children, at all severity levels, are faced with failure in reading in the classroom setting, the greater the probability that comorbid learning and behavioral difficulties will arise, further complicating the remediation task.

Figure 1

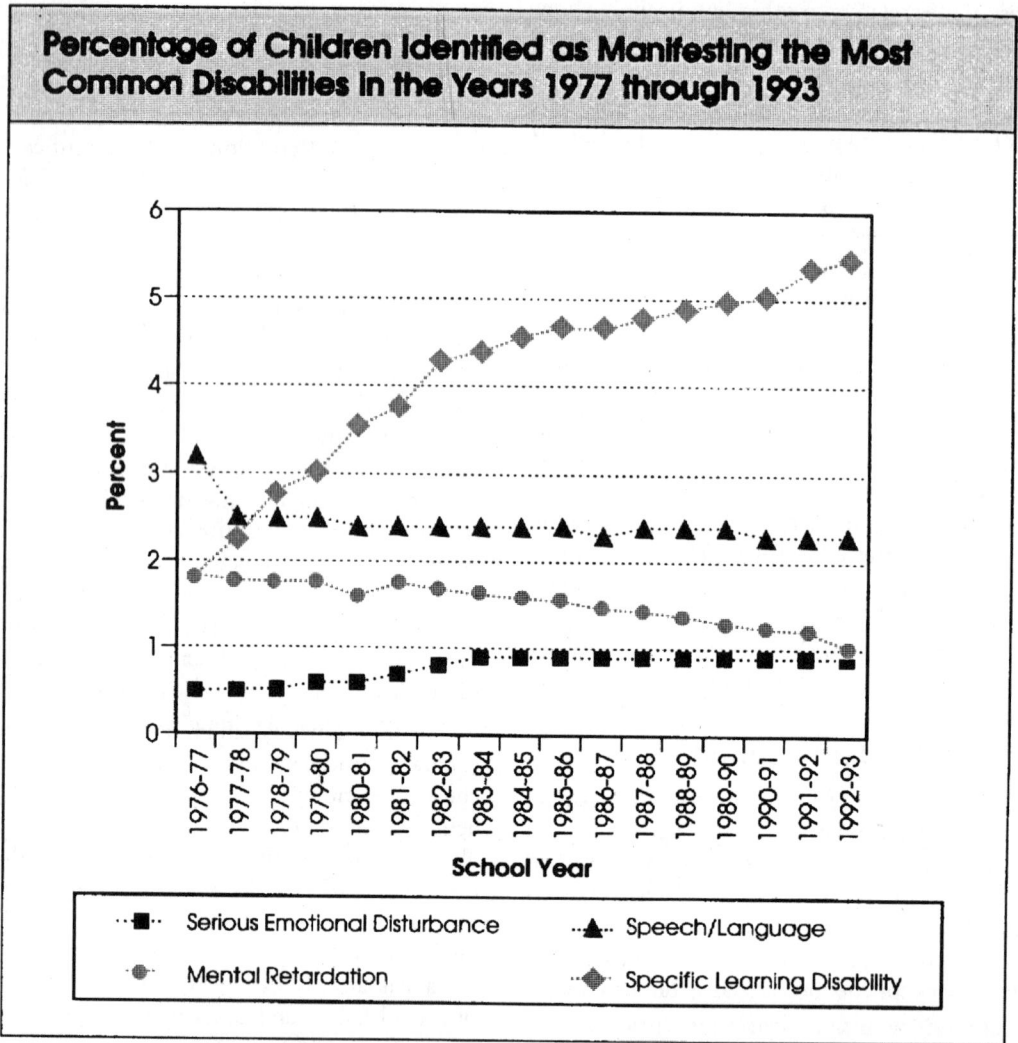

Percentage of Children Identified as Manifesting the Most Common Disabilities in the Years 1977 through 1993

Source: Office of Special Education Programs. *Implementation of the Individuals with Disabilities Education Act: Fifteenth Annual Report to Congress.* Washington, DC: U.S. Department of Education, 1993.

Developing a Diagnostic Standard

If current definitions of learning disability are not useful and if the discrepancy standard is a poor one, why have schools not adopted other means of defining and identifying LD? There are a number of conceptual and methodological barriers to the accurate identification of learning disabilities, and these impediments lead to confusion about definitions, diagnostic issues, and rising prevalence rates.

Multidisciplinary Nature of the Field

Opinions about what constitutes a learning disability vary[6,10] in part because LD is the concern of many disciplines and professions, including education, psychology, neurology, neuropsychology, optometry, psychiatry, and speech and language pathology, to name a few. Each of these disciplines has traditionally focused on different aspects of the child or adult with learning disability, so divergent ideas and contentious disagreements exist about the importance of etiology, diagnostic methods, intervention methods, and professional roles and responsibilities.[10] It is not surprising that so many children are identified because each professional may view the child through his or her own idiosyncratic clinical lens. For example, optometrists may identify a child as having a learning disability if the youngster displays difficulties in visual tracking. Speech and language pathologists, on the other hand, become concerned if the child's vocabulary and syntactic development are not commensurate with expectations. Educators become concerned primarily when development in reading, writing, and mathematics is deficient.

Lack of Specific Identification Criteria

Probably the most significant and persistent problem in the field is the lack of a precise definition and a theoretically based classification system that would allow (1) the identification of different types of learning disabilities and (2) a means of recognizing distinctions and interrelationships between types of learning disabilities and other learning disorders such as mental retardation, attention deficit disorder, speech and language difficulties, and general academic underachievement.[20] At present, the field continues to construct and use vague and ambiguous definitions that rely heavily on the exclusion of alternative diagnoses, such as the IDEA definition shown in Box 1.

Overly Broad Label

Some observers argue that the term "learning disability" is too broad to be of any diagnostic value. Stanovich,[16] a leading proponent of this view, proposes that the general term learning disabilities be abandoned and that definitional and research efforts focus on the specific types of disabilities that are now identified in ambiguous terms.

As noted earlier, the generic term learning disabilities encompasses disabilities in seven categories: (1) listening, (2) speaking, (3) basic reading skills, (4) reading comprehension, (5) written expression, (6) mathematical calculation, and (7) mathematical reasoning. Given the complexity and heterogeneity of each of these disabilities, it seems unrealistic to expect that any definitional clarity can be achieved by grouping them together under one label. To do so only obscures the critical features of each disability and makes research findings difficult to interpret.

Definitions of specific learning disabilities can be more easily and successfully operationalized than generic definitions, as the research on disabilities in basic reading skills shows.[8] To establish valid prevalence estimates for the number of individuals with learning disabilities, the first step should be to establish explicit diagnostic criteria for *each* of the seven specific disability domains. At present, the greatest progress toward this goal has been in the area of disability in basic reading skills.[8]

LD as a Sociological Phenomenon

The simplest explanation for the increasing numbers of children identified with learning disabilities and for the difficulty in understanding and defining LD is that "LD" is not a distinct disability, but an invented category created for social purposes. Some argue that the majority of students identified as having learning disabilities are not intrinsically disabled but have learning problems because of poor teaching, lack of educational opportunity, or limited educational resources.[15] In addition, because the label of LD is not a stigmatizing one, parents and teachers may be more comfortable with a diagnosis of LD than with labels such as slow learner, minimal brain dysfunction, or perceptual handicap. A diagnosis of LD does not imply low intelligence, emotional or behavioral difficulties, sensory handicaps, or cultural disadvantage. Thus, more positive outcomes are expected for children with learning disabilities than for those with mental retardation or emotional disturbance.

Reasons for Increase in Identification of LD

As pointed out, the substantial increase in the identification of LD, as shown in Figure 1, has caused many researchers to question the validity of the data. No doubt, the failure to develop an agreed-upon, objective, operational definition of learning disability gives credence to the concern about the validity of the identification process. Thus, it seems reasonable to assume that at least some of the increase in prevalence can be linked to conceptual, methodological, social, and political factors that spuriously inflate the identification of children with learning disabilities.[5] However, despite the conceptual and methodological shortcomings that have plagued the field with respect to definition and identification practices, there exist a number of possible sound reasons that could account for an increase in the number of children identified with LD.

Some Sound Reasons

As knowledge about learning disabilities grows, some academic difficulties not previously recognized as LD can be identified as such. Greater knowledge also affects the behavior and practices of teachers and parents. Sound reasons for the increase in identification rates are described and discussed in the sections that follow.

■ *Better Research.* Research in the past decade measures underachievement in reading as it occurs naturally in large population-based samples[12,13] rather than as identified by schools, which use widely varying criteria. In addition, much of this new research is longitudinal and has been replicated, providing the necessary foundation for epidemiological studies.[2,12,13,19,21-24] Finally, many of these studies have been specific to LD in reading, rather than LD in general, allowing greater precision.

■ *Broader Definitions.* Prevalence is directly linked to definition. LD in reading has been defined in recent research as *significant difficulties in* reading single words accurately and fluently, in combination with deficits in phonological awareness.[8] Using this definition and stronger longitudinal research methods outlined above, the prevalence for reading disability alone has increased from estimates of less than 5% in 1976 to approximately 17% in 1994.[12]

Both market and legal forces can stimulate the development of new professional specialties whose members have financial incentives to diagnose students with learning disabilities.

Phonological awareness is a critical attribute in learning to read, and children who lack this awareness can be identified in late kindergarten and early first grade. Typical diagnostic questions for kindergartners or first graders involve rhyming skills (for example, "Tell me three words that rhyme with 'cat'") and phoneme deletion skills (for example, "Say 'cat' without the /t/ sound"). The majority of children pick up phonological awareness skills easily by six to seven years of age, but a large minority of children (about 17%) have significant difficulty with these skills and will have great difficulty learning to read, regardless of their intelligence, unless these skills are acquired.

■ *Identification of LD in Girls.* A substantial portion of this increase can be attributed to the fact that females have been found to manifest reading disabilities at rates equal to males, in contrast to previous reports that males with reading disabilities outnumbered females with reading disabilities at a ratio of four to one.[25] This finding necessarily increases the prevalence rate.

■ *Increased Awareness.* Information disseminated in the past decade, particularly concerning the characteristics of reading disability, has increased the number of children referred for assessment of a learning disability.[6]

■ *Understanding of the Impact.* There has been an increase in the recognition that even "mild" deficits in reading skills are likely to portend significant difficulties in academic learning and are, therefore, worthy of early identification, diagnosis, and intervention.[26,27]

Some Unsound Reasons

There is no shortage of horror stories about the misidentification of LD and reports that the category serves as a "catch all" for any youngster who is not meeting the expectations of parents and teachers. Are there legitimate reasons for these criticisms? The answer appears to be yes. Examples are described and discussed in the sections that follow.

■ *Ambiguous Definitions.* The ambiguity inherent in the general definitions of LD (see Box 1) leaves the identification process open for wide interpretation and misinterpretation. Flexible identification decision making allows some children to be identified as having learning disabilities when they do not, while others with learning disabilities may be overlooked.[5] This latitude can be manipulated to increase prevalence rates in response to financial incentives (for example, to qualify for increased state funding), to decrease prevalence rates in response to political movements (for example, inclusion), or to abandon programs that appear too costly.[28]

■ *Social and Political Factors.* Social and political factors also contribute to the inflation of prevalence rates for learning disabilities. In 1976–77, the first year of full implementation of Public Law 94-142, 2.16% of all school-children were served in programs for children with mental retardation (MR) and 1.80% in programs for children with learning disabilities (Figure 1). By the 1992–93 school year, placements for children with MR had decreased to 1.1% while placements for children with LD had increased to 5.4% of the total school population (Figure 1). While these reversed trends mask substantial variations among states, the dramatic changes in identification rates of the two types of disability suggest that attempts to apply less stigmatizing labels may be influencing the identification process.

■ *Number of Professional Specialties Involved.* The large number of professional specialties involved in the identification process provides fertile ground for the overidentification of LD because each specialty brings its own set of diagnostic assumptions, theories, and measures to the assessment task. Inconsistent identification practices allow prevalence rates to escalate. This is a significant problem when there are financial incentives to encourage identification (see the article by Parrish and Chambers in *The Future of Children*, Spring 1996). Both market and legal forces can stimulate the development of new professional specialties (such as language/learning disorder specialist) whose members have financial incentives to diagnose students with learning disabilities, which the specialists will often be employed to treat. Although it may be uncomfortable to mention these factors, they exist and play some role in the increase of prevalence of LD. At the same time, the majority of professionals serving children with learning disabilities appear well intentioned and well informed.

■ *Inadequate Preparation of Teachers.*
Unfortunately, a major factor contributing to invalid prevalence estimates may be the inadequate preparation of teachers by colleges of education. Recent studies have found that a majority of regular classroom teachers feel that they are not prepared to address individual differences in learning abilities within classroom settings.[29] Even more alarming, research suggests that special educators themselves do not possess sufficient content knowledge to address the language and reading needs of children with learning disabilities.[30] Without adequate preparation, teachers have a tendency to overrefer children for specialized assistance because they feel ill-equipped to provide the necessary services.[31]

Interpreting Prevalence Rates

The prevalence of learning disabilities is completely dependent upon the definition used. In most areas, the identification of LD is based largely upon the discrepancy standard and, thus, provides a count of the number of older elementary students (third grade and above) who are achieving significantly below expectations based on IQ. This is, at best, an incomplete definition of LD and one that, for the majority of students with learning disabilities, is based upon an invalid criterion, namely, the discrepancy standard.

Clearly, current definitions allow both overidentification and underidentification of L.D. Depending upon the magnitude of financial incentives and upon unrelated factors (for example, class size, goals for increasing test scores) that often shape the decisions of classroom teachers to refer students with special needs, an individual school district may drastically overidentify or underidentify students with learning disabilities. Therefore, local or national statistics on identification rates for students with LD must be interpreted with caution.

Efforts to Improve Identification

To improve the diagnosis and remediation of learning disabilities, a classification system is needed to identify different types of learning disabilities as well as the distinctions and interrelationships among types of LD and other childhood disorders.[2,20,32] Prospective longitudinal studies are one of the most powerful means to study the different types of LD and their relationships to other disorders and to obtain data for a focused and succinct definition.

Approximately 80% of children identified as having learning disabilities have their primary difficulties in learning to read.

Prospective, longitudinal studies of LD can serve as a platform to (1) identify critical learning and behavioral characteristics that may be manifested in different ways at different developmental periods, (2) develop early predictors of underachievement for different academic domains (for example, reading, written language, math), (3) map the developmental course of different types of learning disabilities, (4) identify commonly co-occurring disorders and secondary behavioral consequences and develop in response to failure in school, and (5) assess the efficacy of different treatment and teaching methods for different types of learning disabilities.

To address this compelling need to establish a valid classification system and definition for LD, Congress enacted the Health Research Extension Act of 1985 (Public Law 99-158). This act called for the development of an Interagency Committee on Learning Disabilities (ICLD), under the lead of the National Institute of Child Health and Human Development (NICHD), to identify critical research needs in LD and to implement comprehensive studies to address issues relevant to identification, prevention, etiology, and treatment.

New Knowledge of Reading Disabilities

Since the inauguration of the NICHD Learning Disability Research Network in 1987, researchers have learned the most about learning disabilities that affect linguistic, reading, and spelling abilities and the least about learning disabilities in mathematics.[2] A number of new findings have also been obtained in the area of attention deficit disorder (ADD) and its relationship to different types of LD, particularly disorders in reading.[12] For brevity, the major discoveries made during the past several years are presented in Table 1. Selected findings are reviewed here. The reader should note that many findings have been replicated by multiple research groups, as cited in Table 1, and that the findings are primarily based on large longitudinal samples. Finally, readers should note that studies being conducted in Canada by Stanovich and Siegel at the Ontario Institute for Studies in Education are included in Table 1 because of their impact on the field and because Stanovich and Siegel serve as consultants to the Yale Learning Disability Research Center (LDRC).

Interventions applied after a child has failed in reading for two or three years may not be effective for several reasons, including the student's declining motivation and impaired self-concept.

As Table 1 shows, a majority of discoveries made during the past decade have been in the area of reading disabilities. This is appropriate. As Lerner pointed out from her analysis of public school referral data in 1989,[33] approximately 80% of children identified as having learning disabilities have their primary difficulties in learning to read. This high rate of occurrence of reading difficulties among youngsters with LD has also been reported by Kavale in his meta-analytic studies.[34] More recent longitudinal and cross-sectional studies have supported the high rate of reading difficulty among children with learning disabilities, but have also found that reading deficits frequently co-occur with other academic and attentional difficulties. For example, Fletcher and his associates at the Yale Center for the Study of Learning and Attention have, as part of a larger classification effort, studied 216 children, 7.5 to 9.5 years of age, who were identified as normal readers, reading disabled, math disabled, both reading and math disabled, normal reading with ADD, and reading disabled with ADD.[21,35] From this sample of children with a variety of learning disabilities, only 25 youngsters were reading at age-appropriate levels.

Research indicates that reading disorders reflected in deficient decoding and word-recognition skills are primarily caused by deficiencies in the ability to segment syllables and words into constituent sound units called phonemes.[16,22,36-38] For example, in a large study of 199 seven- to nine-year-old children who had significant difficulties in decoding and word recognition, more than 85% of the youngsters manifested deficits on measures of phonological awareness. In this investigation, children with and without IQ-reading-achievement discrepancies appeared equally impaired on both the phonological and reading measures.[21] This extremely high frequency of phonological awareness deficits in children with reading disabilities has led Share and Stanovich to conclude: "We know unequivocally that less-skilled readers have difficulty turning spellings into sounds. . . . This relationship is so strong that it deserves to be identified as one, if not the defining, feature of reading disability."[39]

Biological Bases

Several NICHD investigations have indicated that these phonologically based reading disabilities are linked to neurobiological and genetic factors.[2,8,13,40] Functional and structural neuroimaging studies indicate that the poor phonological skills which limit the development of basic reading abilities, are highly related to aberrant neurophysiological processing.[22,40] Moreover, there is increasing evidence from behavioral and molecular genetic studies that the phonological deficits observed in reading disability are heritable.[41,42] Taken together, longitudinal studies of the linguistic, neurobiological, and genetic factors in reading disabilities provide strong and converging evidence that reading disability is primarily caused by deficits in phonological processing and, more specifically, phonological awareness.[8,13,30,37,38,40]

Likewise, the data derived from genetic and neurobiological studies suggest that some reading disabilities are associated with subtle chromosomal[42] and neurological differences,[22,40] indicating that such disabilities are biologically "real" rather than sociopolitically created.

Discrepancy Standard

In addition to the previously discussed problems of the discrepancy standard, Table 1 indicates that the use of a discrepancy formula, which calculates differences between IQ reading scores, is not a valid indicator of reading disability; that is, children with reading disabilities both with and without such discrepancies have similar deficits in phonological awareness and similar genetic and neurophysiological characteristics.[36] At this time, it is not clear whether children with higher IQs respond more favorably to intervention.[7]

Persistent Deficit

Unfortunately, as Table 1 indicates, reading disabilities appear to reflect a persistent deficit rather than a developmental lag. That is, children with

Table 1

Major Findings from Research Programs Supported by the National Institute of Child Health and Human Development

Research Domain	Findings	Research Group*
Definition of learning disabilities	Definitions that measure the discrepancy between IQ and achievement do not adequately identify learning disabilities, particularly in the area of basic reading skills.	Yale Ontario
Reading processes	Disabled readers with and without an IQ-achievement discrepancy show similar information processing, genetic, and neurophysiological profiles. This indicates that the existence of a discrepancy is not a valid indicator of disability in basic reading skills.	Colorado Bowman Gray Yale Ontario
Reading processes	Epidemiological studies indicate that as many females as males manifest dyslexia; however, schools identify three to four times more boys than girls.	Bowman Gray Colorado Yale
Reading processes	Reading disabilities reflect a persistent deficit rather than a developmental lag. Longitudinal studies show that, of those children who are reading disabled in the third grade, approximately 74% continue to read significantly below grade level in the ninth grade.	Yale Ontario
Reading processes	Children with reading disability differ from one another *and* from other readers along a continuous distribution. They *do not* aggregate together to form a distinct "hump" separate from the normal distribution.	Yale Bowman Gray Colorado Ontario
Reading processes	The ability to read and comprehend depends upon rapid and automatic recognition and decoding of single words. Slow and inaccurate decoding are the best predictors of deficits in reading comprehension.	Yale Bowman Gray Colorado Johns Hopkins Florida Houston
Reading processes	The ability to decode single words accurately and fluently is dependent upon the ability to segment words and syllables into phonemes. Deficits in phonological awareness reflect the core deficit in dyslexia.	Yale Colorado Bowman Gray Miami Johns Hopkins Florida Houston
Reading processes	The best predictor of reading ability from kindergarten and first-grade performance is phoneme segmentation ability.	Bowman Gray Yale Florida Houston
Attention	A precise classification of disorders of attention is not yet available; however, operational definitions are emerging.	Yale
Attention	Approximately 15% of students with reading disability also have a disorder of attention. Approximately 35% of students with disorders of attention also have reading disability. However, the two disorders are distinct and separable.	Bowman Gray Yale

*See the related endnote at the end of this article for a detailed description of research groups.

(continued)

Table 1 (continued)

	Major Findings from Research Programs Supported by the National Institute of Child Health and Human Development	
Research Domain	Findings	Research Group*
Attention	Disorders of attention exacerbate the severity of reading disability.	Bowman Gray Miami
Genetics	There is strong evidence for a genetic basis for reading disabilities, with deficits in phonological awareness reflecting the greatest degree of heritability.	Colorado Bowman Gray
Neurology	Regional blood studies indicate that deficient word recognition skills are associated with less than normal activation in the left temporal region.	Bowman Gray
Neurology	PET studies indicate that dyslexic adults have greater than normal activation in the occipital and prefrontal regions of the cortex.	Miami
Intervention	Disabled readers do not readily acquire the alphabetic code because of deficits in phonological processing. Thus, disabled readers must be provided highly structured programs that explicitly teach application of phonological rules to print.	Bowman Gray Florida Houston
Intervention	Longitudinal data indicate that systematic phonics instruction results in more favorable outcomes for disabled readers than does a context-emphasis (whole language) approach.	Bowman Gray Florida Houston

*See the related endnote at the end of this article for a detailed description of research groups.

delays in understanding phonological concepts in first grade are unlikely to catch up later without explicit and informed teaching. Longitudinal studies show that, of the youngsters who are identified in the third grade, approximately 74% remain reading disabled through the ninth grade.[19,43] This appears to be true even when special education has been provided. It should be made clear, however, that interventions applied *after* a child has failed in reading for two or three years may not be effective for several reasons, including the student's declining motivation and impaired self-concept. Instructional difficulties in later intervention abound. For example, the teacher carrying out the interventions may not be properly trained, the interventions may not include explicit and informed instruction in the development of phonological awareness and sound-symbol relationships, the interventions may not be consistently applied and/or may be limited in intensity and duration, and there may be insufficient follow-up or explicit instruction to enable the student to generalize the specific concepts learned to material presented in regular classroom settings.

Distribution of Severity

A significant finding from the Yale LDRC is that reading disability represents the extreme of a normal distribution of reading ability so that there is an unbroken continuum from reading ability to reading disability.[43] The finding that reading disability is part of continuum now places the disorder in the context of other biologically based disorders such as hypertension and obesity.[43] The discovery that reading disability is best conceptualized as occurring along a normal distribution of reading skills underscores the fact that children will vary in their level of severity of the disorder running along a mild-to-severe spectrum, with the majority of children with reading disabilities falling at the mild end. This finding has significant implications. For example, what are the criteria for identifying a child as having a *severe* reading disability, and does this degree of disability warrant entitlement to a greater intensity and duration of specialized interventions?

To answer such questions, the NICHD is embarking on a series of studies to identify the most valid points along the distribution of reading scores that distinguish levels of severity. In part, the validity of different cutoff points for mild, moderate, and severe reading disability is being determined by how children in each severity group respond to different types and intensities of intervention. At this writing, some initial results derived from the Florida State Intervention Project show that children with scores at the extreme lower end of the distributions for both phonological awareness skills and basic reading skills are much more difficult to remediate than children who fall along the distribution in the mild and moderate ranges.[44-46] It is as yet unclear whether children in the more severe range can achieve age- and grade-approximate reading skills, even with intense, informed intervention provided over a protracted period of time.

While children with severe reading disabilities will most likely require a greater amount of time in high-impact intervention programs than children with less severe deficits, as discussed earlier, it is clear that the longer children *at any level of severity* go without proper identification and intervention, the more difficult the task of remediation and the harder it becomes for the children to respond. It is also clear that even children with relatively subtle linguistic and reading deficits require the expertise of a teacher who is well trained and informed about the relationships between language development and reading development.[30] Unfortunately, such teachers are in short supply, primarily because of a lack of programs providing this training.[31]

Co-occurring Disorders

As noted, most children with learning disabilities have more than one of the seven subtypes of learning disabilities. It is also not unusual to find LD co-occurring with certain behavioral or emotional disorders. The most common co-occurring combinations are discussed briefly below.

Reading and Attention Disorders

Attention deficit disorder (ADD) is an increasingly common diagnosis recognized in medicine[47] and psychology[17] although it is not a category of disability recognized under the IDEA. Like LD, ADD is the subject of considerable controversy, and diagnostic criteria for ADD continue to evolve. There is no litmus test for ADD, which is diagnosed on the basis of persistent and maladaptive behavior patterns (inattention, impulsivity, and hyperactivity) that are inappropriate for the child's age. The number of diagnoses of ADD has increased dramatically in the past decade,[48] and one study[12] found 7% of a survey sample of 445 kindergarten students qualifying as "inattentive" on the Multigrade Inventory for Teachers.

Even children with relatively subtle linguistic and reading deficits require the expertise of a teacher who is well trained.

Figure 2[12] indicates that a child identified with reading disabilities is twice as likely as a member of the general population to also meet the diagnostic criteria for inattention (15% versus 7%). Similarly, an individual diagnosed with ADD is at higher risk than a member of the general population of having a reading disability/phonological awareness deficit (36% versus 17%). Despite this co-occurrence, recent studies have indicated that reading disabilities and ADD are distinct and separable disorders.[12,22,49]

Instruction in phonological awareness at the kindergarten level has significant positive effects on reading development during the first grade.

Unfortunately, when children with disabilities in reading also manifest ADD, their reading deficits are typically exacerbated, more severe, and more resistant to intervention.[22] In contrast to reading disabilities, ADD is more prevalent in males. Given the frequent co-occurrence of ADD with reading disabilities and given the tendency of boys with ADD to attract considerable attention from teachers, this combination may make boys with disabilities in reading much more likely than girls with disabilities in reading to come to the attention of teachers and to be referred for testing.

Social Adjustment Problems

In a broad sense, data indicate that learning disability, no matter what the specific type, has a tendency to co-occur with social adjustment problems.[50] Bruck,[51] in her review of the literature related to social and emotional adjustment, concluded that children with learning disabilities are more likely to exhibit increased levels of anxiety,

Figure 2

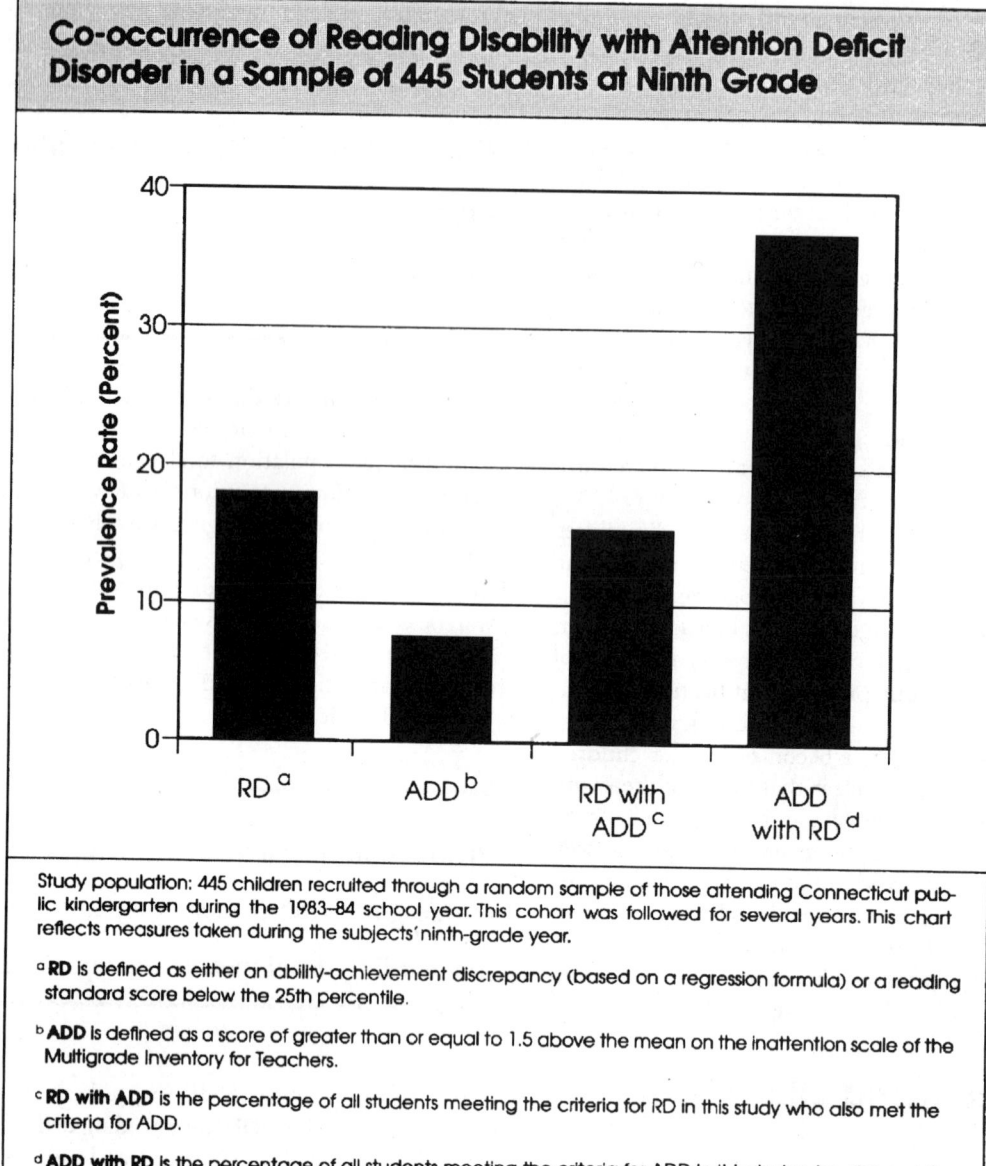

Co-occurrence of Reading Disability with Attention Deficit Disorder in a Sample of 445 Students at Ninth Grade

Study population: 445 children recruited through a random sample of those attending Connecticut public kindergarten during the 1983–84 school year. This cohort was followed for several years. This chart reflects measures taken during the subjects' ninth-grade year.

[a] **RD** is defined as either an ability-achievement discrepancy (based on a regression formula) or a reading standard score below the 25th percentile.

[b] **ADD** is defined as a score of greater than or equal to 1.5 above the mean on the inattention scale of the Multigrade Inventory for Teachers.

[c] **RD with ADD** is the percentage of all students meeting the criteria for RD in this study who also met the criteria for ADD.

[d] **ADD with RD** is the percentage of all students meeting the criteria for ADD in this study who also met the criteria for RD.

Source: Adapted with permission from Shaywitz, S.E., Fletcher, J.M., and Shaywitz, B.A. Issues in the definition and classification of the attention deficit disorder. *Topic in Language Disorders* (1994) 14:1-25

withdrawal, depression, and low self-esteem compared with their nondisabled peers. This comorbidity is persistent. For example, Johnson and Blalock[52] found that, of the 93 adults studied in an LD clinic sample, 36% continued to receive counseling or psychotherapy for low self-esteem, social isolation, anxiety, depression, and frustration. In many instances, it appears that such emotional problems reflect adjustment difficulties resulting from academic failure.[13] Deficits in social skills have also been found to exist at significantly high rates among children with learning disabilities.[53] In general, social skill deficits include difficulties interacting with people in an appropriate fashion (for example, lack of knowledge of how to greet people, how to make friends, and how to engage in playground games or a failure to use knowledge of such skills in these situations). While not all children with learning disabilities exhibit deficits in social skills, there are certain common characteristics among those who do. For example, Bruck[51] reported that children with more severe manifestations of LD are likely to manifest both an increased number of and increased severity of social skills deficits. Moreover, the gender of the child appears to be a factor, with evidence suggesting that girls with LD are more likely to have social adjustment problems.[51]

Reading Disorders with Other Learning Disabilities

There is abundant evidence that it is rare for a child with learning disabilities to manifest only one specific type of learning disability.[3,53] The co-occurrence of learning disorders should be expected given the developmental relationships between listening, speaking, reading, spelling, writing, and mathematics. For example, it is clear that deficits in phonological awareness lead to difficulties in decoding and word recognition which, in turn, lead to deficits in reading comprehension.[16,37,38] Likewise, children with disabilities in reading frequently experience persistent difficulties in solving word problems in math for the obvious reason that the printed word is difficult for them to comprehend.[14]

An important conclusion to draw from the literature on co-occurring disorders is that any intervention or remediation effort must take into account the range of deficits a child may have. More specifically, while an intensive reading intervention may consist of explicit instruction in phonological awareness, sound-symbol relationships, and contextual reading skills, the child may also require elements essential to bolstering self-esteem, and to fostering reading in other content areas such as mathematics, social studies, and science. One cannot expect the intervention for the reading deficit to generalize serendipitously to other domains of difficulty.

LD in Written Expression

Typically, children who display LD in written expression have difficulties in spelling, formulation and expression of ideas, handwriting, and knowledge of grammar and syntax. Unfortunately, well-designed research investigating disorders of written expression is relatively meager. Definitions for disorders of written expression remain vague.[54] Therefore it is not surprising that estimates of the prevalence of such disorders range from 8% to 15%.[13] What is known is that boys and girls display written language deficits at relatively equal rates.[54] Despite the lack of objective and detailed identification criteria, a number of excellent studies have been conducted to identify effective assessment and intervention programs for problems in written expression.[55-57]

The most successful programs tend to ensure that clear linkages are drawn between oral language, reading, and written language. Successful programs also ensure that basic skills development in spelling and writing (graphomotor production) are explicitly taught and/or accommodated and that the student is also taught how to employ strategies to guide the formulation of ideas for writing and the organization of these ideas in writing. These elements are common to many writing programs; however, successful instruction for students with disabilities in written expression depends upon their intensity and explicitness.

LD in Mathematics

Children identified as manifesting LD in mathematics can demonstrate deficits in arithmetic calculation, mathematics reasoning, or both. In general, authorities agree that approximately 6% of the school population have difficulties in mathematics that cannot be attributed to low intelligence, sensory deficits, or economic deprivation.[14,58] While the data are sparse at this time, it appears that deficits in arithmetic calculation skills are more frequently identified than deficits in arithmetic reasoning.[14] However, common sense would suggest that attempts to reason mathematically would be constrained by limitations in calculations skills. Unfortunately, a major difficulty in identifying math learning disabilities accurately is that, like learning to read, learning mathematics concepts is dependent upon the teacher's knowledge of the concepts and ability to present them.[13]

Interventions for Learning Disabilities

Space does not permit an extended review of research on intervention methods for different types of learning disabilities. However, high-quality prospective longitudinal research methods are now being applied to the study of treatment methods for reading disabilities, and that research is summarized here.

Research attempting to identify effective treatment methods for different types and severity levels of reading deficits has been enormously difficult. This is because typical treatment studies have not been able to reliably determine whether the outcomes seen were attributable to the treatment method, the child's general development, the child's previous instruction, the concurrent instruction being provided in the regular classroom, or combinations of these factors. In addition, a majority of treatment studies have been hampered by not having control over teacher expertise and training. Thus, if a treatment method does or does not work effectively, one does not know if it is because of the characteristics of the method, the characteristics of the teacher, or the characteristics of the child.

Since the late 1980s, a number of well-designed longitudinal treatment studies have been conducted. Because these studies have the capability to intervene with children early on and follow them over time, many of the methodological problems described above have been addressed. These intervention studies have provided information about how to prevent reading disabilities as well as how to address reading disabilities once they are detected at later ages.

For example, Blachman and her colleagues[59–61] have shown that instruction in phonological awareness at the kindergarten level has significant positive effects on reading development during the first grade. Within this context, research has demonstrated that proper instruction carried out by informed teachers can prevent reading failure both for children with inherent LD in basic reading skills and for children whose lack of exposure to "language rich" environments and language development activities during the first five years of life places them at risk for reading deficits. For instance, in a series of studies, Blachman[60,61] provided 84 low-income, inner-city children with 11 weeks of intensive instruction, 20 minutes per day, with one teacher instructing a small group of four to five students in several aspects of phonological awareness. Prior to instruction, classroom teachers also received 14 hours of intensive training. At the end of the 11 weeks, children receiving the interventions significantly ($p < 0.0001$) outperformed control children at reading phonetically regular words and at related tasks. A follow-up study conducted in February and May of the first-grade year showed that the gains were maintained if the first-grade curriculum continued the same emphasis on phonological skill development. Similar studies of kindergarten and first-grade children conducted by other researchers[62–64] have yielded similar results.

Unfortunately, not all children with reading disabilities have the benefit of appropriate early interventions. As discussed earlier, most children whose reading disability is not recognized until third grade or later and who receive standard interventions fail to show noticeable improvement. However, intensive instruction of appropriate duration provided by trained teachers can remediate the deficient reading skills of many children. For example, in one study, Alexander and her colleagues[65] provided 65 severely dyslexic children with 65 hours of individual instruction in addition to group instruction in phonemic awareness and synthetic and analytic skills. This intensive treatment approach improved the reading skills of the children from an initial reading score of 77 to an average of 98.4 (mean = 100) on a measure of alphabetic reading skills. Longitudinal studies continue to demonstrate the efficacy of intensive and informed multidimensional treatment programs.[64,66]

Several additional findings have emerged from these longitudinal treatment studies. It is clear that children with severe phonological deficits, leading to poor decoding and word recognition skills, respond to treatment at slower rates than youngsters with mild to moderate deficits.[44,67] In addition, instruction and interventions for reading failure, which focus primarily on context and reading comprehension without commensurate attention paid to phonological awareness, decoding, and word recognition, show limited results.[67–69] Finally, the success of even the best-designed reading intervention program is highly dependent upon the training and skills of the teacher.[22,29–31,38]

Disability in basic reading skills has been a prime candidate for treatment studies because it is the most common form of LD, it is the most objectively identifiable, and more knowledge is available concerning its causes and developmental course. Interventions for other types of learning disabilities have been developed but not studied as extensively and not studied in prospective, longitudinal research. There is as yet no solid indication whether early, effective interventions for disability in basic reading skills will affect the developmental course of other forms of learning disability.

Outcomes

Learning disabilities, sometimes inappropriately conceptualized as a "mild" disorder, may be anything but—they may be persistent and may not respond to general instruction or to inappropriate (for example, whole language) instruction. Unless identified early on and taught by expert teachers using detailed and intensive approaches emphasizing teaching both in phonological awareness and phonics instruction, children who learn poorly in the third grade can be expected to learn poorly throughout middle- and high-school grades. Unfortunately, the majority of children with learning disabilities are still not identified until the third or fourth grade and do not receive appropriate and timely reading instruction. In turn, those students with learning disabilities who graduate from high school are destined for few postschool opportunities. The minority of children with LD who received appropriate early intervention have not been identified for long-term follow-up so their long-term outcomes are speculative, but there is reason for optimism in their significantly improved short-term outcomes.

At present, the long-term outcomes for the majority of individuals with learning disabilities who did not receive appropriate early reading instruction are frequently bleak. It is known from the epidemiological data cited earlier that 75% of the children with disabilities in reading who are not identified until the third grade continue to have reading disabilities in the ninth grade.[24] In a recent review, Martin[70] reported that a considerable percentage (26.7%) of high school students identified as having learning disabilities drop out of school prior to graduation. Another 16% of students with learning disabilities exit school for "unknown" reasons without a diploma. Equally disturbing, Fairweather and Shaver[71] found that only 17.1% of the individuals with learning disabilities whom they followed for three to five years after high school were enrolled in any postsecondary course, including vocational courses. Only 6.7% of the students with learning disabilities participated in two-year higher education programs, and only 1.8% participated in four-year programs.

While these data suggest that individuals with learning disabilities do not markedly improve their academic skills (particularly reading skills) and face limited educational and vocational opportunities, it should not be concluded that individuals with LD cannot be taught. They can, but, as stated throughout this paper, interventions are most likely to be successful if applied early and carried out by expert teachers.

Conclusions

The past decade has witnessed a significant improvement in the quality of research on learning disabilities. Much of this recent research has been longitudinal in nature, thus opening the door to the identification of better predictors of different types of LD, their prevalence, their developmental course, and their response to intervention. Specifically,

■ The definitional issues addressed in this article continue to be the single greatest impediment to understanding learning disabilities and how to help children and adults with LD.

■ Maintaining the term "learning disabilities" makes little sense for scientific purposes, clinical purposes, or school policy purposes. Instead, the field must grapple with the clear need to address each type of learning disability individually to arrive at clear definitional statements and a coherent understanding of etiology, developmental course, identification, prevention, and treatment.

■ Reading disability in the form of deficits in phonological awareness is the most prevalent type of learning disability and affects approximately 17% of school-age children to some degree.

■ While other factors will, no doubt, be identified as contributing to reading disability, deficits in phonological awareness will most likely be found to be the core deficit. Research during the past decade has shown that deficits in phonological awareness can be identified in late kindergarten and first grade using inexpensive, straightforward testing protocols, and the presence of these deficits is a strong indicator that reading disability will follow.

■ Although it is now possible to identify children who are at-risk for reading failure, and some of the instructional conditions that must be in place from the beginning of formal schooling are understood, it is still true that the majority of LD children are not identified until the third grade. Therefore, policy initiatives should focus on the dissemination of existing early identification and early intervention programs.

■ Interventions for reading disability must consist of explicit instructional procedures in phonological awareness, sound-symbol relationships, and meaning and reading comprehension, and should be provided by expert teachers in the kindergarten and first-grade years.

■ In general, teachers remain seriously unprepared to address individual differences in many academic skills but particularly in reading. However, teachers cannot be expected to know what they have not been taught, and clearly colleges of education have let students down. Regrettably, being unprepared takes a toll on teachers. Many teachers worry about their failures with hard-to-teach students, become frustrated, lose confidence, and leave the profession, or discontinue attempting to teach children with special needs. This cycle of events calls for honest and aggressive reform in higher education.

■ While early intervention is *necessary*, it should not be assumed to be *sufficient* to address the multiple manifestations of learning disability. Even those students who receive appropriate phonological instruction at a young age may require continuous and intensive support to deal with other co-occurring disorders.

■ When policymakers consider "inclusionary" models of instruction, they must consider carefully whether those models can provide the critical elements of intensity and the appropriate duration of instruction, along with teacher expertise in multiple teaching methods and in accommodating individual learning differences.

1. Office of Special Education Programs. *Implementation of the Education of the Handicapped Act: Eleventh annual report to Congress.* Washington, DC: U.S. Department of Education, 1989.
2. Lyon, G. R. Research initiatives and discoveries in learning disabilities. *Journal of Child Neurology* (1995) 10: 120–26.
3. Lyon, G. R., ed. *Frames of reference for the assessment of learning disabilities: New views on measurement issues.* Baltimore: Paul H. Brookes, 1994.
4. Lyon, G. R., and Moats, L. C. An examination of research in learning disabilities: Past practices and future directions. In *Better understanding learning disabilities: New views from research and their implications for education and public policies.* G. R. Lyon, D. B. Gray, J. F. Kavanaugh, and N. A. Krasnegor, eds. Baltimore: Paul H. Brookes, 1993, pp. 1–14.
5. Lyon, G. R. Learning disabilities research: False starts and broken promises. In *Research in learning disabilities: Issues and future directions.* S. Vaughn and C. Bos, eds. San Diego, CA: College-Hill Press, 1987, pp. 69–85.
6. Moats, L. C., and Lyon, G. R. Learning disabilities in the United States: Advocacy, science, and the future of the field. *Journal of Learning Disabilities* (1993) 26:282–94.
7. Lyon, G. R. IQ is irrelevant to the definition of learning disabilities: A position in search of logic and data. *Journal of Learning Disabilities* (1989) 22:504–19.
8. Lyon, G. R. Toward a definition of dyslexia. *Annals of dyslexia* (1995) 45:3–27.
9. Zigmond, N. Learning disabilities from an educational perspective. In *Better understanding learning disabilities: New views from research and their implications for education and public policies.* G. R. Lyon, D. B. Gray, J. F. Kavanaugh, and N. A. Krasnegor, eds. Baltimore: Paul H. Brookes, 1993, pp. 251–72.
10. Torgesen, J. K. Learning disabilities: Historical and conceptual issues. In *Learning about learning disabilities.* B. Y. L. Wong, ed. New York: Academic Press, 1991, pp. 3–29.
11. Kirk, S. A. Behavioral diagnosis and remediation of learning disabilities. In *Conference on the Exploration of the Perceptually Handicapped Child.* Evanston, IL: Fund for Perceptually Handicapped Children, 1963, pp. 1–7.
12. Shaywitz, S. E., Fletcher, J. M., and Shaywitz, S. E. Issues in the definition and classification of attention deficit disorder. *Topics on Language Disorders* (1994) 14:1–25.
13. Lyon, G. R. Learning disabilities. In *Child psychopathology.* E. Marsh and R. Barkley, eds. New York: Guilford Press, 1996, pp. 390–434.
14. Fleishner, J. E. Diagnosis and assessment of mathematics learning disabilities. In *Frames of reference for the assessment of learning disabilities: New views on measurement issues.* G. R. Lyon, ed. Baltimore: Paul H. Brookes, 1994, pp. 441–58.
15. Coles, G. *The learning mystique: A critical look at learning disabilities.* New York: Pantheon Press, 1987.
16. Stanovich, K. E. The construct validity of discrepancy definitions of reading disability. In *Better understanding learning disabilities: New views on research and their implications for education and public policies.* G. R. Lyon, D. B. Gray, J. F. Kavanaugh, and N. A. Krasnegor, eds. Baltimore: Paul H. Brookes, 1993, pp. 273–307.
17. American Psychiatric Association. *Diagnostic and statistical manual of mental disorders.* 4th ed. rev. Washington, DC: APA, 1994.
18. Foorman, B. R., Francis, D. J., Shaywitz, S. E., et al. The case for early reading intervention. In *Cognitive and linguistic foundations of reading acquisition: Implications for intervention.* B. Blachman, ed. Mahwah, NJ: Erlbaum. In press.
19. Francis, D. J., Shaywitz, S. E., Steubing, K. K., et al. Measurement of change: Assessing behavior over time and within a developmental context. In *Frames of reference for the assessment of learning disabilities: New views on measurement issues.* G. R. Lyon, ed. Baltimore: Paul H. Brookes, 1994, pp. 29–58.
20. Fletcher, J. M., Francis, D. J., Rourke, B. P., et al. Classification of learning disabilities: Relationships with other childhood disorders. In *Better understanding learning disabilities: New views on research and their implications for education and public policies.* G. R. Lyon, D. B. Gray, J. F. Kavanagh, and N. A. Krasnegor, eds. Baltimore: Paul H. Brookes, 1993, pp. 27–56.
21. Fletcher, J. M., Shaywitz, S. E., Shankweiler, D. P., et al. Cognitive profiles of reading disability: Comparisons of discrepancy and low achievement definitions. *Journal of Educational Psychology* (1994) 95:1–18.
22. Wood, F., Felton, R., Flowers, L., and Naylor, C. Neurobehavioral definition of dyslexia. In *The reading brain: The biological basis of dyslexia.* D. D. Duane and D. B. Gray, eds. Parkton, MD: York Press, 1991, pp. 1–26.
23. Lyon, G. R., Gray, D. B., Kavanagh, J. F., and Krasnegor, N. A., eds. *Better understanding learning disabilities: New views from research and their implications for education and public policies.* Baltimore: Paul H. Brookes, 1993.
24. Shaywitz, B. A., and Shaywitz, S. E. Measuring and analyzing change. In *Frames of reference for the assessment of learning disabilities: New views on measurement issues.* G. R. Lyon, ed. Baltimore: Paul H. Brookes, 1994, pp. 29–58.
25. Shaywitz, B. A., and Shaywitz, S. E., Fletcher, J. M., and Escobar, M. D. Prevalence of reading disability in boys and girls: Results of the Connecticut longitudinal study. *Journal of the American Medical Association* (1990) 264:998–1002.
26. Fletcher, J. M., and Foorman, B. R. Issues in definition and measurement of learning disabilities: The need for early identification. In *Frames of reference for the assessment of learning disabilities: New views on measurement issues.* G. R. Lyon, ed. Baltimore; Paul H. Brookes, 1994, pp. 185–200.
27. Blachman, B. A. Getting ready to read: Learning how print maps to speech. In *The language continuum: From infancy to literacy.* J. F. Kavanagh, ed. Parkton, MD: York Press, 1991, pp. 41–62.
28. Senf, G. Learning disabilities as a sociological sponge: Wiping up life's spills. In *Research in learning disabilities: Issue and future directions.* S. Vaughn and C. Bos, eds. Boston: College-Hill Press, 1987, pp. 87–101.
29. Lyon, G. R., Vaasen, M., and Toomey, F. Teachers' perceptions of their undergraduate and graduate

preparation. *Teacher Education and Special Education* (1989) 12:164–69.
30. Moats, L. C. The missing foundation in teacher education: Knowledge of the structure of spoken and written language. *Annals of Dyslexia* (1994) 44:81–102.
31. Moats, L. C., and Lyon, G. R. Wanted: Teachers with knowledge of language. *Topics in Language Disorders* (1996) 16, 2:73–86.
32. Interagency Committee on Learning Disabilities. *A report to Congress.* Bethesda, MD: The National Institutes of Health, 1987.
33. Lerner, J. W. Educational interventions in learning disabilities. *Journal of the American Academy of Child and Adolescent Psychiatry* (1989) 28:326–31.
34. Kavale, K. A. Potential advantages of the meta-analysis technique for special education. *Journal of Special Education* (1984) 18:61–72.
35. Fletcher, J., Morris, R., Lyon, G.R., et al. Sub-types of dyslexia: An old problem revisited. In *Cognitive and linguistic foundations of reading acquisition: Implications for intervention research.* B. Blachman, ed. Mahwah, NJ: Erlbaum. In press.
36. Stanovich, E. E., and Siegel, L. S. Phenotypic performance profile of children with reading disabilities: A regression-based test of the phonological-core variable-difference model. *Journal of Educational Psychology* (1994) 86:24–53.
37. Adams, M. J. *Beginning to read: Thinking and learning about print.* Cambridge, MA: Cambridge University Press, 1990.
38. Adams, M. J., Bruck, M. Resolving the great debate. *American Educator* (1995) 19:7–10.
39. Share, D. L., and Stanovich, K. E. Cognitive processes in early reading development: Accommodating individual differences into a mode of acquisition. *Education: Contributions for Educational Psychology* (1995) 1:34–36.
40. Lyon, G. R., and Rumsey, J., eds. *Neuroimaging: A window to the neurological foundations of learning and behavior in children.* Baltimore: Paul H. Brookes. In press.
41. DeFries, J. C., and Gillis, J. J. Etiology of reading deficits in learning disabilities: Quantitative genetic analyses. In *Neuropsychological foundations of learning disabilities: A handbook of issues, methods, and practice.* J. E. Obrzut and G. W. Hynd, eds. San Diego: Academic Press, 1991, pp. 29–48.
42. Pennington, B. F. Genetics of learning disabilities. *Journal of Child Neurology* (1995) 10:69–77.
43. Shaywitz, S. E., Escobar, M. D., Shaywitz, B. A., et al. Evidence that dyslexia may represent the lower tail of a normal distribution of reading ability. *New England Journal of Medicine* (1992) 326:145–50.
44. Torgesen, J. K. A model of memory from an information processing perspective: The special case of phonological memory. In *Attention, memory, and executive function.* G. R. Lyon and N. A. Krasnegor, eds. Baltimore: Paul H. Brookes, 1996, pp. 157–84.
45. Torgesen, J. K., and Davis, C. Individual difference variables that predict response to training in phonological awareness. Unpublished manuscript. Florida State University, 1994.
46. Wagner, R. From simple structure to complex function: Major trends in the development of theories, models, and measurements of memory. In *Attention, memory, and executive function.* G. R. Lyon and N. A. Krasnegor, eds. Baltimore: Paul H. Brookes, 1996, pp. 139–56.
47. Dalton, R., and Forman, M. Attention deficit hyperactivity disorder (ADHD). In *Nelson textbook of pediatrics.* 15th ed. R. Behrman, R. Kliegman, and A. Arvin, eds. Philadelphia: W. B. Saunders, 1996, pp. 91–93.
48. Barkley, R. *Attention deficit hyperactivity disorder: A handbook for diagnosis and treatment.* New York: Guilford, 1990.
49. Gilger, J. W., Pennington, B. P., and DeFries, J. D. A twin study of the etiology of comorbidity: Attention-deficit hyperactivity disorder and dyslexia. *Journal of the Academy of Child and Adolescent Psychiatry* (1992) 31:343–48.
50. Bryan, T. Social problems in learning disabilities. In *Learning about learning disabilities,* B. Y. L. Wong, ed. New York: Academic Press, 1991, p. 195–226.
51. Bruck, M. Social and emotional adjustments of learning disabled children: A review of the issues. In *Handbook of cognitive, social, and neuropsychological aspects of learning disabilities.* S. J. Cedi, ed., Hillsdale, NJ: Erlbaum, 1986, pp. 230–50.
52. Johnson, D. J., and Blalock, J., eds. *Adults with learning disabilities: Clinical studies.* New York: Grune & Stratton, 1987.
53. Gresham, F. M. Conceptual issues in the assessment of social competence in children. In *Children's social behavior: Development, assessment, and modification.* P. Strain, M. Guralink, and H. Walker, eds. New York: Academic Press, 1986, pp. 143–86.
54. Hooper, S. R., Montgomery, J., Swartz, C., et al. Measurement of written language expression. In *Frames of reference for the assessment of learning disabilities: New views on measurement issues.* G. R. Lyon, ed. Baltimore: Paul H. Brookes, 1994, pp. 375–418.
55. Beringer, V. W. *Reading and writing acquisition: A developmental neuropsychological perspective.* Madison, WI: Brown and Benchmark, 1994.
56. Graham, S., Harris, K., MacArthur, C., and Schwartz, S. Writing and writing instruction with students with learning disabilities: A review of a program of research. *Learning Disability Quarterly* (1991) 14:89–114.
57. Gregg, N. Disorders of written expression. In *Written language disorders: Theory into practice.* A. Bain, L. Bailet, and L. Moats, eds. Austin, TX: PRO-ED, 1991, pp. 65–97.
58. Norman, C. A., and Zigmond, N. Characteristics of children labeled and served as learning disabled in school systems affiliated with Child Service Demonstration Centers. *Journal of Learning Disabilities* (1980) 13:542–47.
59. Blachman, B. A., ed. *Cognitive and linguistic foundations of reading acquisition: Implications for intervention research.* Mahwah, NJ: Erlbaum. In press.
60. Blachman, B. A., Ball, E., Black, R., and Tangel, D. Kindergarten teachers develop phoneme awareness in low-income inner-city classrooms: Does it make a difference? *Reading and Writing: An Interdisciplinary Journal* (1994) 6:1–17.
61. Tangel, D. M., and Blachman, B. A. Effect of phoneme awareness instruction on the invented spelling of first grade children: A one year follow-up. *Journal of Reading Behavior* (June 1995) 27,2:153–85.

62. Torgesen, J. K., Wagner, R. K., and Rashotte, C. A. Approaches to the prevention and remediation of phonologically based reading disabilities. In *Cognitive and linguistic foundations of reading acquisition: Implications for intervention research.* B. A. Blachman, ed. Mahwah, NJ: Erlbaum. In press.
63. Torgeson, J. K., Morgan, S., and Davis, C. The effects of two types of phonological awareness training on word learning in kindergarten children. *Journal of Educational Psychology* (1992) 84:364–70.
64. Foorman, B. R. *Early interventions for children with reading problems.* Progress Report. NICHD Grant HD 30995. Bethesda, MD: The National Institute of Child Health and Human Development, December 1995.
65. Alexander, A., Anderson, H., Heilman, P. C., et al. Phonological awareness training and remediation of analytic decoding deficits in a group of severe dyslexics. *Annals of Dyslexia* (1991) 41:193–206.
66. Torgesen, J. D. *Prevention and remediation of reading disabilities.* Progress Report. NICHD Grant HD 30988. Bethesda, MD: The National Institute of Child Health and Human Development, December 1995.
67. Torgesen, J. K., Wagner, R. K., and Rashotte, C. A. Longitudinal studies of phonological processing and reading. *Journal of Learning Disabilities* (1994) 27:276–86.
68. Iversen, S., and Tunmer, W. E. Phonological processing skills and the Reading Recovery Program. *Journal of Educational Psychology* (1993) 85:112–26.
69. Foorman, B. R. Research on the great debate: Code-oriented versus whole-language approaches to reading instruction. *School Psychology Review* (1995) 24:376–92.
70. Martin, E. W. Learning disabilities and public policy: Myths and outcomes. In *Better understanding learning disabilities: New views from research and their implications for education and public policy.* G. R. Lyon, D. B. Gray., J. F. Kavanagh, and N. A. Krasnegor, eds. Baltimore: Paul H. Brookes, 1993, pp. 325–42.
71. Fairweather, J. S., and Shaver, D. M. Making a transition to postsecondary education and training. *Exceptional Children* (1990) 57:264–70.

Sources for Table 1:

The Yale Research Group

The principal investigator for the Yale Learning Disability Research Center is Dr. Bennett Shaywitz, professor of pediatrics and professor and chief of pediatric neurology, the Yale University School of Medicine, 333 Cedar Street, New Haven, CT 06510. The Yale Group also consists of Drs. Sally Shaywitz, John Gore, Pawel Skudlarski, Robert Fulbright, Todd Constable, Richard Bronen, and Cheryl Lacadie from Yale University; Drs. Alvin Liberman, Kenneth Pugh, Donald Shankweiler, Carol Fowler, Ann Fowler, and Leonard Katz from the Haskins Laboratories; Drs. Jack Fletcher and Karla Steubing from the University of Texas Medical School; Drs. David Francis and Barbara Foorman form the University of Houston; Dr. Dorothy Aram from Emerson College; Dr. Benita Blachman from Syracuse University; Dr. Keith Stanovich and Linda Siegel from the Ontario Institute for Studies in Education; Dr. Rafael Kloorman from the University of Rochester; and Dr. Irwen Kirsch from the Educational Testing Service.

The Ontario Research Group

Drs. Keith Stanovich and Linda Siegel are professors of psychology and special education at the Ontario Institute for Studies in Education (OISE), Department of Special Education, Toronto, Ontario, Canada M5S 1V6 Canada. They are affiliated with the Yale University Learning Disability Research Center funded by the NICHD, as well as senior level scientists at OISE where funding is obtained primarily through the Canadian Research Council.

The University of Colorado Research Group

The principal investigator for the University of Colorado Learning Disability Research Center is Dr. John DeFries, professor and director of the Institute for Behavioral Genetics, the University of Colorado, Campus Box 447, Boulder, CO 80309-0447. The Colorado research team consists of Drs. Richard Olson, Barbara Wise, David Fulker, and Helen Forsberg from the University of Colorado, Boulder; Dr. Bruce Pennington from the University of Denver; Drs. Shelly Smith and William Kimberling from the Boys Town National Research Hospital in Omaha; Dr. Pauline Filipek from the University of California, Irvine; and Drs. David Kennedy and Albert Galaburda from Harvard University.

The Bowman Gray School of Medicine Research Group

The principal investigator for the Center for Neurobehavioral Studies of Learning Disorders is Dr. Frank Wood, professor of neurology and neuropsychology, Bowman Gray School of Medicine, 300 S. Hawthorne Road, Winston-Salem, NC 27103. Also from the Center are Drs. Rebecca Felton, Cecille Naylor, Mary McFarlane, John Keyes, Mark Espeland, Dale Dagenbach, and John Absher from the Bowman Gray School of Medicine; Dr. Raquel Gur from the University of Pennsylvania; Dr. Connie Juel from the University of Virginia; and Dr. Jan Loney from the State University of New York at Stony Brook.

The Johns Hopkins Research Group

The principal investigator for the Johns Hopkins Learning Disability Research Center is Dr. Martha Denckla, professor of neurology, pediatrics, and psychiatry, Johns Hopkins University School of Medicine, 707 North Broadway, Suite 501, Baltimore MD 21205. The Hopkins research team consists of Drs. Allan Reiss, Harvey Singer, Linda Schuerholz, Lisa Freund, Michelle Mazzocco, and Mark Reader from the Kennedy-Kriger Research Institute at Johns Hopkins; Drs. Frank Vallutino and Donna Scanlon at the State University of New York at Albany; Dr. Mark Appelbaum from Vanderbilt University; and Dr. Gary Chase from Georgetown University.

The Florida State University Research Group

The principal investigator of the Florida State University Learning Disabilities Intervention Project is Dr. Joseph Torgesen, professor of psychology, Florida State University, Tallahassee, FL 33124-2040. Members of the Florida State Research Group are Drs. Richard Wagner and Carol Rashotte from Florida State University; Drs. Ann Alexander and Kytja Voeller from the University of Florida, and Ms. Patricia Lindamood from Lindamood-Bell Learning Processes.

The University of Houston Research Group

The principal investigator for the University of Houston Learning Disabilities Intervention Project is Dr. Barbara Foorman, professor of educational psychology, University of Houston, 4800 Calhoun, Houston, TX 77204. The Houston group also consists of Drs. David Francis and Dorothy Haskell from the University of Houston; Drs. Jack Fletcher and Karla Steubing from the University of Texas Medical School; and Drs. Bennett and Sally Shaywitz from Yale University.

The University of Miami Research Group

The principal investigator for the University of Miami Learning Disabilities Program Project is Dr. Herbert Lubs, professor of pediatrics and genetics, University of Miami School of Medicine, MCCD, P.O. Box 18620, Miami, FL 33101. The Miami group also consists of Dr. Ranjan Dura, Bonnie Levin, Bonnie Jallad, Marie-Louis Lubs, Mark Rabin, Alex Kushch, and Karen Gross-Glenn, all from the University of Miami.

Cognitive Credit Cards

Acquiring Learning Strategies

Alan L. Edmunds

Do you find yourself constantly reminding students with learning disabilities of the cognitive strategies they should or could use when doing schoolwork?

Are students confused about what strategy works with what learning task?

Is the array of learning strategy acronyms, or mnemonics, overwhelming to both you and your students?

Would you like an appealing, organized way to help students help themselves?

This article describes the Cognitive Credit Card (CCC), an individualized approach to learning strategies, that my colleagues and I developed, tested, and modified over a period of 3 years. This article provides feedback by parents, students, and teachers about the benefits of using the CCC, as well as optimum conditions for its use.

Individualized Student Needs

The comments reported here were not gathered under the auspices of a formal study; rather, they were accumulated as the record of what transpired as we developed and tested the CCC. When interpreting these outcomes, keep in mind the individualized nature of both the design and use of the CCC and the individual growth targets for each of the students. Nonetheless, the results were quite consistent from situation to situation.

Because many students with learning disabilities have information-processing problems (see box, "Cognitive Learning Strategy Difficulties"), we designed and implemented the CCC to address these problems. Teachers face many dilemmas in teaching students how to use learning strategies. One way they can overcome these difficulties is by encouraging students to create their own strategies through the CCC process.

The Teacher's Dilemma

Students with learning disabilities often find themselves in a predicament. Their limited strategy repertoire, combined with their limited ability to devise strategies and their limited ability to properly use learning strategies, is a triple whammy. It also presents perplexing problems for teachers:

- If we do not teach students learning strategies, they will not learn efficiently—or they may not learn at all.
- On the other hand, even if we teach students appropriate learning strategies, they still might not use those strategies in the most expeditious manner; and they still might not recognize when they have to stop using an inefficient strategy.
- Further, if students do recognize that their selected strategy is inappropriate or inefficient, they usually cannot switch to an alternative strategy because of their limited repertoire.
- Moreover, for the teaching of learning strategies to be most effective, teachers usually have to monitor and revise the student's implementation of strategies on an ongoing basis. This oversight often leads to students' becoming quite dependent on the teacher for every detail of their learning—the more the teacher tries to help, the less autonomous the student becomes.

Unfortunately, such teacher-support and monitoring tend to reinforce the high external locus of control exhibited by students with learning disabilities (Bender, 1987; Bladow, 1982; Hallahan, Gajar, Cohen, & Tarver, 1978). Despite the well-meaning intentions of the teacher and students, the students might still end up frustrated with their nonsuccess and be unwilling to participate in further learning activities.

Given these problems, many educators could use an approach to successfully teach students to develop, practice, and readily use learning strategies within the context of their schoolwork and, at the same time, help them become productive and autonomous learners.

The objective of our research was to develop a classroom-based learning strategy mechanism that would provide students with sets of non-memory-based, self-mediated cues. These sets of cues would prompt students to *think about their thought processes* as they attempt to solve particular problems or learn particular topics in school. In this instance, a set of cues constitutes a learning strategy.

A Possible Solution: The Cognitive Credit Card

Designing Cognitive Cues

The CCC is a credit card-sized laminated set of cognitive or metacognitive cues designed to elicit thinking *about thinking* as students attempt to learn or solve problems. These cognitive cues must contain little or no subject content matter; yet they have to be specific enough that students can identify what the cues are for—usually accomplished by the heading or title. For example, a specific set of cognitive cues could be designed to prompt students to think about their understanding of, and note-taking on, the play *Macbeth* without providing explanations or notes about the play. This set of cues could also be used, with minor revisions, for other topics requiring similar thinking processes.

In addition, a set of cognitive cues must also contain little or no procedural information. For example, rather than outline or suggest the steps of the scientific method, the cues prompt the students to ask themselves about their understanding and application of the procedures of the scientific method. This set of cues using the scientific method could also be easily adapted for library research or math or other topics whereby a step-by-step or research strategy is required.

Coming Up with a Process

The process of developing a CCC begins when a teacher or student recognizes that the student does not use a particular strategy in trying to learn a particular school topic. Teachers can usually recognize a student's learning-strategy deficit because teachers usually ask students to use particular thinking processes in assigned work.

Students can usually recognize their learning-strategy deficits because of two conditions:

- They are having difficulty learning, and they know they can go to their teachers for help.
- The teacher outlines and demonstrates the benefits of specific cognitive strategies for learning particular topics, and the student wants to take advantage of these learning tools.

Once the students identify the topic, they attempt, with the teacher's guidance, to produce a set of cues that will help them think about their processing of the information. The students determine the cues based on their knowledge that a particular set or series of cues would be beneficial for them for this specific topic. Students acquire this knowledge by engaging in discussions with the teacher about what cues might work best. The student and teacher revise the cues until they are in exactly the form that represents the most meaning for the student. The teacher makes sure that the cues are cognitive prompts and that they provide little or no curricular content and little or no content-specific procedural information. In effect, the CCC becomes a cognitive organizer for a specific topic focusing on *how* the student is to learn, rather than *what* the student is to learn.

"Talking Out" the Cues

It is difficult to outline a specific series of steps for teachers to follow when developing CCCs with their students because the cues used by one student for a particular topic may not be appropriate for another student because of differences in cognitive style, language use, or approaches to problem-solving or learning. This problem is compounded by the fact that the same student will use different cues for similar, but different, school topics. This is consistent with the notion posited by Hagen (1971) and Levin (1976) that learning strategies are most effective when

Cognitive Learning Strategy Difficulties of Students with Learning Disabilities

Students with learning disabilities generally have great difficulty developing learning strategies that significantly enhance the learning of school topics (Hallahan, Kneedler, & Lloyd, 1983; Lerner, 1997; Winzer, 1996). These students tend to have a limited repertoire of learning strategies (Lerner) and they do not readily devise new strategies, particularly for novel problems or situations. They also seem to lack the metacognitive skill of recognizing when a strategy is not producing efficient learning (Torgeson, 1980).

Strategy Use Defined by Limited Success. Instead, students with learning disabilities continue to use their limited number and type of learning strategies for all learning situations only because those particular strategies may have been somewhat successful for them in the past. Thus, they often have difficulty in selecting appropriate strategies for a task or in implementing these strategies in the most appropriate manner.

Research on Metacognitive Strategies. Students with learning disabilities, however, do not seem to lack the ability to carry out the learning task as much as they lack the metacognitive strategies to govern their mental processing during the completion of the task (Adelman & Taylor, 1983; Deshler & Shumaker, 1986). As a result, they have great difficulty managing their thinking while they are trying to learn; yet it often appears to teachers and parents that these students cannot do the required tasks. This often leads to extreme frustration and, too often, the students stop trying to learn.

Despite these problems, the research is quite clear that once students with learning disabilities receive instruction in the use of cognitive and metacognitive learning strategies, they typically do better in school (Deshler, Ellis, & Lenz, 1996; Groteluschen, Borkowski, & Hall, 1990).

The Inherent Problems of Other Strategies. Another facet of this problem is that many learning strategy mechanisms require students to remember *acronyms* (Alley & Deshler, 1979; Deshler, Shumaker, Lenz, & Ellis, 1984), *self-monitoring phrases* (Hallahan, Marshall, & Lloyd, 1981; Hallahan & Sapona, 1983), *mnemonic devices* (Scruggs, Mastropieri, Sullivan, & Hesser, 1993), and the *functional components* of these kinds of strategies. This compounds the difficulties of students with learning disabilities because they typically have poor short-term memory. They exhibit poor coding of information for memory storage (Haines & Torgeson, 1979; Torgeson, 1984) and they are far less mature in their repertoire, awareness, and use of memory strategies (Owings, Petersen, Bransford, Morris, & Stein, 1980). Therefore, the proper rehearsal and storage of usually effective learning strategies is compromised and the retrieval of particular strategies is very difficult.

Mathematics Cognitive Credit Card

This Cognitive Credit Card was used to facilitate the completion of long-division questions. It was designed by a student who felt that there were "just too many things to keep in my head at the same time" while she was doing division questions in class or for homework. Note that this CCC contains specific questions about the procedures and several monitoring questions to enable her to check what she is doing. This particular card was designed in this way because the student was quite capable at doing the calculations; she just seemed to have problems with various processes such as how to get started, decimal placement, place value, and what to do about remainders.

> **Math - Long Division Questions**
> 1. Is the question in the right form?
> 2. Is the smaller number outside and the larger one inside?
> 3. Can the small number go into the large one evenly?
> 4. Do I have to borrow?
> 5. Did I multiply & subtract?
> 6. Are my numbers in the right places?
> 7. Do I need to bring down a number?
> 8. Is there a decimal place in this question?
> 9. Is there a remainder? What form & units?
> 10. Did I check my answer? Does it make sense?

self-generated because they comfortably match the individual's learning style.

Generally, however, a teacher can "talk out" the cues with the student, engaging the student in discovering how he or she would best go about dealing with the topic at hand. Teachers can use questions like these:

- How can you remind yourself about what you have to think of to get started?
- What will you have to think of next?
- How will you ask yourself if you have remembered to think of specific steps in the process?
- How will you check to see if your thinking is working?

The student's answers to these and similar questions are usually effective cognitive cues.

Taking Stock of Repeated Instructions

Another way to proceed is for the teacher to reflect on the number of times they have had to repeat the same cognitive instructions to a student in teaching situations and use these repeated instructions as the basis for a CCC.

In this scenario, the teacher replaces their verbalized cues with a completed CCC. One teacher stated, "To make a good credit card, I just use, or start with, the same questions I have to ask the students when I help them with a problem."

Printing and Using the CCC

Once the student and teacher develop a set of cues for a particular topic, the student or a helper keys it into a word processing program. The computer reduces the font so that the cues can be printed on a credit card-sized piece of paper. Then the student or the teacher laminates the card and punches a hole in one of the corners. The completed CCC is then attached to the student's binder by a fastener. Usually, a cable tie is used so the CCC cannot be detached and risk being lost.

Whenever the student experiences the learning situation that the card is designed for, or needs a reminder, such as during homework, tests, or exams, their personalized cognitive learning strategy is available.

What Students, Teachers, and Parents Think of the CCC

The following outcomes of implementing the CCC reflect the collective feedback of students, parents, and teachers in several schools.

1. *Students became aware that they could devise their own sets of cues that could produce beneficial learning.* This realization not only enhanced learning but, just as important, it provided a much needed boost to self-esteem. Teachers found that the initial set of cues took time, guidance, and encouragement; but for the students, success with a self-designed set of cues was a reward and a motivator. Teachers felt that the greatest contributor to the success of the CCC was that students had significant input in designing their own sets of cues, supporting the position of Hagen (1971) and Levin (1976). After all, we all think about problems, process information, and problem-solve in our own way.

2. *Students quickly learned how to adapt and revise sets of cues to make them applicable to other topics.* Students commented, "It's like knowing all the secrets to getting good grades" and "It is just a matter of figuring out the right combination to use for each subject." Because many individual cues are useful in different subjects, teachers and parents noticed that students started to see the relationships among the various school subjects in terms of thought processes, not just content linkages. This also encourages student understanding of concepts, rather than simply factual information, a criticism

The CCC is a cognitive organizer for a specific topic, focusing on how the student is to learn, rather than what the student is to learn.

of some learning strategies (Andrews & Lupart, 1993; Higbee, 1978).

3. *The students' repertoire of strategies expanded and seemed to be readily available.* Most students ended up with multiple CCCs for a variety of topics. Rather than only having a few strategies because of their limited memory store, students had a wealth of hard-copy strategies to refer to as needed. After several applications, some students internalized some sets of cues. Thus, they had devised, learned, and successfully applied new cognitive and metacognitive strategies and now had additional strategies in their cognitive repertoire. The internalized strategy goes into long-term memory and becomes an asset because children with learning disabilities have no distinct difficulty with long-term memory (Haines & Torgeson, 1979; Ross, 1976; Torgeson, 1984).

4. *In designing and owning a CCC, the student also assumes responsibility for its proper and efficient use.* Teachers noted that

> **Students can develop, practice, and readily use learning strategies within the context of their schoolwork and, at the same time, become productive and autonomous learners.**

having a variety of strategies also helped students make good decisions about the proper applications of certain types of cues/strategies and whether or not the strategy works for them in that situation. By far the most consistently reported fact by teachers was that *the CCC reduced student dependence on the teacher for continual guidance.* Many students indicated that they felt comfortable "trying it without the card" because they knew the card was available, and they did not have to ask the teacher for help if they got stuck. This type of risk-taking is unusual for students who repeatedly experience frustration and failure with academic schoolwork and have high external locus of control. Teachers and parents also reported that many students readily gravitated toward managing their own learning, and they appeared to relish their academic independence and success. Teachers and parents reported that this approach seemed to have given new life to students who were struggling academically and were generally unsatisfied with school.

5. *Contrary to popular belief, students did not feel "identified" by having one or more CCC dangling from their binders.* In fact, the CCC became a badge of honor of sorts, and students were delighted to make them in a multiplicity of colors, shapes, and sizes for a variety of topics, applications, and courses.

6. *By all reports, the most important benefit to emerge from the CCC is that the process is student mediated.* The benefits realized by the students are immeasurable because the CCC is something that they have developed and tried—and it has been successful. This process encourages the student to become an autonomous learner, yet retains the teacher as the guide, moving the student along the continuum of independence as the teacher sees fit.

The anecdotal results reported here were gathered during the ongoing research and development of the CCC and, thus, are considered preliminary. Further research into the efficacy of the CCC, based on these encouraging results, is continuing.

> **Teachers can help students develop a set of cues that prompt the students to think about their thought processes as they attempt to solve particular problems or learn particular topics in school.**

History Cognitive Credit Card

This Cognitive Credit Card, designed by an 11th-grade student, was primarily used to alleviate his perennial problem of not being able to take good notes during class. He did not seem to understand the purpose of taking notes—he just did it because everyone else did it, and he had done so since about Grade 6. He did not know where to start, what was important, what was not important, or what to do with the notes once he was finished. It is evident from the card that he needed numerous cues to manage what he thought about during class time. His note-taking skills were not bad—he got the information down on paper—he just felt that he needed to be a more active learner/listener, an idea he got from one of his teachers. The primary benefits of his use of the card were that he "learned to take a lot fewer notes—just the important ones," and he did not feel lost when it came time to study for a test. After initial success with this CCC, he designed a similar one for taking notes for the readings he did while away from the classroom.

Taking Notes in History Class

- What did I read/study/write about last night?
- How was it related to what we did <u>last</u> class?
- What do I predict the topic will be about today?
- What is the introduction of today's topic?
- Why is this topic important to what I already know?
- How many major/minor points <u>will</u> the teacher make?
- How many major/minor points <u>did</u> the teacher make?
- What kind of questions could be asked on a test?
- Do I have any concerns that need to be cleared up?
- Do I need to talk to the teacher?

Conditions for Using the CCC

We found several conditions under which the CCC system seemed to work best.

First, and most important, the sets of cues cannot contain (a) subject-specific content or (b) subject-specific procedural information. The cues should only make students think about their thinking or think about the task as they are trying to learn or problem-solve. Otherwise, it will be nothing more than a "teacher approved cheat sheet," and no learning benefits will be realized. Teachers who rigorously adhered to these criteria felt secure in allowing students to use their CCCs during tests and exams. In fact, one teacher stated, "The litmus test of a good card was if I felt that it did not give the student an advantage on tests."

Another important condition of the CCC is that students design and use them for more complex and more sophisticated strategies as time goes by, or as the student is capable. The CCC, like any other learning strategy, should be treated like a school subject; as in other school subjects, the teacher must build on the student's prior knowledge and gently challenge the student to develop and design higher-order strategies.

Finally, teachers found the CCC to be most effective with students whose reading abilities were at least at Grade 5 level and with students in their early teens. This finding is consistent with Rohwer's (1971) position that early adolescence is a prime time for such instruction because students are developmentally mature enough not only to profit from such training, but also to apply what they have learned to new circumstances.

References

Adelman, H. S., & Taylor, L. (1983). *Learning disabilities in perspective.* Glenview, IL: Scott, Foresman.*

Alley, G., & Deshler, D. D. (1979). *Teaching the learning disabled adolescent: Strategies and methods.* Denver: Love Publishing.*

Andrews, J., & Lupart, J. (1993). *The inclusive classroom: Educating exceptional children.* Scarborough, Ontario: Nelson Canada.*

Bender, W. N. (1987). Behavioral indicators of temperament and personality in the inactive learner. *Journal of Learning Disabilities, 20,* 280–285.

Bladow, L. (1982). Locus of control of learning disabled and nondisabled children. *Psychological Reports, 50,* 1310.

Deshler, D. D., Ellis, E. S., & Lenz, B. K. (1996). *Teaching adolescents with learning disabilities: Strategies and methods.* Denver: Love Publishing.*

Deshler, D. D., & Shumaker, J. B. (1986). Learning strategies: An instructional alternative for low-achieving adolescents. *Exceptional Children, 52,* 583–590.

Deshler, D. D., Shumaker, J. B., Lenz, B. K., & Ellis, E. S. (1984). Academic and cognitive interventions for LD adolescents: Part II. *Journal of Learning Disabilities, 17,* 170–187.

Groteluschen, A., Borkowski, J., & Hall, C. (1990). Strategy instruction is often insufficient: Addressing the interdependency of executive and attributional process. In T. Scruggs & B. Wong (Eds.), *Intervention research in learning disabilities* (pp. 81–101). New York: Springer-Verlag.*

Hagen, J. W. (1971). Some thoughts on how children learn to remember. *Human Development, 14,* 262–271.

Haines, D. J., & Torgeson, J. K. (1979). The effects of incentives on rehearsal and short-term memory in children with reading problems. *Learning Disability Quarterly, 2,* 48–55.

Hallahan, D. P., Gajar, A. H., Cohen, S. G., & Tarver, S. G. (1978). Selective attention and locus of control in learning disabled and normal children. *Journal of Learning Disabilities, 11,* 231–236.*

Hallahan, D. P., Kneedler, R. D., & Lloyd, J. W. (1983). Cognitive behavior modification techniques for learning disabled children: Self-instruction and self-monitoring. In J. D. McKinney & L. Feagans (Eds.), *Current topics in learning disabilities,* (pp. 207–244). Norwood, NJ: Ablex.

Hallahan, D. P., Marshall, K. J., & Lloyd, J. W. (1981). Self-recording during group instruction: Effects on attention to task. *Learning Disability Quarterly, 4,* 407–413.

Hallahan, D. P., & Sapona, R. (1983). Self-monitoring of attention with learning disabled children: Effects on attention to task. *Journal of Learning Disabilities, 16,* 616–620.

Higbee, K. L. (1978). Some pseudo-limitations of mnemonics. In M. M. Gruneberg, P. E. Morris, & R. N. Sykes (Eds.), *Practical aspects of memory: Current research and issues* (pp. 403–408). Chichester: Wiley.*

Lerner, J. W. (1997). *Learning disabilities: Theories, diagnosis, and teaching strategies.* Boston: Houghton Mifflin.*

Levin, J. R. (1976). What have we learned about maximizing what children learn? In J. R. Levin & V. L. Allan (Eds.), *Cognitive learning in children: Theories and strategies,* (pp. 213–237). New York: Academic Press.*

Owings, R. A., Petersen, G. A., Bransford, J. D., Morris, C. D., & Stein, B. S. (1980). Spontaneous monitoring and regulation of learning: A comparison of successful and less successful fifth graders. *Journal of Educational Psychology, 72,* 250–256.

Rohwer, W. D. (1971). Prime time for education: Early childhood or adolescence? *Harvard Educational Review, 41,* 316–341.

Ross, A. O. (1976). *Psychological aspects of learning disabilities and reading disorders.* New York: McGraw-Hill.*

Scruggs, T. E., Mastropieri, M. A., Sullivan, G. S., & Hesser, L. S. (1993). Improving reasoning and recall: The differential effects of elaborative interrogation and mnemonic elaboration. *Learning Disabilities Quarterly, 16,* 233–240.

Torgeson, J. K. (1980). The use of efficient task strategies by learning disabled children: Conceptual and educational implications. *Journal of Learning Disabilities, 13,* 364–371.

Torgeson, J. K. (1984). Memory processes in reading disabled children. *Journal of Learning Disabilities, 18,* 350–357.

Winzer, M. (1996). *Children with exceptionalities in Canadian classrooms.* Scarborough, Ontario: Allyn & Bacon.*

BooksNow

*To order books marked by an asterisk (*), please call 24 hrs/365 days: 1–800–BOOKS–NOW (266–5766) or (801) 261–1187, or visit them on the Web at http://www.BooksNow.com/TeachingExceptional.htm. Use VISA, M/C, or AMEX or send check or money order + $4.95 S&H ($2.50 each add'l item) to: Books Now, Suite 125, 448 East 6400 South, Salt Lake City, UT 84107.

Alan L. Edmunds *(CEC Nova Scotia Federation), Assistant Professor, Department of Education, St. Francis Xavier University, Antigonish, Nova Scotia, Canada.*

Address correspondence to the author at Department of Education, St. Francis Xavier University, Box 5000, Antigonish, Nova Scotia, Canada B2G 2W5 (e-mail: aedmunds@stfx.ca).

Dropout Prevention: A Case for Enhanced Early Literacy Efforts

LOUIS G. DENTI and GILBERT GUERIN

Teachers and administrators wrestle daily with how best to educate students with learning disabilities and other students who are at risk of school failure. Statistics on the low graduation rates of students with learning disabilities and students from language and ethnic minority populations attest to the limited success of existing programs. At the same time, little attention has been given to how best to prepare teachers and administrators so that they can increase the holding power of schools.

Some probing questions about the goals and content of teacher and administrator preparation are in order. What steps in teacher and administrator preparation will improve the holding power of our schools? What can be done to better prepare teachers, at every grade level, to improve the skills of students who are at high risk of dropping out of school? What can be done to improve teachers' ability to provide early literacy for at-risk students? The answers to these questions could lead to improved instruction for all students and to an increase in the graduation rates of minority students and students with learning disabilities.

In this article, we briefly review current research on dropout issues and describe features of secondary school programs that have high graduation rates. Because early reading skills are linked closely with both school success and graduation rates, we examine that link and the role teacher preparation programs must play to ensure that all students are literate by the end of the primary grades.

Research on the High School Dropout Problem

Factors involved in the high school dropout problem include poverty, minority status, family attitudes, low self-esteem, poor academic skills, economic responsibilities, and pregnancy (Bryk and Thum 1989; Fine 1986). Research has shown that the highest dropout rates occur among students who have learning disabilities or emotional disturbances (U.S. Department of Education 1990), Hispanic and African American students (California State Department of Education 1991), students from low socio-economic backgrounds (Smith and Luckasson, 1992), students with the lowest academic achievement within the learning disabled population (Burstein, Cabello and Hamann, 1993), and students who have been held back and who are absent frequently (Mahood 1990).

Meyen, Vergason, and Whelan (1993) point out that this knowledge unfortunately does not usually result in school policies that improve school holding power. They recommend that the focus should be on school program variables (e.g., curriculum and schedule) and on student behaviors (i.e., those that students can control) that can be altered by teachers and can be shown to result in higher graduation rates. They believe that school programs with the following features have the highest graduation rates:

- Intensive instruction in reading and mathematics
- Explicit instruction in "survival" skills
- Successful completion of courses required for graduation
- Explicit planning for life after high school

The same authors also include vocational education and transition activities within their model programs.

Bryk and Thum (1989) stress a "constellation of structural and normative features" as the critical elements in school holding power. They cite the following school and teacher characteristics as strongly related to high graduation rates:

- A faculty interested in and engaged with students
- An orderly social environment
- A low differentiation among students (e.g., common school experiences and spirit)
- Emphasis on academic pursuits
- Sustained, informal, face-to-face adult-student interactions

---

Louis G. Denti is a professor and Gilbert Guerin is grant director, both in the Division of Special Education and Rehabilitative Services, San José State University.

These elements pose challenges to both regular and special education programs and may provide clues as to why the dropout rates in some schools are so high.

Elementary School Literacy and Reading Needs

Poor reading is one of the most common characteristics of school dropouts. Because the seeds for reading failure are set in the primary grades, dropout prevention needs to begin in those grades. Years ago, Kelly, Veldman, and McGuire (1964) and Lloyd (1978) determined that future dropouts could be predicted with remarkable accuracy by examining students' third-grade reading skills. Slavin et al. (1990) reaffirmed the earlier observation that a child who has not been taught literacy skills in the primary years begins a spiral of failure that often ends in dropping out of school.

Current researchers believe that children should be literate by the end of the third grade. According to Slavin, Karweit, and Wasik (1992–93), prevention is only possible if corrective intervention in reading occurs at an early age. According to Slavin et al. (1994), waiting even until the third grade to assist children is too late to remediate reading problems.

Clay (1987) studied reading problems of children who repeated incorrect reading patterns without either teachers or students making a correction. Clay points out that such children are actually "learning to be learning disabled" (155) by practicing incorrect reading patterns. Unless the incorrect process is interrupted and replaced with the effective literacy skills, the student will fall further behind. Clay believes that children cannot regain normal response patterns on their own, that a teacher must assist.

When education fails and the child develops poor reading skills, the likelihood of special education placement increases (Graham and Johnson 1989). During the past two decades, *learning disability* has become an umbrella term for a vast number of diverse learning and behavior problems (DeStefano and Wermuth 1992). Although placement may help children build new skills, it can also become a catchment that is difficult to escape. Once assigned, the placement is often permanent and the likelihood of dropping out by the tenth grade increases dramatically (Bryk and Thum 1989; Lichtenstein 1988).

Successful Early Intervention Programs

Schools and Parents

Two elements of a successful early intervention program are (a) a focused instructional literacy program in kindergarten through second grade, with the goal of successful reading by the third grade, and (b) increased parent involvement. These elements have been addressed by researchers; the following features, compiled by Feldman (1995), are characteristic of a positive school-based intervention program:

- Takes place in kindergarten through second grade
- Complements the regular language arts program
- Provides more intensive service to students who have been identified as having difficulties in literacy
- Identifies student learning needs based on classroom-level or school-level criteria
- Employs curriculum-based assessment, including teacher observation, to determine needs, monitor progress, and suggest changes
- Increases the total amount of time spent reading and intensifies instruction
- Uses one-on-one tutoring at least four times per week for twenty-five to forty-five minutes with trained tutors
- Is closely coordinated with the core–regular class literacy curriculum
- Includes direct teaching (i.e., modeling, thinking aloud, questioning) of proven literacy acquisition strategies such as phonics, syntax, and semantic clues
- Is essentially an acceleration program and not a long-term remedial program

The literature suggests that schoolwide programs that coordinate early intervention and encourage active parent involvement can prevent reading failure in later years (Levin 1996; Pikulski 1994). These programs require administrators who are able to bring school and community together in support of early literacy. Adams (1990) has addressed family involvement in early literacy programs and has the following suggestions:

- Read aloud to your children daily to increase their memory, knowledge, and judgment.
- Read and discuss with your children the books they are reading at school.
- Encourage your children to write to other family members about what they are reading.
- Discuss stories as you read them with your children.
- Help your children read enjoyable stories as often as possible.
- Take children to the library on a regular basis.
- Encourage selective TV watching that may help promote reading skills.
- Model good reading, that is, read newspapers, magazines, and books.
- Provide computer reading games for your children.

The research on early literacy calls for a renewed contract between school and home if students are to learn to read at grade level by the third grade. Research also substantiates that the intensity of instruction (one-on-one tutorials), ongoing assessment, and early intervention can indeed enhance reading. Moreover, a necessary part of support for early literacy rests within the family. Shaping a positive home environment that values reading and writing can result in children making measurable academic gains at school. Teacher preparation programs that help

FIGURE 1

Teacher and Administrator Competencies in Literacy and Dropout Prevention

TEACHER

- Strategies for systematic and direct instruction of basic reading, writing, and spelling skills, especially in primary grades
- Instructional skills in phonemic awareness, letter shapes, names and clusters (phonics), meaning (semantics), and word sequences (structure), especially in primary grades
- Instructional organization that includes the appropriate use of four grouping levels—whole group, small group, individual, and tutorial
- Skills in collaboration with parents, caregivers, and aides that promote literacy in the primary grades and reading assistance at other grade levels
- Knowledge and skill in classroom and school climate that increase the school's holding power

ADMINISTRATOR

- Skill in establishing the program and organizational conditions that promote school literacy
- Strategies for acquiring the resources (financial and volunteer) needed to provide materials and staff to implement a comprehensive literacy program
- Knowledge and skill in classroom and school climate that increase the school's holding power
- Skill in establishing community awareness, support, and involvement in improving reading and literacy
- Ability to assess and evaluate the effectiveness of school literacy programs and their impact on the dropout rate

---

prospective teachers foster close family and school relationships regarding early literacy are essential.

School Structure Issues

Early literacy programs should allow large numbers of children to receive immediate help in reading and writing and should reduce the need for expensive specialized services in the future. A flexible and adaptable school system can encourage creative early literacy programs. By deploying special education and other specialized resources in a coherent, coordinated, student-centered manner in first through third grades, schools could avert reading problems. The following suggestions can help guide administrators and teachers in restructuring their schools to promote early literacy:

- Develop content standards that identify what students should know and be able to do, from prereading to reading fluency.
- Set performance standards in reading that transcend individual classrooms.
- Assess how well students are learning the essential skills needed for fluent reading.
- Record informal observations of student reading, writing, and social behavior.
- Use a structured reading program to address a beginning reader's need to develop the skills of automatic word recognition in the context of reading texts and supplementary reading materials.
- Establish peer tutoring programs to intensify reading instruction for low-performing students.
- Create a schoolwide ethos—that everyone reads at grade level by third grade.
- Fund library and media centers to equip them with a variety of books.
- Ensure that libraries and media staff assist the classroom teacher in reading instruction.
- Support numerous opportunities for community involvement, such as *Listen to Me Read* programs in which adults listen to children read books in and out of the classroom.

Promising Practices in Early Reading Instruction

The application of best practices in teaching literacy can lead to significant improvement in student skills. Information about empirically validated programs can help beginning teachers make informed instructional decisions. Without background in research on reading, new teachers tend to experiment until they "land on" something that seems to work. In terms of early literacy, primary-grade teachers can no longer afford to experiment. The long-

Resources for Early Literacy

TEACHING THE STRUCTURE OF WRITTEN ENGLISH

LANGUAGE!—This program provides a structured, linguistic base for reading (beginning with phonological awareness), writing, spelling, composition, grammar, vocabulary, and usage. Content is individualized for each student (elementary through high school) and is based on each student's mastery of concepts, rather than a predetermined class schedule or curriculum. Author: Jane Fell Greene; Publisher: Sopris West, 1140 Boston Avenue, Longmont, CO 80501.

Patterns for Success in Reading and Spelling—This program emphasizes integrated teaching of decoding and spelling across a continuum for grades K–8. The curriculum is based on word structure including letter-sound correspondences, syllable patterns, morpheme patterns (e.g., compound words, prefixes, roots, and suffixes), and word origin (i.e., Anglo-Saxon, Latin, and Greek). The program can be useful in small group or classroom settings. Author: Marcia Henry; Publisher: Pro-Ed, 8700 Shoal Creek Boulevard, Austin, TX 78757–6897.

Project READ—This program, designed for regular classroom use, was developed in collaboration with an elementary public school. The primary goal is to provide "competence in applying language as a tool for thinking and for communication." Basic curricular components of the program include decoding, vocabulary, comprehension of narrative text, and comprehension of expository text. Robert Calfee, Project Director, School of Education, Stanford University, Stanford, CA 94305–3096.

PROJECT READ—Based on the Orton-Gillingham model of systematic, multisensory instruction, the program was designed for the elementary classroom teacher and may be used effectively in a resource center as well. Extensions of the program, covering decoding, spelling, comprehension, and written expression, can be used for intermediate and secondary students who are weak in these areas. Authors: Mary Lee Enfield and Victoria Green; Publisher: Language Circle, P.O. Box 20631, Bloomington, MN 55420.

ONE-ON-ONE TUTORING PROGRAMS

Davidson Cross-Age Tutoring Program—This program was developed within a specific school and emerged as a new viable model to teach reading. Fifth- and sixth-grade students are trained to provide intensive one-on-one tutoring sessions four times per week for thirty to forty minutes, using Reading Recovery strategies. Lessons are planned to provide structure, intensity, repetition, and success for students. Certificated adults then monitor students while students work with their tutors one-on-one. Ongoing assessment of each tutee is the key to rapid acceleration in literacy skills. The goal of the program is to monitor children as they move through a carefully selected menu of literacy activities and to ensure they are reading at grade level by third grade. See Nowark 1996; Miracle and Cook 1995.

Reading Recovery—Reading Recovery is designed as an early intervention to reduce the instance of reading failure in at-risk students and is based on the theory that one learns to read by reading. Children are seen thirty minutes daily by a teacher who is specially trained to help the child use strategies that good readers and writers use. The strategies include (a) a basic procedure such as word-by-word matching, (b) self-monitoring activities, (c) cross-checking devices, (d) a search for cues, and (e) self-correction. See Clay 1993; Iversen and Tunmer 1993.

Success For All—This program uses prevention and immediate, intensive intervention (one-on-one tutoring) for all at-risk children to ensure their literacy development. The authors consider students' literacy backgrounds and enlist parental support in an attempt to prevent learning problems. If learning problems do occur, the authors advocate using immediate corrective interventions that are intensive and minimally disruptive to students' progress in the general education program. The program goals are direct: every student reading on grade level by third grade and every student participating as quickly as possible in normalized general education settings. See Slavin, Karweit, and Madden 1989; Slavin, Karweit, and Wasik 1992–93; Slavin, Madden, Karweit, Livermon, and Dolan 1990.

---

term effect of primary-grade instruction is evident in the .80 correlation between achievement in third grade and eleventh grade (McGill-Franzan and Allington 1992).

Comprehensive and effective early literacy programs address the following teaching elements: instruction, curriculum, grouping, and assessment. Effective instruction includes direct teaching, active student participation, and structured group activities. Valid curriculum incorporates a sequence from basic phonological awareness to proficiency in reading, writing, and spelling. Purposeful grouping involves the use of individual, small group, and large group instruction. Active assessment is continuous and monitors individual learning needs and growth. The sidebar, "Resources for Early Literacy," identifies programs that incorporate these variables and programs that use tutoring effectively.

Recommendations for Teacher and Administrator Preparation and Professional Development

By advocating for early literacy programs and making early literacy a priority in teacher and administrator training programs, we can make dropout prevention an issue for preschool, kindergarten, and first- and second-grade teachers. We know that when a child has difficulty in literacy skills by the time he or she enters fourth grade, special education or some other remedial program looms on the horizon. And sadly, when the child enters remedial education, participation in the mainstream becomes problematic. Once the child feels less competent in reading (the most prized basic skill in schools), a spiral of failure begins.

School failure can be averted for many students by providing improved reading instruction and remedial services. To achieve these improvements, teachers and administrators need to be aware of the long-term impact of reading failure, the cumulative effect of years of school failure, and the interventions that lead to school success.

Professional preparation standards and training content need to include specific attention to knowledge and skills in teaching literacy and dropout prevention (see figure 1).

Implications for the Future

Courses at the university level should incorporate the recommendations from the California Department of Education found in *Reading Task Force* (1995), *Every Child a Reader* (1995), *An Analysis of Reading Courses and Reading-Related Courses in Elementary Teacher Education Programs* (Commission on Teacher Preparation and Licensing 1996), and *Teaching Reading* (1996). These reports all maintain that effective reading programs should include a strong literature component, an explicit skills component, ongoing diagnosis, and a powerful early intervention program. They also make recommendations that can provide guidance for school districts to implement a more balanced reading program to include skill components (phonics), along with a more holistic approach (whole language). However, unless preservice and staff development standards make teacher preparation and educational leadership programs accountable for training in early literacy and dropout prevention, these recommendations may have little impact.

The statistics are clear. Poor reading is involved in many social ills—delinquency, low paying jobs, adult crime, and dropping out of school. Teacher training and educational leadership programs that create coursework aimed at decreasing dropout rates can begin to stem the rising tide of special education referrals and the continuing dropout problem. In this way, dropout reduction becomes the explicit responsibility of professional preparation programs and local educational agencies. This comprehensive approach can improve the holding power of our schools and the success of our students.

REFERENCES

Adams, M. J. 1990. *Beginning to read: Thinking and learning about print.* Cambridge, Mass.: MIT Press.

Bryk, A. S., and Y. M. Thum. 1989. The effects of high school organization on dropping out: An exploratory investigation. *American Educational Research Journal* 26 (3): 353–83.

Burstein, N. D., B. Cabello, and J. Hamann. 1993. Teacher preparation for culturally diverse urban students: Infusing competencies across the curriculum. *Teacher Education and Special Education* 16 (1): 1–13.

California Reading Task Force 1995. *Every child a reader.* Sacramento, Calif.: California Department of Education. Bureau of Publications.

California State Board of Education. 1996. *Teaching reading: A balanced, comprehensive approach to teaching reading in prekindergarten through grade three.* Sacramento, Calif.: California Department of Education, Bureau of Publications.

California State Department of Education 1991. *Federal data report for the 1990–91*, OMB Form No. 1820–0523. Sacramento, Calif.: California State Department of Education.

Clay, M. M. 1987. Learning to be learning disabled. *New England Journal of Educational Studies* 22 (2): 155–71.

———. 1993. *Reading recovery: A guidebook for teachers in training.* Auckland, New Zealand: Reed Publishing.

Commission on Teacher Preparation and Licensing. 1996. *An analysis of reading courses and reading-related courses in elementary teacher education programs.* Sacramento, Calif.: Department of Education, Bureau of Publications.

DeStefano, L., and T. R. Wermuth. 1992. IDEA (P.L. 101–476): Defining a second generation of transition services. *Transition from school to adult life: Models, linkages, and policy*, edited by F. R. Ruschl, L. DeStefano, J. Chadsey-Ruscho, L. A. Phelps, and E. Szymanski, 537–49. Sycamore, Ill.: Sycamore.

Feldman, K. 1995. *Building the inclusive classroom: Instructional strategies and curriculum modifications for academically diverse learners.* Medina, Wash.: Institute for Educational Development.

Fine, M. 1986. Why urban adolescents drop into and out of public high school. *Teachers College Record* 87 (3): 391–409.

Graham, S., and L. A. Johnson. 1989. Teaching reading to learning disabled students: A review of research-supported procedures. *Focus on Exceptional Children* 21 (6): 1–12.

Iversen J. A., and W. E. Tunmer. 1993. Phonological processing skills and the reading recovery program. *Journal of Educational Psychology* 85 (1): 112–26.

Kaplan J., and E. Luck. 1977. The dropout phenomenon as a social problem. *Education Forum* 42:41–56.

Kelly, F. J., D. J. Veldman, and C. McGuire. 1964. Multiple discriminant prediction of delinquency and school dropouts. *Educational and Psychological Measurement* 24: 535–44.

Levin, D. 1996. Reflecting on the report of the California Reading Task Force: Every child a reader—a good first step. *The California Reader* 29 (2).

Lichtenstein, S. 1988. *Dropouts: Perspectives on special education.* Concord, N.H.: Task Force for the Improvement of Secondary Special Education.

Lloyd, D. N. 1978. Prediction of school failure from third-grade data. *Educational and Psychological Measurements* 38:1193–1200.

Madden, N. A., R. E. Slavin, N. L. Karweit, L. J. Dolan, and B. A. Wasik. 1993. Success for all: Longitudinal effects of restructuring program for inner-city elementary schools. *American Educational Research Journal* 30 (1): 123–48.

Mahood, W. 1990. Born losers; School dropouts and pushouts. *National Association of Secondary School Principles Bulletin* 65: 45–57.

McGill-Franzan, A., and R. Allington. 1992. The grid lock of low achievement: Perspectives on policy and practice. *Remedial and Special Education* 12: 20–30.

Meyen, E. L., G. A. Vergason, and R. J. Whelan. 1993. *Educating students with mild disabilities.* Denver: Love Publishing.

Miracle, S., and J. Cook. 1995. *Davidson School Cross-Age Tutoring Program.* Vallejo, Calif.: Davidson Elementary School.

Nowark, L. 1996. A study of a cross-age tutoring program which intervenes early to ensure literacy and to reduce referrals to special education. Master's project. San Jose, Calif.: San Jose State University, Division of Special Education and Rehabilitative Services.

Pikulski, J. 1994. Preventing reading failure: A review of 5 effective programs. *The Reading Teacher* 48 (1): 30–37.

Slavin, R. E., N. L. Karweit, and N. A. Madden. 1989. *Effective programs for students at risk.* Boston: Allyn and Bacon.

Slavin, R. E., N. L. Karweit, and B. A. Wasik. 1992–93. Preventing early school failure: What works? *Educational Leadership* (Dec.–Jan.): 10–18.

Slavin, R. E., N. A. Madden, B. Dolan, B. A. Wasik, S. M. Ross, and L. J. Smith. 1994. "Whenever and wherever we choose." The replication of "Success for all." *Phi Delta Kappan* (April): 639–47.

Slavin, R. E., N. A. Madden, N. L. Karweit, B. J. Livermon, and L. L. Dolan. 1990. Success for all: First year outcomes of a comprehensive plan for reforming urban education. *Educational Leadership* 27 (2): 255–78.

Smith, D. D., and R. Luckasson. 1992. *Introduction to special education.* Boston: Allyn and Bacon.

Stevens, R. J., N. A. Madden, R. E. Slavin, and A. M. Farnish. 1987. Cooperative integrated reading and composition: Two field experiments. *Reading Research Quarterly* 22:433–54.

U.S. Department of Education. 1990. *To assure the free appropriate public education of all handicapped children.* Twelfth annual report to Congress on the implementation of the Education of the Handicapped Act, Table 3.7, p. 100, Washington, D.C.: Government Printing Office.

Unit 4

Unit Selections

13. **Distinguishing Language Differences from Language Disorders in Linguistically and Culturally Diverse Students,** Celeste Roseberry-McKibbin
14. **Language Interaction Techniques for Stimulating the Development of At Risk Children in Infant and Preschool Day Care,** William Fowler
15. **Family and Cultural Alert! Considerations in Assistive Technology Assessment,** Jack J. Hourcade, Howard P. Parette Jr., and Mary Blake Huer

Key Points to Consider

❖ How can a culturally sensitive educator decide if language used by a child is dialectally different speech or a language-speech disorder?

❖ What kinds of verbal interactions are most helpful to young children who are learning a language?

❖ Are assistive devices always desirable prescriptions for students with speech and language impairments?

 **Links** www.dushkin.com/online/

18. **Speech and Language Impairment**
    http://www.socialnet.lu/handitel/wwwlinks/dumb.html
19. **YaacK**
    http://www.mrtc.org/~duffy/yaack/toc.html

These sites are annotated on pages 4 and 5.

Speech and Language Impairments

The terms communication, language, and speech are not synonymous. Communication refers to an exchange of information between sender and receiver. It may be through language. However, the exchange may be a movement, a nonlanguage vocal noise, or a symbolized marking in a nonlanguage medium (for example, art, scent, sculpture). Both human and nonhuman species can communicate without language. Language refers to the use of voice sounds (or writing that represents these voice sounds) in combinations and patterns that follow rules that are accepted by the users of the language. Speech refers simply to the vocal utterances of language. The three terms are subsumed in descending order. Communication includes language and speech. Language includes speech. The opposite is not accurate. Communication disorders, as they affect children with disabilities, are usually separated into the subcategories of speech and language impairments.

Speech, the vocal utterance of language, is considered disordered in three underlying ways: voice, articulation, and fluency. Voice involves coordinated effects by the lungs, larynx, vocal cords, and nasal passages to produce recognizable sounds. Voice can be considered disordered if it is incorrectly phonated through the lungs, larynx, and vocal cords (breathy, strained, husky, hoarse) or if it is incorrectly resonated through the nose (hyper-nasality, hypo-nasality). Articulation involves the use of the tongue, lips, teeth, and mouth to produce recognizable sounds. Articulation can be considered disordered if sounds are added, omitted, substituted, or distorted. Fluency involves appropriate pauses and hesitations to keep speech sounds recognizable. Fluency can be considered disordered if sounds are very rapid with extra sounds (cluttered) or if sounds are blocked and/or repeated, especially at the beginning of words (stuttered). Language problems refer to the use of voice sounds in combinations and patterns that fail to follow the arbitrary rules for that language or to a delay in the use of voice sounds relative to normal development in other areas (physical, cognitive, social). Language delays can also be diagnosed in conjunction with other developmental delays (health, sensory, motor, mental, personal, social).

Disordered language is usually more difficult to remedy than delayed language. Disordered language may be due to a receptive problem (difficulty understanding voice sounds), an expressive problem (difficulty producing the voice sounds that follow the arbitrary rules for that language), or both. Language disorders include aphasia (no language) and dysphasia (difficulty producing language). Many language disorders are the result of a difficulty in understanding the syntactical rules and structural principles of the language (form), or are the result of a difficulty in perceiving the semantic meanings of the words of the language (content). Many language disorders are also due to a difficulty in using the language pragmatically, in a practical context (function).

All children with language and/or speech disorders are entitled to assessment as early in life as the problem is realized, and to remediation under the auspices of the Individuals with Disabilities Education Act (IDEA) and its amendments. In addition, they are entitled to a free and appropriate education in the least restrictive environment possible and to transitional help into the world of work, if needed, after their education is completed.

Most speech and language impairments occur in younger children (preschool and primary school) and have been remediated by high school. An exception to this is speech problems that persist due to physical impairments such as damage or dysfunction of lungs, larynx, vocal cords, nasal passages, tongue, lips, or teeth. Another exception is language problems that persist due to concurrent disabilities such as deafness, autism, compromised mentation, traumatic brain injuries, and/or some emotional and behavioral disorders.

The prevalence rates of speech and language disorders are higher than the rates for any other condition of disability in primary school. However, the exact extent of the problem has been questioned because assessment of communication takes a variety of forms. Shy children may be diagnosed with delayed language. Bilingual or multilingual children are often mislabeled as having a language disorder when they simply have different language because they come from linguistically and culturally diverse backgrounds. Many bilingual children do not need the special services provided by speech-language clinicians but do benefit from instruction in English as a second language, bilingual education, or sheltered English.

Speech-language clinicians usually provide special services to children with speech and language impairments in pull-out sessions in resource rooms. Computer technology is also frequently used to assist these children in both their regular education classes and in pull-out therapy sessions.

The first article has been included in this edition of *Annual Editions: Educating Exceptional Children* to stimulate discussion about the sticky problems associated with assessing and diagnosing language disorders. Language differences are not language disorders. The American Speech-Language-Hearing Association (ASHA) has clearly articulated the view that regional, social, or ethnic variations in symbol systems (dialects) should not be considered disorders of language or speech. While a dialect difference is just a difference, disorders existing within a dialectally different language must not be overlooked. A child may have limited English proficiency, but a delay or disorder in the mother tongue or in learning English must not be ignored. The author discusses the diagnostic pie in a conceptual framework that will help educators determine what is what.

The second article in unit 4 is a research-based treatise on how to prevent language delays in infancy and early childhood, especially in children who, historically, have been at risk for language disorders. William Fowler presents data from a series of research projects. He articulates the principles of language development as they are currently known. Fowler also presents several methods that he and his colleagues have devised to increase language stimulation in infant day care and preschool settings. These specific methods and techniques are illustrated with representative case studies to show how successfully they have been used.

The third article included in this unit addresses the question of if and when to provide assistive devices to improve speech and language. The mere fact that the technology exists to improve a speech or language impairment does not make it the most desirable prescription. Decisions about the use of technology must involve families and be sensitive to their routines and needs. Decisions must also be culturally sensitive and be appropriate to each unique student's skill levels.

Distinguishing Language Differences from Language Disorders in Linguistically and Culturally Diverse Students

Celeste Roseberry-McKibbin

Celeste Roseberry-McKibbin is an associate professor in the Department of Communicative Sciences and Disorders, California State University, Fresno.

Introduction

Many educators today view bilingualism as a great linguistic and social advantage (Cummins, 1994; Wong Fillmore, 1993). However, sometimes educators are confronted with linguistically and culturally diverse (LCD) students who appear to be struggling in school. When this happens, one of the first questions usually asked is: "Does this LCD student have a language difference or a language disorder?" In other words, can the problems be traced to cultural differences and/or the student's lack of facility with English, or is there an underlying disability that requires special education intervention? The question of distinguishing a language difference from a language disorder is a very challenging one. (The terms "language disorder" and "language-learning disability" are used interchangeably in this article.)

The "diagnostic pie" is a simple conceptual framework that can help educators begin to distinguish language differences from language disorders. The diagnostic pie paradigm assumes that LCD students speak their primary language and are in the process of learning English as a second language. Bloom and Lahey's (1978) definition of language is central here:

> Language is a system of symbols used to represent concepts that are formed through exposure and experience.

There are practical ramifications of this definition. I am assuming that exposure and

13. Distinguishing Language Differences

experience refer to exposure to good language models, to a variety of "mainstream" experiences (that are consistent with schools' expectations), to literacy, and to environmental and linguistic stimulation. For example, when students come to kindergarten, some educators assume that the children have looked at books; that they have been read to; that they know how to listen in groups; that they have used scissors, crayons, and pencils before. The educators may further assume that children have been taken to stores, zoos, libraries, and other places in the community; that the children have had literacy experiences which prepare them to learn the alphabet, print their names, etc.

Some LCD students come from backgrounds where they have had all these experiences. Some LCD students, especially older ones, may even have a broader experience base than many monolingual English-speaking students who are born and raised in the United States. These LCD students may be bilingual or even trilingual, have traveled in different countries, and be bicultural. These students have a great deal to offer to mainstream American students. Mainstream American students can be enriched and learn many things from these sophisticated LCD students.

Other LCD students come from non-literate backgrounds. They and their families may be non-literate for one or more reasons. Perhaps family members have not had educational opportunities; these opportunities are extremely limited in some countries, especially if the family is of refugee status. Others come from backgrounds where the language is oral only and has not been put in written form. Van Deusen-Scholl (1992) gives the example of a number of Morrocan children in the Netherlands who come from isolated rural areas where no formal education is available; they struggle in the Netherlands' school system. Some of these children speak Berber languages which do not have a tradition of print literacy. Other linguistic groups, such as some Native Americans and speakers of Haitian Creole, have predominantly oral traditions and no written language.

Some educators do not stop to ask themselves whether or not students have had some or any of the usual mainstream experiences that are inherently assumed, like exposure to literacy. And this is often where deficits in students are created: when students' exposure and experiences are different than those expected in the mainstream school environment, then educators may assume that there are deficits inherent in the students themselves.

A centrally important idea in this article is that before educators even begin to ask whether or not a student manifests a language disorder, they must stop and remind themselves of what language really is: a system of symbols that represents concepts formed through **exposure** and **experience**. If a student's background experiences and exposure to life situations and linguistic models are different than those expected by schools, then it follows that their language will represent *their unique backgrounds,* which are not necessarily consistent with those expected by the school.

This difference in students' backgrounds and schools' expectations can lead to misdiagnosis of students and consequent inappropriate placement into special education. Many experts point out that historically in United States schools, disproportionate numbers of LCD children have been placed into special education unnecessarily (Ruiz & Figueroa, 1993). The "diagnostic pie" (see page 89) can help educators begin to conceptualize students' backgrounds and current status, and see that there are various alternatives to special education.

Diagnostic Pie Quadrant 1

Students who fall into this quadrant of the pie are those LCD students who have normal underlying ability to learn language. They come from backgrounds that may be rich in stimulation and general experiences, but the backgrounds have not been consistent with expectations in mainstream United States schools. Some older immigrant students are good examples of this: they had schooling in their country of origin, and generally have a good enough conceptual foundation to succeed academically. If these students are dominant in their primary language and thus are having some difficulty in all-English classrooms, their needs can usually be served best through placement into good bilingual classrooms where both English and the primary language can be developed. If bilingual education is not available, then these students can benefit from Sheltered English or, barring this, English as a second language teaching. Again, if these students are given time, attention, and help, they will generally succeed in school.

Diagnostic Pie Quadrant 2

These students have normal underlying ability to learn language. However, they

---

Student Behaviors to Observe when Distinguishing a Language Difference from a Language Disorder

Teachers can tell when an LCD student might need special education services for a language-learning disability when some of the following behaviors are manifested in comparison to similar peers:

1. Nonverbal aspects of language are culturally inappropriate.
2. Student does not express basic needs adequately.
3. Student rarely initiates verbal interaction with peers.
4. When peers initiate interaction, student responds sporadically/inappropriately.
5. Student replaces speech with gestures, communicates nonverbally when talking would be appropriate and expected.
6. Peers give indications that they have difficulty understanding the student.
7. Student often gives inappropriate responses.
8. Student has difficulty conveying thoughts in an organized, sequential manner that is understandable to listeners.
9. Student shows poor topic maintenance ('skips around').
10. Student has word-finding difficulties that go beyond normal second language acquisition patterns.
11. Student fails to provide significant information to the listener, leaving the listener confused.
12. Student has difficulty with conversational turn-taking skills (may be too passive, or may interrupt inappropriately).
13. Student perseverates (remains too long) on a topic even after the topic has changed.
14. Student fails to ask and answer questions appropriately.
15. Student needs to hear things repeated, even when they are stated simply and comprehensibly.
16. Student often echoes what she or he hears.

If an LCD student manifests a number of the above behaviors, even in comparison to similar peers, then there is a good chance that the student has an underlying language-learning disability and will need a referral to special education.

come from backgrounds where they may have experienced some limitations or differences in environmental stimulation and linguistic exposure. These students may come from backgrounds where society has placed them and their families at profound economic disadvantage. I have worked with many children like this: they have good ability to learn, but life circumstances have curtailed their opportunities to learn and be exposed to various experiences before they come to school. These students often perform poorly on standardized tests, many of which are based on mainstream, White middle-class expectations. If these students have not been exposed to certain experiences and thus developed the conceptual background assumed by these tests, they will often appear "language disordered" simply because the tests do not adequately tap into their unique and indi- vidual backgrounds.

Several years ago, I had the experience of taking the WAIS (Wechsler Adult Intelligence Scale) and being penalized for lack of knowledge of items on the "General Knowledge" subtest. Because I grew up in the Philippines (ages 6–17 years), I had not had the exposure to facts that the WAIS assumed everyone had—and my overall IQ score was lowered because of it! Although I was taking the WAIS mostly out of personal interest, I was poignantly reminded of how often our standardized tests penalize LCD students for not having life experiences consistent with test writers' expectations.

Students in Quadrant 2 will usually show good gains in school if they can receive adequate quantities of input, exposure, and stimulation that may have been unavailable in their homes. These students will benefit from good bilingual education, ESL, and/or Sheltered English programs that enhance both the primary language and English. These students often also need extra stimulation which can be provided through tutoring and participation in school enrichment programs. Unfortunately, these students often are placed into special education programs. Special education is usually unnecessary for students whose underlying language-learning ability is intact. If extra programs outside of special education are provided and the student can attend school consistently enough to benefit from them, usually good academic gains can be made without special education assistance.

Diagnostic Pie Quadrant 3

Quadrant 3 students come from backgrounds where they have had adequate exposure and language stimulation. Their life experiences are often consistent with those assumed by mainstream schools. Often, their parents have given them as much help as possible in the home, and the students still do not succeed in school. Many of them have a history of academic failure. Often, school personnel have given these students opportunities such as extra tutoring and participation in school programs designed to foster academic growth. Despite these measures, however, the students still do not learn and make adequate academic gains. These students have underlying language-learning disabilities that prevent them from learning and using any language adequately despite backgrounds that have attempted to provide environmental and linguistic stimulation.

These students need to be placed into special education so that their unique disabilities can be appropriately addressed. No matter how hard schools and parents try to use traditional methods to assist these students, the students will still struggle because they have underlying language-learning disabilities. As one speech-language pathologist puts it, "These students have a glitch in the computer." Students with these needs will benefit from (ideally) bilingual special education where the primary language is used. Because this ideal option is often not available, these students may be served by special education in English with as much primary language support as possible. Students with disabilities still benefit greatly from being taught concepts initially in their primary language.

Diagnostic Pie Quadrant 4

Students in Quadrant 4 come from backgrounds where there are differences and/or limitations of environmental experience and exposure. These students are very similar to those described in Quadrant 2, except that the students in Quadrant 4 also have underlying language-learning disabilities. These students are very difficult to assess because educators can never be sure whether the students' low test scores are due to background/environment, an underlying disability, or both.

Most educators wrestle with the issue of whether to place these students into Quadrant 2 or Quadrant 4. On the one hand, educators do not want to place into special education a Quadrant 2 student who would be adequately served through additional school enrichment programs such as ESL. On the other hand, educators do not want to deprive Quadrant 4 students of the opportunity to receive special education help because that is what they need. According to Ortiz (1994), we are so afraid of mislabeling LCD students unnecessarily that the pendulum has swung in the other direction: some LCD students who genuinely need special education assistance are not receiving it, and are failing in school year after year.

Quadrant 4 students ideally need bilingual special education with additional enrichment experiences to compensate for limitations/differences of linguistic and environmental experience and stimulation. Barring the provision of these ideal services, Quadrant 4 students may be served by English special education with as much primary language support as possible. They can also benefit from participating in whatever additional enrichment experiences are available.

What to Look For

Comparing LCD students to monolingual English-speaking peers is very biased and provides a poor point of reference from which to make decisions. It is critical to analyze student behaviors in interactions in natural settings **with peers from similar cultural and linguistic backgrounds.** For example, I recently evaluated a 15-year old Russian immigrant ("Viktor") who was having learning difficulties. A major question I asked was: "How does Viktor perform/interact in comparison to other newcomer Russian students who have been in the United States the same length of time that he has?" When we compare students to their linguistic and cultural peers, our decisions will be much more fair and accurate.

I have found that interpreters who work regularly with LCD students are wonderful sources of information in this regard, because they have a great deal of experience with certain populations and thus can validly (albeit subjectively) compare the student in question with other students from the same cultural and linguistic background. I have also found that educators—especially general education classroom teachers—can serve as excellent resources for referral of LCD students who need special services.

Some teachers are fluent in the student's primary language, and can thus make judgments about delays or deviancies in the student's primary language assessment and comprehension. Other teachers, while not speaking a particular student's primary language, have many years of experience working with ESL students. These teachers may have worked, for example, with many Filipino students in the past and may have a number of Filipino students in their current classes. The teachers frequently have a frame of reference for what is "normal" behavior for Filipino learners of English as a second language, and can tell when a particular student is not performing as his/her peers are. While the teachers cannot make the judgment as to whether there is an actual language-learning disability, they can

The Diagnostic Pie

1. Normal Language Learning Ability

Adequate Background

May need one or more of the following:
1. Bilingual education
2. Sheltered English
3. English as a second language instruction

2. Normal Language Learning Ability

Differences and/or limitations of linguistic exposure & environmental experience

May need:
1. Bilingual education Sheltered English, English as a second language
2. Aditional enrichment experiences (e.g. tutoring, etc.)

3. Language-Learning Disability

Adequate Background

May need:
1. Bilingual special education
2. English special education with as much primary language input and teaching as possible

4. Language-Learning Disability

Differences and/or limitations of linguistic exposure & environmental experience

May need:
1. Bilingual special education, English special education with primary language support
2. Additional enrichment experiences

---

refer the student to personnel who have access to Filipino interpreters and who have the resources and background to make this type of diagnosis.

The classroom teacher, then, frequently serves as the "first layer" of the referral process. For example, an African American monolingual English-speaking teacher referred a Filipino kindergartener to me for language testing. In her opinion, his classroom performance was less than optimal and she was concerned that he might have a language-learning disability. This teacher had 15 years of teaching experience. When I asked her how the child compared to other ESL students in her experience, especially Filipino students, she replied "I have never seen a child like this one." She went on to describe some of the student's deviant academic and linguistic behaviors. When I and a Filipino interpreter (who also knew the family) tested the student, it turned out that he had a learning disability that was manifested even in his Filipino languages of Tagalog and Ilocano. In this case, the experienced teacher's insight turned out to be accurate.

Summary

Educators can provide appropriate services to LCD students who may show difficulties in the classroom. Using the "diagnostic pie" as a starting point can help educators to classify students appropriately and thus provide services commensurate with students' background and abilities. When educators suspect that a student may have an underlying language-learning disability that requires special education assistance, they can use the above list as a guideline to assist in differential diagnosis. It is imperative not only to avoid "false positives" in identifying LCD students with special needs, but to avoid "false negatives" that deprive these students of assistance which they need and deserve.

References

Bloom, L., & Lahey, M. (1978). *Language development and language disorders.* New York: John Wiley & Sons, Inc.

Cummins, J. (1994, March). Accelerating second language and literacy development. Paper presented at the California Elementary Education Association, Sacramento, CA.

Ortiz, A. (1994, June). Keynote address. Symposium on Second Language Learners in Regular and Special Education, Sacramento, CA.

Ruiz, N., & Figueroa, R. (1993). Why special education does not work for minority children. Paper presented at National Association for Multicultural Education, Los Angeles, CA.

Wong Fillmore, L. (1993). Educating citizens for a multicultural 21st century. *Multicultural Education Magazine, 1*(1), 10–37.

Language interaction techniques for stimulating the development of at risk children in infant and preschool day care

WILLIAM FOWLER

Center for Early Learning and Child Care, Inc., 29 Buckingham St., Cambridge, MA 02138, USA

It is often assumed that children's language will develop normally in the average, "good" day care and home environments. In fact teachers and parents from all social backgrounds vary widely in the quality of language interaction they furnish to children in the early years. These variations, moreover, are highly correlated with how well children develop language and other skills. Over a series of research projects in both day care and the home, principles and methods have been devised that have been shown to enable both normal and at risk young children to develop high and long-lasting competencies in language and other cognitive and social skills. The approach centers on engaging the whole child to interact with language informally in play and the ordinary routines of child care, both individually and in small groups, and emphasizing both the social, communicative and cognitive functions of language. A variety of specific techniques for use in day care are described and illustrated with several successful cases with at risk children.

Key words: Language, delay, enrichment

When a child of two or three comes into day care saying nothing at all or at best only a few words we say her language is delayed. We are then likely to ask why and begin to think about what to do to help her learn to talk. Yet in a "normal" day care program we almost expect children will learn to talk as a matter of course. Many people assume that a good, average environment furnishes all the language experiences young children need to foster speech development.

Actually, it turns out that both teachers in day care and parents in the home vary enormously in the quality of language they provide for young children. And these large differences have important effects on how children develop, not only in their verbal skills, but also in their overall cognitive development. McCartney (1984), for example, found that the varying quality of language day care teachers used in different day care centers in Bermuda in infants from 19 months on made highly significant differences in the children's language and intellectual development between 3 and 5½ years. Carew (1980) reported that the cognitive experiences guided by language interaction with adults, in both day care and the home, in children between 18 and 34 months, were the chief factors relating to language and cognitive development at age 3. Of special interest is the fact that the children's own experimentation in play activities during infancy showed no effect on later development.

It is important to note that in these and other studies, these differences were true in families and day care centers of all social backgrounds, from the lowest to the highest socioeconomic and educational levels. Huttenlocher and her associates (1991) in a longitudinal study measured the actual range of difference in the amount of parent verbalization and vocabulary development in children in two-parent, well-educated families. The most talkative mothers used vocabularies of 33 more words than the least talkative, which resulted in vocabulary differences between the extremes of 131 words at 20 months and 295 words at 24 months.

It seems clear that the traditional view that what are often considered "good" homes and "good" day care centers typically produce well skilled, verbal children is far from universally true, as these and other studies show (see Fowler, *et al.*, 1992). Given the variation, many programs must be falling short in the quality of attention to language needed to ensure children develop their full potential. Our concerns here are with day care, of course, though effective teachers are likely to express concerns to parents when they feel the child may not be getting enough attention at home.

The Dilemma

But if many ordinary children are not experiencing the kind of interactions they need to foster good verbal skills, how can busy teachers also manage to tend to the special needs of the delayed or at risk child? Is there a way out of this dilemma? If we are going to have millions of the nation's children enrolled in group care from an early age, and to mainstream delayed children as well, can teachers be expected to pay more attention to the language needs of the average child and still take care of the child with special needs? It is one thing to ask parents and child care providers in the home to devote more attention to talking activities with one or two children. It is quite another for teachers in day care to furnish the same high quality to groups of infants, toddlers and preschoolers who often vary widely in skills they bring to group care.

SOME ANSWERS FROM RESEARCH

Some years ago I undertook a series of research projects with infants and preschoolers in group day care and in homes with parents. While two major longitudinal projects in day care (Fowler, 1972; Fowler, 1978) embraced a broad curriculum designed to foster high quality language, cognitive and social development, curriculum goals in the home centered for the most part on guiding parents to enrich the child's language experiences. In all studies, however, the quality of language was a major focus in all daily activities. The day care children came from a wide spectrum of social, ethnic and educational backgrounds, many of them single parent families and all with working mothers, compared to home-reared control families of two parents with non-working mothers. One day care center included a group of high risk infants from largely single-parent families on welfare with less than a high school education. Another included a large number of children from immigrant families with less than a complete high school education. Children entered with widely different levels of developmental competence, including children with various forms of risk and delay and some with bilingual/non-English-speaking backgrounds. It proved possible, nevertheless, to resolve the apparent dilemma of tending to the needs of both the "average" and the "special" child.

Out of that original research has come an approach (since applied in all later projects) to infant and child care of enriching language through play and the informal routines of basic care. The approach is really a whole child, developmental strategy in which language communication is embedded in the activities of daily care. These methods have recently been discussed at length in a recent book and illustrated in a companion videotape, both entitled, *Talking from Infancy: How to Nurture and Cultivate Early Language Development,* (Fowler, 1990a and 1990b). The book includes a chapter on working with language-delayed children.

In these and successive projects children have typically progressed in speech development easily months ahead of norms and no child has failed to develop well in social and general cognitive skills. Both in the projects with infants reared at home (Fowler, 1983; Fowler and Swenson, 1979; Ogston, 1983; Roberts, 1983; Swenson, 1983) and in the day care studies (Fowler, 1972, 1978), children have developed as well and sometimes better than randomized controls (home studies) or comparison groups (day care studies).

In follow-up studies of day care children at ages 4 and 5 (Fowler and Khan, 1974), and as late as age 9 in a study in progress, the day care children scored above average or higher in IQ, language and social skills, as high or higher than children in the home reared comparison group, despite the higher proportion of single parents and the working-mother status of the day care families.

In follow-up studies through high school of infants enriched through guiding parents in the home, most children have developed high competence in multiple skills, including verbal, math and science, are well balanced socially, active in sports and independently motivated intellectually (Fowler, Ogston, Roberts-Fiati and Swenson, 1992, 1993a, b, and c). Over half are creative writers. Throughout our collected studies, ensuring mastery of verbal skills in the early years appears to be central to promoting children's development in cognitive and social skills and later school learning. Further follow-up studies are now in process on the long-term development of these subjects, now approaching early adulthood.

METHODS OF LANGUAGE AND CARE ENRICHMENT

Principles for Stimulating Language Learning

The methods themselves embraced certain core principles and a variety of supporting ones that can easily be applied in virtually any kind of language activity with children. Language is in fact such a convenient educational tool that it requires only the human voice to implement. No external aids are needed, leaving the hands and eyes free to conduct other tasks freely, including the care of the child. Among the most important principles are to:

1. Interact with the child, taking turns in any activity: respond to the child as much as taking initiative.
2. Use language as a tool of social communication, engaging the child in the give and take about personal wants, feelings and interests.
3. Use language to guide the child in understanding how words represent meanings—the world and our ideas about it.
4. Engage the child in a warm and friendly manner, encouraging and personalizing according to the child's style.

Of all these principles, interacting with the child in a balanced way, seems to have an especially critical role. Yet it is apparently the one easiest to overlook. Thus, in the follow-up studies of our original early home intervention studies, turn-taking in language play during infancy proved to be the most powerful predictor of the later language competencies during both early and later development (Fowler, Ogston, Roberts-Fiati, and Swenson, 1993b). How well parents took turns in the language play with their infants turned out to correlate with the children's later SAT scores in high school, significantly with TSWE (Test of Standard Written English) and Reading Comprehension scores.

No doubt many teachers (and parents) use language games with young children to some degree in this way without thinking about it. But in fact adults vary widely in how well they apply them, as the research cited above on teacher differences and how children develop shows. Moreover, the fact that parents furnished with special guidance in our early language intervention research could still vary significantly in the quality of their interacting, underscores the need for special focus on this principle.

Care and consistency in using them becomes of special importance, of course, in the case of children who already have or are moving out of infancy with fewer communication or other cognitive skills than the average child. The complete set of principles is outlined in my book, *Talking from Infancy*.

Applying the Principles in Practice

Principles may sound impressive, and may have worked with parents in the home and with specially structured research programs in day care, but how will they work in the practice of the ordinary day care center? Actually, the research in both the day care and home settings included a substantial number of at risk children, and in any case, these principles have been applied successfully in other group programs and home settings.

Let us consider a variety of situations, drawing on experience in various projects and paying special attention to situations involving a language delayed child in some way. Keep in mind that the focus is on infants at risk or preschoolers with mild to moderate problems of delay or difficulties in verbal communication. Children with severe communication disorders or delays will usually require referral to specialized therapy of some kind. (See especially, Harris, 1990.) Marked hearing loss, organic involvement or severe emotional difficulties are often implicated in such cases.

The delayed or slow-learning child alone

Let us suppose a teacher has some free time to work with a delayed child for a few minutes in some secluded corner of the play room, while the rest of a group of two-year-olds are otherwise engaged. What to do?

The first thing to keep in mind is to identify the stage of language development, in very general terms, the child has attained....

To a large extent, use language according to how well the child can talk, regardless of the child's age. With many delayed children, a few words and perhaps a phrase or two that functions as a hold phrase (a phrase serving as a unit, such as "go bye-bye", in which the individual component words have no separate meaning for the child), is all that some delayed children use. This means that, whereas the average child is well on the way to building a good vocabulary by 20 months and the enriched child as early as about 10 months, the slow child may hardly have gotten any start with words at all by age two.... In any case, even if the child is as old as three or more, the focus in language play needs to be on using single words.

Here are some things to do:

1. *Prepare a set of toys in advance,* choosing items likely to appeal to the child's interests and small objects with frequently used common names (e.g., block, doll, car, truck, ball, clock, spoon). Keep objects in a box or other container, ready to bring them out from time to time to involve the child in repeated sessions. Substitute new toys when the child tires of the toys or new items are needed to expand the child's vocabulary.
2. Engage the child in *play with the toys,* introducing one or two at time and letting the child explore and use them in play spontaneously.
3. *Label each toy as the child handles it.* Be sure to time your naming of the item to the child's attention to the object.

4. *Keep the language simple:* start with the names of small, interesting toys and common objects—nouns, and concrete actions like run, walk, jump, kiss, hug—verbs. Prepositions (up, down, in and out) also function as action terms in the early stages.

5. Keep the play interesting by *introducing variations* of an activity. Engage the child in *sociodramatic play* by pretending that any of the objects are "live" and have them do different social activities (e.g., walk, run, jump, eat, drink, etc.). Social play can often be combined with construction activities with blocks and other building toys.

6. Try to fit in *a series of mini sessions* of 2 or 3 minutes or so several times a day or even only once or twice a day. Such a pattern will quickly start to yield real progress in the delayed child's mastery of verbal skills. Brief time slots of this kind have some realistic chance of being fitted into busy teaching schedules. Should schedules occasionally permit, longer spans of as much as 15 minutes are also productive, as long as the child remains interested.

Avoid Withholding and Correcting Errors

Some teachers withhold opportunities for a child to play with some toy, until the child says a word or phrase. Although sometimes recommended by behaviorist philosophies, in our studies we have found that such withholding strategies are likely to arouse a child's resentment and resistance. Although withholding techniques can be effective in the hands of skilled therapists, too often they lead to subtle or not-so-subtle battles of negative social interaction. The delayed child, especially, often has underlying feelings of failure that lead to the passive resistance of not talking, which is only reinforced by adult withholding. *Warmth, support and encouragement of effort are the most important ingredients to foster learning.*

A better strategy is simply to engage children, including the passive resisters, in the play, letting them start to say words and progress at their own speed in their own way. By the same token, avoid correcting errors (saying the wrong word or choosing a "block" when the teacher has asked the child to put a "ball" in a container). It is particularly important to spare children who have already felt a sense of failure in learning to talk, from meeting another failure experience. A better method is for the teacher simply to label the missed object correctly by making another demonstration in a play task, without referring to the child's "error", and the teacher should continue to do so over a series of play sessions, along with labeling various other objects. In this manner even the slow learning children will gradually understand and eventually say more and more words as they develop confidence.

Avoid Correcting Pronunciation and Grammar

There is also little need to stress correct pronunciation, following some model of standard English or even some dialect. Adequate pronunciation and adequate mastery of grammatical forms (e.g., pronouns, plurals, tenses, and sentence structures) will gradually be shaped as teachers demonstrate the correct or useful forms while interacting with the child. The same is true when the child uses the wrong label, mispronounces a word, uses "you" when "I" is meant, or uses present tense when past tense is called for. All these errors will be most easily corrected sooner or later by the children themselves as they come to grasp the relevant concept.

Teachers need only to label objects and actions correctly themselves, to use correct pronominal designations, and to employ tenses properly for the child gradually to understand and correct his or her own errors. Giving multiple, varied and accurate examples in the course of play furnishes all the material a child needs to make cognitive inferences of various rules for correct usage. At the same time, modeling in the course of play keeps the activity lots of fun for the child, without the burden of being labeled "wrong". The advantage of this focused language activity, anchored in manipulating objects directly, over the ordinary adult speech of everyday life, which is too often much of what children have to make inferences from, is that the language is simplified, relevant and more accessible in helping the child make useful inferences.

OTHER DEVICES AND SITUATIONS

Many programs and teaching situations may not allow much room for scheduled play time alone with any child on a regular basis. But even if they do, what about the rest of the day, the 6 to 7 or more hours of the day spent in working with groups of children? Actually, the routines of child care for children under two, and often up to 2½ or more, typically require individualized care for a number of activities, especially changing diapers and beginning toileting routines, dressing and undressing on departure and arrival or even movement to and from the playground in inclement weather, feeding and eating routines, and washing and bathing activities. If nothing else, such activities represent large blocks of otherwise lost learning time and they are in fact ideal settings for engaging the child in language learning. Indeed, some infant-toddler enrichment projects have been based on embedding cognitive and language interactions in just such routines (Lally, Mangione and Honig, 1986).

Basic care routines

Think about the routines of getting dressed or washing hands. Activities repeated several times a day become demanding tasks to be gotten through with each child in turn, hopefully with sensitivity and warmth—but in any case executed with despatch to get on to the main "business" of care, activities of some kind in the play room or on the playground. But what if such routines involved a teaching goal, in which one could see progress in the child's development, almost day to day, from one's efforts?

Language interaction is just such an activity. A few well-timed words said during each routine, repeated every time, will in a matter of days bring about noticeable progress. Use vocabulary of the names of clothes—shirt, sock, diaper, pants, and the concrete actions performed each time—sit, stand, lie, up, down. These terms are used so often that the prespeech infant is soon showing evidence of understanding, then imitating here and there and finally saying them. In the same way, the delayed child will begin to make up for time lost.

The same flexible, informal style, *timing* the saying of each key word to your or the child's action, will engage the child's interest in language, in the same way individual play sessions do. Equally important, the tasks become rewarding to the teacher and the child is also involved in gradually learning about the steps to master her or his own self-care.

Small group activities

But can caregivers use language effectively in the same focused manner with groups of infants and preschoolers? Two-to-five-year-olds in most centers are of course regularly assembled into groups of different sizes around a table for eating or on the floor for singing, story time, and circle activities, or to observe plants, frogs or other phenomena for "science" learning. Much of the time, however, the flow of words may not relate closely to the item talked about. If the pace is not too fast, and some children are not left on the periphery in an oversized group, language and understanding will be far enough along in the average child for them to learn something about the activity. For infants under two, however, and even many two-year-olds, and especially the child with very little language, little understanding may get through—certainly not in understanding words, parts of speech and syntax. Keep in mind that the so-called "average" child is a mathematical myth. In any group of children of the same age, language skills often vary widely. For example, the skills of a group of two-year-olds may range from the child who spouts sentences to the one who only occasionally stumbles through two or three words. What to do?

How about breaking up main groups of 8 two-year-olds or 12 three-year-olds into more manageable groups of 3 and 4 each? But how can this be done when there is only a single teacher for each set of 8 or 12 children? One way to accomplish this is to find a relatively quiet corner to engage 3 or 4 children at a time in a separate language activity for a few minutes while the rest of the children are engaged in free play. If there is no such corner, set up one. Arrange an area with a small table and chairs. Just a throw rug will do sometimes. Give the activity additional focus and shield the group from intrusions from other children by placing two toy shelves to form an angle. Leave only a small entry way, blocked by a small chair that can quickly be removed for teacher exit in an emergency.

Groups of 3 or 4 little ones in a close circle are small enough so that every child can see every block, truck, or nose on a doll, at the exact moment the toy is labeled by the teacher. The teacher can also easily go from child to child, asking each one in turn to "put a block in a box" or "make the doll walk", without a long waiting period in between. Small groups thus combine the advantage of children learning in groups with highly focused individual attention. Extended discussions of engaging small groups of children in interactive play in language and concept learning activities may be found in my text, *Infant and Child Care* (Fowler, 1980).

It is also easy to keep track of each child's individual needs in small circle groups. Tailor your comments and requests according to the child's level. For example, with one child it may be important to stick to the simplest nouns—ball, car and bell. With another, use verbs—roll, walk and jump; and with still another a few more abstract terms like adjectives—round, big and little, can be woven in. When there are wide gaps between levels, then hesitant and slower children sometimes become intimidated and the fast and confident ones become bored. Some of these problems can be handled by involving the fast learners in leadership roles. It is vital to ensure that even the slowest child gets turns in performing tasks. Another alternative is to organize groups on the basis of skill levels instead of age. On this basis a group might consist of 4 children, all of whom are only beginning to say their first few words, yet range in age from 12 to 20 months or even more.

By rotating the small subgroups, every child gets a turn with this relatively individualized form of language play with toys. It is often useful to make up different combinations of children from time to time to vary the kind of stimulation and play interests children provide for one another. But little ones sometimes feel more secure if they can count on a familiar friend in their group.

Parent and other teacher assistants

Teacher assistants can add a great deal to a program, but too often they are not used for much more than setting out and putting away toys and art materials and moving groups of children from activity to activity. When aides are assigned to watch over children in free play, at least for short periods, the teacher can be free to engage a small group in language play, or even occasionally an individual child with special learning needs. Taking time

14. Language Interaction Techniques

to guide an assistant (or parent assistant) in techniques of handling and guiding children multiplies the amount of individual teacher attention for children. Many assistants can readily learn to work effectively in the language interactions activities, certainly individually in toy play and the child care routines, if not so easily in groups.

KEEPING TRACK OF EACH CHILD'S PROGRESS

Perhaps the most pleasant reward for a teacher is observing children's progress in development. Language growth is one of the easiest areas in which to chart a child's progress. Such charting takes more time and the changes are often difficult to perceive in the development of such concepts as number or size. But language development follows a highly visible course from sounds, to words, phrases, sentences, and sequential telling about things in a string of phrases and sentences. It is true that the first understandings of words are some times tricky to verify, and documenting progress in the different parts of speech and forming sentences (syntax) can be more technical. But even here, rather simple day-to-day (or perhaps every other day or so) records will shed light on a child's learning in these areas, at least enough to ascertain that a child is actually progressing. Especially, for the delayed or slow learner, written records will supply information to reassure teachers of progress that casual memory may overlook.

The child's first understanding of words is easily verified by asking a child to give you the [toy] dog or cow, when three or four toys to choose from are placed in front of him or her. In this way, if children can repeatedly pick the right one, you can judge they understand a given word. They show *word recognition*. Varying the setting broadens the child's experience and gives evidence of how generalized the child's understanding is. But don't press the child with repeated requests and usually avoid asking, "What is this?" This task requires the child to *recall* a word, a much more abstract task, which will come spontaneously with practice in play.

Written records or charts need consist only of a single page in a notebook or chart posted on the wall, one page for each child, with two columns, one for the date and a second for the sound, word or phrase a child is heard to use that day. A third column could also describe the circumstances when the child said something, such as "imitating the teacher" or "in response [to] looking at a picture of a duck." This additional information, while furnishing more insights on how the child is learning, may not be necessary except for a child with special difficulties.

Perhaps the *most important value of recording progress in language is to guide teachers on what to do next with a child*, especially with the slower children or those with special difficulties in pronunciation, use of adjectives, or forms of syntax. Checking over a child's record for the past week or two, for example, will reveal not only whether a certain child is learning much slower than others of a similar age, but that this child is learning no verbs, only the simplest nouns, or forms no phrases except occasional rote imitations (e.g., "big truck" or "go out") without ever applying them alone to new situations. A teacher can then zero in on desirable steps—using more examples with simple verbs or applying the same simple phrase to slightly varying situations, such as "more cars," "more blocks," etc.

Because time demands are of the essence of all teaching, jotting down any new term when a teacher has an odd moment free or at the end of the day, will probably serve very well. Don't give up if some term is missed or two or three days go by with no notations. Even spotty records can furnish valuable information on how well a child's language is progressing. This is particularly true in the early stages for infants up to 18 months or age two, and above all for the delayed and slow learning child.

Early records are the easiest to keep, because new sounds for the typical 6 months old, new words for the typical 12 months old and new phrases for the typical 20 months old start out slowly—one or two for the first week or two or even for several weeks. Gradually, the rates for most children accelerate at each stage, however. At some point in each successive stage, children grasp the concept of how to make new sounds, then that words have meaning—that they stand for things, and then that words can be put together (in phrases, later sentences) to describe actions and events of and about things. It is when these shifts occur that children learn new terms more and more rapidly and it becomes both increasingly difficult and relatively unimportant to keep track of the new terms. Just move on to recording progress for the next stage, from the now rapidly expanding vocabulary to the first halting, occasional phrases, or the rapid production of two word phrases to the beginning of constructing 3 or more word sentences.

SOME EXAMPLES

John[1]

John came from a well-off, college-educated family. When he entered our program at one year, it was almost immediately evident to everyone that he had a strange way of relating to people, and that there were none of the usual signs that he responded in any way to what a teacher said. Although lack of words is hardly surprising at one year, lack of any response to the human voice through smiling or gesture is. John usually totally ignored the speaker or looked very blank, and quite often

---
[1]All names of children are pseudonyms to preserve privacy.

looked right past the speaker, though tests given before entering day care had established that he had no hearing loss. In fact, John never made any rapport at all with adults or other children. It was quite evident that communication of any kind, gestural, vocal, or verbal, was out of the question with John. Yet, curiously, when the psychologist (myself) attempted to engage him in play with toys to diagnose his patterns, he did interact in manipulating the toys, though maintaining his usual stance of avoiding vocal communication and all except furtive eye contact. There was a distinct paranoid quality of complete mistrust and emotional blockage of relations with others. Later it was revealed that the mother could not stand infants, John included.

Because the center had a training program for students, we were able to assign an interested student, who soon formed a close attachment to John, as his main caregiver. With staff guidance she engaged John daily in toy play and frequently cared for him in basic routines. Gradually, she added more and more language into her play with him and involved him with the other children and teachers, with whom he was initially quite distant. Over the course of the 18 months he attended the program, John formed a close attachment to this student and gradually expanded relations to other caregivers and the children in play. By the time he was 2½, at graduation, he was speaking well in sentences and he was admitted to another pre-school program, where he adapted well, despite being the youngest child attending by several months. Especially interesting were changes in the mother's perceptions of John as an interesting, verbal little boy she came to accept and love, no longer the dependent infant she initially could not abide.

Terry and Mary

Two infants from a poor, inner city English Canadian single parent family on welfare, Terry was only 13 months older than his younger sister, Mary. The mother had only an 8th grade education and a much below average IQ. Terry's developmental test scores were also extremely low when he entered day care at 3½ months. Over the course of 14 months in the program his language skills blossomed and his test scores rose to very high average levels, which were maintained through the last follow-up with him at age 4½.

By the time his sister entered day care at 4 months, the mother had been engaged in a year of parent education and Mary had enjoyed the daily undivided attention of her mother during her early months while Terry attended day care. Mary's test scores were about average at entry. Her language and other test scores also rose to very high average like Terry's while she was in the program, but were found to have receded to average levels over the course of her final follow up at just over age 3. Given her circumstances, the mother could apparently sustain the care and stimulation of one child, the older boy, but not two, once the children no longer attended day care.

Ed

The language focus of our day care program was particularly important for Ed. Despite his college-educated family background, when he enrolled at 14 months Ed could neither imitate nor say any words, though he had good perceptual-motor skills. By the time he left the program 16 months later, his language and other skills were all at the superior level and remained this high when last followed up at age 4½. Had he been in a program where nothing but free play prevailed without much teacher-child interaction and attention to language, his mild language delay might have expanded to become serious, since he was also getting little attention to his language at home. The mother was working at two jobs and the father was chronically ill.

CONCLUSION

Children having a wide range of language and other skills, including children from high risk backgrounds, can be accommodated in day care for infants and preschoolers, just as children with a wide range of other learning problems and emotional styles are regularly fit into the ordinary environment. The "average" or "ordinary" child is in fact an extraordinarily varying individual, who because of different backgrounds, varies in both the pace of development and the variety of courses followed. Within the average environment, a teacher strategy of bringing language into special focus, and anchoring it in the child's "natural" world of play to enhance accessibility, will enable the fast, the moderate, the slow and the different child all to progress in their own ways to acquire language and related cognitive skills at minimal acceptable levels of competence.

References

Bzoch, K. R. and League, R. (1971) *Receptive Expressive Emergent Language Scale.* Tallahassee, FL: Tree of Life Press.

Carew, J. V. (1980) Experience and the development of intelligence in young children at home and in day care. *Monographs of the Society for Research in Child Development,* **45**, Serial no. 187.

Fowler, W. (1972) A developmental learning approach to infant care in a group setting. *Merrill-Palmer Quarterly,* **18**, 145–175.

Fowler, W. (1978) *Day Care and Its Effects on Early Development: A Study of Group and Home Care in Multi-Ethnic Working Class Families.* Toronto: Ontario Institute for Studies in Education.

Fowler, W. (1980) *Infant and Child Care: A Guide to Education in Group Settings.* Boston: Allyn and Bacon.

Fowler, W. (1983) *Potentials of Childhood.* Vol. 2: *Studies in Early Developmental Learning.* Lexington, MA: Lexington Books.

Fowler, W. (1990a) *Talking from Infancy: How to Nurture and Cultivate Early Language Development.* Cambridge, MA: Brookline Books.

Fowler, W. (1990b) (same title) Cambridge, MA: Center for Early Learning and Child Care.

Fowler, W. and Khan, N. (1974) *The Later Effects of Enfant Group Care: A Follow-up Study.* Toronto: Ontario Institute for Studies In Education.

Fowler, W. and Swenson, A. (1979) The influence of early language stimulation on development. *Genetic Psychology Monographs*, **100**, 73–109.

Fowler, W., Ogston, K., Roberts-Fiati, G. and Swenson, A. (1992) *The influence of early language term development of abilities: Identifying exceptional abilities through educational intervention*. Paper presented at the 1992 Esther Katz Rosen Symposium on the Psychological Development of Gifted Children: Developmental Approaches to Identifying Exceptional Ability. (To be published in Proceedings by the American Psychological Association).

Fowler, W., Ogston, K., Roberts-Fiati, G. and Swenson, A. (1993a) Accelerating Language Acquisition. In K. Ackrill (ed.) *The Origins and Development of High Ability*. Chichester, UK: Wiley.

Fowler, W., Ogston, K., Roberts-Fiati, G. and Swenson, A. (1993b) Increasing societal talent pools through early enrichment. Paper presented at A Gifted Globe: Tenth World Congress on Gifted and Talented Education. Toronto, Ontario, Canada, August 8 to 18, 1993. Submitted for publication in Proceedings.

Fowler, W., Ogston, K., Roberts-Fiati, G. and Swenson, A. (1993c) *The longterm development of giftedness and high competencies in children enriched in language during infancy*. Paper presented at the 1993 Esther Katz Rosen Symposium on the Psychosocial Development of Gifted Children: Relating Life Span Research to the Development of Gifted Children (To be published in Proceedings by the American Psychological Association).

Griffiths, R. (1970) The *Abilities of Young Children*. London: Child Development Research Centre.

Harris, J. (1990) *Early Language Development: Implications for Clinical and Educational Practice*. London: Routledge.

Huttenlocher, J., Height, W., Bryk, A., Seltzer, M. and Lyons, T. (1991) Early vocabulary growth: Relation to language input and gender. *Developmental Psychology*, **27**, 236–248.

Lally, J. R., Mangione, P. L. and Honig, A. S. (1986) Syracuse University Family Development Research Project: Long-Range Impact of Early Intervention on Low Income Children and Their Families. In D. R. Powell (Ed). *Parent Education as Early Childhood Intervention: Emerging Directions in Theory Research, and Practise* (pp. 79–104), Norwood, NJ: Ablex.

McCartney, K. (1984) Effect of quality day care environment on children's language development. *Developmental Psychology*, **20**, 244–260.

Menyuk, P. (1977) *Language and Maturation*. Cambridge, MA: MIT Press.

Ogston, K. (1983) The effects of gross motor and language stimulation on infant development. In W. Fowler (ed.) *Potentials of Childhood*. Vol. 2. Lexington, MA: Lexington Books.

Roberts, G. (1983) The effects of a program of stimulation in language and problem solving on the development of infants from lower-income, black Caribbean immigrant families. In W. Fowler (ed.) *Potentials of Childhood*. Vol. 2. Lexington, MA: Lexington Books.

Swenson, A. (1983) Toward an ecological approach to theory and research in child language acquisition. In W. Fowler (ed.) *Potentials of Childhood*. Vol. 2. Lexington, MA: Lexington Books.

Family and Cultural Alert!

Considerations in Assistive Technology Assessment

*Jack J. Hourcade,
Howard P. Parette, Jr.,
Mary Blake Huer*

Imagine yourself as a special educator in San Francisco who comes across his student and her family in a restaurant. You are excited that your student has such a wonderful chance to use her new augmentative communication device, but you are disappointed to see that it is nowhere in sight, and that her father is speaking for her.

Or, imagine that you are a special educator teaching at the high school level in San Antonio. One day you learn to your dismay that your student with severe mental retardation, who in your opinion had been making excellent progress in using her electronic communication device, is no longer using the device. Her parents have apparently and suddenly become discouraged and disinterested in its ongoing use.

These and similar professional disappointments are inevitable if we as special educators are not sensitive to family and cultural issues in assessing technology needs of students with disabilities. In the first example, the girl's family is uncomfortable with the way the device draws attention to them, and so they prefer not to take it out and use it in public. In the second example, the teacher failed to realize that the Hispanic girl had just had her *quincancera,* a celebration of her 15th birthday. In the Hispanic culture, this frequently serves as a milestone to demonstrate the growing independence of the girl, and marks a significant transition on the way to adulthood. Her failure to use the device has resulted from her parents' viewing her as an increasingly independent adult, and deciding to let her make her own decisions about whether to use the device.

Selecting Assistive Technology Devices

Assistive technology devices are pieces of equipment used to increase, maintain, or improve the functional capabilities of students with disabilities. Recommendations for these devices are often included in individualized education programs (IEPs) for students with disabilities.

Involving Families

While family participation in IEPs is theoretically mandated by law; in reality, the involvement of family members in team decision making is often limited. When we fail to involve the family in decisions about possible uses of assistive technology devices, assistive technology *abandonment* (Batavia & Hammer, 1989; Parette, in press), a failure/refusal to use the device, can result. Such an outcome represents a waste of increasingly scarce fiscal resources available to school systems.

Assessing Students' Skills

Assessment of student skills and abilities in special education has long relied on formal testing procedures, but over the past few years, less formal approaches to gathering information from families for decision making have become more common. Informal assessment strategies are particularly important in assistive technology decision making, because few standardized instruments are available.

Informal information-collection strategies require from special education teachers a high level of sensitivity to families and their needs. In particular, there are three specific needs reported by families as being especially important for professionals to understand in considering technology devices for students (Parette & VanBiervliet, 1995). Specifically, professionals should use the following guidelines:

- Understand family needs for *information* about assistive technology devices.
- Recognize the impact on, and changes in, *family routines* the assistive technology will cause.
- Consider the extent to which family members desire themselves or their children to be *accepted in community settings.*

A research base incorporating data provided by families throughout the United States is now beginning to emerge (Parette & VanBiervliet, 1995). Using these data, we discuss specific and practical recommendations to help teachers become more sensitive to family needs during assistive technology decision making in each of these three areas.

Sensitivity to Family Need for Information

Parents need information, and *how* that information is provided can be as important as *what* is provided.

Researchers have frequently noted the importance of providing families with basic information regarding assistive technology devices (e.g., Angelo, Kokoska, & Jones, 1996). One particularly useful source of information on assistive devices is ABLEDATA. This U.S. Department of Education-sponsored database contains detailed descriptions on approximately 21,000 products from more than 3,000 manufacturers. ABLEDATA is accessed through a low-cost CD-ROM, *Cooperative Database Distribution Network for Assistive Technology* (CO-NET), available through the Trace Center at the University of Wisconsin. This CD-ROM also contains 16 easy-to-use national directories of disability-related services that cover certain states, plus regional and nationwide data sources (CO-NET, 1996). Teachers and family members may use the CO-NET CD-ROM to learn of the range of assistive technology devices and to identify possible solutions for a particular child in the classroom setting.

While we can simply tell parents about some device, or even show it to them, it is often more helpful for parents to view another child actually using that device. This is especially useful if the child is similar culturally or ethnically to their child. Videotapes are a powerful format for this; they can help the family to see the use of the device in a real-life setting. Seeing an adaptive device being used successfully by another child is a convincing way to communicate the potential impact of assistive technology.

When a technological device is provided, a frequent though typically unasked question is who actually owns the device. When devices are purchased by the school system, families must understand that the school continues to own the device. If the child is to use the device off school grounds, families should understand the school's policies regarding such issues as responsibility for theft and damage. Some families will understandably be reluctant to use an expensive piece of equipment if they perceive that they will be held accountable for any damages. If teachers are involved in helping families obtain assistive technology devices through funding mechanisms other than schools, the actual ownership of the device must be understood by all.

Sensitivity to Changes in Family Routines

The introduction of any technology device into a child's life is likely to have *unanticipated effects* on both the child and the family.

Often we as special educators do not adequately consider how a family's life can change when a child begins using some adaptive device. The overall high demands of caring for children with disabilities in general have been well documented (e.g., Miller & Hudson, 1994). These demands may be especially challenging with children with severe disabilities, the very children most likely to receive assistive technology devices.

Sometimes, in our professional excitement over the possibilities some device offers a child, we fail to consider the changes and stresses that the device can cause in the home. Computerized electronic assistive technology devices may require much training on the part of the child and family before they can be effectively used. Unfortunately, family members who participate in training sessions often report *information overload*

Cultural sensitivity is an important issue to consider when proposing technological devices for children with disabilities.

during such experiences. More information is provided during intensive training than can possibly be used or remembered by the family. As a result, the device may be used incorrectly, inadequately, or not at all.

Special educators also must be aware that training can place a variety of stresses on families over and above those typically associated with having a child with a disability. For example, attendance at a remote site to receive training might require the parent to resolve such practical problems as obtaining time away from work, arranging for child care for other siblings, and managing transportation and related travel expenses (if the training is a multiple-day experience).

Certain devices may require family members to assume responsibilities for assistance in using or transporting the device. If the device is heavy, complex, or cumbersome, family members may quietly choose not to use it.

As special educators, before meeting with parents to discuss technology devices we must spend time identifying and considering these and other possible changes in family routines the device may require. When we do so, we significantly increase the likelihood the device will be used productively.

Sensitivity to Family Needs for Acceptance

Some families prefer to *blend in,* and feel that an assistive technology device makes the child (and the family) more noticeable.

When working with family members to identify appropriate assistive technology devices that may be used in community settings, special educators must first seek to learn if the family members are comfortable with, and are likely to use, an assistive technology device in the public settings the family frequents. It is understandable that some family members might feel uncomfortable

---

Family Issues to Consider in Introducing Assistive Technology

- When we fail to involve the family in decisions about possible uses of assistive technology devices, assistive technology abandonment can result.
- Informal information-collection strategies require from special education teachers a high level of sensitivity to families and their needs.
- Parents need information, and how that information is provided can be as important as what is provided.
- The introduction of any technology device into a child's life is likely to have unanticipated effects on both the child and the family.
- Some families prefer to blend in, and feel that an assistive technology device makes the child (and the family) more noticeable.
- Families and teachers may have very different perceptions and values, based in part on the differing cultural backgrounds they bring to the IEP table.
- A family's values will affect the nature and extent of family participation in assistive technology decision making.

using certain devices in public. For example, when the family attends church services, the child may not be able to *whisper quietly* using certain communication devices. Thus, family members may choose not to use the device in that setting.

If such reservations are widespread, the device may still have considerable usefulness at home. It may not help the child's overall inclusion, however, into the mainstream of society.

If the family feels that the device is too obtrusive, the special educator and the rest of the IEP team might brainstorm to identify other less conspicuous options. Perhaps a less expensive or lower technology solution would be less obtrusive and noticeable and would serve the overall purpose better. For example, a communication picture book might well be preferable in a church setting to a more sophisticated electronic device.

Cultural Sensitivity

In proposing technological devices for children with disabilities, we as special educators must be careful to be especially sensitive to important issues that are too frequently overlooked. A significant aspect of this is understanding that families and teachers may have very different perceptions and values, based in part on the *differing cultural backgrounds* they bring to the IEP table.

This issue is especially significant to us in special education, given the continuing overrepresentation of students from minority racial and cultural backgrounds (e.g., Ysseldyke, Algozzine, & Thurlow, 1992). We sometimes forget that individuals from cultural backgrounds different from our own may see the world quite differently from us. In such cases, the quality of the special educational services provided both to students and family members will be impaired (Hetzroni & Harris, 1996; Parette, 1995; Trivelli, 1994; Soto, Huer, & Taylor, in press).

A variety of issues relevant to special education differ systematically across cultures in America. These include:

- Perceptions of disability held by family members.
- Attitudes toward the education system.
- Priorities regarding services deemed important for the child and family.
- Ideas regarding the importance and process of child care.
- Family perceptions of ability to collaborate with professionals.
- The extent to which life circumstances are viewed as being overwhelming.

When we as special educators consider the possible use of an assistive device for a child, we must recognize cultural-specific differences in how families might perceive these issues. Assistive technologies are playing an increasingly prominent role in the provision of services to children and youth with disabilities. In our excitement over the possibilities these technologies may offer to students with disabilities, we may fail to consider that our perceptions of the advantages and disadvantages of these devices may be quite different from the perceptions of the family of the student.

Parents need information, and how that information is provided can be as important as what is provided.

Teachers must realize that the Euro-American values of independence and self-sufficiency are not values shared by family members from all cultures. Some cultures, for example Asian and Native American cultures, are more collectivist in nature. Often in these cultures children are viewed less as individuals in their own right, and more as parts of the family and the community. A certain degree of dependence on the family throughout life is expected and valued. Thus, the typical special education goal of increased independence that an assistive technology device might help with may not be seen as important to these families.

In addition, families having a collectivist orientation typically wish to fit in, and to avoid being perceived as being different from others. For example, some families in the African-American community may prefer not to have attention drawn to their children in social settings (Parette & VanBiervliet, 1995). An assistive device that is obtrusive and does just this may be a poor choice.

In terms of other information we share with parents, special educators might be careful not to let their own cultural backgrounds filter the information they share with families. For example, many of us from Euro-American cultural backgrounds may automatically assume that mothers will wish information regarding how assistive technology devices may be used for socialization purposes and in community settings, while fathers are more interested in repair, maintenance, and programming (Angelo et al., 1996). However, as is the case with many generalizations, such an assumption may be invalid for family members from non-Euro-American backgrounds.

As educators, we should also consider the way we share information with family members from differing cultural backgrounds. Family members from certain cultural backgrounds may mistrust Euro-American school personnel. In such cases, having a representative from a community support system (e.g., a church or community action group) join the IEP meeting can help resolve this communication problem. It is often helpful to ask community resource or support personnel who are from the same cultural backgrounds of families to help us in providing information regarding assistive technology devices to families, and learning their needs.

Perhaps needless to say, having a language interpreter is necessary when English is not the primary language of the family. Even when parents do speak English, if it is not their first language, an interpreter can help in conveying subtleties and complexities that otherwise might not be understood.

Augmenting Our Perceptions

One way to think about family issues and cultural background is to see them as the air. Though air is crucial to our existence, we are so immersed that we seldom even notice or consider it. Some families with whom special educators will work in assistive technology assessment will demonstrate strong cultural identifications; others will not. Regardless of how strong or weak these values appear to be, they will nonetheless affect the nature and extent of family participation in assistive technology decision making.

A family's unique historical and cultural backgrounds influence factors such as the following:

- A family's willingness to seek help.
- The family's communication styles.
- The amount and type of participation family members choose.
- The goals the family selects.
- Which family members will be involved in school intervention efforts.

Special educators can become more effective in working with all families across cultures by recognizing their own cultural identities and values, and considering how these may be shaping their present professional beliefs (Hanson, Lynch, & Wayman, 1990).

Figure 1 offers some guidelines for special educators to consider as they work with families in assistive technology decision-making processes. In an era when diminishing fiscal resources for school services is the reality, sensitivity to family and cultural considerations will help to ensure that the most appropriate devices are selected for the children of all families.

References

Angelo, D. H., Kokoska, S. M., & Jones, S. D. (1996). Family perspective on augmentative and alternative communication: Families of adolescents and young adults. *Augmentative and Alternative Communication, 12,* 13–20.

Batavia, A. I., & Hammer, G. (1989). Consumer criteria for evaluating assistive devices: Implications for technology transfer. In J. J. Presperin (Ed.), *Proceedings of the 12th Annual Conference of the Rehabilitation Engineering Society of North America* (pp. 194–195). Washington, DC: RESNA Press.

CO-NET (Cooperative Assistive Technology Data Base Dissemination Network). (1996). *HyperABLEDATA Database,* CO-NET CD ROM version (8th ed.). Madison, WI: Trace Research and Development Center.

Hanson, M. J., Lynch, E. W., & Wayman, K. (1990). Honoring the cultural diversity of families when gathering data. *Topics in Early Childhood Special Education, 10,* 112–131.

Hetzroni, O. E., & Harris, O. L. (1996). Cultural aspects in the development of AAC users. *Augmentative and Alternative Communication, 12,* 52–58.

Miller, S. P., & Hudson, P. (1994). Using structured parent groups to provide parental support. *Intervention in School and Clinic, 29*(3), 151–155.

Parette, H. P. (1995, November). *Culturally sensitive family-focused assistive technology assessment strategies.* Paper presented at the 11th Annual International Early Childhood Conference on Children with Special Needs, Orlando, FL. (ERIC Document Reproduction Service No. ED 387 996)

Parette, H. P. (in press). Effective and promising assistive technology practices for students with mental retardation and developmental disabilities. In A. Hilton & R. Ringlaben (Eds.), *Effective and promising practices in developmental disabilities.* Austin, TX: PRO-ED.

Parette, H. P., & VanBiervliet, A. (1995). *Culture, families, and augmentative and alternative communication (AAC) impact: A multimedia instructional program for related services personnel and family members.* Grant funded by the U.S. Department of Education, Office of Special Education and Rehabilitative Services, Office of Special Education Programs Special Projects (No. H029K50072).

Soto, G., Huer, M. B., & Taylor, O. (in press). Multicultural issues in augmentative and alternative communication. In L. L. Lloyd, D. H. Fuller, & H. H. Arvidson (Eds.), Augmentative and alternative communication. Boston: Allyn & Bacon.

Trivelli, L. U. (1994). The impact of human and multicultural diversity on assistive technology outreach and services. NARIC Quarterly, 4(3), 1, 6–8.

Ysseldyke, J. E., Algozzine, B., & Thurlow, M. L. (1992). *Critical issues in special education* (2nd ed.). Boston: Houghton-Mifflin.

Figure 1. Family and Cultural Issues Questionnaire

Question	Yes	No	Notes
1. Has the family clearly communicated concerns, needs, and goals about the child?			
2. Are the family's and child's daily routines identified?			
3. Would the family like a support group to convey information or training regarding assistive technology devices?			
4. Would the family prefer a community leader or liaison to convey information regarding assistive technology devices?			
5. Has a range of possible technology solutions for the child and family been explored?			
6. Do family members and the child want an assistive technology device?			
7. Are family expectations of the assistive technology assessment process clearly understood?			
8. Does the family understand issues related to funding and ownership of the assistive technology device?			
9. Do all family members understand how assistive technology devices may affect family routines?			
10. Have the various settings where the child might use assistive technology devices, and resulting demands/consequences of device usage there, been identified?			
11. Do families want to use devices in community settings?			
12. Are the family expectations of the assistive technology device clearly understood prior to purchase?			

Source: Copyright 1997 by Howard P. Parette. Used with permission.

Jack J. Hourcade *(CEC Chapter #225), Professor, Elementary Education and Specialized Studies, Boise State University, Idaho;* **Howard P. Parette, Jr.** *(CEC Missouri Federation), Professor, Department of Elementary, Early, and Special Education, Southeast Missouri State University, Cape Girardeau;* **Mary Blake Huer,** *Professor, Department of Speech Communication, California State University, Fullerton.*

This article is supported in part by Grant No. H029K50072 from the U.S. Department of Education to the first author. Opinions expressed herein are those of the authors alone and should not be interpreted to have agency endorsement.

Address correspondence to H. P. Parette, Jr., Elementary and Special Education, Southeast Missouri State University, One University Plaza, Cape Girardeau, MO 63701.

Unit 5

Unit Selections

16. **Collaborative Planning for Inclusion of a Student with Developmental Disabilities,** Jane E. Doelling, Suzanne Bryde, Judy Brunner, and Barbara Martin
17. **Children with Down Syndrome: Implications for Adult-Child Interactions in Inclusive Settings,** Dolores J. Appl
18. **Getting the Student with Head Injuries Back in School: Strategies for the Classroom,** Mary Steensma
19. **Identifying Depression in Students with Mental Retardation,** Laura M. Stough and Lynn Baker

Key Points to Consider

❖ What strategies can make transition from special education in primary school to regularized education in middle school easier for a child who is developmentally disabled?

❖ How can children with Down Syndrome be helped to interact successfully with adults and other children in inclusive education settings?

❖ Can students who have sustained traumatic brain injuries return successfully to their school classes? What strategies assist their reintegration?

❖ What is diagnostic overshadowing and how does it affect the diagnosis of depression in students with developmental disabilities and/or traumatic brain injuries?

 Links   www.dushkin.com/online/

20. **Autism Society Early Interventions Package**
    http://www.autism-society.org/packages/early_intervention.html
21. **Disability-Related Sources on the Web**
    http://www.arcofarizona.org/dislnkin.html
22. **Gentle Teaching**
    http://utopia.knoware.nl/users/gentle/

These sites are annotated on pages 4 and 5.

Developmental Disabilities and Traumatic Brain Injuries

Children with disabilities of mentation have been the focus of much of the attention of the changes to a kinder, gentler, more "politically correct" vocabulary in the 1990s. Children who have cognitive skills falling two standard deviations below the norm for their age may be considered mentally challenged or developmentally disabled. Children who have sustained brain damage through traumatic brain injury may also fall two standard deviations below the intellectual norm for age, but the preferred term for them is traumatically brain injured, not developmentally disabled. Each are recognized as separate disability categories by IDEA.

Children with significantly subnormal intelligence were once classified as "educable," "trainable," or "custodial" for purposes of placement. These terms are strongly discouraged today. Even severely developmentally disabled children are educable and can benefit from some schooling. The current preferred categorical terms for children who are developmentally challenged are "intermittent," "limited," "extensive," and "pervasive." These terms refer to how much support the individuals need to function as capably as possible.

The U.S. Individuals with Disabilities Education Act mandates free and appropriate public school education for every child, regardless of mentation. While the legal windows on education are from ages 6 to 16 in the United States, individuals with developmental disabilities are entitled to a free and appropriate education from age of assessment (birth, early childhood) to age 21. This encompasses parent-child education programs and preschool programs early in life and transitional services into the community and world of work after the public school education is completed.

A child with developmental disabilities who is in the "intermittent" classification needs support at school, at times when special needs arise, and at times of life transitions. This terminology is generally used for children whose disabilities do not create an obvious and continual problem. These children have slower mentation but also have many abilities. The level of support classified as "limited" is usually used for children whose disabilities create daily limitations on their abilities, but who can achieve a degree of self-sufficiency after an appropriate education. Limited refers to the period of time from diagnosis until adulthood (age 21). The "extensive" support classification extends the support throughout the lifespan for individuals whose developmental disabilities prohibit them from living independently. The "pervasive" support classification is used infrequently. It is only for those individuals whose disabilities prevent them from most activities of self-help. Pervasive support is intensive and life-sustaining in nature.

The majority of children with developmental disabilities can be placed in the intermittent support classification. To casual observers, they often do not appear to have any disabilities. However, their ability to process, store, and retrieve information is limited. In the past, this group of children was given IQ measurements between two and three standard deviations below the mean (usually an IQ below 70 but above 55). Intelligence testing is an inexact science with problems of both validity and reliability. The current definition of developmental disability endorsed by the American Association on Mental Deficiency (AAMD) does not include any IQ scoring results other than to use the phrase "subaverage intellectual

functioning." It emphasizes the problems that individuals with developmental disabilities have with adaptive skills such as communication, self-care, home living, social skills, community use, self-direction, health and safety, functional academics, leisure, and work.

The causes of developmental disabilities (DD) are unclear. About one-half of all individuals with DD are suspected of having sustained some brain damage prenatally, neonatally, or in childhood. (Brain damage after age 18 that results in impaired mentation is not referred to as DD.) Several hundred factors have been identified that can singly or in combination alter brain functioning or destroy neurons. Most of these factors are silent killers. We lack the technology to detect even small areas of brain damage, much less to determine what caused them. Among the better-known factors that damage brain tissue are very early birth and/or very low birth weight, anoxia, malnutrition, drugs, viruses, radiation, trauma, and tumors. Children with more severe functional disabilities (those classified in the limited, extensive, and pervasive categories) usually have other symptoms of neurological damage and are entitled to special services under the category of multiple disabilities.

The first article in this unit depicts the transition of a boy with developmental disabilities from special education in primary school to regular education in middle school. The authors emphasize the collaborative efforts of the school staff, how they shared leadership roles, and how they attended to due process. The problems encountered by the school, the student, and the family and also the factors that contributed to the inclusive education success are presented.

Children with Down Syndrome (DS) are described in the second article. The author points out that while Down Syndrome is a collection of characteristic symptoms, each child with DS has his or her own unique strengths and needs. Dolores Appl provides useful guidelines for including children with DS in inclusive educational settings.

The third article is on traumatic brain injury. It suggests ways to help students, who were previously functioning at a much higher cognitive level, to reenter school successfully after their brain injury.

Unit 5 ends with an article that addresses the problem of depression in students with developmental disabilities. Depression is a common problem in students with cognitive disabilities. It is also difficult to recognize due to the coexisting symptoms of intellectual deficits. The problem of diagnostic overshadowing is discussed by the authors.

Collaborative Planning for Inclusion of a Student with Developmental Disabilities

Jane E. Doelling, Suzanne Bryde, Judy Brunner & Barbara Martin

It appears that many education professionals in both general and special education are experiencing confusion regarding the concept of inclusion. There is a misconception regarding corresponding legal mandates pertaining to provision of services to students with disabilities. In a recent position statement, The Council for Exceptional Children (1993) cites the need for increased collaboration and greater emphasis on inclusive practices. Inclusion in itself is not a legal mandate; however, implementing the Individual Educational Plan (IEP) in the least restrictive environment is a component of the Individuals with Disabilities Education Act (IDEA) of 1990. Full inclusion programs typically offer students with disabilities services in the general education classroom with little or no time in special education settings. IDEA mandates that placement decisions be made by a multidisciplinary team and that a continuum of service delivery options be maintained.

The setting in which educational services for students with disabilities are provided remains a major issue, particularly in middle level and secondary education where students are expected to spend a great deal of time in content classes. Nolet and Tindal (1993) suggest that demands for response in content classes may directly affect students' ability to use content information and that low performing students benefit from accommodative instruction that includes modeling of problem solving solutions and rich contextual clues. Most general educators agree that inclusion is a positive practice, but do not feel prepared to serve students with disabilities. A support system with shared involvement is necessary for successful inclusion (Simpson, & Myles, 1993).

The current paradigm shift to less restrictive models for educating students with disabilities requires collaborative planning, routine modification of instructional materials, and the inclusion of parents and peers as important components of the educational process (Bradley & Fisher 1995). The following discussion will focus on clarifying issues surrounding inclusion, as well as a description of specific action taken to implement an appropriate educational program for Matt, an 11-year-old student with autism, entering a middle school program. Emphasis is placed on the collaborative efforts of school staff, the importance of shared leadership roles, adherence to appropriate due process, and analysis of the instructional environment in planning and implementing an inclusive educational program appropriate to individual needs.

History

Matt had previously received educational services in a self-contained language development classroom with limited integration in general education classes at the elementary level. The greatest concerns expressed by Matt's family and the school team were social interaction and severely delayed communication. Matt was functioning at approximately an eight-year-old level with the exception of expressive language which fell below other areas. He rarely initiated interaction with peers and had developed limited interest in age-appropriate leisure activities. Previous success with implementing behavioral change

Jane E. Doelling, Suzanne Bryde, and Barbara Martin teach at Southwest Missouri State University in Springfield. Judy Brunner is a middle school principal in the Springfield Public Schools in Missouri.

Figure 1
Functional Behavioral Analysis and Interventions

A. Setting Task
Hall transition to music

Antecedent
Student transition to music with limited supervision from teachers posted at each end of the hall.

Intervention
Modeling and guided practice of appropriate hall behavior and increased adult proximity to Matt. Fade proximity with practice.

Implementor
All educators collaborate.

Behavior(s)
Matt followed behind peer in line. Touched peer on shoulder 5 times in 2 minutes.

Consequence(s)
Peer tolerant of first two touches. Turns to Matt and shouts "stop" for the last three touches. Matt smiles.

Direct instruction in appropriate interaction skills. Generalization sessions implemented in natural contexts (luncheon, hall, classroom).

Special educators

Function
Request for interaction/attention. Difficulty with self monitoring.

Develop monitoring/cueing system. (Card that reads "Hands down" and "Act like a teenager.")

Special educators

Monitoring and check for appropriate behavior.

All educators collaborate

B. Setting/Task
General Education Classroom—social studies class discussion on protection of natural resources.

Antecedent
Teacher asked student to open social studies text, survey the passage, and brainstorm information gleaned from survey.

Intervention
Develop prior knowledge for lesson through vocabulary lessons, survey of pictures, participation in hands on activities.

Implementor
Special educators.

Behavior(s)
Walked to the back of the room. Repeatedly stacked and unstacked library books for duration of 15 minute discussion. Did not comply to verbal directive to return to seat.

Consequence
Matt told to return to seat. Teacher ignored behavior since Matt's activity was not disruptive.

Include structured, parallel lesson to be implemented independently on a visual schedule.

Special educators

Function
Escape/avoidance. Protest of non-meaningful activity. Confusion.

Structure cooperative group activity appropriate to diverse abilities (e.g. recycling school materials, identifying community resources and how to care for them).

All educators collaborate

---

was credited with determining the reasons for Matt's behavior through an analysis of environmental variables and planning intervention accordingly. (See Figure 1)

The middle school Matt was to attend had implemented a collaborative teaching model that involved core teams of three content teachers in general education with one special services consultant/teacher assigned to each team. The district had no autism specialist and the middle school teachers were apprehensive about working with a student that presented such unique challenges. The family requested that the next IEP include age-appropriate tasks and specific plans for including Matt with typical peers. They expressed long range goals for Matt that included independent living and employment in a competitive or semi-supported setting; however, they noted their concern that this did not seem

> **Figure 2**
> **Agenda for the Transition Team**
>
> 1. Review the IEP and all available diagnostic and programming data in the following areas: social, behavioral, academic, health, adaptive, and cognitive to determine Present Level of Performance (PLP).
> 2. Determine IEP goals and objectives appropriate to meeting needs identified in the PLP.
> 3. Determine placement and services appropriate to implementing goals and objectives.
> 4. Determine accommodations necessary for implementation of goals and objectives across settings (i.e. grading alternatives, curricular and material modifications, physical arrangements, teaching and student response modes).
> 5. Assign a liaison/case manager to coordinate the collaborative process and implementation of the IEP.

possible without exposure to typical language and social models. A systematic plan of transition was developed in order to ease the movement to middle school for Matt, his family and school personnel.

Phase One: Planning the Transition

The special education director and middle school principal assumed leadership roles for initial transition planning. A meeting was arranged with the family and included elementary team members as well as the team from the receiving middle school. Due to questions regarding Matt's placement and the content of his IEP, it was essential to set an agenda for the meeting that reflected sensitivity to the family's requests and adherence to due process. Figure 2 includes the agenda for the transition team.

By reviewing major instructional goals for the district and comparing them to Matt's Present Level of Performance (PLP), the team addressed the family's wishes regarding inclusion of Matt in age-appropriate academic activities. For example, the team related district curriculum goals such as listening and reading comprehension skill development to the needs identified in Matt's diagnostic report and corresponding IEP. For the benefit of general education professionals, as well as Matt's family, it was noted in the IEP that Matt would not be expected to master all district curriculum goals presented at his chronological age level and that modification was fair and appropriate based on diagnostic data documenting the effects of Matt's disability.

It was the decision of the team that full inclusion would not meet all specified IEP goals and objectives at that time. Matt needed specialized language, occupational therapy, and special education services to meet individual needs. However, it was also determined that many of the goals and objectives of Matt's IEP could be attained in both special and general educational settings.

In an effort to alleviate confusion regarding the district's policy on inclusion, a brief explanation had been added to both the student and faculty handbooks. A portion of the district policy is provided here:

- Decisions regarding services and educational placement will be based on a multidisciplinary evaluation and a detailed IEP developed by the family and educational team.
- Regardless of disability, students will be fully included in general education programs, when deemed appropriate by the IEP team. A full continuum of service delivery options should be maintained by the school district as full inclusion may not meet the needs of all students.
- Those students whose IEP does not include full inclusion requirements should be placed in the least restrictive environment possible based on the student's needs and the continuum of available services.

Finally, it was determined that Mr. Brown, the special education teacher assigned to one of the established middle school teams would serve as liaison, case manager, and integration specialist for Matt's program. This determination was based on the team's record of success in regard to meeting educational goals and Mr. Brown's experience with developmental disabilities.

Phase Two: Preparing for the Transition

In an effort to address programmatic barriers to collaboration, district administrators agreed to provide transitional support by providing an additional plan hour for Matt's team leader, Mr. Brown. A commitment was also made to provide an instructional aide for Matt. It was noted the support of the individual aide would be phased out as Matt progressed since the ultimate family and school goal was developing his independence. Further, Mr. Brown received specialized training in autism to serve as a consultant for the middle school, thus enhancing a site-based approach to program management. Conceptual barriers to inclusion were addressed through district supported staff development and team planning coordinated by Mr. Brown. Other team members attended various staff development activities supported by the district. To facilitate transition to the middle school setting, several ecological variables affecting Matt's performance were analyzed. Examples from the functional behavioral analysis that assisted the team in program planning are noted in Figure 1. The provision of contextual cues within a structured environment had been noted as important to behavioral control and supported in data collected and the professional literature on autism. Based on this analysis of behaviors, the team implemented a plan that included a visual schedule with clear criteria for assigned tasks and a physical arrangement that reduced frustration.

Phase Three: Implementing the Program

The majority of the goals and objectives on Matt's IEP were to be implemented across settings. Because several different implementors were involved, it was necessary to establish a system for effective collaborative planning and systematic communication. An agenda for planning sessions was established by the team with a focus on five areas: (a) instructional content, (b) methods of presentation, (c) participant roles, (d) evaluation procedures, and (e) lesson accommodations. In an effort to further improve communication and consistency of programming, Matt carried his individual schedule across settings. Mr. Brown followed a rotating instructional schedule, alternating days in inclusive settings while still providing direct instruction to students in special education settings. This system allowed him to work with students on IEP objectives as well as assist the general education teacher with inclusive programming.

Providing services in inclusive settings required each team member to share leadership roles and all team members to be consultants in their varied areas of expertise. A primary barrier expressed by general educators on Matt's team was time involved in development of an alternate curriculum for Matt as well as concern with the appropriateness of the academic curriculum. Mr. Brown took the lead in designing a curriculum that included prevocational skills crucial to independent adult functioning yet, when possible, parallel to the general education curriculum. General educators typically took lead roles in collaborative planning sessions involving the discussion of content for future instructional units. Alternative lessons plans were maintained on disk by Mr. Brown and other building specialists to be disseminated among instructional teams so that they could be modified and appropriately implemented for diverse learners.

Providing Matt with a means to more readily communicate with individuals across settings was imperative to successful integration, socialization, and behavioral control; therefore, speech and language therapy was provided in individualized sessions, as well as the general education settings, hall transitions, and luncheon. To ensure that language programming goals were clear, each team member was provided with a data collection form containing five communication skills specific to Matt's IEP. In addition, each member kept brief records regarding progress to share in collaborative planning sessions.

Due to Matt's expressive communication problems, a small photograph album with line drawing illustrations was employed. Sight words and phrases were attached to each picture; therefore, the system could be used to enhance reading and vocabulary skills. The low technology system was chosen for its flexibility and its potential for promoting communication between Matt and his peers and adults.

With desks arranged in a format that promoted face-to-face interaction, Matt was assigned to cooperative learning groups. An additional peer mediated strategy found to contribute to positive outcomes for Matt and his peers was peer tutoring (Dettmer, Thurston, & Dyck, 1993). Mr. Brown and the general education team members discussed cooperative roles appropriate to various curricular assignments and Matt's role in these assignments. Teachers analyzed cooperative lessons and structured them to provide rich contextual cues including schedules, material organizers, and self-monitoring forms. Specific cooperative group behaviors were targeted for direct instruction in language therapy and in the special education setting.

These included passing papers, making eye contact, requesting assistance, taking turns, and listening. Peers were selected as cooperative group partners on the basis of their expressed interest in working with Matt and because they were noted to be appropriate social and academic models.

It was apparent that positive behavioral intervention could not be separated from academic and communication instruction. Priorities identified in the team planning process included expanding Matt's repertoire of leisure activities, replacing socially inappropriate behaviors with appropriate skills, and developing friendships. It was determined that serving as an office worker would provide opportunity to apply social and academic skills. Matt was paired with a peer for some office activities and conducted other jobs independently. Opportunities were structured for Matt to interact, take direction, and request assistance from secretaries, administrators, or other adults in the building in an effort to generalize targeted social behaviors.

Peer networks were expanded from the original cooperative group members by rotating a peer in and out of the cooperative group on a periodic basis. In addition, Matt was assigned to a home room group that met twenty minutes daily. Each home room group in the building chose a theme or area of interest to pursue and Matt's group met in the gymnasium due to their interest in weight lifting and physical development. Matt's occupational therapist designed a program to be implemented in daily sessions and appropriate to Matt's physical ability and sensory integration needs. In addition to meeting social and motor development goals, mathematics goals were implemented by having Matt and a peer monitor physical progress.

Summary

Support for collaborative efforts to provide services to students with disabilities in inclusive settings became a district priority. Some faculty meetings and district inservice days were reserved for team meetings as educators' schedules were organized to promote collaborative planning. District policies and philosophy clearly reflected inclusive educational practices; however, programming decisions continued to be based on individual student needs, attributes of the school, and the expertise of building professionals.

It is important to note that variables and processes noted to contribute to success for Matt may not generalize to all students with disabilities; and, of course, problems with implementation did occur. Although there is a need for further research that validates effective collaborative and inclusive practices, the existing literature does support many of the practices implemented in Matt's educational program. These include the use of cooperative learning techniques; analysis of the instructional environment to determine variables affecting learning; problem solving strategies; and the shared leadership and consultative roles demonstrated by administrators, instructional team members, and ancillary staff (Dettmer, Thurston, & Dyck, 1993; Ysseldyke, Christenson, & Kovaleski, 1994). Matt did not master all district curricular goals; however, partial inclusion in the general education setting did contribute to the increased success with language, social, and academic goals of Matt's IEP.

Programmatic collaborative barriers noted in the literature (Johnson, Pugach, & Hammitte, 1988 [as cited in Heron & Harris, 1993]; Dettmer, Thurston, & Dyck, 1993) included scheduling problems, lack of resources, and lack of shared planning time and lack of role clarification. These were primarily addressed through administrative support and as a part of district reorganization. Conceptual barriers to collaboration and inclusion also corresponded to those noted in the literature and these included philosophical differences and lack of knowledge regarding diverse populations. In Matt's case, administrative support was essential, particularly for establishing a school climate that reflected the shared responsibility of educating all students. Therefore, professional credibility and the resolve of all team members are required to alleviate any conceptual barriers that may exist.

Educators want instructionally relevant strategies for teaching students with special needs and brainstorming alone may not lead to effective intervention (Ysseldyke, Christenson, & Kovaleski, 1994). Previously, emphasis was placed on the special educator as an outside or impromptu consultant and on the operation of parallel, segregated service delivery systems. It is essential that instructional models stress collaborative planning and problem solving that address the needs of education professionals, as well as a diverse student population.

As noted in Matt's program, decisions evolved from analysis of the learning environment along with assessment of learner characteristics. This emphasis on environmental analysis may include consideration of instructional presentation, physical accommodations, teacher expectations, academic engaged time, and adaptive instruction as recommended by Ysseldyke and others (1994). In summary, the following guidelines are offered to middle level educators planning collaboratively for inclusion of children with disabilities:

1. Conduct data review and planning sessions (IEP meetings) prior to placement in inclusive settings. These team sessions should include a consideration of family, professional, and peer needs along with a review of all present-level information for the particular child to be included. Long term goals (including post graduation goals) and corresponding short term objectives must be developed with clear delineation of settings for implementation, acceptable standards of performance, evaluation procedures, accommodations, and roles of various professionals.

2. Determine training, support service, and organizational needs as deemed appropriate from review of IEPs and general instructional goals. A focus on strengthening site-based management, collaborative opportunities, and the reallocation of available resources to meet the needs of diverse learners is essential to successful inclusion. Professional development needs may include enhancement of expertise in academic or behavioral strategies while organizational restructuring may call for reassignment of personnel or the reorganization of teams, planning times, or instructional schedules.

3. At collaborative planning sessions conduct ongoing evaluation of student performance and modify classroom instruction and IEPs accordingly. Collaborative sessions should include analysis of the effectiveness of instructional content, teaching methods, classroom organization, evaluation procedures, and professional roles. Analysis must be based on measurable outcomes for *all* students in the setting and IEPs may need to be revised prior to the expected annual review.

4. In collaborative planning sessions, determine how district curriculum goals and instructional methods can be modified to meet the needs of individuals with IEPs. Partial participation, alternative grading systems, peer coaching, and reduced assignments may all be appropriate. Inclusion in general education may not mean that students with IEPs are expected to master all objectives of the inclusive setting.

5. Delineation of professional roles should be based on analysis of the needs of all students within the setting. Although the general educator is basically responsible for presentation of content, and the special educator responsible for accommodation, roles may change. In collaborative instructional partnerships, flexibility, respect for individual expertise, and equal participation are stressed.

Educators demonstrate a wide range of skills and training; therefore, no single collaborative model is likely to be successful. General education teachers must clearly identify concept and principles they view as critical and special education teachers must support this process by providing expertise in formatting content information (Nolet & Tindal, 1993). Further, a continuum of services to meet the needs of individuals with varied needs must be maintained. Placement in collaborative, integrated settings remains an individualized decision based on the specific goals and objectives targeted in the IEP by a multidisciplinary team.

References

Bradley, D. F., & Fisher, J. F. (1995). The inclusion process: Role changes at the middle level. *Middle School Journal*, 26(3), 13–19.

The Council for Exceptional Children (1993). CEC policy on inclusive schools and community settings. *Supplement to Teaching Exceptional Children, 25(4)*

Dettmer, P., Thurston, L. P., & Dyck, N. (1993). *Consultation, collaboration, and teamwork for students with special needs.* Needham Heights, MA: Allyn & Bacon.

Heron, T. E., & Harris, K. C. (1993). *The educational consultant.* Austin, TX: Pro-ed.

Nolet, V., & Tindal, G. (1993). Special education in content area classes: Development of a model and practical procedures. *Remedial and Special Education*, 14(1), 36–48.

Simpson, R. L., & Myles, B. S. (1993). General education collaboration: A model for successful mainstreaming. In E. L. Meyen, G. A. Vergason, & R. J. Whelan (Eds.), *Challenges facing special education* (pp. 63–78). Denver, CO: Love.

Ysseldyke, J. E., Christenson, S., & Kovaleski, J. F. (1994). Identifying students' instructional needs in the context of classroom and home environments. *Teaching Exceptional Children*, 26(3), 37–41.

Children With Down Syndrome:

Implications for Adult-Child Interactions in Inclusive Settings

Dolores J. Appl

Dolores J. Appl is a doctoral candidate, Early Childhood Special Education, University of Illinois, Champaign.

In this article, Dolores Appl reviews research on children with Down Syndrome, highlighting physical, medical, intellectual, language, and behavioral characteristics that provide valuable information for caregivers and teachers in planning and intervention. The author reminds readers, however, that considerable variation exists among children with DS. Each child is a unique individual with his or her own strengths and needs. Appl's reviews of research on parent-child interactions provide helpful guidelines for caregivers and teachers working in inclusive settings. She advises readers that interactions and environments must be adjusted to support the uniqueness of each child for his or her optimal growth.—S.J.S.

In 1866, John Langdon Down described characteristics of a chromosomal disorder that since has been named Down syndrome (DS). The most common form of DS is Trisomy 21, a congenital condition marked by the addition of a third part to the 21st chromosome. With this extra genetic material comes the likelihood of physical and intellectual complications. Since Down's initial description of the characteristics, considerable research has been conducted on DS. Although a cure or prevention has not yet been found, research shows that the limitations associated with DS are not as uniformly extensive as once thought. While the exact upper developmental limits or the changes over the life span are not yet fully understood, intervention can help children with DS reach their full potential (Nadel, 1988; Wishart, 1988). Research that compares the development and learning of children with DS to that of children who are developing typically provides valuable information for planning and implementing intervention.

Although DS is a relatively common and well-known syndrome, misconceptions about it can lead to stereotyping (Wishart, 1988). Not only can this be disconcerting to parents, the children may be disadvantaged by lower expectations. Low expectations are apt to adversely affect the learning environment and are related to low performance (Kozma, 1986a; Spiker & Hopmann, 1997; Wishart, 1988).

Knowledge of DS characteristics and parents' response to them can inform the practice of other adults working with children who have DS. Because children with DS and other disabilities increasingly are included into child care and preschool settings where children who are developing typically also attend, this information is particularly important for adults working in inclusive environments.

Characteristics of Down Syndrome

Although children born with DS are more likely than typically developing children to possess certain characteristics, not all children will be affected similarly, nor will the degree of involvement be the same. In addition, certain characteristics, such as those related to language development, may become more obvious with age. Moreover, characteristics found in individuals with DS also may be found in individuals with other syndromes. It is not now known whether any characteristics are unique to DS (Kasari & Hodapp, 1996). Therefore, educators should not uniformly apply characteristics to all children with DS. Rather, the characteristics should be used as a means for understanding and supporting individual children with DS within the specific contexts of their physical and social environments (McCollum & Bair, 1994). Therefore, we must remember that considerable variation exists in the physical development, medical conditions, mental abilities, and behavior of individuals with DS. Children with DS, like all children, have unique personalities, strengths, and needs (Cicchetti & Beeghly, 1990a; Kasari & Hodapp, 1996; National Down Syndrome Congress, 1994; National Information Center for Children and Youth with Disabilities, 1994; Spiker & Hopmann, 1997).

Physical and Medical Characteristics

Common physical characteristics of children with DS include the distinctive appearance of their facial features, head shape, feet, and hands. These characteristics do not interfere with their development and learning, nor is there any connection between the number of distinctive features and mental ability (Kozma, 1986a).

However, hypotonia, or low muscle tone, which is present in many infants with DS, *is* likely to affect learning and development. Hypotonia tends to be present to some extent in all muscles of those afflicted, causing the muscles to feel flaccid and floppy. However, the degree of low tone varies among different children with DS and in different parts of the body in the same individual. Fortunately, hypotonia diminishes with age and early intervention can minimize its negative effects (Kozma, 1986a; McConnaughey, 1986).

Hypotonia affects the strength and movement of children with DS and often is accompanied by excessive joint flexibility, which reduces stability in the children's limbs. Consequently, many children with DS experience delays in the development of major motor skills. These delays can hinder their ability to explore and gain mastery over their environment. In addition, hypotonia can negatively affect other areas of development, including language and feeding skills (Fetters, 1996; Kozma, 1986a; McConnaughey, 1986).

In addition to the above physical differences, children with DS have a higher incidence of medical problems than children who are developing typically. Common conditions include cardiac defects, respiratory and intestinal problems, vision and hearing difficulties, hypothyroidism, vertebrae instability, umbilical hernia, and obesity. With early detection, however, most of these problems are treatable, and most individuals with DS lead healthy, full lives (Kozma, 1986b; Spiker & Hopmann, 1997).

Intellectual Characteristics

While the medical conditions associated with DS are treatable, the mental retardation associated with the syndrome cannot be treated medically. Fortunately, psychoeducational methods of intervention, which involve working directly with the children and their caregivers within their physical and social environments, may minimize the effects of mental retardation (Spiker & Hopmann, 1997). Most children with DS score in the mild-to-moderate range of retardation, although some are normal or near normal (Kozma, 1986a; McConnaughey, 1986). Young children with DS tend to perform poorly on both motor and mental tests of early learning (Wishart, 1988). This is not surprising, given the motor skills required for successful performance on these tests. Thus, over-reliance on test scores must be avoided, particularly because it could lead to lowered expectations for the children. Although the size and structural complexity of the brains of children with DS are less than that of children developing typically, it is not known how this specifically affects their mental functioning (Kozma, 1986a). It *is* known that many children with DS have shorter attention spans, make slower progress, and are less motivated than peers developing typically (McConnaughey, 1986).

The Edinburgh Longitudinal Study of Early Learning in Infants and Young Children investigated object concept development in children with and without DS (Wishart, 1988). Object concept development is considered a primary achievement during infancy, as well as a prerequisite for language development (Spiker & Hopmann, 1997). Findings from this study showed that the children with DS, unlike their peers who were developing typically, had difficulty consolidating tasks they had recently learned into new developmental demands. When encouraged, however, the children were able to retrieve the necessary information as long as the new task was not too far removed from their current level of functioning.

When tasks were presented that were more than one step beyond their current ability levels, the children protested or tried to divert the examiner's attention away from the task. The children again participated when the task was adjusted one step closer to their current level of functioning. The findings from this study indicate that the exploratory and motivational styles of children with DS may be less than optimal for development (Spiker & Hopmann, 1977; Wishart, 1988). These findings also imply that the zone of proximal development (ZPD), Vygotsky's term for the area slightly beyond a child's current competence (Rogoff, 1990), may be narrower for children with DS than for children developing typically.

Language Characteristics

The expressive language of children with DS tends to be far below their mental age. These delays are thought to be related to factors such as intermittent hearing losses, auditory processing difficulties, oral-motor hypotonicity, and structural differences (Gibbs & Carswell, 1991; Mahoney, Glover, & Finger, 1981).

Not only is the speech of many children with DS delayed, it is often unintelligible. The errors they produce are inconsistent and somewhat resistant to therapy. Although children may have difficulty with spontaneous speech, they tend to be able to imitate words correctly. The difficulties are thought to be related to tongue size, low muscle tone, chronic upper respiratory conditions, and frequent middle ear infections. Consequently, some children with DS may rely more on visual attention than on auditory attention (Dodd, McCormack, & Woodyatt, 1994). Hence, speech and language therapy, as well as total communication (the simultaneous presentation of manual signs and speech), is often recommended for children with DS.

Behavioral Characteristics

The varying presence of the above characteristics contributes to the behavior of children with DS. For example, many infants with DS, particularly those with more involved cognitive delays, show muted and delayed facial expressions. This characteristic decreases with age, however. In fact, after infancy, many children with DS show similar or greater facial expressiveness than children developing typically. The quality of facial expressions in children with DS may make it difficult for adults to read their cues accurately (Kasari & Hodapp, 1996; Kasari, Mundy, Yimiya, & Sigman, 1990). When adults misread children's cues, they may become less involved and provide fewer opportunities for interactions. Or, they may increase their involvement in a manner that may be intrusive or that the child might find overstimulating (Cicchetti & Beeghly, 1990b). Thus, the child's behavior is likely to influence, as well as be influenced by, interactions with adults (Kasari & Hodapp, 1996).

Research shows that children with DS interact with their mothers differently than do peers of the same mental age who are developing typically. Infants with DS have been found to take a less active role and use more meaningless vocalizations than do children who are developing typically (Mahoney & Robenalt, 1986). Additional differences have been found in attention skills, nonverbal requests for objects, and exploratory skills of children with DS (Landry & Chapieski, 1989). In addition, many children with DS have higher arousal thresholds than children developing typically. Consequently, they may take longer to react to stimuli, and longer to calm down once they have reacted (Cicchetti & Beeghly, 1990b).

Delay or Difference?

An unresolved issue in the literature on children with DS is whether their unique characteristics represent developmental delays or differences. While the sequence of development is similar in children with DS and children who are developing typically (Hodapp & Zigler, 1990), children with DS often experience delays in their developmental skills (Wishart, 1988). For these children, the trajectory of development is not as constant as that of children developing typically, and the rate of development tends to decline (Hodapp & Zigler, 1990; Wishart, 1988). But the delays represent more than "development in slow motion" (Cicchetti & Beeghly, 1990b, p. 54). They can lead "to significant differences in the unfolding of subsequent developmental processes? (Wishart, 1988, p. 17). Hence, the development of children with DS appears to differ both qualitatively and quantitatively (Cicchetti & Beeghly, 1990a).

In terms of intervention, we must consider the possibility that children with DS have both delays and differences. If we only look at the delays, we might approach children from a maturationist perspective and wait for them to "catch up." If we only look at the differences, we might approach the children as having deficits to "fix." By looking at delays as well as differences, we can determine children's current levels of functioning and provide experiences slightly above those levels. At the same time, we can seek ways to adapt experiences that build upon children's strengths and meet their needs. Thus, intervention would "take into account the unique characteristics of the child, the age- and stage-level of functioning, the experiences to which the child has been exposed, and the stability of environmental conditions" (Cicchetti & Beeghly, 1990b, p. 31). Moreover, we should consider and learn from children's relationships with primary caregivers, as well as with certain aspects of caregiving environments (Cicchetti & Beeghly, 1990b).

Adult-Child Interaction Research

If development is viewed as encompassing the "mutual involvement of children and their social world" (Rogoff, 1990, p. 27), then it makes sense to examine children's early social contexts, such as adult-child interactions. Interactions between infants and their primary caregivers (most often their mothers) provide a window through which to view development. There is considerable research involving mothers and children with and without DS. The findings have important implications for adults who are working and developing relationships with young children who have DS in preschool and child care settings.

Interaction Behaviors of Mothers of Children with Down Syndrome

Researchers have found that mothers of children with DS have more trouble reading their children's cues than do mothers of children who are developing typically (Landry & Chapieski, 1989). In a study by Kasari et al. (1990), children with DS exhibited more frequent shifts in their neutral and positive affect expressions than children matched according to mental age who were developing typically. The frequency of these shifts may contribute to mothers' difficulties in reading the cues of children with DS. These shifts could likewise be challenging for other caregivers.

Mothers of children of DS respond to their children as often as mothers of children developing typically. Mothers of children with DS have been found to take a more dominant role, however, which may be due to their infants' less active roles (Mahoney & Robenalt, 1986). Researchers also have reported that mothers of children with DS use directives more often than mothers of children who are developing typically. Their findings may have to do with the type of directives used. Mothers of children who are developing typically tend to use questions to give directions. Although researchers may not consider questions to be directives, they can be an implicit type of directive. It is possible that mothers of children with DS have found that their children do not respond to questions, and so they rely on commands or explicit directives (Maurer & Sherrod, 1987). Other caregivers and teachers may want to think about how they give directions and whether their method is effective for children with DS.

Joint Attention Within Interactions

Early interactions between infants and their primary caregivers frequently involve both partners visually attending to the same object in the environment. This skill is referred to as "joint attention," and is instrumental in social interaction learning (Harris, Kasari, & Sigman, 1996; Landry & Chapieski, 1989). During a child's first months of life, caregivers promote joint attention by pointing and showing objects. During the second half of the first year, children who are developing typically begin to physically explore objects. Active and sustained object exploration helps children learn about their worlds. For infants, a close relationship exists among cognitive processing, attentional capacity, and active exploration of objects (Landry & Chapieski, 1989).

In a study by Harris et al. (1996) in which children were matched according to mental age, caregivers and children with DS spent more time in joint attention than did dyads in which the children were developing typically. In addition, the caregivers of children with DS were more likely to select the toys on which the dyad focused than did the caregivers of children developing typically. In those cases where the toys were selected by children with DS, however, joint attention lasted longer, and an association was found 13 months later that showed improved language skills. For children developing typically, the researchers found no difference in later language skills between using child-selected and adult-selected toys. This finding is further supported by research showing that children with DS have difficulty shifting their focus of attention, and that doing so may provide fewer opportunities to attend to language (Harris et al., 1996). In addition, findings from the Kasari et al. (1990) study indicated that children with DS looked less often toward objects out of their reach than children developing typically, which may be related to nonverbal object requesting differences. Because these studies are correlational, it is difficult to draw implications about facilitating language development around child-selected versus adult-selected toys. They do provide support, however, for attending to children's cues and following their leads.

Implications for Early Childhood Caregivers and Teachers

Several implications can be drawn from the literature on adult-child interactions in general as well as from the research focusing on children with DS. Research on parent-child interactions confirms the importance of considering each child's history, the immediate context and task demands, and the child's strengths and needs as he or she interacts with other children. Researchers also have identified effective adult interaction characteristics, which include warmth, attentiveness, and responsiveness. Children who interact with warm, attentive, and responsive caregivers tend to function at a higher level than children who do not have caregivers with these characteristics (Landry & Chapieski, 1989).

The findings about parent-child interaction in general provide helpful guidelines for adults interacting with all children in child care, preschool, and primary school settings. Implications from research studies involving children with DS can then be applied according to specific adult-child interactions (McCollum & Bair, 1994). One such implication concerns adult and child roles. Because children with DS may take a less active role in interactions (Mahoney & Robenalt, 1986), adults working with these children may need to assume a more active role than they would with children who are developing typically.

A teacher might be uncomfortable taking an active role if he or she views the adult role as a dichotomy of child-directed versus teacher-directed. This perspective may be based on the early guidelines for developmentally appropriate practice (Bredekamp, 1987) in which didactic, teacher-directed approaches, when used "almost exclusively," were consider[ed] inappropriate. The revised guidelines, however, emphasize the need for both child-initiated and teacher-structured activities (Bredekamp & Copple, 1997). Adults working with children with DS should use a continuum of teaching strategies ranging from indirect to direct, depending on the needs and interests of the individual children involved and the specific situation.

Deciding on an approach to take requires reading the child's cues, which, as the research indicates, can be a difficult task. Yet, it is especially important to be able to read a child's cues when trying to jointly attend to objects. Doing so allows the adult to follow the child's lead in deciding upon which objects to attend to; increased attention is related to increased language proficiency about the objects (Harris et al., 1996). Therefore, teachers need to persevere in their attempts (McCollum & Bair, 1994). Doing so in a warm, attentive, and responsive manner is likely to lead to success and help expand children's learning opportunities. Teachers and other caregivers can learn from parents who are "able to match their children's needs for support" within interactions, thus succeeding "at setting the stage for participation, practice, and ultimately, development" (McCollum & Bair, 1994, p. 99).

A final implication from the research pertains to the use of questions when giving directions. Questions allow for choices. Although it is important to offer children choices, adults should not do so if they are not prepared to accept the child's choice. For example, asking children if they want to put their coats on when it is time to go home on a wintry day is inappropriate. Yet, adults often give directions this way. This habit may be additionally troublesome for children with DS, who may have difficulty understanding such implicit directives (Maurer & Sherrod, 1987).

Differences in interaction styles may reflect that the optimal environment for children developing typically (Maurer & Sherrod, 1987). Adults working with young children need to be able to adjust their interactions and structure children's activities and environments in ways that support each child (Rogoff, 1990). They must provide learning environments that are optimal for all children, knowing that one size may not fit all! Research on children with DS illustrates the need for ongoing, continuous individualization. The research also challenges us to reconsider our views of normalcy and deficiency, in order to help all individuals reach their maximum potential.

References

Bredekamp, S. (Ed.). (1987). *Developmentally appropriate practice in early childhood programs serving children from birth through age 8.* Expanded edition. Washington, DC: National Association for the Education of Young Children.

Bredekamp, S., & Copple, C. (Eds.). (1997). *Developmentally appropriate practice in early childhood programs* (Rev. ed.). Washington, DC: National Association for the Education of Young Children.

Cicchetti, D., & Beeghly, M. (1990a). Preface. In D. Cicchetti & M. Beeghly (Eds.), *Children with Down syndrome: A developmental perspective* (pp. ix–xiii). New York: Cambridge University Press.

Cicchetti, D., & Beeghly, M. (1990b). An organizational approach to the study of Down syndrome: Contributions to an integrative theory of development. In D. Cicchetti & M. Beeghly (Eds.), *Children with Down syndrome: A developmental perspective* (pp. 29–62). New York: Cambridge University Press.

Dodd, B., McCormack, P., & Woodyatt, G. (1994). Evaluation of an intervention program: Relation between children's phonology and parents' communicative behavior. *American Journal on Mental Retardation, 98,* 632–645.

Fetters, L. (1996). Motor development. In M. J. Hanson (Eds.), *Atypical infant development* (pp. 403–448). Austin, TX: Pro-ed.

Gibbs, E. D., & Carswell, L. E. (1991). Using total communication with young children with Down syndrome: A literature review and case study. *Early Education and Development, 2,* 306–320.

Harris, S., Kasari, C., & Sigman, M. D. (1996). Joint attention and language gains in children with Down syndrome. *American Journal of Mental Retardation, 100,* 608–619.

Hodapp, R. M., & Zigler, E. (1990). Applying the developmental perspective to individuals with Down syndrome. In D. Cicchetti & M. Beeghly (Eds.), *Children with Down syndrome: A developmental perspective* (pp. 1–28). New York: Cambridge University Press.

Kasari, C., & Hodapp, R. M. (1996). Is Down syndrome different? Evidence from social and family studies. *Down Syndrome Quarterly, 1*(4), 1–8.

Kasari, C., Mundy, P., Yimiya, N., & Sigman, M. (1990). Affect and attention in children with Down syndrome. *American Journal of Mental Retardation, 95,* 55–67.

Kozma, C. (1986a). What is Down syndrome? In K. Stray-Gundersen (Ed.), *Babies with Down syndrome: A new parents guide* (pp. 1–25). Kensington, MD: Woodbine House.

Kozma, C. (1986b). Medical concerns and treatments. In K. Stray-Gundersen (Ed.), *Babies with Down syndrome: A new parents guide* (pp. 47–65). Kensington, MD: Woodbine House.

Landry, S. H., & Chapieski, M. L. (1989). Joint attention and infant toy exploration: Effects of Down syndrome and prematurity. *Child Development, 60,* 103–118.

Mahoney, G., Glover, A., & Finger, I. (1981). Relationship between language and sensorimotor development of Down syndrome and nonretarded children. *American Journal of Mental Deficiency, 86,* 21–27.

Mahoney, G., & Robenalt, K. (1986). A comparison of conversational patterns between mothers and the Down syndrome and normal infants. *Journal of the Division of Early Childhood, 10,* 172–180.

Maurer, H., & Sherrod, K. B. (1987). Context of directives given to young children with Down syndrome and nonretarded children: Development over two years. *American Journal of Mental Deficiency, 91,* 579–590.

McCollum, J. A., & Blair, H. (1994). Research in parent-child interaction: Guidance to developmentally appropriate practice for young children with disabilities. In B. L. Mallory & R. S. New (Eds.), *Diversity and developmentally appropriate practices: Challenges for early childhood education* (pp. 84–106). New York: Teachers College Press.

McConnaughey, F. (1986). Your babies' development. In K. Stray-Gundersen (Ed.), *Babies with Down syndrome: A new parents guide* (pp. 109–131). Kensington, MD: Woodbine House.

Nadel, L. (1988). Introduction. In L. Nadel (Ed.), *The psychobiology of Down syndrome* (1–3). Cambridge, MA: The MIT Press.

National Down Syndrome Congress. (1994). *Down Syndrome.* Atlanta, GA: Author.

National Information Center for Children and Youth with Disabilities, (1994). *General information about Down syndrome.* Washington, DC: Author.

Rogoff, B. (1990). *Apprenticeship in thinking: Cognitive development in social context.* New York: Oxford University Press.

Spiker, D., & Hopmann, M. R. (1997). The effectiveness of early intervention for children with Down syndrome. In M. J. Guralnick (Ed.), *The effectiveness of early intervention* (pp. 271–305). Baltimore, MD: Brookes.

Wishart, J. G. (1988). Early learning in infants and young children with Down syndrome. In L. Nadel (Ed.), *The psychobiology of Down syndrome* (pp. 7–50). Cambridge, MA: The MIT Press.

GETTING THE STUDENT WITH HEAD INJURIES BACK IN SCHOOL:

Strategies for the Classroom

Strategies for successfully returning students with head injuries to school

By Mary Steensma

In 1979, when he was 12 years old, Jamie was hit by a car while riding his bike. In the seconds it took for the car to hit his bike and his head to hit the pavement, Jamie went from being a gifted sixth-grade boy to being a student with head injuries in the special education system. There were no programs to help him, and no support groups for parents. The schools had no information or guidance for designing programs to meet Jamie's needs.

In 1989, when he was 12, Matt was hit by a car while riding his bike. He too went from being a gifted sixth-grade boy to being a head injured student in the special education system. But here Matt's story differs from Jamie's. In December 1989, after weeks of outpatient therapy and 3 months in a transitional educational program, he returned to his class in school. Matt's head injury did change his life: Things are not the way they used to be for Matt or his family. But in his case, the school and his parents had information and assistance, and Matt's transition back to school was more successful than Jamie's.

In a review of educational studies of children with head injuries, Telzrow (1987) noted that these children do not make a good educational adjustment. She cited studies showing that the majority of head injured students (56%) in special education classes are in programs for students with physical handicaps and mild to profound levels of retardation (Brink, Garrett, Hale, Woo-Sam, & Nickle, 1970). Students whose brain injuries have resulted in significant character change and difficult behavior have often been placed in behavior disorder classrooms. The less severely brain injured students are often placed in learning disability or resource rooms.

But students who suffer head trauma differ from students with emotional disturbance, learning disabilities, or mental retardation in one important way: Their disabilities are acquired suddenly and result from neurological damage to specific areas of the brain. The head injured student may retain skills and information, and IQ scores may return to within the normal range (Chadwick, Rutter, Brown, Schaffer, & Traub, 1981).

When students are released from the hospital or in-patient facility, they should be medically recovered from the injury, but they are rarely ready to return to school—and the school is rarely ready to receive them. The students still have a variety of cognitive and emotional problems that affect their educational adjustment, and typically these problems are not addressed in reintegrating them to their school. Optimally, these deficits should be addressed during a transition period of several months in a setting with a low teacher/student ratio and minimal distractions. A classroom with a 1:3 ratio and a maximum class size of six is preferable to a classroom with a ratio of 1:3 and a maximum of 12 students.

The students who have had recent head injuries often are not aware of how the injury has affected their behavior and ability to do schoolwork. Like people who have experienced the death of someone close, they may go through the stages of grief—denial, anger, bargaining, and depression. Without an effective transition program to help the students become aware of their new deficits, they may build up a wall of denial and defensive behaviors to cope with the effects of the accident. This may become as debilitating as the injury itself.

Transition Program Structure

The primary goal of a transitional program is to place students back in their school districts in programs that best meet their current needs. To be successful, the transitional program should begin immediately after primary rehabilitation needs have been met. The students are given neuropsychological evaluations to isolate specific cognitive and neurobehavioral problems. During the initial months, all classroom activities should take place in a self-contained classroom with a high degree of control and a low staff-student ratio. Telzrow (1987) emphasizes the importance of this, as well as McCabe and Green's (1987) study of three severely brain injured adolescents. The adolescents showed a need for consistent, authoritative handling in a controlled structure. Without this, they exhibited a "fight or flight" reaction. Program goals in the first few months are to increase the students' awareness of how the injury has affected them, to develop coping strategies, and to build tolerance for classroom activities.

When school reintegration begins, the program enters a new phase. Teacher and staff members receive in-service training on head trauma and the special needs of the students as outlined in the Individualized Education Plan developed by the transition classroom teacher. The students are reintegrated slowly to build tolerance for larger classes, room transitions, and the variety of people with whom they must interact.

Classroom Strategies

Head injured students need to relearn how to learn. Although many skills are preserved and students' IQs may be within the normal range, the ability to draw on their knowledge and skills is impaired. Because the students do not respond well to traditional classroom strategies, teacher and students often become angry and frustrated. Six common deficits that students exhibit—and some classroom strategies for working around them—are discussed in the following paragraphs.

Problem: Structure

Head injured students have lost some of the ability to organize their work and environment. The impact on their school work is obvious in the inability to take notes or write an essay with a logical structure. But the students may also be unable to keep track of their books and assignments or to organize their morning routines. These problems are less obvious signs of an inability to organize and may be attributed instead to carelessness or resistance to school.

Strategy. The teacher must build the structure around the students and teach compensatory techniques. For example: Keep one set of books at school and one

> *"Without an effective transition program to help the students become aware of their new deficits, they may build up a wall of denial and defensive behaviors to cope with the effects of the accident. This may become as debilitating as the injury itself."*

at home to eliminate the problem of forgotten books. To reduce confusion and lost notebooks, use a five-subject notebook instead of five separate notebooks. Schedule a resource room or study hall at the end of the day to allow the students to "check in" with a staff member and make sure all assignments are recorded and understood.

Problem: Abstraction

Head injured students find it difficult to summarize, draw conclusions, and differentiate fact from opinion. This often makes essay questions on tests or assignments and higher level math concepts quite difficult.

Strategy. Initially, essay questions and reports must be avoided as methods of testing students' knowledge in content area subjects, since students are unable to effectively retrieve information using this approach. Information must be kept concrete and learned gradually in a structured manner. New information is broken down into smaller units and reinforced in writing. Progress takes time and repetition. Finding the main idea or summarizing a story must be taught with specific steps to follow, one at a time. These steps should be presented in writing and kept in the students' notebooks.

Problem: Attention and Concentration

Cognitive and physical fatigue are important factors affecting students' ability to make the transition back into school. Head injured students tire quickly and may be physically unable to sustain concentration through a full day at school and additional activities or studying at night.

Cognitively, students rapidly reach a "saturation" level where they simply stop processing information. Like a water glass that begins overflowing when you reach the top, head injured students may simply stop hearing the instructions given to them halfway through a 45-minute class period.

In addition to being unable to sustain attention and concentration, head injured students are very sensitive to distraction. Asking the students to read or take a test in a regular classroom of 12 to 20 students is equivalent to trying to compute your taxes at a Rolling Stones concert.

Strategy. Lessons initially are kept to 15 or 20 minutes and are increased gradually. Even after the student's tolerance has been increased to 30 to 40 minutes in a transitional classroom, he or she will suffer some cognitive and physical fatigue when placed back in regular classes at school. This can be compensated for by alternating content area subjects such as History and English with time spent in the resource room, lunch, gym, and so forth. This allows time for the students to "down load" information from one class before beginning another. Since students will begin to fatigue as the day goes on, classes that allow more flexibility should be scheduled for the later periods in school. In addition to alternating the content area subjects with catch-up periods and making sure that the content area subjects are not scheduled for final periods, the student's course load must be reduced to only those classes required for graduation.

Problem: Transition

For head injured students, transitions always seem to create problems. The primary focus is usually on the students' difficulties with physical transitions—from home to school, or from class to class. Equally difficult are the students' mental transitions within a specific subject, and from one format to another. For example, students may have difficulty transferring math problems from the book to paper, or switching from fraction problems to decimals while completing a worksheet.

Strategy. The physical transition of head injured students back into school must be thought of as a desensitization process. It must be taken step by step with a safety net positioned underneath.

For example: Students are ready to leave the transitional classroom and join a regular ninth-grade class.

Step 1: They visit the first class they will join, walking through the route to the class and bathrooms. This visit is kept simple and covers only the essentials. Lockers, homerooms, and other important places are introduced gradually, one at a time.

Step 2: Students are met at their bus by someone they know and are escorted to class. Initially there are no changes from class to class.

Step 3: Class changes are practiced, walked through, and added one at a time. Class changes are made with someone from the class, if possible.

Throughout the desensitization process, students continue to attend the self-contained transitional classroom. The hours in this classroom are reduced gradually as students are reintroduced to their regular classes. This continued contact with the self-contained classroom acts as a safety net to handle any problems that may occur during the transition.

Transitions within subject areas, or from one subject to the next, can be handled for head injured students much as teachers handle students with learning disabilities. Transitions on a worksheet page are reduced and clearly delineated. Pages from books or workbooks can be copied so the students do not need to make the transition from book to paper. If possible, outlines in content area subjects should be handed out on worksheets—not placed on the board to be copied by students.

Problem: Writing

Neurological damage may cause partial paralysis in head injured students that affects the physical ability to write. It may also affect students' ability to organize or express thoughts. Students' writing speed often is reduced as well. Particularly for junior high or high school students, this makes re-entry difficult because so much of the work involves taking notes, writing reports, and answering written homework questions.

Strategies. For lectures and instructions that must be recorded, a micro-cassette recorder is effective. Students can carry it to all classes and record information inconspicuously, and the information can then be played back and repeated at the students' speed.

Often, writing must be retaught as a skill in a very structured fashion. The steps of brainstorming, organizing information, constructing topic sentences, supplying details, and summarizing must be set out in writing for reference each time students write.

As mentioned previously, teachers should hand out preprinted lecture notes, assignments, and other information given orally. Students with handwriting problems may be able to learn to use a computer effectively for outlining and word processing and should be allowed to use the computer as a compensatory strategy.

Problem: Processing Speed

Most students who have had a head injury process information more slowly. This means the students' auditory, visual, or reaction speed may be slower than before the accident. How the students process information depends on the seriousness and site of the head injury. The slowed processing speed may affect the students' ability to read assignments, listen to directions, and take notes.

Strategies. All textbooks students use in school also should be recorded on tape. This allows students to listen to the text while following it in the book. All standard junior high and high school textbooks are available on tape through Recording for the Blind for blind, physically, and perceptually handicapped students. Recording for the Blind headquarters are located at 20 Roszel Road, Princeton, NJ 08540. This service can be reached toll free outside New Jersey by calling 1–800/221–4792. With the special-format tapes used by Recording for the Blind, students can control the playback speed.

Testing procedures must be modified so that time limits are eliminated or extended.

Conclusion

Head injured students can return to school successfully. However, it takes more time, intervention, and money than the average special education student gets. Students with head injury require a highly structured, consistent program that changes as their needs change. School staff members must understand and be trained to deal with the cognitive and psychological changes caused by the head trauma and the grieving process that follows. Students are atypical in their performance and needs, and they cannot be judged by standard test data. If the school is able to meet students' needs in the early stages of their re-entry, their chances for a successful re-entry are good. This in turn will reduce their special education needs as they continue in school.

Mary Steensma, MA, is a teacher and consultant who helps students with head injuries re-enter regular classrooms. Address: Mary Steensma, 211 Mildorf St., Rochester, NY 14609.

References

Brink, J.D., Garrett, A.L., Hale, W.R., Woo-Sam, J., & Nickle, V.L. (1970). Recovery of motor and intellectual function in children sustaining severe head injuries. *Developmental Medicine and Child Neurology, 12,* 565–571.

Chadwick, O., Rutter, M., Brown, G., Shaffer, D., & Traub, B. (1981). A prospective study of children with head injuries: II. Cognitive sequelae. *Psychological Medicine, 11,* 49–61.

McCabe, R.J.R., & Green, P. (1987). Rehabilitating severely head-injured adolescents: Three case reports. *Journal of Child Psychology, 28,* 111–125.

Telzrow, C.F. (1987, November). Management of academic and educational problems in head injuries. *Journal of Learning Disabilities, 20,* 536–545.

Identifying Depression
in Students with Mental Retardation

Laura M. Stough
Lynn Baker

The belief that people with mental retardation are always happy, carefree, and content is a misconception. In reality, students with mental retardation are at risk for the same types of psychological disorders as are students without cognitive deficits (Crews, Bonaventura, & Rowe, 1994; Johnson, Handen, Lubetsky, & Sacco, 1995; Sovner & Hurley, 1983).

Many researchers have actually found a *higher* rate of depressive disorders in people with mental retardation (e.g., Borthwick-Duffy & Eyman, 1990; Menolascino, 1990; Reiss, 1990). Teachers should be aware of this increased risk for depression so that they can appropriately refer their students for diagnosis and treatment. In this article, we present suggestions for detecting and treating childhood depression.

Figure 1. Signs of Major Depression

Look for five or more of these symptoms in the same 2-week period. These symptoms should represent a *change* from the person's previous typical level of functioning:
- Depressed or irritable mood most of the day, nearly every day.
- Decreased interest in pleasurable activities.
- Significant weight loss or weight gain.
- Sleeping problems.
- Activity level has increased or decreased.
- Fatigue or energy loss.
- Feelings of worthlessness or guilt.
- Loss of concentration.
- Thoughts of death.

Source: Adapted from the *Diagnostic and Statistical Manual of Mental Disorders-Fourth Edition,* by the American Psychiatric Association, 1994, Washington, DC: Author.

Prevalence and Symptoms of Depression

Although little research has investigated the precise prevalence of depression in children with mental retardation, special education teachers will likely encounter students with depression. Several studies have suggested that these children exhibit symptoms of sadness, loneliness, and worry at a much higher rate than do their peers without disabilities (e.g., Matson & Frame, 1986; Reiss, 1985). These studies estimated that as many as 10% of children with mental retardation suffer from depression, in contrast to the lower prevalence rate of 1%–5% in children without mental retardation (Cantwell, 1990).

Clinical depression is usually determined by a psychologist or psychiatrist, who uses the *Diagnostic and Statistical Manual of Mental Disorders, Fourth Edition* (DSM-IV; American Psychiatric Association, 1994) to make the diagnosis. To be formally diagnosed as "depressed," a child must experience *five different clinical signs of depression* over a 2-week period. The primary symptom is that the student exhibits either an overall depressed mood or a loss of interest in daily activities (also called *anhedonia*). Some students may express this depressed mood in the form of persistent irritability, rather than by sadness or withdrawal.

The remaining four symptoms are expressed as *changes* in a student's usual functioning. These changes may be expressed as either an increase or decrease in any of the following areas: (a) appetite or weight; (b) sleep habits; (c) activity level; (d) energy level; (e) feelings of worthlessness or guilt; (f) difficulty thinking, concentrating, or making decisions; or (g) recurrent thoughts of death or suicidal ideations, plans, or attempts (see Figure 1).

Causes of Depression

Students may experience depression as a result of a negative life event, such as the loss of a parent, stresses at home, or adjustment to a new environment. This type of reactive depression is normal and is not a cause for concern unless the depressive symptoms linger and significantly interfere with a student's typical level of functioning. In other cases, there may not be a clear precursor for the depression, yet the student consistently is in a depressed mood. It is when this mood persists over a 2-week period that a teacher should observe the child for other signs of depression.

Students with *mild* mental retardation seem to be at risk for depression because they often can perceive that their peers without disabilities are able to accomplish tasks that they themselves cannot (Eaton & Menolascino, 1982). They may also be aware, via negative peer experiences, that they are different and viewed negatively by society. These observations can then lead to a higher risk for depression and low self-esteem. Conversely, people with *severe* mental retardation are not as likely to be diagnosed with depression as those with mild retardation, but this may be because of their limited ability to verbally express feelings of sadness or hopelessness, rather than an actual decreased risk for depression (Charlot, Doucette, & Mezzacappa, 1993; Pawlarcyzk & Beckwith, 1987). As a result, depression may be easily overlooked in people with severe mental retardation.

Difficulty of Detection and Diagnosis in Students with Mental Retardation

Teachers, parents, and direct care workers are usually the first to notice that a child with

> As many as 10% of children with mental retardation suffer from depression, in contrast to the lower prevalence rate of 1%–5% in children without mental retardation.

mental retardation is having a problem; however, they often find it hard to determine if the problem is behavioral or emotional (Borthwick-Duffy, 1994). Often, diagnosticians and psychologists tend to attribute symptoms of depression to a student's limited cognitive functioning, rather than to the depression that the student is experiencing. This underdiagnosis of depression is called *diagnostic overshadowing,* in that the depression is deemphasized because the student additionally is labeled as mentally retarded (Crews et al., 1994; White et al., 1995).

The lack of understanding that most psychologists have about students with mental retardation usually results from the lack of exposure that psychologists have had with this population. Phelps and Hammer estimated that fewer than 25% of professionals in the area of psychology receive information about mental retardation in their graduate programs (as cited by Nezu, 1994). As a result, the teacher's input to the psychologist about a student's emotional well-being is extremely important.

The classroom teacher continually monitors the cognitive, social, and emotional well-being of students. Although many students with mild mental retardation can verbalize their feelings of depression, those with more severe limitations tend to express their depression primarily through changes in their behavior. The teacher can help detect these changes in students' behavior by being sensitive to variations in their overall mood or activity level. Teachers can help identify when a student's behavior has changed in its frequency, intensity, or duration.

For example, some students with mental retardation who are experiencing depression become more aggressive (Reiss & Rojahn, 1993). In these cases, the teacher can give valuable input about how typical the aggressive behavior is and when the behavior first was exhibited by the student. Such input can offset the previously mentioned "overshadowing" in correctly diagnosing depression in students with mental retardation.

Detecting Symptoms in the Classroom

Behavioral Markers

It is most common for a person who is depressed to exhibit an overall mood of sadness. Children with mental retardation, however, may express their sadness through withdrawing and decreasing their social interactions with their peers. Alternatively, they may change the way in which they interact with their peers, becoming irritable or even aggressive toward them. Also, teachers should pay attention when students exhibit new, inappropriate behavior, such as noncompliance or distractibility. In some cases, students may even begin to express their depression through self-injurious behavior. Although behavioral markers such as these may stand out, they may also be quite subtle: A depressed student may simply not seem to take pleasure in activities that he or she previously enjoyed.

Physical Markers

People with depression usually experience changes in their *vegetative functioning,* or eating and sleeping patterns. Students with mental retardation may also exhibit these signs. Teachers should be aware of changes in overall activity level (either a decrease or an increase) in their students. A student who usually is calm and methodical may show signs of hyperactivity, whereas a student who usually maintains a high level of activity may become withdrawn and slow to respond to stimuli. Changes in weight or

> Students with *mild* mental retardation seem to be at risk for depression because they often can perceive that their peers without disabilities are able to accomplish tasks that they themselves cannot.

interest in food can also be markers of depression. Again, the teacher should look for changes in usual student patterns: the formerly thin student who puts on a substantial amount of weight quickly or the voracious eater who suddenly has no appetite.

Sleep behavior can also be a sign of depression, either increased sleeping or a decrease in the hours the student sleeps. A common occurrence for someone who is depressed is to have little difficulty going to sleep but then awaken in the early morning.

Figure 2. Ideas for Treating Students' Depression Across Life Settings

Skill Building
- Develop the student's communication skills.
- Try a social skills unit to develop interpersonal skills.
- Focus on problem-solving.
- Teach conflict resolution.

Resource Networking
- Work with the family to find needed community resources.
- Start a parent support group in your school.
- Obtain literature from a mental health center about depression.

Expression Opportunities
- Develop nonverbal means for student expression: music, dance, art.
- Role-play potentially stressful situations and appropriate solutions.
- Use films and stories to teach problem-solving.

Relationship Opportunities
- Have pets in class.
- Have students write or draw to pen pals.
- Provide appropriate peer-group opportunities.
- Invite volunteers from the community to develop supportive friendships.
- Find group activities outside the school setting appropriate for the student.

Teachers should be aware that sleepy or lethargic students may be suffering from these sleep disturbances during the night.

Treatment of Depression in Children with Mental Retardation

The Individuals with Disabilities Education Act (IDEA) not only ensures the right to free and appropriate educational services, but also to related services, such as psychological assessment and counseling. Many times the school district has programs or staff that can help a student diagnosed as depressed. Once the student has been assessed, the teacher can work closely with the school psychologist or counselor to provide supportive therapy for the student.

The teacher can also discuss with the family any additional support needs that they might have as these needs may contribute to the stress that the student is experiencing. Loss of employment, death of a family member, or economic hardships can all affect the student's level of depression. Teachers should be aware of changes in their students' home environments to help determine if a student is depressed—as opposed to, for example, simple being oppositional. These support needs often occur across settings, for example, at family outings or at recreational activities (see Figure 2).

Examining the settings in which a student functions on a regular basis can help pinpoint obstacles or difficulties that the student is experiencing in these areas, for example, appropriately talking to peers at the community pool. Knowledge of these difficulties thus can help the teacher target instructional objectives for the student in the classroom, such as learning social skills training.

Psychological Services

Psychological services in the mental health community are limited for people with mental retardation. One reason for this may be the bureaucratic structure of these services. Typically, services for people with mental retardation and services for people with mental health needs are provided separately. This separation of services often results in a quandary between agencies as to who should provide services and, often, in a lack of services for the person who is "dually diagnosed."

The most popular forms of psychological services used for children without cognitive limitations experiencing depression may also be used with children with mental retardation. The most popular forms of therapy for children with depression are behavioral therapy, social and adaptive skills training, psychotherapy, and the use of psychiatric medications. These and additional treatment modalities are listed in Figure 3.

Figure 3. Possible Types of Therapy Appropriate for Use with Students with Depression

Individual psychotherapy: The student discusses issues with a counselor or psychologist on an individual basis. The focus is on the student's perceptions and behaviors. The student is usually guided to make his or her own interpretations and goals for change.

Group psychotherapy: Usually a group is formed around a common problem that each member of the group shares to some degree. Groups are usually facilitated by a professional counselor or psychologist. The involvement and support of the other group members are part of the therapeutic treatment.

Family therapy: The family meets with a psychologist or counselor who moderates while problems and solutions are generated by the family members. Family interactions, perceptions, and roles are the areas of focus and change.

Skills training: Building social skills allows the student to engage in social situations while he or she receives modeling and coaching from a therapist or teacher. These social situations allow the student to practice skills in particular deficit areas.

Psychodrama: Guided by a psychologist or counselor, the student acts out themes or roles that represent areas of concern and unresolved conflict. The drama provides emotional release and insight into these areas of concern.

Art therapy: A nonverbal therapy, usually directed by a psychologist, counselor, or art therapist, art therapy uses art as the milieu in which emotions and thoughts can be expressed freely.

Music therapy: A nonverbal therapy, usually directed by a psychologist, counselor, or music therapist, music therapy uses music to help students express and release emotions.

Play therapy: A psychologist or counselor works with the student as he or she plays with toys or other materials that permit expression of conflict issues.

Psychopharmacology: This type of therapy uses prescription drugs to treat medical problems associated with mental disorders.

> When we ignore signs of depression in children with mental retardation, these children become at risk for being misunderstood, underestimated, and untreated.

Because children with mental retardation are a heterogeneous group, the mental health provider must make modifications in these approaches and techniques. Rubin (1983) suggested that providers should consider the following characteristics of a child when providing psychological services to a student with mental retardation:

- Intellectual aptitude.
- Capacity for relationships.
- Neurological functioning.
- Communication skills.

In addition, the mental health provider should always be apprised of the student's current medication intake and medical history.

Final Thoughts

Intellectual functioning does not seem to offset depression; in fact, those with mild mental retardation seem to be at an even greater risk for depression. We say, "seem to be," because of the paucity of recent research in this important area. In addition, many treatment techniques for depression that have proven successful in persons without retardation remain untested in those with mental retardation (Sevin & Matson, 1994).

Children with mental retardation experience pain, loss, and depression as do other people. When we ignore signs of depression in children with mental retardation, these children become at risk for being misunderstood, underestimated, and untreated.

References

American Psychiatric Association. (1994). *Diagnostic and statistical manual of mental disorders* (4th ed.). Washington, DC: Author.

Borthwick-Duffy, S. A. (1994). Epidemiology and prevalence of psychopathology in individuals with mental retardation. *Journal of Consulting and Clinical Psychology, 62*, 17–27.

Read More About It

General Information on Depression and Mental Retardation
Borthwick-Duffy, S. A., & Eyman, R. K. (1990). Who are the dually diagnosed? *American Journal on Mental Retardation, 94*, 586–595.

Charlot, L. R., Doucette, A. C., & Mezzacappa, E. (1993). Affective symptoms of institutionalized adults with mental retardation. *American Journal on Mental Retardation, 98*, 408–416.

Matson, J. L., & Barrett, R. P. (1990). Affective disorders. In J. L. Matson & R. P. Barrett (Eds.) *Psychopathology in the mentally retarded* (pp. 121–146). New York: Grune & Straton.*

Menolascino, F. J. (1990). The nature and types of mental illness in the mentally retarded. In M. Lewis & S. M. Miller (Eds.), *Handbook of developmental psychology* (pp. 397–408). New York: Plenum.*

Treatment and Counseling
Hurley, A. D. (1989). Individual psychotherapy with mentally retarded individuals: A review and call for research. *Research in Developmental Disabilities, 10*, 261–275.

Nezu, C. M., Nezu, A. M., & Gill-Weiss, M. J. (1992). *Psychopathology in persons with mental retardation: Guidelines for assessment and treatment.* Champaign, IL: Research Press.*

Petronko, M. R., Harris, S., & Kormann, R. J. (1994). Community-based behavioral training approaches for people with mental retardation and mental illness. *Journal of Consulting and Clinical Psychology, 62*, 49–54.

Schroeder, S. R., Schroeder, C. S., & Landesman, S. (1987). Psychological services in educational settings to persons with mental retardation. *American Psychologist, 42*, 805–808.

Borthwick-Duffy, S. A., & Eyman, R. K. (1990). Who are the dually diagnosed? *American Journal on Mental Retardation, 94*, 586–595.

Cantwell, D. P. (1990). Depression across the early life span. In M. Lewis & S. M. Miller (Eds.), *Handbook of developmental psychopathology* (pp. 293–310). New York: Plenum.*

Charlot, L. R., Doucette, A. C., & Mezzacappa, E. (1993). Affective symptoms of institutionalized adults with mental retardation. *American Journal on Mental Retardation, 98*, 408–416.

Crews, W. D., Bonaventura, S., & Rowe, F. (1994). Dual diagnosis: Prevalence of psychiatric disorders in a large state residential facility for individuals with mental retardation. *American Journal on Mental Retardation, 98*, 688–731.

Eaton, L. F., & Menolascino, F. J. (1982). Psychiatric disorders in the mentally retarded: Types, problems, and challenges. *American Journal of Psychiatry, 139*, 1297–1303.

Johnson, C. R., Handen, B. L., Lubetsky, M. J., & Sacco, K. A. (1995). Affective disorders in hospitalized children and adolescents with mental retardation: A retrospective study. *Research in Developmental Disabilities, 16*, 221–231.

Matson, J. L., & Frame, C. L. (1986). *Psychopathology among mentally retarded children and adolescents* (Vol. 6). Beverly Hills: Sage.*

Menolascino, F. J. (1990). The nature and types of mental illness in the mentally retarded. In M. Lewis & S. M. Miller (Eds.), *Handbook of developmental psychology* (pp. 397–408). New York: Plenum.*

Nezu, A. M. (1994). Introduction to special section: Mental retardation and mental illness. *Journal of Consulting and Clinical Psychology, 62*(1), 4–5.

Pawlarcyzk, D., & Beckwith, B. E. (1987). Depressive symptoms displayed by persons with mental retardation: A review. *Mental Retardation, 25*, 325–530.

Reiss, S. A. (1985). The mentally retarded, emotionally disturbed adult. In M. Sigman (Ed.), *Children with emotional disorders and developmental disabilities: Assessment and treatment* (pp. 171–193). Orlando, FL: Grune & Stratton.*

Reiss, S. A. (1990). Prevalence of dual diagnosis in community-based day programs in the Chicago metropolitan area. *American Journal on Mental Retardation 94*, 578–585.

Reiss, S. A., & Rojahn, J. (1993). Joint occurrence of depression and aggression in children and adults with mental retardation. *Journal of Intellectual Disability Research, 37*, 287–294.

Rubin, R. L. (1983). Bridging the gap through individual counseling and psychotherapy with mentally retarded people. In F. J. Menolascino (Ed.), *Mental health and mental retardation: Bridging the gap* (pp. 119–128). Baltimore: University Park Press.

Sevin, J. A., & Matson, J. L. (1994). An overview of psychopathology. In D. C. Strohmer & H. T. Prout (Eds.), *Counseling and psychotherapy with persons with mental retardation and borderline intelligence* (pp. 21–78). Brandon, VT: Clinical Psychology Publishing.*

Sovner, R., & Hurley, A. (1983). Do the mentally retarded suffer from affective illness? *Archives of General Psychiatry 40*, 61–70.

White, M. J., Nicholas, C. N., Cook, R. S., Spengler, P. M., Walker, B. S., & Look, K. K. (1995). Diagnostic overshadowing and mental retardation: A meta-analysis. *American Journal on Mental Retardation, 100*, 293–298.

BooksNow

*To order books marked by an asterisk (*), please call 24 hrs/365 days: 1-800-BOOKS-NOW (266–5766) or (801) 261–1187, or visit them on the Web at http://www.BooksNow.com/TeachingExceptional.htm. Use VISA, M/C, or AMEX or send check or money order + $4.95 S&H ($2.50 each add'l item) to: Books Now, Suite 125, 448 East 6400 South, Salt Lake City, UT 84107.

Laura M. Stough (CEC Texas Federation), Senior Lecturer; and **Lynn Baker,** Doctoral Candidate, Department of Educational Psychology, Texas A&M University, College Station.

Address correspondence to Laura M. Stough, Department of Educational Psychology, Texas A&M University, 704 Harrington Tower, College Station, TX 77843–4225 (e-mail: stough@acs.tamu.edu).

Unit 6

Unit Selections

20. **Teaching Students to Regulate Their Own Behavior,** Lewis R. Johnson and Christine E. Johnson
21. **"Look! I'm on TV!" Using Videotaped Self-Modeling to Change Behavior,** Tom Buggey
22. **How to Defuse Defiance, Threats, Challenges, Confrontations . . . ,** Geoff Colvin, David Ainge, and Ron Nelson

Key Points to Consider

❖ What are the five steps of behavioral self-regulation? Are students with emotional and behavioral disorders willing to use self-regulation of their behaviors? Why or why not?

❖ How will students react to an edited version of their own behaviors on television that shows only compliant acceptable behaviors?

❖ What should adults be aware of to defuse confrontational scenes in the classroom? How can a classroom environment be made more conducive to education?

 Links www.dushkin.com/online/

23. **Resources in Emotional or Behavioral Disorders (EBD)**
    http://www.gwu.edu/~ebdweb/index.html

These sites are annotated on pages 4 and 5.

Emotional and Behavioral Disorders

The 1990s gave rise to a strange and tragic way for children with emotional and behavioral disturbances to vent their frustrations. They took a weapon to school and engaged in a shooting spree. While the actual incidence of school shootings was not large, many children with distressed lives threatened to adopt copy-cat behaviors. What would make a young person (frequently on the cusp of puberty) think about committing such a grotesquely absurd act? An easy, often-cited reason is that they are barraged with images of violence on the news, in music, on videos, on TV programs, and in movies. It is too facile: The barrage is aimed at everyone, yet only a few decide that they want to become violent and harm others. Aggressive, acting-out children commonly come from homes where they see *real* violence, anger, and insults. They often feel disconnected, rejected, and afraid. They do not know how to communicate their distress. They may appear to be narcissistic, even as they seek attention in negative, hurtful ways. They usually have fairly easy access to weapons, alcohol, and other substances of abuse.

The identification and assessment of students with emotional and behavioral disturbances is controversial. Labels are discouraged because of their effects on self-concept and self-esteem. A student can benefit more from an individualized profile of his or her strengths, aptitudes, and achievements, plus a characterization of the dimensions of behavior in which he or she has specific needs. This profile, on the individualized education plan, needs to be updated frequently as progress is made, and/or as new needs arise.

The Individuals with Disabilities Education Act (IDEA) uses serious emotional disorder as a category into which students are placed for educational and related services. The numbers of students identified as falling into this category help determine a state's eligibility for federal funding of special education each year. This categorization for statistical and monetary purposes does not describe the severity of the emotional or behavioral disorder. This category encompasses about 9 percent of the students served by special education in the United States each year.

The 1994 revision of the *Diagnostic and Statistical Manual of Mental Disorders* (4th edition) *(DSM-IV)* uses serious behavioral disorders as a category into which students are placed for identification and assessment purposes. Behavior disorders are subsumed under the category of disorders usually first diagnosed in infancy, childhood, or adolescence. Among the *DSM-IV* disorders of childhood are disruptive behaviors, eating disorders, tic disorders, elimination disorders, separation anxiety disorders, and reactive attachment disorders.

For educational purposes, children with behavior disorders are usually divided into two main behavioral classifications: (1) withdrawn, shy, or anxious behaviors; and (2) aggressive, acting-out behaviors. The debate about what constitutes a behavior disorder, or an emotional disorder, has not been fully resolved. In 1990, the U.S. Department of Education elected to remove autism from its list of emotionally disordered behaviors and gave it a separate classification under IDEA.

An alliance of educators and psychologists proposed that IDEA remove the term "serious emotional disturbances" and instead focus on disordered behaviors that adversely affect educational performance. Conduct usually considered a sign of emotional disorder, such as anxiety, depression, or failure of attachment, can be seen as behaviorally disordered if it interferes with academic, social, vocational, and personal accomplishment. So, also, can conduct, eating, elimination, or tic disorders, and any other responses outside the range of "acceptable" for school or other settings. Such a focus on behavior can link the individualized educational plan curriculum activities to children's behavioral response styles.

Should children with chronic and severe behavior disorders, especially those that interfere with the education processes in the regular classroom, be allowed to enroll in inclusive education programs? IDEA ruled yes, both in its original form and in amendments written more recently. Although teachers, other pupils, and school staff may be greatly inconvenienced by the presence of one or more behaviorally disordered students in every classroom, the law is clear. The school must "show cause" if a child with disruptive behavior is to be moved from the regular classroom to a more restrictive environment.

Inclusive education does not translate into acceptance of disordered behaviors in the regular education classroom. Two rules of thumb for the behavior of all children, however capable or incapable, are that they conform to minimum standards of acceptable conduct and that disruptive behaviors be subject to fair and consistent disciplinary action.

The first article in this section is concerned with teaching students who have emotional and behavioral disorders to regulate their own behavior. Self-regulation compels children to compare their behaviors to predetermined standards of acceptable behavior and to self-assess the degree of compliance. Students only receive positive reinforcement for behaviors that meet the criteria. This motivates them to think more carefully before they act.

The second article in unit 6 describes the use of videotapes and television to allow students with emotional and behavioral disorders to see themselves on TV. It focuses on televising correct behaviors. Students use the self-modeled appropriate behaviors on TV to learn how to use their own nonaggressive, compliant behaviors more frequently. The authors encourage readers to remember that appropriate responses can alter situations. Several steps are given that can help students control their own behavior. Teachers can learn to create an environment more conducive to education.

Teaching Students to Regulate Their Own Behavior

> During the 1994–95 school year, 43% of all students with disabilities were served in general education classrooms (18th Annual Report, 1997).

> Children and Adults with Attention Deficit Disorders (CHADD) estimates that there are 3.5 million children with ADHD (CHADD, 1993).

> Of the 5.4 million children nationwide with disabilities, 8.7% are identified as emotionally disturbed/behavior disordered, and 80% of these children are co-diagnosed with ADHD (Mathes & Bender, 1997).

Lewis R. Johns • Christine Johnson

Before general education teachers refer a child to special education services, the teachers must implement program modifications and strategies and document that the modifications were insufficient to remedy the student's problem. For these reasons, general educators and special education teachers/consultants need methods to successfully include students with disabilities in general education programs.

A Question of Generalization

Sometimes, consultants and classroom teachers collaboratively develop prereferral interventions or behavior management plans that require the teacher to monitor, record, and issue contingent reinforcers. This type of behavior management program is time-consuming; and if more than one student in the class is "on a plan," it can be overwhelming.

In 1973 Glynn, Thomas, and Shee described an effective procedure for general education teachers to employ so students can self-monitor and improve their on-task behavior. Although recent research has focused on the use of self-regulation techniques for students with disabilities in special education settings, it is peculiar that the technique is not used more in general education classrooms as prereferral interventions and to facilitate inclusion of students with disabilities.

Self-regulation techniques can be used with students from preschool age through postsecondary age when educators adapt the level of sophistication to the age group. One limitation of self-regulation training conducted by special education teachers in the special education setting is the lack of generalization of the behavior change in the general education setting.

One way to facilitate generalization of skills is to provide the training in the setting in which you want the generalization to occur (Guevremont, Osnes, & Stokes, 1988). In this article we present a description of self-regulation and the specific procedures for teaching students to employ self-regulation of classroom work-study behavior.

Components of Self-Regulation

Self-regulation requires students to stop, think about what they are doing, compare their behavior to a criterion, record the results of their comparison, and receive reinforcement for their behavior if it meets the criterion (Webber, Scheuermann, McCall, & Coleman, 1993). Self-monitoring involves all the steps in self-regulation, except the issuing of reinforcement.

When you begin the program, first teach students to ask the monitoring question aloud. Then, as the program becomes more

Self-regulation requires students to stop, think about what they are doing, compare their behavior to a criterion, record the results of their comparison, and receive reinforcement for their behavior if it meets the criterion.

routine, students ask the monitoring question in a whisper. In the initial stages of self-regulation, use a tone sounded in the classroom at random intervals to cue the students to ask the question. Cued monitoring is much more effective than uncued monitoring. When you must conduct a training session outside the general classroom, the use of the same tone aids in maintaining the skills across settings.

The Steps of Self-Regulation

Students use the following sequence of steps to use self-regulation:

1. Self-observation—looking at one's own behavior given a predetermined criterion.
2. Self-assessment—deciding if the behavior has occurred, through some self-questioning activity.
3. Self-recording—recording the decision made during self-assessment on a private recording form.
4. Self-determination of reinforcement—setting a criterion for success, and selecting a reinforcer from a menu of reinforcers.
5. Self-administration of reinforcement—administering a reinforcer to oneself (Glynn et al., 1973).

> According to Barkley (1990), 3%–5% of all school-age children may have attention deficit hyperactivity disorder (ADHD).

Target Behavior

Self-regulation is most widely used during independent seatwork; however, you may apply the technique to a variety of classroom activities. Here are kinds of behavior commonly targeted by self-regulation:

- Staying on task.
- Assignment completion (productivity).
- Appropriate classroom behavior (such as staying in one's seat).
- Accuracy of completed work (percent correct).

The student should focus on positive behavior. The choice of a target behavior for self-regulation is important and may be individually selected, depending on student needs.

Initially, you may want to select a single target behavior for the entire class group. Then, after the students learn the technique, you may want to select different kinds of behavior to target to meet the needs of individual students. Although teachers most frequently select on-task behavior, improvement in on-task behavior may not promote improved academic outcomes. Researchers have found that a *combination* of types of target behavior, including both work-study and accuracy of assignment completion, seems to work best (Rooney, Polloway, &

Hallahan, 1985). Young students respond to task completion as a criterion, whereas older students respond best to completion of tasks with an accuracy criteria (Maag, Reid, & DiGanni, 1993).

Procedure

Before you begin a self-regulatory program, collect program data to determine the students' current level of performance regarding the behavior problem. The special education teacher/consultant or a classroom assistant can collect preintervention "on-task" data using an interval observation method on several students over several visits.

For interval observation, the observer records "+" or "−" every 10 seconds to indicate if the student was on/off task during that interval. The observer then divides the number of intervals marked "+" by the total number of intervals in the observation to get a percentage of time on task (see Figure 1). Then the teacher begins the procedure for teaching the students to self-regulate their behavior, as follows:

1. Model the procedure, using a suitable behavior. Model being cued to engage in self-observation/recording by a tone provided by an audiotape (available from ADD Warehouse; see box, "Internet Sites").
2. Students observe you modeling the procedure.
3. The students practice self-observation/
4. recording on a single behavior.

> **Internet Sites for ADHD**
>
> **Children and Adults with Attention Deficit Disorders**
> http://www.chadd.org
>
> **Teaching Children with ADHD**
> http://www.kidsource.com/kidsource/content2/add.html
>
> **A.D.D. Warehouse (catalog)**
> http://www.addwarehouse.com
>
> **ADD Treatment Information**
> http://www.mediconsult.com/add/shareware/decad_brain/cope.html

The Five Steps of Self-Regulation

1. Self-observation.
2. Self-assessment.
3. Self-recording.
4. Self-determination of reinforcement.
5. Self-administration of reinforcement.

5. Students employ the procedure daily.
6. The students graph their own observation data, in a manner appropriate to the age and ability of students.
7. Introduce self-reinforcement, such as "I did a good job staying on task," to the students. Better grades and teacher praise are effective reinforcers of accurate and honest self-recording.
8. Collect posttraining data over several observation sessions.
9. Suggest that some students self-observe and record a different behavior, based on individual student need.
10. With each student, review the weekly self-recording data. Introduce the concept of self-determination of a goal and self-reinforcement.

To teach students to use the self-regulation procedure, use the following direct instruction approaches—modeling and guided practice.

Format for Training Grade 2 Students: Modeling

1. "Class, I am concerned that when a student correctly responds to a question, I have not been providing praise as regularly as I should have. I need to find a way to improve how I respond to students who answer my questions."
2. *Thinking aloud,* say: "I will use this tape, which makes a sound every so often to remind me to ask myself, 'Did I offer praise for correct student answers?' If I did offer praise since the last tone, I will put a mark in the *yes*

Figure 1. Classroom Observation of "On-Task" Student Behavior

Student	1	2	3	4	5	6	7	8	9	10	11	12	13	14	15	16	17	18	19	20	%

column on my record sheet if I said something like 'thank you' or 'that's correct.' " (See Figure 2 for the recording sheet.)
3. "Class, what am I going to ask myself?" Group response—
4. "Class, if I said something like 'thank you' or 'that's correct' to a student, what will I mark?" Group response—

You should then begin the tape, which has several tones at intervals of 2–4 minutes, and then begin a short group lesson that lends itself to individual student responding. At the sound of each tone, the teacher will ask in a volume so all students can hear, "Did I offer praise?" Each time, record on the chalkboard or on an overhead a mark in the "Yes" or "No" column.

Self-regulation techniques can be used with students from preschool age through postsecondary age. Self-regulation is most widely used during independent seatwork.

After the short lesson is done, "think aloud," making comments about the number of marks in each column and how the students responded to the lesson. This think-aloud action is necessary to demonstrate to the students the relationship between the data collection and an evaluation of the outcome—the lesson.

After you have fully modeled the self-regulation procedure with the "think alouds," begin training the class using the single target behavior, such as on-task behavior.

Format for Training Group 2 Students: Guided Practice

1. Distribute a "Check Yourself" recording form to each student, and make a "Yes/No" box on the chalkboard. Say, "Class, when you hear the tone, ask yourself, 'Am I working?' " Provide examples of what is considered working and not working. This aspect of training is important so students will be able to make a quick decision and record it without asking you about a common task-related behavior. (Figures 3 and 4 show variations on the "Check Yourself" student form.)
2. Begin the tape of the tones and continue talking: "When you hear the tone, ask yourself in your quiet voice, 'Am I working?' Put a check mark in the 'Yes' box or the 'No' box. Are you always going to be working or listening to the lessons? No, sometimes you won't. That's OK. This strategy will help you become a better student. It is not possible to always be working on an assignment."
3. Continue teaching the group lesson started during the modeling phase and the tape of the recorded tones. When the class hears the first tone, the students (with your assistance) ask out loud, "Am I working?" You answer "Yes" and record a check in the "Yes" box on the chalkboard. Each student will record the response on his or her record sheet. The procedure continues with tones at random intervals, which are frequent enough to allow four or five recordings within a 10–15-minute time period.
4. At the conclusion of the lesson, say, "You did a good job asking the 'Am I working?' question and recording your answer. We will practice this again later."

Graphing and Record Keeping

Graphing the self-recording data can be an excellent activity for upper elementary age students to help them keep a long-term record of their performance and begin to set behavior goals. Older students can compute and record the percentage of "Yes" responses. Younger students may need to count total number of checks, "Yes" and "No," and record that total on a graph. Then they will count just the "Yes" check and record that total on the graph. The goal is to make the distance between the total number of checks and number of "Yes" checks as small as possible. (See Figure

Figure 2. Teacher Recording Form

"Did I offer praise?"

Yes	No

Figure 3. Student Recording Form for One Behavior

Yes	No

20. Teaching Students to Regulate Their Own Behavior

Figure 4. Student Recording Form for Several Types of Behavior

	Yes	No
"Am I working?"		
"Did I stay in my seat?"		
"Did I do my work?"		

5 for an example of student data and a sample graph.)

Benefits and Potential

The strengths of the self-regulatory program include the following:

- Reduced teacher time for monitoring and responding to student behavior.
- The ability to vary the target behavior from simple on-task behavior to the complex self-monitoring of strategy usage.
- The ability to individualize target behavior to accommodate a variety of student ability levels.

The teaching of self-regulation has the potential of providing students with a skill that will have an ongoing benefit as students become self-directed, lifelong learners.

References

18th Annual Report affirms CEC's policy on inclusive settings. (1997). *CEC Today, 3*(7), 1.

Barkley, R. A. (1990). *Attention-deficit hyperactivity disorder: A handbook for the diagnosis and treatment.* New York: Guilford.*

Children and Adults with Attention Deficit Disorders. (1993). *CHADD facts 8: The national organization working for children and adults with attention deficit disorders.* Washington, DC: Author.*

> **Researchers have found that a combination of types of target behavior, including both work-study and accuracy of assignment completion, seems to work best.**

Glynn, E. L., Thomas, J. D., & Shee, S. M. (1973). Behavioral self-control of on-task behavior in an elementary classroom. *Journal of Applied Behavior Analysis, 6*(1), 105–113.

Guevremont, D. C., Osnes, P. G., & Stokes, T. P. (1988). The functional role of preschoolers' verbalizations in the generalization of self-instruction training. *Journal of Applied Behavior Analysis, 21*(1), 45–55.

Maag, J. W., Reid, R., & DiGanni, S. A., (1993). Differential effects of self-monitoring attention, accuracy, and productivity. *Journal of Applied Behavior Analysis, 26*(3), 329–344.

Mathes, M. Y., & Bender, W. N. (1997). The effects of self-monitoring on children with attention-deficit/hyperactivity disorder who are receiving pharmacological interventions. *Remedial and Special Education, 18*(2), 121–128.

Rooney, K. J., Polloway, E. A., & Hallahan, D. P. (1985). The use of self-monitoring procedures with low IQ learning disabled students. *Journal of Learning Disabilities, 18*, 384–389.

Webber, J., Scheuermann, B., McCall, C., & Coleman, M. (1993). Research on self-monitoring as a behavior management technique in special education classrooms: A descriptive review. *Remedial and Special Education, 14*(2), 38–56.

BooksNow

*To order books marked by an asterisk (*), please call 24 hrs/365 days: 1–800–BOOKS–NOW (266–5766) or (801) 261–1187, or visit them on the Web at http://www.BooksNow.com/TeachingExceptional.htm. Use VISA, M/C, or AMEX or send check or money order + $4.95 S&H ($2.50 each add'l item) to: Books Now, Suite 125, 448 East 6400 South, Salt Lake City, UT 84107.

Lewis R. Johnson (CEC Chapter #345), Assistant Professor, Department of Special Education; **Christine E. Johnson**, Graduate Student, Department of Speech Pathology, Arkansas State University, State University.

Address correspondence to Lewis R. Johnson, P.O. Box 1450, Arkansas State University, State University, AR 72467 (e-mail: Ljohnson@kiowa.astate.edu).

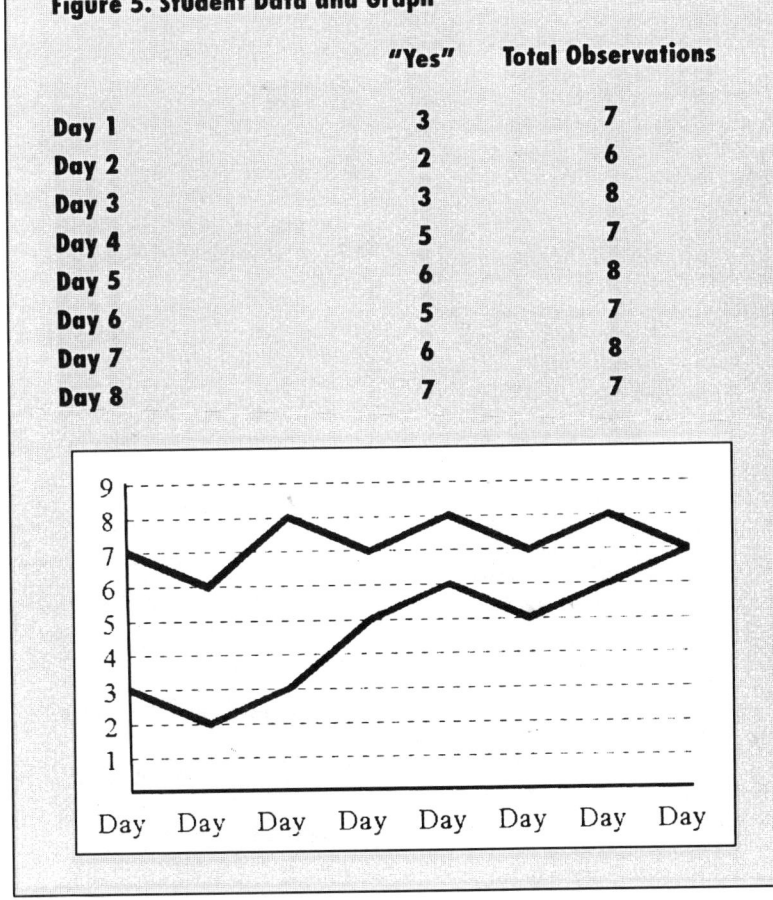

Figure 5. Student Data and Graph

	"Yes"	Total Observations
Day 1	3	7
Day 2	2	6
Day 3	3	8
Day 4	5	7
Day 5	6	8
Day 6	5	7
Day 7	6	8
Day 8	7	7

"Look! I'm on TV!"

Using Videotaped Self-Modeling to Change Behavior

Tom Buggey

The history of self-modeling as an instructional strategy dates back almost 30 years. The first research study of videotaped self-modeling (VSM) in educational settings was carried out by Creer and Miklich (1970). They set out to use videotapes to modify noncompliant and aggressive behavior in children. Creer and Miklich videotaped children over time and edited out all examples of negative behavior. They then compiled examples of students exhibiting compliant and nonaggressive behavior to include in the final VSM tape. Shortly after beginning to view the tapes, the students were exhibiting less of the undesirable behaviors throughout the school day.

Research on the Efficacy of Self-Modeling

Since this pioneering study, other researchers have verified the efficacy of VSM in treating children with various disorders:

Attention disorders (Dowrick & Raeburn, 1977; Woltersdorf, 1992).
Depression (Kahn, Kehle, Jenson, & Clark, 1990).
Aggressive/disruptive behavior (Creer & Miklich, 1970; McCurdy & Shapiro; 1988).
Elective mutism (Pigott & Gonzales, 1987).
Responding behaviors in children with autism (Buggey, Toombs, Gardner, & Cervetti, 1998).
Motor problems (Dowrick, 1983; Dowrick & Dove, 1980).

Researchers have also used VSM effectively to train both children and adults in the following important skills:

Parenting skills (Meharg & Lipsker, 1991).
Life skills (Dowrick & Hood, 1981).
Social skills (Hosford & Brown, 1976).
Language behavior (Buggey, 1995, 1996).
Cognitive skills (Schunk & Hanson; 1989).

The ages of participants in these studies have ranged from preschoolers (Buggey, 1995, 1996) to adults (Dowrick & Hood, 1981; Meharg & Lipsker, 1991).

In virtually all these studies, VSM produced results that accelerated quickly from baseline performance, were maintained in follow-up assessment, and were effectively generalized. Researchers who have compared peer modeling to self-modeling have found that self-modeling has produced equivalent or better results (McCurdy & Shapiro, 1988; Schunk & Hanson, 1989). (See box, "What Does the Research Say About Modeling?" for a discussion of adult, peer, and self-modeling.)

A striking example of the generalization effect associated with VSM was presented by Dowrick (1983). In this case study of a 6-year-old girl with cerebral palsy, the targeted behavior was stepping over obstacles. At the beginning of the study, the girl could not lift her feet over obstacles over 2 inches high.

The researcher set up an obstacle course for the girl to navigate with the assistance of aides. The aides would physically assist her over obstacles of various heights by manipulating her legs and offering balance support. The author videotaped this process and subsequently edited the tape, eliminating all views of the aides to create a video that illustrated the girl navigating the course without assistance.

The girl watched the tape, and within hours she was successfully navigating the obstacle course without physical assistance. The author then accompanied her on a walk and found that she could climb stairs and navigate street curbs. This result of VSM training is a dramatic example of the generalization effect reported in much of the literature surrounding the method.

Another strength of the VSM technique is the limited instructional time needed to produce obvious results. The research with preschoolers, school-age children, and adults indicated that exposure to VSM tapes for only 3–5 minutes per day was sufficient to produce considerable behavior change. Considering these findings, it is somewhat surprising that educators have not more widely accepted and used VSM in instructional settings.

Technological Requirements for VSM

A possible barrier to the use of VSM by more professionals and parents is lack of understanding of the technology needed to carry out the procedure. Two elements are needed for children to function as their own models:

- The audio/video technology that allows children to view themselves.
- The manipulation of children's behavior so that they can function (or appear to be functioning) beyond their present level.

Teachers who have access to a camcorder and a VCR have the necessary technology

VSM uses a medium of instruction in which children have been immersed for most of their lives; it allows children to become the stars.

What Does the Research Say About Modeling?

Having students imitate modeling behaviors has long been a mainstay of instructional practice. Adult modeling and, more recently, peer modeling (Levin, Glass, & Meister, 1984; Robertson & Weismer, 1997; Scruggs & Richter, 1985) have attained important status as teaching strategies. One of the great advantages of peer modeling is that it allows teachers to delegate their instructional responsibilities among students in the class, thus providing more time for individualized instruction. At the same time, peer modeling serves to build the confidence and prestige of those serving as models.

There is evidence to suggest that a peer may even represent a more influential model than the teacher. Researchers have found that the most effective models tend to be individuals close to the observing child's age, with similar characteristics (gender, personality, race, and mood), and who function only slightly above the level of the observer (Bandura, 1969; Thoresen & Hosford, 1973). Concerning the similarity of model and observer, video models who exhibit absolute mastery of a task are not as effective as those who display some task anxiety, yet are effectively learning to cope with a situation (Hosford & Mills, 1983).

These findings, along with other benefits experienced by peers when acting as models in the classroom (such as increased prestige, improved retention by practicing recently acquired skills and knowledge, and learning of responsibility) lead to the question of whether a child, given the opportunity to view himself or herself performing well at an advanced level, would serve as an even better model than a peer. No peer or adult could exhibit characteristics as close and relevant to the individual as when that child serves as both model and imitator. Also, children having difficulty mastering a task could benefit from the added prestige and confidence received by observing their own success.

Editing on the VCR and Camcorder

In two studies (Buggey, 1995, 1996), we used a VCR with the capacity for two cassettes for editing. Manipulating the *pause* button limited break-up between edited segments. The average time needed to select video segments, edit the tape, and produce a finished self-modeling tape of 3–5 minutes, using a dual VCR, was just over 1 hour. If dual VCRs are unavailable, you can obtain the same effect by joining two conventional VCR units. Although most VCRs are set up for this type of linkage, you may need to purchase extra cables.

If dual VCRs are unavailable, or if the necessary technical skills still seem somewhat intimidating, there is an even simpler procedure. In a recent study (Buggey et al., 1998), we edited videotapes by plugging a camcorder into the VCR and using the *play, pause,* and *record* buttons. While the VCR was on *pause* and *record,* we viewed the original tapes of children in the camcorder. When we found a desired behavior, we rewound the camcorder to the start of the behavior. Then we pressed the *play* button on the camcorder while simultaneously releasing the *pause* button on the VCR. When the desired video sequence was complete, we pressed the *pause* button on the VCR. We repeated this process until we had captured 3 minutes of positive behavior on the self-modeling tape.

Although most schools now have access to VCRs, many may not possess camcorders. These small, hand-held video cameras are versatile and have many applications in a school setting. The prices of camcorders have fallen over the past 5 years to the point where a device of fair quality can be purchased for under $400.

Arranging the Videotaping

Once the technology is in place, all you need is a method for arranging and videotaping positive child behaviors. Two major methods have been used in VSM research to assist students in performing (or appear to be performing) beyond their present developmental levels: taping role-plays and taping natural behavior.

Taping Role-Plays

The less time consuming of these methods is to have the student role-play or imitate the target behavior. Role-playing and imitation are especially effective when working with language and with social behavior. Children can often imitate correct language forms before they adopt them into their everyday use.

For example, we used VSM to train preschoolers to use forms of the verb *to be*

to produce VSM tapes. Techniques involved in producing videotapes for VSM are not complicated. The technology needed to construct VSM interventions should be available to most professionals and many parents.

21. "Look! I'm on TV!"

> **Teachers who have access to a camcorder and a VCR have the necessary technology to produce VSM tapes.**

(Buggey, 1995). We videotaped these children imitating the use of short sentences with the words *am, is,* and *are.* We edited the tapes to include their best imitations and then showed them to the children for 3–5 minutes each morning. Audio recordings made during recess indicated that the students were using the new forms in natural situations soon after intervention began. Generalization of the verb use had also occurred without specifically targeting that outcome.

Similarly, children who exhibit behavior difficulties can usually role-play correct responses to social situations that they do not typically perform. Educators commonly use role-playing strategies, such as "Social Skills Stories" (Johnson & Susnik, 1995), to promote social behavior change. This method requires students to role-play specific social situations and responses that are problematic for them. Videotaping the role-playing activity would provide a tape of the student successfully performing the behavior needed for the given social situation. The tape could be viewed by the student in the morning before classes, or on an as-needed basis. If you follow this procedure, take care to ensure that the tape is viewed only in a positive light. Showing the video following negative behaviors to illustrate how the student *should* be behaving could be problematic. It is better to let the student view the video in neutral situations and accompany the viewing with praise.

Another reason for having a student role-play an activity rather than taping his actual behavior deals with confidentiality. It is sometimes difficult to videotape a child in a classroom setting without including peers in the video. Unless you have permission from all who might be included, problems with confidentiality and privacy can arise. This situation might occur when training proper classroom transition skills. Some children experience difficulty on the way to lunch, the restroom, or special classes like art and music. Specific difficulties can include pushing, flailing arms, banging a lunch box, or not staying in line. Videotaping the student on the way to lunch is possible; however, it may draw undue attention to the child. Further, compact lines may make it impossible to isolate the child in the viewfinder. It would be easier to arrange a role-playing situation with one or two other peers to simulate proper transition behaviors. The videotape produced for this situation can include an introduction praising the child for positive transition behavior and could be discreetly shown to him or her before major transitions.

Taping Natural Behavior

The second method for obtaining tapes of desired behaviors is more time-consuming. It requires taping a person's behavior over time and editing the tape so that only exemplars of the behavior are present in the final product. People who tend to be nonimitative, such as those with autism, are candidates for this technique. This method also requires that baseline forms of the behavior be demonstrated by the person being taped.

For example, we trained elementary-age students with autism in responding to questions (Buggey et al., 1998). The intervention took place during play situations in the homes of the children. We videotaped all sessions in their entirety. We asked questions throughout the play period, but received only limited responses. We edited hours of tapes to obtain 3–5 minutes of the students responding correctly. For one child, examples of correct responses were so rare that we repeated those we found to produce 3 minutes of viewable tape. We showed the tapes to the children at the beginning of subsequent play sessions, and then the sessions continued as usual.

All the children in this study doubled their rate of responding during intervention. Two of the three parents related that they saw significant changes in responding behaviors in their child's daily activities, thus lending support to the generalization factor. Although this method of collecting examples for VSM is time-consuming, it may be appropriate for some students who have not responded well to other interventions or do not readily imitate.

Using Self-Modeling as a Positive Behavior Support

VSM by its very nature focuses on the positive. Negative types of behavior are simply ignored or eliminated during the editing process. In light of the new positive-behavior-support elements required in the Individuals with Disabilities Education Act (IDEA), VSM might be a viable solution to meet the behavioral intervention needs of some students. Its positive approach would fulfill the intent of IDEA.

It is possible that self-modeling could have applications in offsetting problems arising from low self-esteem in children and youth. Researchers have found that positive role models are successful in motivating students who are at risk for school and societal problems (Struchen & Porta, 1997; Willoughby-Herb & Herb, 1993–94). When children come out of at-risk environments

> Researchers have used VSM effectively to train both children and adults in life skills, parenting skills, social skills, and cognitive skills.

and are successful in life, they often attribute their achievements to someone in their lives who helped them feel less powerless (Kotulak, 1996).

Through self-modeling, children can learn to empower themselves. Having children and youth viewing themselves in positive role-modeling situations may provide them with an image of how they could be. High school transition programs could make use of this technique to reinforce or train students in the types of behavior needed for jobs and parenting. With young children, VSM might be used to offset the low self-esteem typically found in children from at-risk environments.

Unfortunately, research on the effect that VSM has on self-esteem is extremely limited. The relationship of positive adult role-models to the success of children from at-risk environments, however, should warrant examination of whether self-modeling could produce similar results.

Precautions and Challenges

Besides the confidentiality issues addressed previously, educators should take other precautions when using videotaped self-modeling. Although VSM is an inherently positive technique, we must always use videotapes with sensitivity and respect for the individual. Anytime we as professionals deal with behavior change, we must be careful to eliminate cultural and personal bias when selecting target behaviors. This is especially true of self-modeling, where we are asking children to view themselves in a slightly altered condition. Selecting target behaviors that are too advanced or unreasonable could possibly increase a viewer's sense of hopelessness and frustration.

The student's individualized education program (IEP) should determine whether a behavior is addressed though self-modeling. It is also important that we use the videotapes (both unedited and edited) solely for intervention or training purposes. Using unedited tapes to demonstrate negative behaviors to parents can be problematic and should be done only at the request of parents, if at all.

According to researchers, behavior change with VSM should occur soon after intervention begins. If gains are not made relatively quickly, the teacher may want to discontinue or alter the intervention.

Final Thoughts

The use of videotaped self-modeling appears to be a logical extension of the established methodologies of adult and peer modeling. VSM also uses a medium of instruction in which children have been immersed for most of their lives. Children are bombarded, for better or worse, by role models on television. VSM allows children to take center stage on television. They become the stars. Participation in VSM is usually highly motivating to the student and could serve to increase self-esteem and confidence.

Interestingly, little research has been conducted to determine why VSM has proven successful. Whether gains can be attributed to increased motivation and confidence, or to actual modeling of behaviors (or to a combination of both) remains unanswered. Although this method has been in use for almost 30 years, it has not become a mainstream teaching technique. The common theme of research findings indicates the power of videotaped self-modeling, for people of all ages.

References

Bandura, A. (1969). *Principles of behavior modification.* New York: Holt, Rinehart & Winston.

Buggey, T. (1995). An examination of the effectiveness of videotaped self-modeling in teaching specific linguistic structures to preschoolers. *Topics in Early Childhood Special Education, 15,* 434–458.

Buggey, T. (1996). *Efficacy of videotaped self-modeling with preschoolers with language delay.* Memphis, TN: The University of Memphis. (ERIC Document Reproduction Service No. ED 390 211)

Buggey, T., Toombs, K., Gardner, P., & Cervetti, M. (1998). Self-modeling as a technique to train response behaviors in children with autism. Manuscript submitted for publication.

Creer, T. L., & Miklich, D. R. (1970). The application of a self-modeling procedure to modify inappropriate behavior: A preliminary report. *Behavior Research and Therapy, 8,* 91–92.

Dowrick, P. W. (1983). Self-modeling. In P. W. Dowrick & J. Biggs (Eds.), *Using video: Psychological and social applications* (pp. 105–124). New York: Wiley.*

Dowrick, P. W., & Dove, C. (1980). The use of self-modeling to improve the swimming performance of spina bifida children. *Journal of Applied Behavior Analysis, 13,* 51–56.

Dowrick, P. W., & Hood, M. (1981). Comparison of self-modeling and small cash incentives in a sheltered workshop. *Journal of Applied Psychology, 66,* 394–397.

Dowrick, P. W., & Raeburn, J. (1977). Video editing and medication to produce a therapeutic self-model. *Journal of Consulting and Clinical Psychology, 45,* 1156–1158.

Hosford, R. E., & Brown, S. E. (1976). Innovations in behavioral approaches to counseling. *Focus on Guidance, 8,* 1–11.

Hosford, R. E., & Mills, M. E. (1983). Video in social skills training. In P. W. Dowrick & J. Biggs (Eds.), *Using video: Psychological and social applications* (pp. 125–140). Chichester, England: Wiley.*

Johnson, A. M., & Susnik, J. L. (1995). *Social skills stories: Functional picture stories for readers and nonreaders K–12.* Solana Beach, CA: Mayer-Johnson.*

Kahn, J. S., Kehle, T. J., Jenson, W. R., & Clark, E. (1990). Comparison of cognitive-behavioral, relaxation, and self-modeling interventions for depression among middle-school students. *School Psychology Review, 19,* 196–211.

Kotulak, R. (1996). *Inside the brain: Revolutionary discoveries of how the mind works.* Kansas City, MO: Andrews & McMeel.*

Levin, H., Glass, G., & Meister, C. (1984). *Cost-effectiveness of four educational interventions.* Stanford, CA: Institute for Research on Educational Finance and Governance, Stanford University.*

McCurdy, B. L., & Shapiro, E. S. (1988). Self-observation and the reduction of inappropriate classroom behavior. *Journal of School Psychology, 26,* 371–378.

Meharg, S. S., & Lipsker, L. E. (1991). Parent training using videotape self-modeling. *Child & Family Behavior Therapy, 13,* 1–26.

Pigott, H. E., & Gonzales, F. P. (1987). Efficacy of self-modeling in treating an electively mute child. *Journal of Clinical Child Psychology, 16,* 106–110.

Robertson, S. B., & Weismer, S. E. (1997). The influence of peer models on the play scripts of children with specific language impairment. *Journal of Speech, Language, and Hearing Research, 40,* 49–61.

Schunk, D. H., & Hanson, A. R. (1989). Self-modeling and children's cognitive skill learning. *Journal of Educational Psychology, 81,* 155–163.

Scruggs, T. E., & Richter, L. (1985). Tutoring learning disabled students: A critical review. *Learning Disability Quarterly, 8,* 286–298.

Struchen, W., & Porta, M. (1997). From role-modeling to mentoring for African American youth: Ingredients for successful relationships. *Preventing School Failure, 41,* 119–123.

Thoresen, C., & Hosford, R. (1973). Behavioral approaches to counseling. *Behavior modification in education.* Seventy-second Yearbook of the National Society for the Study of Education, Part 1. Chicago: University of Chicago Press.

Willoughby-Herb, S. J., & Herb, S. L. (1993–94). The importance of men as role models in literacy. *Catholic Library World, 64,* 46–50.

Woltersdorf, M. A. (1992). Videotape self-modeling in the treatment of attention-deficit hyperactivity disorder. *Child & Family Behavior Therapy, 14,* 53–73.

BooksNow

*To order books marked by an asterisk (*), please call 24 hrs/365 days: 1–800–BOOKS–NOW (266–5766) or (801) 261–1187, or visit them on the Web at http://www.BooksNow.com/Teaching Exceptional.htm. Use VISA, M/C, or AMEX or send check or money order + $4.95 S&H ($2.50 each add'l item) to: Books Now, Suite 125, 448 East 6400 South, Salt Lake City, UT 84107.

Tom Buggey *(CEC Tennessee Federation), Associate Professor of Special Education, RISE Project Director, College of Education, The University of Memphis, Tennessee.*

Address correspondence to the author at The University of Memphis, 401–C Ball Building, Memphis, TN 38152 (e-mail: buggey.tom@coe.memphis.edu).

Article 22

HOW TO DEFUSE CONFRONTATIONS
DEFIANCE THREATS CHALLENGES

The T-Shirt attention getter...
Prohibited cookies on the bus...
Profanity in class...
Outright refusal to do classwork...
Chair-throwing...

A comprehensive system of behavior management has three critical components: prevention, defusion, and follow-up.

Geoff Colvin
David Ainge
Ron Nelson

Do some of your students engage in confrontational behavior like this? Here's a litany of such behavior: attention-getting, defiance, challenges, disrespect, limit testing, verbal abuse, blatant rule violations, threats, and intimidation. Some students test the patience of teachers who have what they thought was an effective behavior-management system. This article presents teacher-tested ways to *defuse* such behavior and allow the students to learn and participate in positive ways.

Special education teachers have always had the task of managing students who display seriously disturbing behavior. More recently, these teachers are expected to provide support and consultation to general education teachers who need assistance on managing the behavior of all students in inclusive classrooms. Special education teachers can assist other educators in a comprehensive system of behavior management composed of three critical components: prevention, defusion, and follow-up (see box, "Three Approaches to Behavior Management").

We focus here particularly on *defusion*, an approach that is helpful with students who are continually confrontational. Such behavior not only leads to class disruption, but also can readily escalate to more serious behavior—and threats to the safety of both staff and students. Let's look at some examples of confrontational behavior and then explore how we can deal with it.

Three Confrontational Students

- Joe steps onto the school bus holding a monster cookie in his hand. Above his head is a large sign that reads, "No food on the bus." Joe looks at the driver, takes a huge bite of the cookie, and takes another step on the bus. The bus driver points to the sign and says quite emphatically, "Look, no food on the bus. You'll have to give me that cookie." Joe says equally emphatically, "No," and takes another bite. The driver looks him right in the eye and says, "If you don't give me the cookie, you will not ride the bus." Joe says, "So," takes another bite of the cookie, and begins to move toward his seat. The driver calls transportation to have the student removed from the bus.

- Sarah walks into the classroom wearing a T-shirt displaying a toilet bowl with an arrow coming up out of the bowl and a written statement underneath, "Up your AZ." Some students giggle, and another asks, "Where did you get that?" The teacher comes over and says, "Sarah, that shirt is not acceptable in a public school. You had better go to the restroom and turn it inside out." Sarah looks at the teacher and says, "I'm not gonna do that. My dad gave it to me and you can't make me turn it inside out." The teacher says that if she does not cooperate, she will be sent to the office. Sarah throws her book down and heads to the back of the room.

- Jamie is sitting at his desk, arms folded, shoulders rounded, feet firmly planted on the floor, and staring at the floor with a scowl on his face, while the rest of the class is working on an independent math assignment. The teacher eventually approaches Jamie and prompts him to start on his math. He scowls and says in a harsh tone that he can't do it. So the teacher offers to help him. He says he still can't do it. The teacher provides more detail with the explanation and directs him to make a start. He says he hates math. The teacher tells him that he needs to start or he will have to do his math during the break. He utters a profanity and storms out of the room.

22. How to Diffuse Defiance, Threats, Challenges, Confrontations

What Happened?

In each case, the supervising staff person reacts to a problem behavior in a direct manner. There is a high likelihood that the student *expects* a response. In fact, the student not only expects a response, but he or she expects a *particular* response.

For all practical purposes, the staff person is *already set up for confrontation*. In other words, the student displays engaging behavior that is highly likely to elicit a predictable response from staff that includes a clear direction. The student refuses to follow the direction, which engages staff further, leading to ultimatums and additional problem behavior.

Moreover, if the staff person becomes confrontational at this point, there is a strong likelihood that the student will react with more serious behavior. In effect, we can see a pattern—a cycle—of successive interactions beginning with problem behavior leading to more serious behavior, such as throwing a book (Sarah), continuing to disregard requests (Joe), or profanity (Jamie). These vignettes have five common features:

1. The student displays defiant, challenging, or inappropriate behavior.
2. The supervising staff person reacts to the problem behavior and provides a direction in opposition to the student's behavior.
3. The student challenges the direction by not complying and by displaying other inappropriate behavior.
4. The staff person reacts to the non-compliance and presents an ultimatum.
5. The student takes up the challenge of the ultimatum with further defiance and exhibits hostile and explosive behavior.

What Strategies Can Help?

When students exhibit confrontational behavior, you need approaches that are likely to defuse the problem behavior, rather than lead to more serious behavior. Defusing strategies minimize the likelihood that interactions between you and the student will escalate the confrontation. We have found five defusing strategies that work—in order of least intrusive student behavior to more serious confrontational behavior. These strategies range from ignoring the behavior to delaying a response and allowing the student to calm down.

Focus on the Task to Defuse Minor Attention-Getting Behavior

Students often display minor problem behavior to secure attention: talking out in class, moving out of their seats, starting work slowly, and pencil tapping. Once you respond to such behavior, the student may exhibit more attention-getting behavior. The basic approach for managing this level of problem behavior is to use a *continuum* of steps based on the level of attention you provide:

- Attend to the students exhibiting expected behavior, and ignore the students displaying the problem behavior.
- Redirect the student to the task at hand. Do not respond to or draw attention to the problem behavior.
- Present a choice between the expected behavior and a small negative consequence (such as a loss of privilege).

For example, Michael is out of his seat wandering around the room while other students are seated and engaged in a class activity. The teacher moves among the students who are on task, acknowledges their good work and ignores Michael. Michael continues to move around the class. The teacher approaches him and says privately, "Michael, listen, it's math time. Let's go," and points to his seat. Michael still does not return to his seat. The teacher secures his attention and says calmly and firmly, "Michael, you have been asked to sit down and start work or you will have to do the work in recess. You decide." The teacher follows through on whatever Michael chooses to do.

Present Options Privately in the Context of a Rule Violation

Sometimes students will break a rule to challenge you. They know you will react and give a direction. The student will then refuse to follow the direction. In this way, a confrontation scene is established. For example, in the cases of Joe and Sarah, the staff member gave the students a direction that the students refused to follow—the cookie was not turned in to the driver, the T-shirt was not turned inside out. Here are steps to follow in such cases:

- State the rule or expectation.
- Request explicitly for the student to "take care of the problem."
- Present options for the student on how to take care of the problem.

In this way, you lessen the chance of confrontation when you present options and focus how the student might decide to take care of the problem, rather than whether the student follows a specific direction.

For example, the bus driver might have quietly said something like this to Joe: "Look, there is no food on the bus, thank you. You had better take care of that. You can eat it before you get on or leave it here and collect it later." Note the options the bus driver might have provided.

Or, to deal with Sarah's offensive T-shirt, the teacher might take Sarah aside and say, "Sarah, that shirt is not OK in a public school. It has a rude message. You can turn it inside out, get a shirt from the gym, or wear a jacket."

Reduce Agitation in a Demand Situation

Sometimes students are already agitated when they enter a situation. When you or other people place demands on them, their behavior will likely escalate.

For example, Jamie's body posture and tone of voice suggest he is upset. When the teacher tries to prompt him to work, even in

> *First, communicate concern to the student. Then allow the student time and space. Give the student some choices or options.*

a very reasonable manner, his behavior escalates to storming out of the room. Here, the teacher might have used agitation-reduction techniques.

Signs of Agitation. Students show agitation by either increasing distracting behavior or decreasing active, engaged behavior (Colvin, 1992). Here are common signs of increases in *distracting behavior*:

- Darting eyes
- Nonconversational language
- Busy hands
- Moving in and out of groups
- Frequent off-task and on-task behavior
- Starting and stopping activities
- Moving around the room

Paradoxically, sometimes agitation doesn't seem to live up to its name. Some students can be agitated and not show it. Watch for the following *decreases in behavior* and a lack of engagement in class activities:

- Staring into space
- Subdued language
- Contained hands
- Lack of interaction and involvement in activities
- Withdrawal from groups and activities
- Lack of responding in general
- Avoidance of eye contact

Techniques for Reducing Agitation. Once you recognize that the student's behavior is agitated, your primary goal is to use strategies to calm the student down and assist him or her to become engaged in the present classroom activity. Because these

The most important thing to remember is that your responses can change things.

strategies are supportive in nature, you need to use them *before* the behavior becomes serious; otherwise, you risk reinforcing the seemingly endless chain of inappropriate behavior. The critical issue is *timing*. Use the following techniques at the *earliest* indications of agitation:

Teacher support: Communicate concern to the student.

Space: Provide the student with an opportunity to have some isolation from the rest of the class.

Choices: Give the student some choices or options.

Preferred activities: Allow the student to engage in a preferred activity for a short period of time to help regain focus.

Teacher proximity: Move near or stand near the student.

Independent activities: Engage the student in independent activities to provide isolation.

Movement activities: Use activities and tasks that require movement, such as errands, cleaning the chalkboard, and distributing papers.

Involvement of the student: Where possible, involve the student in the plan. In this way, there is more chance of ownership and generalization to other settings.

Relaxation activities: Use audiotapes, drawing activities, breathing and relaxation techniques.

Now let's replay Jamie's situation. This time, the teacher determines that Jamie seems to be agitated—he shows a *decrease* in behavior. The teacher says, as privately as possible, "Jamie, it's time for math. Are you doing OK? Do you need some time before you start?" In this way, the teacher is recognizing the agitation, communicating concern to Jamie, and giving him time to regain his focus.

Preteach and Present Choices to Establish Limits and Defuse Noncompliance

Use this strategy to establish limits and to defuse sustained noncompliance. Essentially, the student is refusing to follow the teacher's directions.

For example, suppose that Scott has been off task and distracting other students for several minutes. The teacher has tried to provide assistance, redirect him, and give a formal direction to begin work. Scott refuses to cooperate. At this point, the teacher wants to communicate to him that "enough is enough," and to establish some classroom limits. When the teacher tries to establish limits, however, Scott may become more hostile and aggressive.

The following steps in the preteaching strategy can establish limits without escalating the behavior. Role-playing these steps can help students learn how to use self-control.

Preteach the procedures: Carefully rehearse the procedures with the student, give explanations, model the steps, and describe the consequences. Do preteaching at a neutral time when the student is relatively calm and cooperative.

Deliver the information to the students without being confrontational:

1. Present the expected behavior and the negative consequence as a decision; place responsibility on the student.
2. Allow a few seconds for the student to decide. This small amount of time helps the student calm down, enables face saving in front of peers, enables you to pull away from the conflict, and leaves the student with the decision.
3. Withdraw from the student and attend to other students. You thus help the student focus on the decision, not attend to you.

Follow through: If the student chooses the expected behavior, briefly acknowledge the choice and continue with the lesson or activity. If the student has not chosen the expected behavior, deliver the negative consequence. Debrief with the student and problem solve.

For example, if Sarah refused to take care of the T-shirt problem, the teacher could say. "Sarah, you have been asked to take care of the shirt (expected behavior), or I will have to make an office referral (negative consequence). You have a few seconds to decide." The teacher moves away from Sarah and addresses some other students or tasks. The teacher follows through on the choice made by the student.

Disengage and Delay Responding in the Presence of Serious Threatening Behavior

Students may escalate to a point of serious confrontational behavior involving threats or intimidation. For example, the teacher may have presented options, given the student

Defusing strategies minimizes the likelihood that interactions between you and the student will escalate the confrontation.

Three Approaches to Behavior Management

Prevention. The teacher places a strong focus on teaching desirable behavior and orchestrating effective learning activities. These proactive strategies are designed to establish a positive classroom structure and climate for students to engage in productive, prosocial behavior.

Defusion. Teachers use strategies designed to address problem behavior after the behavior has commenced. The goal here is to arrest the behavior before it escalates to more serious behavior and to assist the student to resume class activities in an appropriate manner.

Follow-up. A teacher or an administrator may provide consequences for the problem behavior and endeavors to assist the student to terminate the problem behavior and to engage in appropriate behavior in the future.

The goal of these approaches is to provide information to the student on the limits of behavior and to use problem-solving strategies to enable the student to exhibit alternative appropriate behavior in subsequent events (Biggs & Moore, 1993; Colvin & Lazar, 1997; Kameenui & Darch, 1995; Myers & Myers, 1993; Sprick, Sprick & Garrison, 1993; Sugai & Tindal, 1993; Walker, Colvin, & Ramsey, 1995).

time, and provided a consequence: "Eric, you are asked to start work or you will have to stay after school. You have a few seconds to decide." Eric walks over to the teacher and says, "I know where you live."

Suppose a more serious situation occurs, such as this real incident: An administrator told a student to go to the in-school suspension area or he would call his probation officer. The student picked up a cup of coffee from the secretary's desk, moved to the administrator, held the coffee in his face, and said, "You call my P.O. and I will throw this in your f_____ face."

In each of these cases, there is a direct threat to a staff member and the danger that the student's behavior may escalate. Whether the student's behavior becomes more serious *depends on the staff member's initial response to the threat.* The primary intent of this strategy is to avoid responding directly to the student's behavior and to disengage momentarily and then to redirect the student.

We are *not* suggesting that this strategy is all you need to do. Rather, the primary purpose of this strategy is to defuse a crisis situation. Once the crisis has been avoided, you should follow up and address the previous threatening behavior so that such behavior does not arise again. Here are steps to use in disengaging and delaying:

Break the cycle of successive interactions by delaying responding: This pattern consists of successive hostile or inflammatory interactions between you and the student—the student challenges you to respond. The first step is to *delay responding,* because the student is expecting an immediate response. To delay responding, very briefly look at the student, look at the floor, look detached, and pause.

Prevent explosive behavior by making a disengaging response: Do not leave the student waiting too long; otherwise, an "extinction burst" may occur. That is, if events do not go the way the student expects them to, he or she may exhibit explosive behavior, such as throwing a chair at the wall (or staff, or another student), or throwing the coffee cup. To prevent this burst, disengage swiftly and engage in something neutral or unrelated (Lerman & Iwata, 1995). For example, say to the student, "Just a minute," and move on and pick up something on your desk.

Return to the student, redirect, and withdraw: If the student has not exhibited further problem behavior and is waiting, simply return to the student and present the original choice.

For example, approach the student and say, "You still have a moment or two to decide what you wish to do," and withdraw. If the student engages in more serious behavior, implement emergency procedures and policies established by the school or district.

Follow through: If the student chooses the expected behavior, acknowledge the choice briefly and debrief later. If the student does not choose the expected behavior, deliver consequences and debrief later.

> *Sometimes students will break a rule to challenge you; others are already agitated when you try to correct them.*

Debrief: The debriefing activity is designed to help the student problem solve by reviewing the incident and events leading up to the incident, identifying the triggers, and examining alternatives. The debriefing finishes with a focus or agreement on what the student will try to do next time that would be an appropriate response to the situation (Sugai & Colvin, in press).

Now Let's Debrief

How many Sarahs and Jamies and Erics do you know? Are you tired of throwing up your hands and sending these students to the office, or facing hostility and muttered challenges—or even threats to your own safety? Are you equally concerned that these students (and other students in your class) may be missing out on learning opportunities?

The most important thing to remember is that *your responses can change things.* Go back to the section on "Disengage and Delay Responding" and memorize it. Then follow the steps in "Preteaching," and you are on your way to helping students control their own behavior and create a better environment for learning.

References

Biggs, J. B., & Moore, P. J. (1993). *The process of learning.* New York: Prentice Hall.

Colvin, G. (1992). *Video program: Managing acting-out behavior.* Eugene, OR: Behavior Associates.

Colvin, G., & Lazar, M. (1997). *The effective elementary classroom: Managing for success.* Longmont, CO: Sopris West.

Kameenui, E. J., & Darch, C. B. (1995). *Instructional classroom management: A proactive approach to behavior management.* White Plains, NY: Longman.

Lerman, D., & Iwata, B. (1995). Prevalence of the extinction burst and its attenuation during treatment. *Journal of Applied Behavior Analysis, 28,* 93–94.

Myers, C. B., & Myers, L. K. (1993). *An introduction to teaching and schools.* Fort Worth, TX: Rinehart and Winston.

Sprick, R., Sprick, M., & Garrison, M. (1993). *Interventions: Collaborative planning for students at risk.* Longmont, CO: Sopris West.

Sugai, G., & Colvin, G. (in press). Debriefing: A proactive addition to negative consequences for problem behavior. *Education and Treatment for Children.*

Sugai, G., & Tindal, G. (1993). *Effective school consultation: An interactive approach.* Pacific Grove, CA: Brooks/Cole.

Walker, H., Colvin, G., & Ramsey, E. (1995). *Antisocial behavior in school: Strategies and best practices.* Pacific Grove, CA: Brooks/Cole.

Geoff Colvin *(Oregon Federation), Research Associate, Special Education and Community Resources, University of Oregon, Eugene.* **David Ainge,** *Senior Lecturer, Special Education Department, James Cook University, Queensland, Australia.* **Ron Nelson** *(CEC Chapter #374), Associate Professor, Applied Psychology Department, Eastern Washington University, Spokane.*

Address correspondence to Geoff Colvin, Special Education and Community Resources, University of Oregon, Eugene, OR 97405 (e-mail: geoff_colvin@ccmail. uoregon.edu).

Unit 7

Unit Selections

23. **Schools for the Visually Disabled: Dinosaurs or Mainstays?** Michael J. Bina
24. **A Child with Severe Hearing Loss Joins Our Learning Community,** Mary Jane Blasi and Lori Priestley
25. **Multimedia Stories for Deaf Children,** Jean F. Andrews and Donald L. Jordan

Key Points to Consider

❖ Are schools for the visually disabled dinosaurs or mainstays? Defend your answer.

❖ How can a reserved, overwhelmed young child with a hearing loss become a confident, happy child with a hearing loss in his or her first year of school?

❖ What are multimedia stories? How can they help children with hearing impairments?

 **Links**   www.dushkin.com/online/

24. **British Columbia Education, Skills, and Training: Special Education Branch**
    http://www.bced.gov.bc.ca/specialed/hearimpair/toc.htm
25. **The New York Institute for Special Education**
    http://www.nyise.org/index.html

These sites are annotated on pages 4 and 5.

Vision and Hearing Impairments

Blindness and deafness are uncommon, and are even becoming rare as medical technology increases and infectious diseases, malnutrition, and acquired causes of sensory loss decrease. Students with vision or hearing impairments whose disabilities can be ameliorated with assistive devices are more common in the school population. Regular education can usually meet their individualized needs appropriately. However, students with visual and/or hearing disorders whose problems cannot be resolved with technological aids need the procedural protections afforded by law. They should receive special services from birth (or age of diagnosis) through age 21, in the least restrictive environment, free of charge, with semiannually updated individualized family service plans (IFSPs) until age 6, and annually updated individualized education plans (IEPs) and eventually individualized transition plans (ITPs) through age 21. The numbers of children and youth who qualify for these intensive specialized educational programs are small.

Children with visual disabilities that cannot be corrected are the smallest group of children who qualify for special educational services through the Individuals with Disabilities Education Act (IDEA). In order to be assessed as visually disabled for purposes of receiving special educational services, a child must have low vision, which necessitates large print or magnification of print, or be blind, which necessitates use of hearing (audiotapes, records) or touch (braille, long cane) aids to be educated.

The educational definition of visual impairment focuses on what experiences a child needs in order to be able to learn. Legally, a child is considered to have low vision if acuity in the best eye, after correction, is between 20/70 and 20/180 and if the visual field extends from 20 to 180 degrees. Legally, a child is considered blind if visual acuity in the best eye, after correction, is 20/200 or less and/or if the field of vision is restricted to an area of less than 20 degrees (tunnel vision). These terms do not accurately reflect a child's ability to see or read print. One must consider the amount of visual acuity in the worst eye, the perception of light and movement, the field of vision (a person "blinded" by tunnel vision may have good visual acuity in a very small field of vision), and the efficiency with which a person uses any residual vision.

Children with visual impairments that prevent reading print are usually taught to read braille. Braille is a form of writing using raised dots that are "read" with the fingers. It takes many years to learn to read braille, and instruction should begin in preschool. In addition to braille, children who are blind are usually taught with Optacon scanners, talking books, talking handheld calculators, closed-circuit televisions, typewriters, and special computer software. In early childhood, many children with low vision or blindness are given instruction in using the long cane. Although controversial for many years, the long cane is increasingly being accepted. A long cane improves orientation and mobility and alerts persons with visual acuity that the user has a visual disability.

Hearing impairments are rare, and the extreme form, legal deafness, is rarer still. In order to be assessed as hard-of-hearing for purposes of receiving special educational services, a child needs some form of sound amplification to comprehend oral language. In order to be assessed as deaf for purposes of educational programming, a child cannot benefit from amplification. Children who are deaf are dependent on vision for language and communication.

When children are born with impaired auditory sensations, they are put into a classification of children with congenital (at or dating from birth) hearing impairments. They should be assessed as early as possible and started in early-childhood special educational programs for the hearing impaired.

When children acquire problems with their hearing after birth, they are put into a classification of children with adventitious hearing impairments. If the loss of hearing occurs before the child has learned speech and language, it is called a prelinguistic hearing impairment. If the loss occurs after the child has learned language, it is called a postlinguistic hearing impairment.

Children with hearing impairments are subsumed into etiological (causative) divisions of disability as well as being classified as hard-of-hearing or deaf and congenitally or adventitiously impaired. Children whose hearing losses involve the outer or middle ear structures are said to have conductive hearing losses. Conductive losses involve defects or impairments of the external auditory canal, the tympanic membrane, or the ossicles. Children whose hearing losses involve the inner ear are said to have sensorineural hearing impairments. They are difficult or impossible to correct with surgery, medicine, or sound amplification.

Many professionals working with individuals who are deaf feel that a community of other people who are deaf and who use sign language is less restrictive than a community of people who hear and who use oral speech. The unity of individuals who are deaf has benefits. The debate about what has come to be known as the deaf culture has not been resolved.

The first article in this unit deals with the pros and cons of inclusion in general education classes for students with visual disabilities. The author argues that special schools or special classes may be less restrictive for children with severe visual disorders than public schools with regular classroom placements.

The second article is a story of a child with severe hearing loss who is warmly included in a general education classroom. Harry brought a phonic ear and a cued speech transliterator with him. His teacher used a voice amplifier. The rest of Harry's classmates asked and received answers to questions about hearing loss. This story has implications for the inclusive education of all students with disabling conditions.

The material for thought in the unit's third selection is how the World Wide Web can enhance the education of children with hearing impairments. Jean Andrews and Donald Jordan review the benefits of new multimedia technology. Children with impaired hearing can use built-in video dictionaries of sign language on the Web. Print can be augmented with graphics, animation, and movies. Multimedia stories can also be used for children with speech and language impairments and learning disabilities. Teachers who have used multimedia labs and CD-ROM stories relate that their students increase both their vocabularies and their enjoyment of learning.

Schools for the Visually Disabled: Dinosaurs or Mainstays?

Michael J. Bina

In an age of inclusion, specialized schools for the visually disabled play an integral part of the continuum of placements offered for students with disabilities.

Schools for blind or visually disabled children have existed in the United States for more than 169 years. Some ask, Why have they survived this long? Has not inclusion made these placement options obsolete? If federal and state laws mandate education in the least restrictive environment, why do local school districts still send children to segregated settings? Are the high per capita costs justifiable? Should not the resources for these schools be redirected to local education agencies to improve services in students' home communities?

These are fair and not uncommon questions asked by the general public, legislators, and even many educators. For answers, we must listen carefully to current students, former students, local school leaders, and parents whose children attend or have attended these schools. Schools for blind children may seem an outdated service delivery model, but as Jim Durst, principal of the Indiana School for the Blind, recognizes, the educational outcomes of students prove that these placement options are justifiable, legitimate, and critically essential "for some children all of the time and for all children some of the time."

Obsolete and Unnecessary?

The inclusion movement has not eliminated the need for specialized schools for blind children. In fact, to a large extent it has increased the need for specialized services to enable children with visual disabilities to succeed in regular classrooms.

For students with visual disabilities to be meaningfully and successfully included in regular programs and to keep up with their classmates, they must have educational support services, reading and writing skills, and materials in accessible formats. To expect a child without skills to be successful in a regular education setting without supports would be as ill-advised as immersing a nonswimmer in the deep end of a pool with a sink-or-swim expectation. Although students might survive the experience, they certainly wouldn't enjoy it or thrive to their full potential.

Today, local directors of special education schools refer blind children to schools for the blind to help them thrive rather than just survive—so that they can better integrate themselves into their local schools. Often, these referrals are for short-term placements in the school's on-campus program, summer school enrichment or compensatory skill training, or consultative outreach services that support children remaining in their local districts.

In 1900, the blindness field was the first disability group to integrate or mainstream students in public schools. Even before the advent of the Education for All Handicapped Children Act, approximately 93 percent of students with visual disabilities were already placed in their local school districts, with 7 percent in specialized schools. Although this ratio has remained the same, many specialized schools report increasing referrals for outreach services and summer and regular on-campus enrollment. The U.S. trend shows not a diminishing need but rather a legitimate placement option in response to the steadily increasing demands from local districts. Schools for the blind are not a substitute for public school programs but are an important complementary option.

Least Restrictive Environment

Educators in local schools are committed to fulfilling the spirit and letter of the federal and state legislation that mandates that all children with disabilities be educated with their nondisabled peers to the maximum extent possible.

However, some school districts find its implementation impossible owing to circumstances over which they have no control.

For example, Mr. Adams, a rural area director of special education, has been unable for the past five years to recruit qualified staff to meet the needs of visually disabled students in his district because of a national specialized-teacher shortage. Only 33 U.S. universities offer preservice training programs for teachers of the visually disabled. Unfortunately, these 33 programs graduate fewer than 200 students each year. The demand throughout the United States far outweighs the supply of graduates from each program. This is compounded by the very high yearly attrition rate of specialists. Mr. Adams, therefore, must refer many of his district's visually disabled students to the school for blind children.

In another scenario, Mr. Sands, a director of special education in a large Indiana community, is fortunate to have recruited and retained qualified teachers for visually disabled students. Even though his district has qualified staff, he makes occasional referrals for placements to the school for blind children. He refers students who have difficulty achieving academically in the regular classroom and who need more intensive and individualized instruction than what is locally available. In these cases, the individualized education program team has determined that a school for blind children is the least restrictive environment—or the most productive setting. Many students benefit from immersion in a learning environment where all the staff in every class and dormitory can instruct and reinforce critical blindness-specific skills, such as Braille reading and writing, orientation and mobility (independent travel) and daily-living skills.

Rebecca, a high school sophomore from Mr. Sands's district, attended her first five grades at a school for the blind, returning to her neighborhood school for junior high. Her family, Mr. Sands, and his staff determined that Rebecca would benefit from returning to the school for the blind for at least the first two years of high school. Rebecca, who also attends a nearby local high school part-time, has taken advantage of the school's revolving door policy, in which students can come and go depending on their changing needs. Rebecca's parents and the staff from both schools agree that placement cannot be a one-size-fits-all solution: The question is not which option is best—they both are.

In another situation, Ms. Dare, a director of special education in the state's largest city, utilizes a school for the blind on a daily basis for students in her district who are having difficulty in large school settings. Often, these students can attend both schools, taking academic courses at the school for the blind, for example, and vocational courses at the local high school. These children can go home every evening, but frequently they stay overnight in the dormitory to take advantage of recreational programs, such as swimming, dances, Boy Scouts or Girl Scouts, or Special Olympics; on- or off-campus jobs; extracurricular competitive sports, such as track and field, swimming, or wrestling; or band, choral, speech, or debate activities.

Real-World Connections

Shawn, who was born blind, has a twin sister who is fully sighted. Although he attended a school for the blind for his entire school career, he was able to have the best of both worlds by attending a nearby local high school part-time. Now an alumnus of the school, Shawn told me,

> I knew when I was in high school that I was getting a good education because I could compare it to what my twin sister was getting from our public school. But until I got to college, I really didn't recognize how very well prepared I was.

Shawn described how the pre-med students in his fraternity house frequently sought his assistance with English themes, research papers, and math assignments. He knew that his abilities to match subjects with verbs, to organize his thoughts on paper, and to calculate numbers were superior in many cases to his fraternity brothers' abilities. He also felt more mature than his fraternity brothers because of his early dormitory experience dealing with, and adapting to, others.

Shawn's dormitory experience also helped him work independently. When he went home on weekends, he taught his parents, who tended to be overprotective, how he could do things for himself and why they needed to let him. His parents struggled with his living away from home, particularly in the early grades. However, when they saw his progress—his strong "can do" attitude, his confidence, his happiness, and his many friends—they realized that this sacrifice was necessary for his current and future independence and success.

Shawn just earned his college degree and is currently employed as a social worker. He lives in an apartment and does his own cooking, shopping, and other household chores. He travels in the community independently, using skills he learned in orientation and mobility, a related service that was not available in his home school.

Not all students are exactly like Shawn. Blind and developmentally delayed, Megan just graduated from a school for the blind. Unlike Shawn, she will not go to college or live independently in an apartment. But with the assistance of a job coach, she is employed, and she lives in a supervised group home. Megan, too, was not sheltered from "real world" realities or segregated from the community.

Shawn's and Megan's career experiences began in their early grades, and later both had on- and off-campus jobs. Shawn attended the local high school for academic enrichment and social experiences; Megan went off campus to gain experience working in a community adult workshop. Both Shawn and Megan moved from their dormitories into three-bedroom houses while in high school, and both were expected to shop for groceries, prepare food, clean the house, and meet other responsibilities. Shawn lived in one of the school's independent living houses without a live-in supervisor; Megan lived in a semi-independent living program with ongoing staff supervision. Shawn earned a pass to travel off campus independently to any location; Megan went many places in the community with adult supervision. Megan was required to open and maintain a checking account at a local bank where she deposited her check each week and conducted financial transactions.

Both Shawn and Megan also distinguished themselves in extracurricular activities. Shawn was a wrestler, competing with other blind athletes on the national level and with public school opponents in state competitions. He also developed powerful speaking skills, which led to participation in state and national oratory contests, and had challenging roles in school plays. His parents, proud of his extensive involvement, often asked Shawn if he ever had time to sleep! Megan was widely recognized for her singing. Twice she sang the national anthem at the state Special Olympics competition, and she sang in the school's chorus that traveled around the state and country.

The Cost of Value

These are impressive achievements. A state government official, after attending graduation at a school for the blind, commented on how well prepared the graduates appeared and how much progress they had made at the school. A school administrator replied, "Yes, but you are well aware of the criticism our school receives for the high per pupil cost and perceived 'expensiveness.'" The state official responded,

> How can they place a value on what these children were provided, what they have clearly gained, and what we know they are going to accomplish because of our investment in them? Look at the value rather than the cost.

In a similar conversation, Mrs. Botkin, whose teenage son is visually disabled and autistic, said,

> They can either pay now to make my son independent or *he* will pay in the future if he does not get the services he needs. We must decide whether we are going to socialize our children in less expensive programs that do not have all the essential services or we are going to instruct them and make sure they get skills. My son's success is only possible in a program that costs more.

The per capita cost statistics are often misleading. If all the services provided at a school for the blind could be replicated in the local district, the cost per capita would be the same in both settings. However, because blindness is a low-incidence condition and each district does not have large numbers of visually disabled students, the local services would likely be less economical than those in a centralized setting where the ratio of staff to students is higher and therefore the cost is less per pupil.

A colleague employed in a large Illinois public school reported that the per capita costs of students in her district were comparable to the instructional costs at a school for blind children. She indicated that because her district provided comprehensive and intensive full services, costs were higher than those in a local district that provided only the bare essentials, such as an itinerant teacher working with a student only one or two times a month. She defined full services as highly adapted technology; a full complement of specialized itinerant and resource teachers; and such related services as orientation and mobility, physical and occupational therapy, and special transportation. In her district, transportation costs were high because of the need to bus children extensively throughout the large metropolitan area.

Another factor is that the specialized school's costs include not only the educational expenses but also the provisions for food, housing, supervision, utilities, and other expenses over a 24-hour day. These costs are not included in public school expenditure figures. When comparing costs in both settings, we must match services for services. To say that one option with fewer services is less expensive is unfair. The more expensive options provide more services.

But shouldn't the resources be redirected to local education agencies to improve services in students' home communities? This appears to be a logical strategy given the least restrictive language in the law. However, because qualified specialists are typically not available, local districts are not likely to fill all the positions needed and would have to regionalize programs to consolidate services. Therefore, students would still be unable to attend their neighborhood schools, and some students would end up without any services. Specialized services would lose their effectiveness if they were scattered throughout the state. The state would also lose a major resource center and would no longer be able to provide outreach services.

Least Restrictive or Most Productive?

Are schools for the visually disabled dinosaurs on the verge of extinction or credible placements of distinction? Consider the impact that blindness has on learning for such students as Megan and Shawn, the role that specialized schools play in overcoming their potentially devastating disabilities, and the ever-increasing demands for these services from local districts.

All these examples illustrate the value and necessity of providing a continuum of service options when students need alternatives to their local school programs. Schools for visually disabled students are an integral part of this continuum of options. A district may call upon the specialized school when it is unable to recruit specialized staff and provide services locally. Whenever a particular student is not achieving to his or her potential, school leaders can turn to this "more restrictive"—or potentially more productive—setting.

Michael J. Bina is Superintendent of the Indiana School for the Blind, 7725 N. College Ave., Indianapolis, IN 46240 (e-mail: binami@speced.doe.state.in.us).

A Child with Severe Hearing Loss Joins Our Learning Community

Mary Jane Blasi and Lori Priestley

There was much anxiety in our first-grade classroom. The rest of the school was buzzing in its usual way. The hustle and bustle of teachers and students was abundant in the hallways, but we were in our own little world. Anxious yet focused, we were preparing a program we had never attempted before. Finally, the moment everyone anticipated—the arrival of our new class member—was here.

Harry walked in slowly, with reserve. For him, everything was new: the school, the people, the situation, the experience. His crystal blue eyes absorbed the richness of the environment around him. He appeared overwhelmed by the chatter of the people wanting him to feel welcome. Harry stared intently, smiling occasionally at the attempts to make him feel at home, but he obviously wanted to be left alone to make his own adjustment. He hurried to his seat.

Harry, with profound hearing loss, wore two hearing aids that were connected to a cassette-player-like box held by suspender straps at his waist. This apparatus is sometimes called a "phonic ear."

The classroom teacher, Mary Jane, wore a microphone that amplified her voice. Harry also had a transliterator (interpreter), Lori.

Because Harry had had difficulty in preschool with lipreading and sign language, his family had decided to supplement his learning with *cued speech*, a system of hand cues that enhance lipreading. With Lori as the facilitator of communication, cued speech was to become Harry's link with the classroom environment.

Initially, the first-graders had many questions. We addressed each concern. There were no secrets. Educating ourselves and the class was crucial. Ultimately our challenge was to educate the school as well.

We as a learning community reaped many valuable benefits. We as teachers experienced the precious rewards and dynamic power of a collaborative team. This was a turning point in our careers.

Although our experience was with a child who could not hear speech (he hears only some sounds), we hope our observations and reflections will prove valuable to teachers of other children in inclusive classrooms.

Creating a community of learners

A general educator, a cued speech transliterator, and a class of caring, compassionate children comprised our learning community. We experienced every emotion conceivable, but our union as a community gave us the support we needed to succeed. Our community became the vehicle for exploration. The innate acceptance and uninhibited minds of the children became the true magic of our community. We grew together in a way few others were able to understand.

We wanted our classroom to be warm and inviting but, most important, our own. We labeled everything, in keeping with our goal of providing a print-rich environment, and selected songs to make everyone feel welcome.

It may be hard to imagine how a child with a hearing loss could enjoy the simplicity of a song, but Harry certainly did. In the beginning it was awkward for us all. But with wonderful song cards designed by children's musician Raffi and Lori cueing the words, "Down by the Bay" became Harry's favorite song. We soon lost our awkwardness.

We shared basic educational philosophies, which proved paramount in providing a positive and stimulating environment. We established a successful learning community by first becoming "active learners" ourselves. Open and honest communication was equally important. We developed an atmosphere of trust by valuing the importance of dialogue. The ownership our community shared was essential in establishing the bond we needed to succeed.

Many hours were spent developing an awareness of serious hearing impairment and other disabilities. The class began reading Jeanne Peterson's *I Have a Sister, My Sister Is Deaf* (1977), a beautiful story about the author's childhood experiences. Developing an awareness of cued speech also was important because our new classmate had no other mode of communication and was just beginning to learn the system. We allowed time for practicing cues as well as working on class cue projects, which created an understanding and acceptance of cued speech.

We introduced cued speech to the school community by designing a school showcase. It read, "Can you cue—Hello, how are you?" We often found people eagerly attempting to cue. The school community was very accepting and supportive of Harry and made an effort to make him feel at home. From the principal with his "Just Cue It!" shirt to the cafeteria workers who eagerly interacted with him, Harry found many people attempting to communicate with him. In an odd sort of way, we were all in the same boat: we were faced with something new and were doing our best to make it work.

We learned to appreciate the benefits of whole language in conjunction with cued speech. When experimentation is the mainstay of the daily routine, emphasis is placed on that which is truly meaningful. The most valuable experiences allow true meaningful communication. We enjoyed the simplicity of thoughts yet worked very hard at the skill of communicating.

Lori remembers her first really meaningful conversation with Harry, an experience from which we learned a great deal. The two were on their way to the computer lab for another session of cued speech and language practice when Lori saw a peculiar expression on Harry's face. She stopped and motioned for Harry to join her at a nearby table. Harry sat down and said quite simply, "I'm tired." Lori, who was tired too from a trying morning with her new puppy, started talking about her unsuccessful attempts to train the pup.

Harry's eyes lit up, he cued rapidly in response, and Lori knew he was truly understanding her every word. They sat laughing and enjoying the immense rewards of true communication. The antics of Lori's puppy were a popular discussion topic for the rest of the year.

Harry, as part of a whole language classroom, benefited from a variety of learning experiences. The

---

What Is Cued Speech?

Cued speech was developed by Dr. Orin Cornett, a physicist and vice president for planning at Gallaudet University in Washington, D.C. Dr. Cornett was motivated by the knowledge that most severely hearing-impaired people do not read proficiently and do not make maximum use of what should be their "window on the world"—reading. This is because children with hearing losses do not learn spoken language before learning to read (Cunningham-Walker 1987).

Cued speech is a system of hand cues that enhances lipreading. Eight different handshapes represent consonant sounds and four hand positions represent vowel sounds. The hand cues, used near the lips, match what is being said to clarify ambiguities. Spelled out are grammatical constructs and changes in language that are difficult to differentiate in sign or lipreading. Cues can be used for words without standard signs—for example, for names, funny sounds ("Yikes!"), and idioms ("Cool, man")—promoting vocabulary growth and development. Cued speech aids in increasing reading skills by corresponding exactly to the words read, allowing the child to focus on the meaning of the message.

children worked on research projects throughout the year in cooperative learning groups. Each child was responsible for a part of the work, reflective of the group as a whole. Harry's excellent reading ability helped his partners with their initial research work, and he closely watched Lori's cues to understand his responsibilities. He helped the children with the content of the readings and they helped him understand what he was to do. As we worked on these projects Harry rehearsed at home so he could report his part of his group's research project clearly at school.

The numerous "pull-out" sessions for Harry were both a necessity and a problem for us. Harry needed to learn cueing, but he did not want to leave his classroom and friends. He received speech-language services daily, for 30 minutes, and was pulled out of our classroom usually during our lengthy language arts time. Initially Lori went with him to pull-out sessions, but because of his ongoing quest for independence she eventually remained in the classroom, working with other children while he was gone.

On Mondays and Thursdays Harry met with an audiologist for another half-hour session. These two days were particularly fragmented and exhausting. Initially this was a real problem, but Harry adapted, working tirelessly to complete his assigned work before lunch and the long-awaited recess. We admired his fortitude. Lori or Mary Jane clarified assignments and helped him with any difficulties, allowing him to complete his work along with his classmates.

Fortunately the therapists working with him were honest, open, and flexible, and we worked together to minimize Harry's time away from class. Our dialogue with the speech-language pathologist was ongoing, and she devised some creative approaches to Harry's isolation by including other children from our class in her sessions. What a hit that turned out to be! Every time she appeared at our door the children excitedly waved their hands, each wanting to be the one selected to cue with Harry that day.

Many children were picking up cues themselves, cueing to each other as well as practicing from literature during our daily Drop Everything And Read (DEAR) time. They took turns going to speech class with Harry, learning language and cues and diminishing Harry's sense of being singled out to leave our community.

During the first days of school, crucial in establishing a classroom community, many well-meaning professionals came to see Harry, anxious about his adjustment. These interruptions became a difficult issue, and in exasperation Mary Jane turned to the principal. He reinforced that Mary Jane, though not an expert in deaf education, was in charge of the classroom and her decisions regarding Harry and the class were to be respected. These procedures, established early on, helped maintain a calmer atmosphere in our environment.

The principal was an integral member of our support network, a real advocate for Harry, and our dialogue with him was continuous throughout the year. His open door, support, and honest communication proved invaluable. All teachers working in inclusive situations need to enlist the support and advocacy of their principal.

Harry's school day

Harry always had less time than everyone else. He rode the shuttle bus from his home to school and arrived just as the school day began. He settled in his seat with homework assignments and the storybooks he had previewed with his mother.

Our mornings were routine, beginning with a reading of plans for the day. During these opening exercises Lori was always near the teacher, cueing dialogue and songs for Harry. Lori's role was to provide cues for all the words as well as environmental sounds and interruptions, such as announcements on the school intercom.

Harry's sense of humor eased many initial situations and allowed us to learn about deafness, cued speech, and sound-enhancing equipment with a minimum of anxiety. One day Harry raised his hand to answer a question, came up to the front of the class to write on the board, and then looked puzzled—he had no idea what to do! He started to giggle, we started to laugh, and the class joined in. His sense of humor and willingness to take risks quickly eased Harry into our community and provided a valuable lesson for the other children: that learning is a process, not a right or wrong answer.

Henry Kisor, in *What's That Pig Outdoors?* relates a similar outlook in his schooling: "I still had that sunny good humor which helped wary hearing children to accept my deafness despite my odd, breathy speech and the necessity of facing me when they spoke to me" (1990, 56). Harry embodies the qualities that we, as teachers, are constantly striving to instill in all of our students: independence, positive self-esteem, risk-taking, curiosity, humor, expressiveness, enthusiasm, and excitement about learning and the world.

Collaboration at School

Collaboration was essential. Our collaborative efforts began with a professor from Gallaudet University who spent two days training the classroom teacher, transliterator, resource teacher, resource instructional assistant, and speech-language pathologist in the basics of cued speech. He defined our roles and offered avenues to pursue for further training in deaf education and cued speech.

Our training was compact and stressful. We were inundated with rules and procedures based on each person's role. We became active learners; after all, we had only a few days to digest all of this information before making it come together in the classroom. The professor's strongest recommendation was that we attend a cue camp weekend in Virginia.

Funded by our school, we traveled to Jamestown, Virginia, for a three-day immersion in deaf culture. Cue camps are weekend or week-long (summer) events and provide the opportunity for families and professionals to discuss common concerns, provide support for each other, and have fun. Many families attend cue camp year after year. We were impressed by the support, courage, and love they displayed for each other. These people have faced and accepted obstacles in their lives with the attitude of "Let's get on with it"—in other words, "Just cue it!"

Our days were filled with interaction with the families, workshops, and dialogues with teachers. In a workshop for beginning cuers, we watched a video that simulated deafness. We were directed to read what the speaker was saying, and we watched the film over and over until someone deciphered enough words of the Declaration of Independence that we figured out what was being recited. The task was difficult, but given a context of prior knowledge, reminiscent of our whole language background, we could figure out the words.

We were exhausted after this experience. Throughout the year we recalled our intense concentration as we thought of the tremendous and exhausting focus that was always expected of Harry.

A psychologist presented a workshop on the stages of grief. We learned about the stages of grief that parents progress through when experiencing the loss of the "perfect child" they expected at birth. We learned the importance of working through these stages to promote acceptance and mental health. A critical piece in our training was developing the understanding of loss and determining where each family might be in the grief process. It helped us develop a deeper understanding of Harry and his family and gave us ideas for helping them to keep moving forward.

Strengthened by a better understanding of deafness, we returned to our classroom. The speech-language pathologist was eager to share new ideas, and our collaboration with her was enhanced by our new learnings from cue camp. We established a caring support network for ourselves and continually reflected and reevaluated our work to appropriately serve Harry as well as the other children in our class. Not only did we share ideas and concerns but also frustrations that we experienced along the way.

Following warm-up exercises the children returned to their seats for writing in their word books and journals as well as reading in heterogeneous or skills-as-needed groups. Our early writing was based on the "key word" ideas of Sylvia Ashton-Warner, as described in her book *Teacher* (1963). She says that first words must have intense meaning for a child, for it is here that the love of reading is born. The longer this reading is "organic," the stronger it becomes. Among Harry's favorite words were Batman and Riley, his dog's name.

As the children wrote, we circulated, available to all for conferencing and nurturing their thoughts. We always met the children at eye level, kneeling by their desks to talk quietly, personally. During this time Lori focused on cueing with Harry, acting as a tutor as well as a transliterator. We found the "stretch" (phonetic) spelling we used corresponded quite naturally with cued speech. Every sound was cued, with Harry picking up the same sounds and progressing with or beyond his classmates with his writing.

We found many advantages to cued speech. We noticed that for unfamiliar words the beginning reader can see the correct number of syllables, the correct consonants and vowels for use in reading and writing.

After writing we gathered to share our stories, make comments, and ask questions. The children took turns in the Author's Chair. At times we teachers became exasperated with the children's repetitious remarks: "I like your printing," "What's your favorite part?" "Why did you write about that?" Harry's comment invariably was, "I like your picture."

We worked hard to expand the children's thinking and questioning, suspecting that somehow we were not getting them into a depth of meaningful conversation. We brainstormed other possible comments and modeled thoughtful remarks but to little avail.

Then we came upon Thomas Newkirk's *Listening In* (1992), which describes the talk of a community of first- and second-grade learners. In explaining the persistence of the same questions, Newkirk says,

> Our problem with understanding it, I believe, stems from the assumption that six and seven year olds buy into an adult model of asking questions to resolve perplexities, seek information, explore motives. But do the students in these groups feel such a compelling need to know the reader's favorite page, day after day, week after week? I doubt it. Instead they see the opportunity to ask a sanctioned question as a way of participating in the group. It is the asking that is central; the answer is of secondary importance, and they often don't listen to it.... The formula questions are like a free pass that allows anyone to enter a conversation. (p. 39)

We realized that Harry's "I like your picture" made him a part of our community.

After lunch we all enjoyed DEAR time, with everyone finding a cozy spot to read, alone or with a friend or two. Harry loved this time because he loved books and catalogs. He assisted friends in reading and understanding texts. His personal motivation to learn about the world through literature served as a model for the other children.

After DEAR time the children usually participated in a special area class—music, art, library, or physical education (Harry's favorite). During this time Mary Jane, sometimes with Lori's assistance, prepared for math. By this time of day we were all tired, Harry sometimes more than others. Math concepts seemed to be more difficult for him to grasp. We incorporated *Mathematics Their Way* (1976) activities, a manipulatives math program designed by Mary Baratta-Lorton to develop understanding and insight into the patterns and relationships of math through the use of patterns, blocks, geoboards, unifix cubes, graphs, and so on. Children work in collaboration, with emphasis on the learning process. In this collaborative situation Harry observed his classmates to clarify his thinking as well as his own manipulation of the materials.

During math time Harry needed Lori's assistance as a cuer and tutor. The concepts of tens and ones and of money were especially difficult for him. We conferred with his mother on this and came up with the idea of saving money at home, with Harry continually counting the amounts and paying for services, such as eating at fast-food restaurants.

After math we went outside for a much-needed break. Harry excelled at sports and was always involved in a game of kickball or soccer. Communication was not a problem here with a group of peers!

Mary Jane's daughter, aware of Harry and his athletic abilities, told her about Kenny Walker, a deaf player for the Denver Broncos. Mary Jane wrote a short letter to Mr. Walker describing Harry. Within a week Harry received a handsome autographed picture with a personal note that read, "Harry, keep up the good work and *never give up!*" We all were moved by the gesture of a strong football player who had so much in common with a strong little boy.

Implications for teachers

Although our story is based on experiences with inclusion of a child with hearing loss, we believe there are critical points for all teachers to consider when faced with including a challenged child in a regular learning environment. Most important, teachers must educate themselves—seek out information and resources that will help them understand the special challenges faced by the child. Teachers can prepare the class by reading appropriate literature and talking with the children. All questions should be answered as openly and honestly as possible.

Teachers should educate the school community, including administrators, support staff, other teachers, and children. Our showcase, for example, sparked a schoolwide interest in cued speech. Reach out to others. Collaborate with school staff and the parents. A trusting, working relationship with the child's parents is critical. Enlist the support of your principal or director to become an advocate for you, your special-needs child, and your class. Education at all levels and collaboration are essential components of successful inclusive programs.

Conclusion

Harry became an active participant in the learning community, always moving forward and making the best of every situation. When he visited the second-grade class at the end of the school year, he appeared secure. He no longer looked down at the floor as he walked, and he intermingled with his peers happily and confidently. The embarrassment of wearing his phonic ear and having a transliterator was gone.

Collaboration with Home

Like all children, Harry carried his knowledge from school to home and from home to school. The help and dedication his home environment provided helped him achieve success. Harry's mother is a tireless advocate for him in every aspect of his life. Although we had not discussed our views of literacy, we soon realized that we shared a common view: literacy and a love of books would be Harry's "window on the world." Harry's mom especially wanted him to acquire an extensive vocabulary, the same as hearing children. His favorite story was *Knots on a Counting Rope* (1987) by Bill Martin and John Archambault, which recounts the loving relationship between an Indian boy who cannot see and his grandfather.

A major concern in deaf education is the lack of language skills and vocabulary. Throughout Harry's early years he and his mother had written multitudes of language experience stories and compiled scrapbooks with photos and stories about every family outing and vacation. As Karen Smith says, "Literature [is] a universal language that binds people together and helps them create understandings of what it means to be a member of a community of learners and of the greater community of humankind" (in Short & Pierce 1990, 16).

We had high expectations for Harry and in no way planned to "water down" the curriculum. We outlined procedures that we thought would work for home/school collaboration, then reflected, evaluated, and adapted as the year progressed. We used plastic storage bags for transport of storybooks that were to be read daily in class. When Harry's mother saw the plastic bag, she knew there was work to do at home. She reviewed the stories daily, cueing, clarifying, and elaborating on the story or vocabulary.

The enthusiasm and accepting nature of the community helped Harry make a difficult transition. His peers, with all of their eagerness, helped Harry feel like "one of the bunch" by readily accepting his situation and becoming a part of it. They were instrumental in helping Harry begin to cue and become more comfortable with his deafness.

The children's attitude was reflected in a hallway encounter one morning. Harry and a new friend, Jeremy, were on their way to the nurse's office when another child passed them slowly, staring at Harry and his phonic ear. "What's wrong with him?" the child asked, pointing. Jeremy replied simply, "He's deaf. So what?" and he and Harry went on about their business.

As Harry's teachers we became more aware of how important it is to work with every individual child. We learned from our research, workshops, collaboration, and ongoing dialogue with professionals and the family, from our reflections with each other, and most important, from a six-year-old boy who sometimes was tired but *never gave up!* We believe, "as Jay Lemke (1985) argues, [that] schools are not 'knowledge delivery systems' but human social institutions in which people influence one another's lives" (in Pierce & Gilles 1993, 17).

Epilogue

Today Harry is in sixth grade and doing well. His mother reports that the transition to middle school was easy and that Harry has mastered cueing.

References

Ashton-Warner, S. 1963. *Teacher.* New York: Simon & Schuster.
Baratta-Lorton, M. 1976. *Mathematics their way.* Reading, MA: Addison-Wesley.
Cunningham-Walker, J. 1987. Children who cue. *The Voice* 3: 12–17.
Kisor, H. 1990. *What's that pig outdoors? A memoir of deafness.* New York: Penguin.
Newkirk, T. 1992. *Listening in.* Portsmouth, NH: Heinemann.
Pierce, J., & C. Gilles, eds. 1993. *Cycles of meaning.* Portsmouth, NH: Heinemann.
Short, K., & K. Pierce, eds. 1990. *Talking about books.* Portsmouth, NH: Heinemann.

Resources for children

DePaola, T. 1980. *Now one foot, now the other.* New York: G. P. Putnam's Sons.
Litchfield, A. 1976. *A button in her ear.* Niles, IL: Albert Whitman.
Martin, B., & J. Archambault. 1987. *Knots on a counting rope.* New York: Henry Holt.
Peterson, J. 1977. *I have a sister, my sister is deaf.* New York: Harper & Row.
Powers, M. 1986. *Our teacher's in a wheelchair.* Niles, IL: Albert Whitman.
Simon, N. 1976. *Why am I different?* Niles, IL: Albert Whitman.
Twinn, M. 1989. *Who cares about disabled people?* Singapore: Child's Play.

For further reading

Boggs, C., ed. 1990. *The cued speech journal.* Raleigh, NC: National Cued Speech Association.
Bredekamp, S., & C. Copple, eds. 1997. *Developmentally appropriate practice in early childhood programs.* Rev. ed. Washington, DC: NAEYC.
Daisey, M., ed. 1994. *Center lines.* Raleigh, NC: National Cued Speech Association.
Derman-Sparks, L., & the A.B.C. Task Force. 1989. *Anti-bias curriculum: Tools for empowering young children.* Washington, DC: NAEYC.
Vygotsky, L. 1978. *Mind in society.* Cambridge, MA: Harvard University Press.

Multimedia Stories for Deaf Children

Jean F. Andrews
Donald L. Jordan

It's hard to beat the feel of a book between the hands—feeling its soft cover, turning crisp pages, and smelling the ink. The low cost of books and their easy portability—carrying them to the couch, backyard, bathtub, pool, and the beach—entice us. But the whir and wonder of technology has captivated many teachers. Multimedia stories on the Web, for instance, can lead children with language and reading disabilities to read print augmented with graphics, animation, and movies.

Using Multimedia Technology

Multimedia technology allows authors to develop stories in two or more languages. Each language, then, can be accessed by the click of a button on each page. Multimedia applications are especially useful for deaf children because video dictionaries of sign language can be built right into the stories. This article describes our U.S. Department of Education-funded project and shows how teachers can use the Web to research their stories—and put these stories on the Web.

Phase 1: We set up a multimedia laboratory with state-of-the-art hardware and software.

Phase 2: Our staff (graduate students in deaf education and computer science) developed scripts and multimedia stories centering on the Mexican-American culture. These student-authors used library sources, as well as the Web, for information (see Figures 1 and 2 for Web sources). Native users of American Sign Language provided sign language translations and native-Spanish-speaking students provided the Spanish translations. Our computer science students set up a Web server to distribute our stories.

Phase 3: We provided summer workshops for teachers, teaching them to use the Web and to develop their own multimedia stories for their students. We placed teacher-authored stories on the Web.

Phase 4: We set up a research plan to follow the progress of Mexican-American deaf children over 1 year to see how they learned language using this new technology.

Designing Projects for Mexican-American Deaf Children

We developed materials and activities for Mexican-American deaf children because they are the fastest growing minority group in the U.S. school-age population of deaf children, particularly in Texas, where we work. In fact, these are more than 7,000 deaf children from Spanish-speaking homes in the United States, and this number is growing (Schildroth & Hotto, 1996). These children have difficulty learning English; and on

Stories centered on Mexican-American cultural themes written at different reading levels helped students with a wide range of hearing loss meet their language and cultural needs.

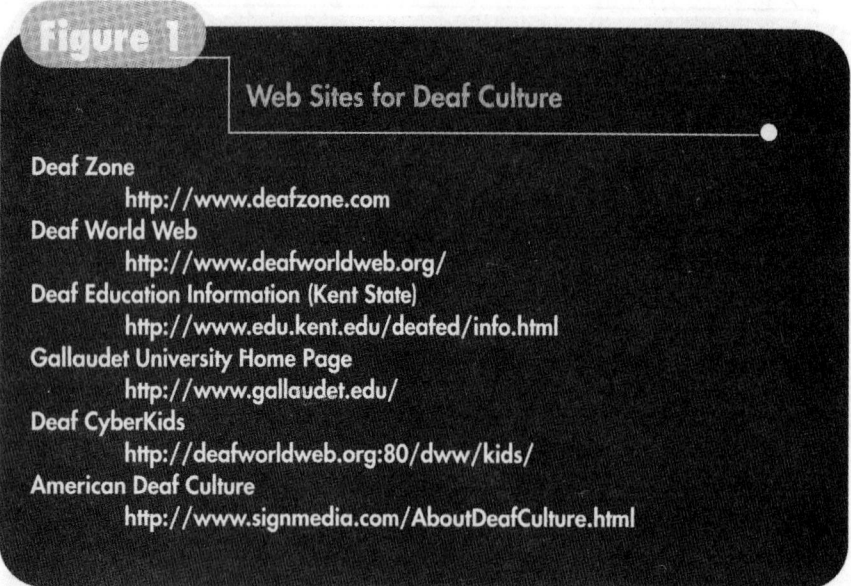

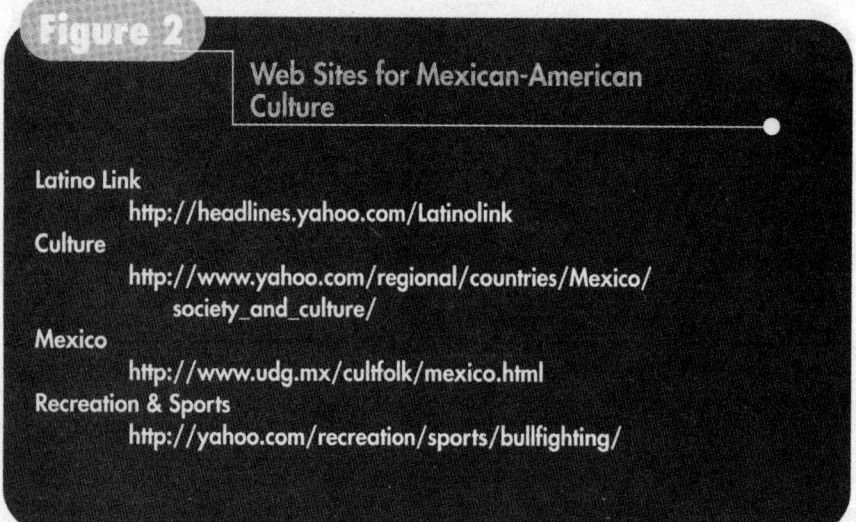

standardized tests that measure reading, language and mathematics, many score 2–3 years below their Anglo peers who are deaf (Allen, 1994; Gerner de Garcia, 1993).

School has been difficult for Hispanic deaf students because of cultural and linguistic differences. Cultural influences can be Spanish, Mexican, Puerto Rican, Dominican Republican, Cuban, Latin or South American origin, or mixed. These students' language learning may be fragmented. For example, children may use some spoken and written English, American Sign Language (ASL), gestures, and home signs. They may also speak and lip-read the Spanish language. In addition, they may use some spoken English and sign language, or a mixture of these. And even further, if families recently emigrated from Mexico or South America, these deaf children may use an indigenous sign language. Such a mixture of codes and languages can make learning academic subjects in English difficult for deaf Mexican-American students.

Mexican-American deaf youth must also navigate through three different cultures—Hispanic, American, and deaf cultures. Even though they might eat ethnic foods and celebrate the religious and historical holidays of their families, these cultural events have little meaning because few family members can explain these events to them in sign language. Consequently, many deaf Mexican-American children have grown up not fully understanding their home culture.

To meet their language and cultural needs, we designed a project to develop stories centered on Mexican-American cultural themes written at different reading levels—elementary, junior high, and high school. We added translations in ASL. We also provided written and spoken texts in Spanish and English because some Mexican-American deaf and hard-of-hearing children may benefit from hearing and reading Spanish words. We wanted our multimedia stories to be accessible to children with a wide range of hearing losses. (See Figures 3 and 4, for other uses of multimedia stories.)

Personalizing Dictionaries and Stories

Multimedia technology lets you explore information at your own pace. It combines printed text, narration, words, sounds, music, graphics, photos, movies, and animation on one computer "page." These pages can be linked together sequentially or can branch off into new pages called *hypermedia*.

For deaf children who use ASL, printed texts can be supported with sign language video (or movie) dictionaries. These videos can include facial expressions, head tilts, eyebrow raises, and body movements, the elements that encode the grammar of ASL (Pollard, 1993). No longer must deaf students turn to the teacher or sign language interpreter to ask what a word in a story means. They can simply press a button—and a person will appear on the screen, explaining the word in sign. This person could be the teacher, thus personalizing the dictionary.

For example, one Mexican-American folktale we designed is called "The Tracks" or "Las Vias." In this story, on one page is the phrase "piled up." If the student does not know the meaning, he can click on this "hot word" (which is colored red to differentiate from the other black text). By clicking on this hot word, the student is linked to a movie clip of a deaf adult signing the concept "piled up." All pages contain hot words where the child can get a sign language translation. Students can also click on the button and have whole paragraphs signed to them (see Figure 5).

Hard-of-hearing children can choose these sign language translations or turn up the sound track volume of the story or use both. If the Hispanic child knows some Spanish words, he or she may click on a button to translate the paragraph into Spanish. Stories formatted in multiple ways pro-

Multimedia applications are especially useful for deaf children because video dictionaries of sign language can be built right into the stories.

vide options for children to choose the mode that best meets their needs. Along the way, they learn about their Mexican-American culture in stories that are motivating and entertaining to read.

Creating Mexican-American Stories

Faculty and graduate students of Mexican-American heritage decided what Mexican-American cultural themes should be used. We purchased a library of 150 books, including Hispanic history, literature, encyclopedias, and references. We bought books on holidays, food, and traditions, and we purchased videotapes and magazines. We also found Internet resources on Hispanic and deaf cultures (see Figures 1 and 2).

With Web-related information, we developed stories about folktales, animal stories, Mexican-American history, famous Hispanic Americans, holidays, crafts, foods, and entertainers. An important topic was also added—successful Hispanic-deaf persons to provide role modeling to deaf children.

Our graduate students teamed up to write short two-page scripts. They calculated a reading grade level using the Flesch-Kincaid readability formula on Microsoft Word 6.0. After stories were edited, computer-science research assistants designed a "book" using the ToolBook software. Then the computer-graphics students designed pictures for the story. We also scanned pictures from books, calendars, and magazines. Teachers who made materials for *classroom-use only* could use pictures from books and magazines. However, we wrote original stories or rewrote folktales which had been written more than 75 years ago in order to not violate copyright laws. These stories we will commercially market.

Other graduate students worked on the sign language videos of the script. Deaf students fluent in ASL signed scripts in American Sign Language. Other students used videocapturing equipment to mesh the sign language with the text of each story. One of our graduate students from Mexico who was fluent in Spanish translated our stories into written and spoken Spanish.

Other graduate students designed comprehension tests or games for each story (Pollard, 1993). The games provided the teachers with a tool to measure reading comprehension. The students could push a button to see how many points they scored after each game. For example, in one game, the student pressed a button to see a sentence signed into ASL. The student's task was to translate the ASL sentence into English. At the bottom of the screen were a group of scrambled words. The student had to drag the words and put them into the right slots that would show a grammatically correct English sentence.

Figure 3. Other Uses for Our Trilingual Multimedia Stories

* Hispanic hearing children learning English as a second language. Pictures, animation, photos, and videos can support the children's learning of home and school language.
* Anglo college and high school deaf and hearing students who are learning Spanish as a second language.
* Hearing children with language and reading difficulties. Signs support the children's learning of printed text (Vernon & Andrews, 1990).
* Hard-of-hearing Hispanic students. The stories may support their further learning of printed Spanish.
* Hearing adults (interpreters, teachers, parents) learning sign language. The multimedia stories may provide instruction in sign language.

Figure 4. Multimedia Stories Support Second-Language Learning

* Multiple translations of text (in English, Spanish, and ASL) provide students with options in learning English.
* Observing children using multimedia stories can increase our understanding of how children acquire and develop a second language.
* Trilingual multimedia materials provide "comprehensible input" (Krashen, 1996) in the child's first language.
* Trilingual stories may help the child bridge learning from one language to another (Cummins, 1988).

For example, in "The Tracks," students come upon scrambled words. They push on the "hot button" PLAY and see a video clip of a sentence signed in ASL. It is their job to unscramble the words to make a correct English sentence. If they succeed, they get a smiley face on the screen (see Figure 6).

Producing a CD-ROM and a Public Web Site

After we edited the stories, we transferred the files and pressed them to a CD-ROM disk (Andrews & Jordan, 1998). We also made copies of the CD-ROMs for the teachers participating in the research component of the project.

Mexican-American deaf children in the area were invited to the multimedia lab at our university to read the stories and comment on them. We have also loaded up some of the stories on the World Wide Web for national distribution. You can access our stories through our Web page (http://www.deafed.lamar.edu/).

Training Teachers

An important part of our project was to teach educators how to develop their own multimedia stories. During two summers, 20 teachers who worked primarily with Mexican-American deaf children attended a 2-week multimedia workshop. Some teachers had no experience with Windows applications; others had used ToolBook before. In the two summers, the teachers learned basic and advanced competencies with ToolBook software.

Skills included accessing the Internet (e-mail, newsgroups, file transfer protocol, World Wide Web). Teachers also learned how to operate a CD-ROM drive, view the internal and external components of the computer, use scanners, and create and save simple books on ToolBook. Further, they learned the basics of ToolBook software, viewed commercial CD-ROM software, and used the Internet to download and save audio and video files. Teachers created text and buttons in ToolBook; and they recorded, saved, and captured sound and video and in-

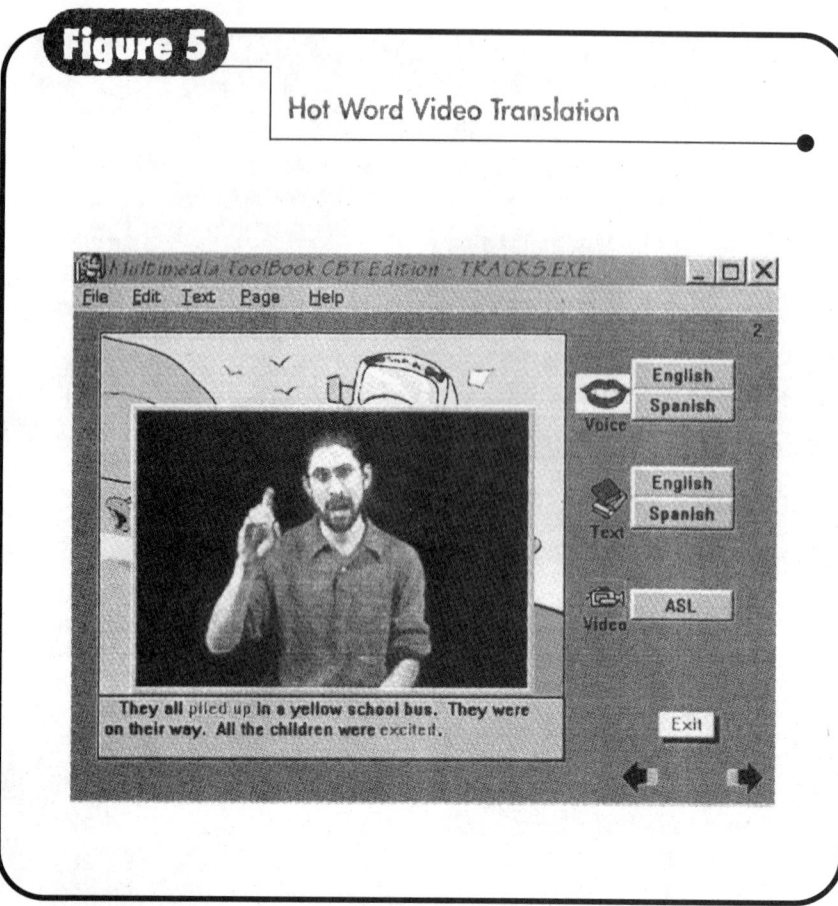

Figure 5 Hot Word Video Translation

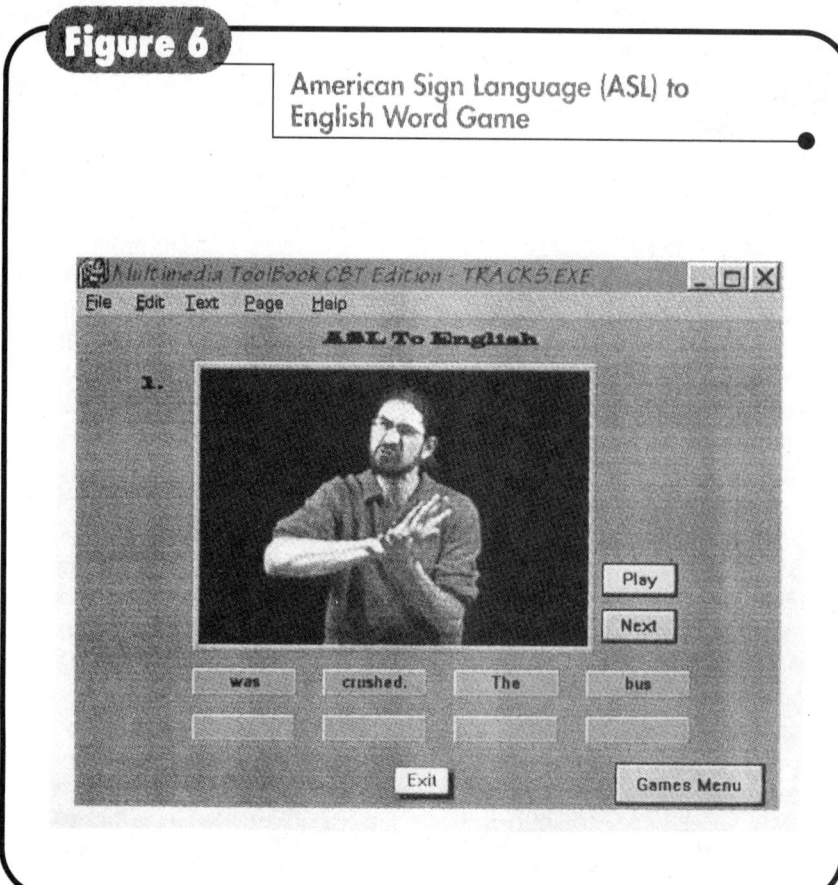

Figure 6 American Sign Language (ASL) to English Word Game

corporated them into their books. They composed a story with a Mexican-American theme and storyboarded it into pages, shared files over the network, transferred files over a network, and completed a CD-ROM storybook. Teachers completed one story, and our staff pressed it to a CD-ROM so they could use it with their Mexican-American students. See our Web page for titles of stories our teachers created.

Conducting Classroom Research

Of the 20 participating teachers, 7 took multimedia computers from our university setting to their home classrooms. Teachers would use the computers with the students to create additional books using ToolBook software. These teachers worked in classrooms with at least 80% Hispanic-deaf children in McAllen, Corpus Christi, Zapata, Austin, Baytown, San Antonio, and Beaumont, Texas. These 7 teachers will study the language learning of 10 Hispanic-deaf children as they use multimedia technology during the third and final year of the project.

So far, commentary on the use of technology in the schools has been anecdotal or testimonial, rather than data on the children's performance in reading. (An exception to this is data on math score improvements using computers.) In view of this lack of data, our study will use in-depth literacy assessments to determine how deaf children learn language from reading multimedia stories in Phase 4 of our project.

The seven teachers who received computers and took them to their classrooms will follow the progress of two or three students over a full school year (September 1997—June 1998). A set of literacy measures will be given to the children. These will be standardized tests and portfolio or performance assessments.

The *literacy portfolio* is a collection of a student's work and records of progress of achievement assembled over time. In contrast to standardized tests, literacy portfolios measure students on high-quality, performance-based, meaningful tasks. These tasks include reading and discussing significant books and articles, writing reflective responses to meaningful topics, researching and writing reports, and compiling a log of books and stories read (Valencia & Calfee, 1991). Based on current reading research, we put together a battery of different tasks to measure literacy development.

Using these techniques, we can provide a detailed description of 10 Mexican-American deaf students and how they develop English literacy skills using technology, as well as other literacy activities in their curriculum over a full school year. Even though researchers have reported smaller studies of the language and communication abilities of

Hispanic deaf children (Gerner de Garcia, 1993; Luetke-Stahlman & Weiner, 1984), to our knowledge, no one has examined Mexican-American deaf students' literacy development over time.

Communicating Early Results

We have started to collect data on Mexican-American deaf children using our CD-ROM multimedia stories. More detailed studies will be made in the 1998–99 school year, the final year of our project. So far, teachers report that their students enjoy using the sign language videos with the English print. This has increased vocabulary learning. One teacher reported that one of her students used the vocabulary hot words independently by pushing the ASL translation button to get the meaning in sign.

Another teacher reported that the stories with Mexican-American themes have generated class discussions about identity and customs (piñatas, 15th birthday party, immigrants, and language). For example, a Vietnamese deaf child who recognized that her skin color was the same as the Mexican-American signer in one story, asked if she was Mexican too. This started a class discussion on ethnic background and skin color. One teacher's story about the *Quinceanera,* or the 15th birthday party, an important rite of passage for young Hispanic girls, generated lots of discussion. Two students who were going through the ceremonies themselves did not understand the meaning behind it. The CD-ROM story provided explanations to these girls—for example, the meaning of the white dress, the church service, and the necklace worn by the girl in the story.

One teacher reported that her deaf students were learning Spanish words and bringing them home to show to their parents. Many of these Mexican-American deaf children came from homes where neither English nor signing was used. Thus, the CD-ROm stories raised the children's awareness of their home family's native language.

Another teacher reported that groups of her students used the CD-ROM stories independently. Students would gather around each other and take turns as the "teacher" to see if their classmates could read the text, then check the ASL translation for meaning. Our anecdotal reports are still preliminary, but we plan more comprehensive portfolio assessments of students' reading skills; and we plan to build case studies of Mexican-American deaf children and their language development.

Final Notes

The Web offers a valuable resource for researching stories. Teachers and students have access to libraries of print, graphics, and videos on the deaf culture, sign language, and the Mexican-American culture.

The Web can also be used to distribute teacher and student stories world-wide. It is easy to download our stories with the graphics, print, and Spanish translations. The sign language videos, however, may take longer to download. The technology for crisp, clear sign language videos with fast transmission rates is not here yet. But with compressed video techniques and faster computers and

> **No longer must deaf students turn to the teacher or sign language interpreter to ask what a word in a story means. They can simply press a button—and a person will appear on the screen, explaining the word in sign.**

modems, this technology is emerging fast. Schools must have computers with high-speed modems or direct lines to the Internet. Currently, the download time for our sign language translations is slow and cumbersome. We anticipate that the technology will soon allow faster transmission of sign language videos. In the meantime, we will continue our development of stories and put them on the Web for experimentation in preparation for new technology.

Our four-phase project—setting up a multimedia lab, developing stories, training teachers, and assessing the progress of deaf children as they use our CD-ROM stories—is an attempt to make a positive impact in improving literacy for deaf children from the Mexican-American heritage. With computer costs decreasing and with improvements in technology, multimedia on CD-ROMs and on the Web will continue to be excellent tools to bring deaf Mexican-American children into the 21st century.

References

Allen, T. (1994). *Who are the deaf and hard-of-hearing students leaving high school and entering postsecondary education?* Washington, DC: Office of Special Education and Rehabilitative Services, U.S. Department of Education.

Andrews, J. & Jordan, D. (1998). *The tracks and the wise stones: 2 Mexican American folktales retold in American Sign Language, English and Spanish.* A CD-ROM available now. Lamar University, Beaumont, TX 77710.

Cummins, J. (1988). Second language acquisition with bilingual education programs. In L. Beebe (Ed.), *Issues in second language acquisition* (pp. 145–166). New York: Newbury.*

Gerner de Garcia, B. (1993). *Language in use in Spanish-speaking families with deaf children.* Unpublished doctoral dissertation, Boston University.

Krashen, S. (1996). *Under attack: The case against bilingual education.* Culver City, CA: Language Education Associates.*

Luetke-Stahlman, B., & Weiner, F. (1984). Language and/or system assessment for Spanish preschoolers. In G. Delgado (Ed.), *The Hispanic deaf: Issues and challenges for bilingual special education* (pp. 106–121). Washington, DC: Gallaudet University Press.

Pollard, G. (1993). Making accessible to the deaf CD-ROM reading software. Austin, TX: Texas School for the Deaf.*

Schildroth, A., & Hotto, S. (1996). Changes in student and program characteristics. *American Annals of the Deaf, 141*(2), 68–71.

ToolBook II Assistant, Software. (1996, 1997). Published by Asymetrix Corp., Belview, WA.

Valencia, S., & Calfee, R. (1991). The development and use of literacy portfolios for students, classes, and teachers. *Applied Measurement in Education, 4*(4), 333–345.

Vernon, M., & Andrews, J. (1990). *The psychology of deafness: Understanding deaf and hard-of-hearing persons.* White Plains, NY: Longman.*

Books Now

*To order books marked by an asterisk (*), please call 24 hrs/365 days: 1–800–BOOKS–NOW (266–5766) or (702) 258-3338 and ask for ext. 1212; or visit them on the Web at http://www.BooksNow.com/TeachingExceptional.htm. Use VISA, M/C, or AMEX or send check or money order + $4.95 S&H ($2.50 each add'l item) to: Books Now, 448 East 6400 South, Suite 125, Salt Lake City, UT 84107.

Jean F. Andrews (CEC Texas Federation), *Department of Communication Disorders and Deafness, Lamar University, Beaumont, Texas.*

Donald L. Jordan, *Department of Business and Management Information Systems, Lamar University, Beaumont, Texas.*

Address correspondence to Jean F. Andrews, Department of Communication Disorders and Deafness, Lamar University, P.O. Box 20076, Beaumont, TX 77710 (e-mail: JPhelan200@aol.com).

Unit 8

Unit Selections

26. **Training Basic Teaching Skills to Paraeducators of Students with Severe Disabilities,** Marsha B. Parsons and Dennis H. Reid
27. **The Unexpected Benefits of High School Peer Tutoring,** Amy Wildman Longwill and Harold L. Kleinert
28. **Perspectives on Technology in Special Education,** A. Edward Blackhurst

Key Points to Consider

❖ Can paraeducators make a difference in the education of students with multiple disabilities? How can paraeducators be taught specialized skills quickly?

❖ How many people benefit from a high school peer tutoring program? Who are they? Why do each of them reap benefits?

❖ Can teachers access state-of-the-art technology to assist in their education of students with multiple disabilities? How? Can research and practice be brought closer together? Explain.

 Links www.dushkin.com/online/

26. **Activity Ideas for Students with Severe, Profound, or Multiple Disabilities**
http://www.palaestra.com/featurestory.html
27. **Related Services Research Project: Abstract**
http://www.uvm.edu/~mgiangre/RSRPab1.html

These sites are annotated on pages 4 and 5.

Multiple Disabilities

Children and youth with multiple disabilities were kept out of the public eye until very recently. We were scarcely aware that they existed. This population of individuals was typically hidden in their parents' homes or put into institutions. A child placed in the category of multiple disabilities may have learning disabilities and/or speech and language impairments, mental retardation, autism, traumatic brain injuries, emotional and behavioral disorders, visual impairments, hearing impairments, orthopedic impairments, or health impairments. While a child with multiple disabilities does not need to be disabled in every category set forth by the IDEA in order to be so labeled, each child with MD is very special and very needy. Most of them have more than two co-occurring areas of exceptionality.

The practice of deinstitutionalization (removing individuals from hospitals and large residential institutions and placing them in homes), and the legal initiatives requiring free and appropriate public education for all children with disabilities in the least restrictive environment, has closed some of the cracks through which these children once fell. However, the needs of many children with multiple disabilities are not yet being met.

One of the problems that looms largest in the collection of enigmas that hinder appropriate education for children with MD is lack of acceptance and preparation by society and by the school system for their inclusion. Society practices a form of discrimination against many people who are different and/or in a minority in some settings (ageism, racism, sexism). Advocates for the rights of disabled individuals have used the term "handicapism" to describe a similar prejudice and discrimination directed at disabled members of our society. The greater the disability, the greater the evinced prejudice. A disability (not able) does not translate the same as a handicap (hindrance, not at an advantage). The words should not be used interchangeably. A person who is not able to do something (walk, see, hear) has a disability but does not have to be handicapped. Society imposes handicaps (hindrances) by preventing the person with the disability from functioning in an alternative way. Thus, if a person who cannot walk can instead locomote in a wheelchair, he or she is not handicapped. However, if a building has no ramps, and is inaccessible to a wheelchair user, then society has imposed a handicap by preventing access to that particular property of the environment. There are millions of ways in which properties of our environment, and characteristics of our behavior, prevent persons with disabilities from functioning up to their potentialities. Therefore, society is "handicappist" and practices handicapism.

Public schools have resisted the regular education initiative (REI) that calls for general education classes rather than special education classes to be primarily responsible for the education of students with disabilities. The inclusive school movement, which supports the REI, would have special education teachers become consultants, resource specialists, collaborative teachers, or itinerant teachers rather than full-time special education teachers. While arguments for and against the REI have not been resolved, most educators agree that an appropriate education for each child with a disability may require a continuum of services. Some children, especially those with multiple disabilities, may require an environment more restrictive than a general education classroom in which to have the types of assistance they need to function up to their potentialities. Teacher education typically does not offer comprehensive preparation for working with children with MD who require extensive special educational services. In addition, children with MD often require related services (for example, chemotherapy, physical therapy, psychotherapy, transportation) to enable them to learn in a classroom environment.

Many children and youth with MD suffer from a lack of understanding, a lack of empathy, and handicapist attitudes that are directed at them. They present very special problems that few teachers are equipped to solve. Often the message they hear is, "Just go away." The challenge of writing an appropriate individualized education plan (IEP) is enormous. Updating the IEP each year and preparing an individualized transition plan (ITP), which will allow the child with MD to function as independently as possible after age 21, is mandated by law. These children will not go away. They must be served. Excuses such as no time, no money, and no personnel to provide appropriate services are unacceptable.

The first article in this unit suggests that paraeducators can play a very important role in giving one-on-one services to students with MD in inclusive education settings. A major need is to provide inservice training for paraeducators. This selection describes a one-day workshop which gives paraeducators an overview of effective methods of teaching adaptive skills to students with MD. Many highly successful teaching strategies can be learned quite quickly in this program.

The second article of unit 8 reports on the unexpected benefits of high school peer tutoring. The authors describe a peer tutoring program that has achieved phenomenal success in Danville, Kentucky, since its initiation in 1983. They describe how to set up a program and how to evaluate its usefulness, citing research that documents its effectiveness as a learning tool and as a social tool. Students with multiple disabilities are not the only recipients of benefits from peer tutoring. The tutee, parents, teachers, and the community all have positive outcomes from high school peer tutoring programs.

The unit's final article discusses the uses of new technology to make appropriate, individualized services to students with disabilities more feasible in general education classes. Computers can be adapted to make many areas of instruction more applicable to their specific needs. The author, A. Edward Blackhurst, reviews the dramatic evolution of technology in education and presents information on the technology of teaching, as well as medical, instructional, and assistive technology.

ns, 1996).

Training Basic Teaching Skills to Paraeducators of Students with Severe Disabilities
A One-Day Program

Marsha B. Parsons
Dennis H. Reid

> Lakeisha beams at the teacher as she demonstrates her new skills at setting the table with plates, cups, forks, and napkins.
>
> The new paraeducator can't wait to report that he successfully taught Jon to put on his coat independently.
>
> Finally conquering the copy machine at her workplace, Susan proudly delivered 30 copies of the newsletter to her co-workers.

Since the early 1970s, a technology for teaching students with severe disabilities has been evolving. Research behind the development of this teaching technology has indicated that the strategies for teaching students with severe disabilities are somewhat different from strategies used with students who have mild or moderate disabilities. Whereas the latter students may benefit substantially from teaching strategies based on verbal instruction, students with severe disabilities often require more individual instruction, using a high degree of physical guidance.

This article shows that when teachers and other staff members proficiently use physical guidance in conjunction with other teaching strategies, such as task analysis, prompting, reinforcement, and error correction, students with severe disabilities can learn useful skills (Parsons, Reid, & Green, 1993). And paraeducators can quickly learn to assist students with their learning.

Paraeducators in Inclusive Settings

The valuable role paraeducators can play in teaching students with severe disabilities is currently well recognized and is becoming even more important as greater numbers of students with severe disabilities receive their education in inclusive settings. Whereas special education teachers often learn appropriate teaching strategies during their preservice training, paraeducators rarely have specific preservice training in how to use the teaching strategies that constitute "best practice" for these students. Hence, a major need in special education is to provide inservice training for paraeducators in effective methods of teaching adaptive skills to students with severe disabilities.

Teaching-Skills Training Program

We developed the Teaching-Skills Training Program (TSTP) to ensure that human service personnel are adequately prepared to teach people with severe disabilities. We conducted research over a 5-year period to meet each of four criteria for successful staff training (see box, "Characteristics of Successful Staff Training Programs"; Jensen, Parsons, & Reid, 1997; Parsons et al., 1993; Parsons, Reid, & Green, 1996; Reid & Parsons, 1996).

In initial research conducted to validate the program's effectiveness, we taught 9 direct-support staff and 4 supervisors in a resi-

TSTP is efficient because the program can be conducted in one 8-hour workday.

dential program for people with severe disabilities to apply basic teaching strategies, with at least 80% proficiency (Parsons et al., 1993). In subsequent research, we trained 24 staff members, including group home personnel, paraeducators, and undergraduate teaching interns, to teach with 80% proficiency using TSTP (Parsons et al., 1996). Acceptability research has indicated that staff respond favorably to the training pro-

> The role of paraeducators is becoming even more important as greater numbers of students with severe disabilities receive their education in inclusive settings.

cedures (Parsons et al., 1993; Reid & Parsons, 1996). Finally, TSTP is efficient because the program can be conducted in one 8-hour workday (Parsons et al., 1996).

Since the initial validation research, educators have used TSTP to successfully train more than 300 paraeducators and other support personnel. Equally important, students with severe disabilities have made progress toward acquiring adaptive skills when their paraeducators have used the skills they learned during the program (Parsons et al., 1993).

To illustrate, graduates of TSTP have taught children with severe disabilities in an inclusive preschool program the following skills:

- Wash hands.
- Recognize numbers and letters of the alphabet.
- Operate a cassette player.
- Eat with a spoon.
- Respond to one-step directions.

In a school classroom for students with severe multiple disabilities, other graduates have taught students the following skills:

- Drink from a cup.
- Press a switch to activate a radio or TV.
- Use augmentative communication devices.

Other graduates have used the teaching strategies developed through TSTP to teach job skills to adults with severe disabilities—at the workplace.

Characteristics of Successful Staff Training Programs

Research has delineated four characteristics of successful staff training programs (Reid, Parsons, & Green, 1989). Each of these characteristics is particularly relevant in selecting a program for training paraeducators to teach students with severe disabilities.

1. Training focuses on *performance-based skills:* The training emphasizes what staff *do* when teaching their students. Although many programs provide interesting and *potentially* useful knowledge regarding teaching processes, such programs rarely train staff specifically how to apply the knowledge in actual teaching situations. How well paraeducators translate knowledge about the teaching process into the action of teaching directly affects the quality of education students receive.

2. Training is conducted *efficiently:* When paraeducators attend training away from the students' classrooms, schools and districts often must hire substitute personnel to assist with instruction, as well as with other essential routines, such as transportation and lunch. For school systems to have the resources to maintain well-trained paraeducators, cost factors must be contained by providing staff training as quickly as possible.

3. Training must be *effective:* In one sense, declaring that staff training should be effective seems to be asserting the obvious. School systems, however, frequently invest large sums of money in a staff training program with little, if any, verification of the program's effectiveness. Educators must examine the effectiveness of a training program from two perspectives:

- The program should result in staff mastery of the skills taught by the program. Staff should not complete the training until they achieve a criterion of satisfactory, hands-on teaching performance.
- The program is truly effective only if students learn when staff use their newly acquired teaching skills.

4. For long-term success of staff training programs, the training must be *acceptable* to staff. When staff dislike the training process, they are less willing to be involved in the training. Staff's negative reactions to training also result in unpleasantness for the staff trainer, which can cause the individual charged with staff training duties to become reluctant to conduct the training.

Figure 1. Sample Activity Illustrating the Rationale for Using Task Analyses

Why Is a Task Analysis Important When Teaching a New Skill?

1. If you were asked to teach someone to prepare a place setting incorporating a plate, cup, napkin, knife, fork, and spoon, draw the placement of the items on a placemat. Assume that the placemat is already on the table in the appropriate place.

2. Compare what you have drawn to the drawings of others in the group. How many place settings among the group were exactly like yours?

3. Draw a place setting following the task analysis provided by the instructor.

4. Compare what you have drawn by following the task analysis to the drawings of others in the group. How many place settings were exactly like yours?

Task Analysis for Place Setting

1. Place the plate in the center of the placemat.
2. Place the napkin directly beside and to the left of the plate.
3. Place the fork on the napkin.
4. Place the knife directly beside and to the right of the plate.
5. Place the spoon directly beside and to the right of the knife.
6. Place the cup directly above the tip of the knife.

8 ❖ MULTIPLE DISABILITIES

Types of prompts range from mild forms of assistance, such as gesturing to the student, to more directive prompts, such as physically guiding the student through a skill.

We teach staff that if the level of assistance they provide at first does not enable the student to correctly complete a step in the task analysis, they should gradually increase assistance—level of prompting—until the student successfully performs the step (see box, "Using the Least-to-Most Assistive Prompting Strategy").

Reinforcement and Error Correction

The third and fourth teaching competencies work together. *Reinforcement* is the means by which a paraeducator can increase the likelihood across successive teaching sessions that a student will perform the skill that the paraeducator is attempting to teach. We teach staff that a reinforcing consequence is more than a reward or provision of a preferred item. A consequence provided in the context of a teaching program can be regarded as a reinforcer only if student performance of the skill improves over time. Hence, one of the most important skills of paraeducators who teach people with severe disabilities is determining what constitutes reinforcement for a given student, and effectively providing that reinforcement to encourage student learning. Praise and attention are effective reinforcers for many students. Also, engaging in preferred activities following teaching sessions can function as a reinforcer.

When a student incorrectly performs a step within a skill, a staff member must deal

Using the Least-to-Most Assistive Prompting Strategy

When teaching a student to put on her coat, the first step of the task analysis is to pick up the coat. If the student does not pick up the coat independently, the paraeducator might begin by saying to the student, "Pick up your coat."

If the verbal prompt does not result in the student's picking up the coat, the paraeducator might tell her to pick up the coat while simultaneously pointing to the coat.

Subsequently, if the combined verbal and gestural prompt as just described does not evoke the student's picking up the coat, the paraeducator might tell the student to pick up the coat while guiding her hand toward the coat (verbal and partial physical prompts).

Teaching Skills

TSTP focuses on four basic teaching competencies: task analysis, least-to-most assistive prompting, reinforcement, and error correction.

Task Analysis

We teach staff that to use task analysis, they should list each specific behavior in performing a targeted skill sequentially, in the order the behavior should occur for the skill to be performed correctly. They teach the kinds of behavior, or steps, in the order specified in the task analysis to facilitate learning so that each step becomes a signal for the performance of each subsequent step in the task analysis. Figure 1 illustrates a task analysis for teaching students how to set a table for lunch or dinner.

Least-to-Most Assistive Prompting

Providing assistance on a continuum of least-to-most prompting involves giving a student only the assistance necessary to correctly complete each step of the task analysis. Types of prompts range from mild forms of assistance, such as gesturing to the student, to more directive prompts, such as physically guiding the student through a skill.

TSTP focuses on four basic teaching competencies: task analysis, least-to-most assistive prompting, reinforcement, and error correction.

with the *error* in a manner that promotes student learning. In essence, errors are opportunities for students to practice the wrong way of completing a skill and should be prevented whenever possible. We teach

158

paraeducators to prevent errors by increasing the assistance provided on a given step when they see that the student is about to make an error. When the staff member cannot prevent an error, he or she immediately stops the student and has the student repeat the step of the task while providing enough assistance to prevent the error from occurring a second time. For example, when a student who is learning to use a copier loads the paper incorrectly, the paraeducator should stop the student, remove the paper, and provide more assistance so that the student loads the paper a second time with no mistake.

Training Format

For paraeducators in our program, we use a training format consisting of classroom-based instruction, on-the-job monitoring and feedback, and follow-up supervision.

Classroom-Based Component

The primary purpose of the classroom-based training is to familiarize paraeducators with the *rationale* for each teaching competency (task analysis, prompting, and so forth) and the terminology used in describing the teaching process.

For example, using the activity shown in Figure 1, we show the rationale for using a *task analysis* to ensure that staff members teach students a skill in a consistent way. When several staff trainees draw a place setting without the task analysis, almost invariably the placement of cups, plates, and other items will differ across the staff trainees. Thus, if each trainee were teaching a student the task, the task would differ each time it was taught, so that a student with severe disabilities would find it difficult to learn to perform the task. If all trainees follow the task analysis when drawing the place setting, however, the completed drawings should look the same.

A second purpose of the classroom-based training is to begin training staff in the *performance skills* necessary to teach students with severe disabilities by having trainees practice the skills in a role-play situation. We limit the group size of classroom-based training to six trainees. Working with a small group allows the instructor sufficient time for the instruction, observation, and feedback necessary to ensure that each trainee acquires the teaching competencies.

During classroom-based training, we teach prospective paraeducators the skills of task analysis, prompting, reinforcement, and error correction, one at a time. We provide a rationale for using each skill to teach people with severe disabilities, and we demonstrate both correct and incorrect applications of each skill. Trainees practice and receive feedback about their performance from the instructor until each trainee can perform each respective teaching skill proficiently in a role-play situation (see box, "Modeling, Practice, and Feedback").

On-the-Job Monitoring and Feedback

The primary purpose of on-the-job monitoring and feedback is to ensure that trainees can apply the teaching skills learned during the classroom-based component in an actual teaching situation with their students. The instructor observes the trainee's teaching in the classroom and provides feedback regarding the trainee's application of the teaching skills. Through monitoring, the instructor determines the trainee's proficiency in applying each of the teaching competencies.

Using an Observation Form. To facilitate the instructor's job in this respect, we use the form shown in Figure 2, in conjunction with the criteria listed in Table 1. The form in Figure 2 guides the instructor in focusing on whether or not the trainee performs each of the teaching skills proficiently.

To use the observation form, the observing instructor lists steps of the task analysis (e.g., steps for setting a table) in the appropriate order along the left side of the form. As illustrated in Figure 2, the observer scores each teaching skill under the column labeled for the respective skill on the line corresponding to the designated step of the

---

Modeling, Practice, and Feedback

Instructor demonstration of a teaching skill, followed by trainee practice of the skill with subsequent feedback from the instructor, is the most important aspect of classroom-based training.

Modeling. When training paraeducators how to use a least-to-most assistive prompting strategy, the instructor first demonstrates a prompting sequence in a teaching program with a staff trainee who plays the role of a student.

Practice. Each trainee practices implementing the prompting strategy, with another trainee playing the role of the student.

Feedback. After the trainee practices the prompting strategy, the instructor provides the paraeducator feedback regarding the accuracy of his or her prompting.

> **In small groups, paraeducators role-play effective teaching strategies.**

task analysis. The observer scores each performed skill as being either correct (+) or incorrect (−). Nonapplicable (NA) is scored if there is no opportunity to perform one of the teaching skills for a given step of the task analysis. Table 1 shows the specific criteria for scoring a teaching skill as correct.

Providing Feedback. Following observation of the student-teaching session, the instructor provides the trainee with feedback by explaining the teaching skills that were correctly and incorrectly performed. For those teaching skills that the trainee performed incorrectly, the instructor describes or demonstrates how the skill should have been performed.

The trainee's teaching proficiency is calculated by dividing the total number of *correctly* implemented teaching skills across all program steps by the *total* number of all skills taught, and multiplying by 100%. This calculation results in a percentage of correct teaching skill application, as illustrated in Figure 2. We consider a staff trainee *proficient* when he or she scores at least 80% correct during two separate observations of student teaching.

Follow-up Supervision

We designed the final component of TSTP, follow-up supervision, to ensure that paraeducators maintain their teaching skills at the 80% proficiency level. Establishing maintenance procedures is essential for the long-term success of staff training programs (Reid et al., 1989, Chapter 4). This part of the program, of course, lasts longer than 1 day!

Follow-up supervision entails implementing a schedule for continued observation of staff teaching and provision of feedback. The frequency of follow-up sessions is determined by how proficiently a given paraeducator continues to teach—the more proficient the teaching skills, the less frequently observations with feedback are needed, and vice versa.

Role of Special Education Teachers and Administrators

We have successfully implemented TSTP using two different staff training models: direct training and pyramid training.

Figure 2. Sample of a Completed Form for Observing Teaching Proficiency

Teaching-Skills Observation Form

Trainee: Anna   Instructor: Mary   Student: Joe
Skill: using a table napkin   Date: 5-22-98

+ correct
− incorrect
NA nonapplicable

TRAINING STEPS	ORDER	PROMPTS	REINFORCES	ERROR CORRECTION
STEP 1 pick up napkin	✚ − NA	✚ − NA	✚ − NA	+ − N̸A
STEP 2 wipe mouth	✚ − NA	+ − N̸A	+ − ✚	+ ∕ NA
STEP 3 replace napkin in lap	✚ − NA	+ − N̸A	✚ − NA	+ − N̸A
STEP 4	+ − NA	+ − NA	+ − NA	+ − NA
STEP 5	+ − NA	+ − NA	+ − NA	+ − NA
STEP 6	+ − NA	+ − NA	+ − NA	+ − NA
STEP 7	+ − NA	+ − NA	+ − NA	+ − NA
STEP 8	+ − NA	+ − NA	+ − NA	+ − NA
STEP 9	+ − NA	+ − NA	+ − NA	+ − NA
STEP 10	+ − NA	+ − NA	+ − NA	+ − NA

OBSERVATION SUMMARY

CORRECT TEACHING SKILLS / # CORRECT AND INCORRECT TEACHING SKILLS = 6/7 × 100% = 86%

Feedback: Nice job! Appropriate prompting on step 1; use more assistance during error correction to avoid another error

---

Table 1. Definitions for Correct Application of the Basic Teaching Skills

Teaching Skill	Definition for Correct Application
Order	The steps of the task analysis are taught in sequence so that each step taught is preceded by the specific step listed in the task analysis.
Prompt	Each successive prompt (if more than 1 prompt is used) provided for a given step in the task analysis involves more assistance than the previous prompt.
Reinforcement	A positive consequence is provided following the last correct step of the task analysis and is not provided following any incorrectly performed step. Reinforcement could be provided following any correctly performed step but must be provided following the last correctly performed step.
Error Correction	When the student incorrectly performs a step of the task analysis (i.e., a behavior incompatible with the step), the student is required to repeat the step; and a more assistive prompt is provided on the second trial. The prompt on the second trial should provide sufficient assistance so the student completes the step without another error.

Direct Training

A model that works well in settings where fewer than 10 staff require training involves having one instructor directly train all staff. The instructor is responsible for the classroom-based training, on-the-job observations, and follow-up supervision for all staff in a school or agency. The instructor may be a principal, supervising teacher, or educational consultant—essentially, anyone with experience using the teaching strategies, observing staff performance, and providing feedback. The *Teaching-Skills Training Program Instructor's Manual,* available from the authors, serves as a guide in implementing the program (Reid & Parsons, 1994).

Pyramid Training

In school systems where a large number of staff require training, other researchers have successfully used the *pyramid* staff training model (Demchak & Browder, 1990). Using the pyramidal model, one instructor initially trains all *supervising teachers,* who, in turn, directly train the paraeducators whom they supervise. The type of training teachers should receive is twofold:

• Teachers may need to complete TSTP to ensure that the teachers themselves are proficient in the skills they will be training to paraeducators.

• Teachers should be trained in the supervisory skills of systematically observing the teaching skills of others and providing feedback to improve the teaching process. This focused supervisory training for teachers is often essential to the successful training of paraeducators because, although teachers are expected to supervise paraeducators, few teachers have had training in effective strategies for supervision.

Supervisory training for teachers should include practice in observing another staff member teach, completing the observation form, and giving feedback in a role-play situation. A protocol for teachers to use as a guide for giving diagnostic feedback is presented in Figure 3. Once a teacher is competent in observing and providing feedback in a role-play situation, the instructor observes the teacher on the job as the teacher

---

Through on-the-job monitoring, the instructor determines the trainee's proficiency in applying each of the teaching competencies.

> Focused supervisory training (in observation and feedback methods) for teachers contributes to the successful training of paraeducators.

observes the paraeducator conduct a teaching session. When the teacher can provide accurate feedback to the paraeducator regarding the latter's teaching skills, then the teacher independently observes and provides feedback to the paraeducator several times each week until the paraeducator can perform the basic teaching skills.

Research has indicated that when teachers complete TSTP, as well as the additional supervisory training, they can train paraeducators to implement the basic teaching skills through observation and feedback in the classroom and *without the paraeducators participating in the classroom-based component* (Jensen et al., 1997). Moreover, these researchers found that the supervisory training improved the teacher's *own teaching skills* when those skills were below the 80% proficiency criterion prior to training. The supervising teacher provides follow-up supervision for paraeducators through intermittent observations and feedback.

Figure 3 shows a checklist that supervising teachers can use to guide their feedback sessions. This form actually constitutes a "task analysis" for providing feedback, beginning with setting a positive tone and ending with making a positive statement.

Student and Parent Input

The highly effective teaching strategies espoused by the Teaching-Skills Training Program require brief teaching sessions involving one student at a time. Individual instruction, however, is only one component of a quality educational experience for students with severe disabilities. Students and family members should have significant input into which skills warrant teaching in this manner and how much time should be directed to individual teaching services versus other valuable educational supports.

When individualized teaching, embedded within the daily routine, is deemed necessary, the TSTP provides paraeducators with the requisite teaching skills to improve student achievement.

References

Demchak, M., & Browder, D. M. (1990). An evaluation of the pyramid model of staff training in group homes for adults with severe handicaps. *Education and Training in Mental Retardation, 25,* 150–163.

Jensen, J. E., Parsons, M. B., & Reid, D. H. (1997). *Multiple effects of training teachers to improve the data recording of teacher aides.* Manuscript submitted for publication.

Parsons, M. B., Reid, D. H., & Green, C. W. (1993). Preparing direct service staff to teach people with severe disabilities: A comprehensive evaluation of an effective and acceptable training program. *Behavioral Residential Treatment, 8,* 163–185.

Parsons, M. B., Reid, D. H., & Green, C. W. (1996). Training basic teaching skills to community and institutional support staff for people with severe disabilities: A one-day program. *Research In Developmental Disabilities, 17,* 467–485.

Reid, D. H., & Parsons, M. B. (1994). *Training to teach in a day: The teaching skills training program instructor's manual.* Morganton, NC: Carolina Behavior Analysis and Support Center, Ltd.*

Reid, D. H., & Parsons, M. B. (1996). A comparison of staff acceptability of immediate versus delayed verbal feedback in staff training. *Journal of Organizational Behavior Management, 16*(2), 35–48.

Reid, D. H., Parsons, M. B., & Green, C. W. (1989). *Staff management in human services: Behavioral research and application.* Springfield, IL: Charles C Thomas.*

Books Now

*To order books marked by an asterisk (*), please call 24 hrs/365 days: 1-800-BOOKS-NOW (266-5766) or (801) 261-1187, or visit them on the Web at http://www.BooksNow.com/TeachingExceptional.htm. Use VISA, M/C, or AMEX or send check or money order + $4.95 S&H ($2.50 each add'l item) to: Books Now, Suite 125, 448 East 6400 South, Salt Lake City, UT 84107.

Marsha B. Parsons, *Associate Director, Carolina Behavior Analysis and Support Center, Ltd., Morganton, North Carolina.* **Dennis H. Reid,** *Associate Professor, Louisiana State University Medical Center, New Orleans.*

Address correspondence to Marsha B. Parsons, Carolina Behavior Analysis and Support Center, Ltd., P.O. Box 425, Morganton, NC 28680.

Figure 3. Protocol for Giving Diagnostic Feedback to a Staff Member Following the Observation of a Teaching Session

Supervisor's Feedback Checklist

Staff Trainee _____ Student _____ Skill _____

Supervisor _____ Location _____ Time _____ Date _____

Feedback Components

Check each component included in your feedback to the trainee. Check NA (nonapplicable) for components 4 and 5 if no teaching errors were made.

	Yes	No	NA
1. Set a positive tone for feedback session			
2. Began diagnostic feedback with positive feedback			
3. Gave appropriate positive feedback.			
4. Identified each skill category with teaching errors			
5. For each category with teaching errors, described how the teaching skill should have been performed correctly			
6. Solicited questions for feedback from trainee			
7. Referenced current training status			
8. Ended feedback session with a positive statement			

The Unexpected Benefits of High School Peer Tutoring

Amy Wildman Longwill
Harold L. Kleinert

Flexible scheduling, course credits, and alternative assessments are some characteristics of an innovative peer tutoring program in Danville, Kentucky. And students with disabilities, who receive the tutoring, are not the only beneficiaries.

This article describes how high school peer tutoring programs can enhance educational outcomes, including increased academic performance, for students both with and without moderate and severe disabilities. Moreover, we describe how peer tutoring programs can play an important role for all participants as high schools increasingly undergo fundamental educational restructuring. Finally, we note how peer tutoring programs can promote greater levels of general education class participation and community inclusion for students with significant disabilities.

Fundamental Changes in High School Programs

Over the past decade, significant changes in best practices have occurred at the high school level in both general and special education services for students with moderate and severe disabilities. In general education, restructuring has resulted in the following strategies:

Interdisciplinary projects
Block scheduling
Alternate portfolios
Reciprocal teaching and learning
Course credit for peer tutoring
Student-produced adaptations
Cooperative learning
Natural supports
Community links
Developing career interests
Genuine friendships

- *Block scheduling*, for example, students attending four classes per semester, with each class lasting 90 minutes instead of 60, to allow for greater in-depth exploration of specific topics.
- *Increased interdisciplinary learning opportunities*, for example, an ecology assignment in which students are required to integrate writing, mathematics, and biology skills into a single, applied project on recycling and its impact on pollution in their own community.
- *Performance-based assessment*, in which students are evaluated more by the solutions they develop to address actual problems rather than the knowledge they can feed back on more traditional pen-and-pencil tests (Brandt, 1992; Falvey, Gage, & Eshilian, 1995).

Best practices for high-school age students with moderate and severe disabilities have likewise undergone a significant shift during this time. Following a renewed focus on essential life outcomes (Hardman, McDonnell, & Welch, 1997) teachers have placed greater emphasis on the development of social interaction skills, genuine friendships, and support networks for students with significant disabilities at the high school level, and the importance of learning *along with* (and not always *from*) their peers without disabilities (Coots, Bishop, Grenot-Scheyer, & Falvey, 1995; Giangreco, Cloninger, & Iverson, 1993). Moreover, reflected in the newly enacted 1997 Amendments to the Individuals with Disabilities Education Act (IDEA) is the requirement that the learning results of students with significant disabilities be included in general state and district student assessment measures—that these students' educational outcomes are a part of school accountability, too.

These fundamental changes in school practice at the national level have had their counterpart in Kentucky. As a result of the Kentucky

27. Unexpected Benefits of High School Peer Tutoring

High school peer tutoring programs can enhance educational outcomes, including increased academic performance, for students both with and without moderate and severe disabilities.

Education Reform Act of 1990 (KERA), educators have established a set of 57 learner outcomes, or academic expectations. These outcomes are meant for *all* students, including students with moderate and severe disabilities. Thus *all* students, including those with severe disabilities, take part in the state's performance-based assessment and accountability system (Steffy, 1993; Ysseldyke, Thurlow, & Shriner, 1992). While students with and without *mild* disabilities are collecting their best work for their required math and writing accountability portfolios, students with *moderate and severe* cognitive disabilities are participating in the state's assessment system through the Alternate Portfolio (Kleinert, Kearns, & Kennedy, 1997).

Finally, these national and state reforms have had a significant impact at the local level. For example, Danville, Kentucky, High School (DHS) incorporated block scheduling for all students at the start of the 1995–96 school year. To emphasize a more interdisciplinary curricular approach, the principal implemented a school-wide policy that students must complete one entry for their required writing portfolio from *every* class, including electives. At the same time, students with moderate and severe disabilities had begun developing their own Alternate Portfolios, as an integral part of the school's score in Kentucky's mandatory assessment and accountability system.

All these changes—for students with moderate and severe disabilities and for general education students—have prompted educators in Kentucky to take a new look at high school peer tutoring. Specifically, we needed to ask how peer tutoring can focus on these essential outcomes for all students, with activities designed so that students are learning with and from each other.

Peer Tutoring in Danville

Peer tutoring is not a new program at Danville High. In fact, peer tutoring, as a formal credit elective, originated in Kentucky at DHS in 1983. As was typical in many such programs, peer tutoring at DHS was initially set up to provide social interactions between students with and without disabilities. Students without disabilities enrolled in peer tutoring to receive academic course credit. The course required students to complete a series of self-study modules in such areas as beliefs and attitudes, legal rights of people with disabilities, educational programming needs, and family issues; take multiple choice type tests on their readings; and do class projects (Guiltinan & Kleinert, 1987; Kleinert et al., 1991). Students also received grades for their daily work and their interactions with the students with moderate and severe disabilities for whom they acted as tutors. The instructors hoped that, from these more formally structured interactions, friendships would develop (and, sometimes, real friendships did occur).

With the emergence of both general and special education reforms, however, it was time to make changes in peer tutoring, as well. What has evolved at DHS is a series of activities and assignments that allow peer tutors to learn about issues of concern to people with disabilities, to learn with students with disabilities as they work on projects together, and to develop deeper insights into the nature of human relationships and social policy (e.g., inclusion, full community participation). These activities have allowed peer tutors to develop an awareness of significant life issues and to develop their own opinions and beliefs about these issues. (See box "Setting Up a Peer Tutoring Program.")

Some of the peer tutor topics for both reading and writing assignments have included the desirability, benefits, and potential drawbacks of including students with severe disabilities in general education classes at the high school level; opportunities for peer tutors to develop their *own* strategies for adapting and modifying general education class activities to meet the needs of a student with a moderate or severe disability; the meaning and importance

---

What the Research Says About Peer Tutoring

Extensive research on peer tutoring can be viewed in three categories:

- Peer tutoring is a well-recognized strategy for increasing instructional effectiveness in programs for students with moderate and severe cognitive disabilities and enhancing interactions with peers without disabilities (Haring, 1991; Haring, Breen, Pitts-Conway, Lee, & Gaylord-Ross, 1987; Helmstetter, Peck, & Giangreco, 1994; Salisbury, Gallucci, Palombaro, & Peck, 1995; Sprague & McDonnell, 1984; Thousand & Villa, 1990).
- Peer tutoring offers many benefits to students both with and without disabilities, as well as to their parents and teachers (see Figure 1), as noted extensively throughout the literature.
- Much of the research has focused on social and educational outcomes for the *tutee* (Helmstetter, Peck, & Giangreco, 1994; Kishi & Meyer, 1994).

Figure 1
Benefits of Peer Tutoring

For Students with Moderate and Severe Disabilities:
- Opportunities for sustained, positive interactions and friendships (Haring, 1991; Stainback, Stainback, & Wilkinson, 1992)
- Increased opportunities to practice needed skills (Sprague & McDonnell, 1984)
- Age-appropriate role models (Kleinert, Guiltinan, & Farmer, 1991)
- Development of prosocial behaviors and communication skills (Staub & Hunt, 1993)
- Promotion of equity among students and the discovery of hidden strengths of students with significant disabilities (Salisbury, Gallucci, Palombaro, & Peck, 1995)

For Peers without Disabilities:
- Increased acceptance of individual differences (Helmstetter, Peck, & Giangreco, 1994)
- A deeper sense of social justice and advocacy for others (Falvey, Gage, & Eshilian, 1995)
- Increased self-esteem and knowledge of self (Peck, Donaldson, & Pezzoli, 1990; Helmstetter et al., 1994)
- Better understanding of how to communicate with and provide assistance to people with moderate and severe disabilities (Clayton, 1993; Staub & Hunt, 1993)

For Special Education Teachers:
- Increased instructional time for students in school and community settings (Sprague & McDonnell, 1984)
- More age-appropriate expectations for their students (Kleinert et al., 1991)
- Opportunities to become more personally and professionally integrated into the school's general education programs (Clayton, 1993)

For Parents of Students with Moderate and Severe Disabilities:
- Increased skill gains for their son or daughter
- Enhanced opportunities for the development of friendships for their son or daughter (Kleinert et al., 1991)

For Parents of General Education Students:
- An interest in pursuing a career in the helping professions on the part of their son or daughter
- Increased enthusiasm for school on the part of their son or daughter (Kleinert et al., 1991)

of friendships in all of our lives; and the pros (or cons) of the Americans with Disabilities Act as an instrument of social justice and basic human rights. The new peer tutoring assignments relate closely to the academic expectations that have been identified for all Kentucky students (Steffy, 1993). For example, here are two of these outcomes:
- Students recognize issues of justice, equality, responsibility, choice, and freedom, and apply these democratic principles to real-life situations.
- Students use critical thinking skills in a variety of situations that will be encountered in life.

Each activity requires peer tutors to develop a written product, usually from a reading assignment and always from a writing prompt. Students are required to relate the topics to their own experiences and to their activities in peer tutoring; they are graded on both the quality and logic of their ideas, as well as the clarity of their writing.

Indeed, one of the most valuable aspects of peer tutoring in Kentucky today is that peer tutors are often providing assistance to students with moderate and severe disabilities in the development of Alternate Portfolio entries, while the students without disabilities are simultaneously able to complete requirements for their *own* portfolios. Peer tutoring has thus evolved more into a context of learning *together*, helping one another and supporting each other's efforts. Such a context provides a more fertile ground for the development of genuine friendships, and lessens the potentially negative impact of peer tutors seeing themselves as extensions of the teacher, as opposed to participating as true learning partners of students with significant disabilities (Kleinert, 1996).

For example, all students at DHS are required to take a Writing Workshop Class as a part of developing their school accountability portfolios. Together, peer tutors and students with significant disabilities work on their "Letters to the Reviewer" (a state requirement for both general writing portfolios and Alternate Portfolios). They also work together to compile their own Table of Contents, design their own Cover Page, and assemble their portfolio entries. For a student with a significant disability whose primary mode of communication is a picture communication system, a peer may help that student to develop a written description of what the student has communicated through pictures.

For many of the same reasons, peer tutoring also provides an excellent framework for increasing the meaningful participation of students with moderate and severe disabilities in general education classes. If a peer tutor is enrolled in the same class as a student with a disability, that peer tutor can be an excellent source of natural support for the student with a disability. Indeed, one of the required peer tutor assignments (identifying potential adaptations in general education class activities)

27. Unexpected Benefits of High School Peer Tutoring

Setting Up a Peer Tutoring Program

1. Create with your school administration and other interested faculty a framework for a high school peer tutoring course. Develop a course syllabus, including course overview, learning objectives, and required activities and assignments, and decide who may enroll in the class (at DHS enrollment is usually limited to 11th and 12th graders).
2. Include the new course in your high school's description of course offerings. Make sure that eligible students, faculty, and guidance counselors are all aware of the new elective.
3. Ensure that students can enroll in the peer tutoring course through the same process that they register for their other courses. (Some teachers have also found it helpful to personally interview prospective peer tutors.)
4. Do not accept more peer tutors than you can actively engage in learning activities with students with disabilities, and limit the number of peers who may sign up for the course during each scheduled period of the day.
5. On the first day of class, give peer tutors the essential information they need about the course (e.g., grading, assignments, behavioral expectations). Stress the importance of learning together and that students are expected to support each other.
6. Schedule writing assignments (based on required readings and school and community learning experiences) approximately every 2 weeks. Initial assignments are due weekly; toward the end of the course, more in-depth projects are due at approximately 3-week intervals.
7. Make writing assignments reflective and insist on the student's best work. You may want to coordinate the development and grading of these assignments with members of your school's English faculty.
8. Ensure that students with significant disabilities and peer tutors are given a range of opportunities throughout the course to engage in cooperative learning activities in both school and community settings, as well as the opportunities to develop friendships.
9. For students who have completed the peer tutoring course but who wish to continue their learning, consider offering a more advanced course on an independent study basis (this should be developed as an individualized learning contract between the student, teacher, and school principal).
10. Frequently evaluate the impact of your peer tutoring program; seek the input of students (with and without disabilities), parents, and other teachers, as well as your own observations and data on student learning.

provides a wealth of ideas for both special and general education teachers. In the context of that assignment, students read an article about curricular modifications to enhance general education class participation for students with significant disabilities (see Tashie et al., 1993). Students must then develop ways, through the use of a general education class activity analysis (Roger, Gorevin, Fellows, & Kelly, 1992), to adapt oneของ their *own* classes for an individual student with a significant disability. Peers have developed a number of practical and innovative strategies for adapting course content and instruction across a variety of classes (e.g., English, art, history, and music). Here are some of their ideas:

- In art class, instead of having Richard, who has severe disabilities, draw a picture, he could paste pictures from magazines.
- When completing research papers, Tony could work with picture symbols on a topic or theme of his choice. He could use the pictures, arranged or copied from his communication system, for a research report.
- When a large reading assignment is required, peers could write summaries of each reading for Karla. This would help the student who was developing the summary learn the material and help Karla understand the basic themes or ideas.
- In typing class, when there are longer assignments, Tom could type his personal identification information or what he did in the community that day.
- As a part of the yearbook class, Lauren could classify photographs into activity categories such as school classes, clubs, and sports.
- In biology, for an oral research presentation to the class, Derrick could develop a collage of local fruits and vegetables, and the best places to purchase the seeds for those plants.

Besides providing an essential link to academic classes, peer tutors can also provide a natural link to the community for students with significant disabilities. Many peer tutors work in the community on a part-time basis and introduce students with disabilities to their co-workers in their own jobs. Peers also may provide support to students with disabilities in their respective job searches. For example, one of the requirements of the peer tutoring class is that both peer tutors and students with disabilities develop their own job resumés; of course, they work on this together.

Yet it is important to remember that this community-linking goes both ways. Because students with significant disabilities usually participate in community-based instruction (CBI) extensively at the secondary level, many of them are already familiar with their community. For example, when a new discount store opened in Danville, students with moderate and severe disabilities often chose that new store as a site to work on their purchasing skills. Two of the peer tutors, assigned to provide assistance with shopping and budgeting skills, commented what a help the students (with disabilities) were to them in learning their way around the new store.

Peer tutors love to go on community-based instruction themselves,

> ### Reflections of a Peer Tutor
>
> *This is my second semester as a peer tutor. That in itself says a lot about my feelings toward the class. You don't see me signing up for plant physiology for a second semester! I have learned more about my true identity and aspirations in this class than I ever dreamed to. The values and experiences that I have gained will be important to me for years to come. It is easy to express my growth as a person through writing about peer tutoring. Several pieces that I have written will be included in my senior writing portfolio.*
>
> *The particular prompt I am writing from instructs me to write an introduction to peer tutoring for future peer tutors. It will include advice, suggestions, and examples of what it takes to be a successful peer tutor.*
>
> *Day one. I know what you are thinking, unless you have had a personal encounter with students with disabilities prior to now, you feel the same way that everyone else does. You are somewhat nervous, intrigued, and even frightened. Don't be—sit back, take a deep breath, and get over it!*
>
> *It will take time and patience to become a good peer tutor. It will not happen overnight. The students will not magically adjust to you, or fall in love with you, neither you with them, but it won't take long....*
>
> *I can honestly say that I know I have gained just as much from being a peer tutor as the students have from me. I have grown immensely as a peer tutor, and filled an empty place in my heart....*
>
> *Soon I will be moving on to college, and few classes have prepared me for the next phase of my life like peer tutoring. I have learned about happiness, diversity, patience, strength, determination, and above all, life in its true essence.*
>
> *Katie Corcoran*
> *Danville High School*

and the longer class periods facilitated by block scheduling has increased opportunities for their participation. In addition to providing carefully planned assistance on targeted CBI skills to students with moderate and severe disabilities, peer tutors continue to gain skills in budgeting, nutrition, banking, and overall shopping. Peers continue to comment about how much they learn when they go on CBI with students with disabilities.

Evidence of Learning Together

As noted previously, students with moderate and severe disabilities in Kentucky must complete Alternate Portfolios as the students in the general assessment system simultaneously complete writing and math portfolios. For students in the Alternate Portfolio assessment, the special education teacher must enable these students to show evidence of extensive interactions with peers and reliance on natural supports, as well as clear documentation of students' performance of learned skills across a wide range of school and community settings. This evidence is presented through a series of portfolio entries (see Kleinert et al., 1997).

Peer tutors are valued resources in documenting each of these Alternate Portfolio assessment requirements. Peer tutors frequently develop friendships with students with disabilities that go well beyond the classroom. Peers collaborate with students with disabilities within and outside of the school, in such activities as going to youth group, out for pizza on Saturday night, or to the movies; researching topics at the school and public libraries; and going Christmas shopping together. Peers collaborate on community instruction while shopping, banking, eating at a fast food restaurant, and participating in community recreation and leisure activities. Each of these instances can provide an appropriate context for showcasing both learned skills and valued social relations at an exemplary performance level for students in Kentucky's alternate assessment system (Kleinert et al., 1997). This documentation can take the form of written or photographic entries (e.g., a portfolio entry centered on community recreation/leisure activities in which the student engages), course projects developed together, or examples of instructional programming and student self-evaluation data across school and community settings. Finally, peer tutors may assist students with moderate and severe disabilities in completing their entries and assembling the entries into a finished portfolio.

As peer tutors provide this support, they also are developing their own portfolio entries. Essays on the meaning and purpose of friendship, the essential need for all students to be an integral part of their community, or what they have learned from their peer tutoring experience have provided the context for outstanding writing entries. Students have even used their peer tutoring assignments as a part of their college admission application, as evidence of their best writing.

Encouraging Self-Evaluation

As a culminating activity for their peer tutoring experience, tutors are required to complete a self-evaluation matrix during the latter part of the semester. For this assignment, each peer determines five characteristics they believe essential for a peer tutor. They then must describe that characteristic, as it would be shown at four different performance levels (novice, apprentice, proficient, and distinguished—the four levels that are used to score students' work in Kentucky's overall assessment and accountability system). Finally, using their own rubric, peers must evaluate their performance. They must also complete a written explanation for their score. Here are some of their final comments on the course and on their own performance:

- "This class will have more meaning than *any* other classes on your schedule.... Expect the class to be one you will remember for a lifetime."
- "You are there for support, not to do students' work, a job they are supposed to be doing.... You will have learned that students with disabilities are capable of doing anything you are."

Peer tutoring continues to evolve at DHS in a way that reflects rapidly changing educational practices and paradigms for students both with and without moderate and severe disabilities. The teachers have experienced a renewed excitement and challenge related to peer tutoring, as they attempt to integrate the learning experiences of their students into a curriculum reflecting high expectations for all.

References

Brandt, R. (1992). On performance assessment: A conversation with Grant Wiggins. *Educational Leadership, 49*(8), 35–37.

Clayton, J. (1993). *Peer power manual for middle school students.* Lexington: Kentucky Statewide Systems Change Project, Human Development Institute, University of Kentucky.*

Coots, J., Bishop, K., Grenot-Scheyer, M., & Falvey, M. (1995). Practices in general education: Past and present. In Falvey, M. (Ed.), *Inclusive and heterogeneous schooling: Assessment, curriculum, and instruction* (p. 18). Baltimore: Paul Brookes.*

Falvey, M., Gage, S., & Eshilian, L. (1995). Secondary curriculum and instruction. In Falvey, M. (Ed.) *Inclusive and heterogeneous schooling: Assessment, curriculum, and instruction* (p. 355). Baltimore: Paul Brookes.*

Giangreco, M., Cloninger, C., & Iverson, V. (1993). *Choosing options and accommodations for children.* Baltimore: Paul Brookes.*

Guiltinan, S., & Kleinert, H. (1987). *High school peer tutoring manual.* Frankfort: Division of Exceptional Children Services, Kentucky Department of Education.

Hardman, M., McDonnell, J., & Welch, M. (1997). Perspectives on the future of IDEA. *Journal of the Association for Persons with Severe Handicaps, 22,* 61–76.

Haring, T. (1991). Social relationships. In Meyer, L., Peck, C., & Brown, L. (Eds.), *Critical issues in the lives of people with severe disabilities* (p. 204). Baltimore: Paul Brookes.*

Haring, T., Breen, C., Pitts-Conway, V., Lee, M., & Gaylord-Ross, R. (1987). Adolescent peer tutoring and special friend experiences. *Journal of the Association for Persons with Severe Handicaps, 12,* 280–286.

Helmstetter, E., Peck, C., & Giangreco, M. (1994). Outcomes of interactions with peers with moderate or severe disabilities: A statewide survey of high school students. *Journal of the Association for Persons with Severe Handicaps, 19,* 263–276.

Kishi, G., & Meyer, L. (1994). What children report and remember: A six-year follow-up of the effects of social contact between peers with and without severe disabilities. *Journal of the Association for Severe Handicaps, 19,* 277–289.

Kleinert, H. (1996). *Kentucky classrooms—Everyone's welcome: A practical guide to learning and living together.* Lexington: Human Development Institute, University of Kentucky.

Kleinert, H., Guiltinan, S., & Farmer, J. (1991). *High school peer tutoring manual—revised edition.* Frankfort: Division of Exceptional Children Services, Kentucky Department of Education.

Kleinert, H., Kearns, J., & Kennedy, S. (1997). Accountability for *all* students: Kentucky's Alternate Portfolio assessment for students with moderate and severe cognitive disabilities. *Journal of the Association for Persons with Severe Handicaps, 22,* 88–101.

Peck, C., Donaldson, J., & Pezzoli, M. (1990). Some benefits nonhandicapped adolescents perceive for themselves from their social relationships with peers who have severe handicaps. *Journal of the Association for Persons with Severe Handicaps, 15,* 241–249.

Roger, B., Gorevin, R., Fellows, M., & Kelly, D. (1992). *Schools are for all kids: School site implementation level II training.* San Francisco: California Research Institute, San Francisco State University. (ERIC Document Reproduction Service No. ED 365 052)

Salisbury, C., Gallucci, C., Palombaro, M., & Peck, C. (1995). Strategies that promote social relations among elementary students with and without severe disabilities in inclusive schools. *Exceptional Children, 62,* 125–137.

Sprague, J., & McDonnell, J. (1984). *Effective use of secondary age peer tutors: A resource manual for high school teachers.* Eugene: Center on Human Development, University of Oregon.

Stainback, W., Stainback, S., & Wilkinson, A. (1992). Encouraging peer supports and friendships. *TEACHING Exceptional Children, 24*(2), 6–11.

Staub, D., & Hunt, P. (1993). The effects of social interaction training on high school peer tutors of schoolmates with severe disabilities. *Exceptional Children, 60,* 41–57.

Steffy, B. (1993). Top-down—bottom-up: Systemic change in Kentucky. *Educational Leadership, 51*(1), 42–44.

Tashie, C., Shapiro-Barnard, S., Schuh, M., Jorgensen, C., Dillon, A., Dixon, B., & Nisbet, J. (1993). *From special to regular, from ordinary to extraordinary.* Concord: Institute on Disability/University Affiliated Program, University of New Hampshire. (ERIC Document Reproduction Service No. ED 387 963).

Thousand, J., & Villa, R. (1990). Sharing expertise and responsibilities through teaching teams. In Stainback, W., & Stainback, S. (Eds), *Support networks for inclusive schooling: Interdependent, integrated education.* (p. 162). Baltimore: Paul Brookes.

Ysseldyke, J., Thurlow, M., & Shriner, J. (1992). Outcomes are for special educators too. *TEACHING Exceptional Children, 25*(1), 36–50.

Books Now

*To order books marked by an asterisk (*), please call 24 hrs/365 days: 1-800-BOOKS-NOW (266-5766) or (702) 258-3338 and ask for ext. 1212; or visit them on the Web at http://www.BooksNow.com/TeachingExceptional.htm. Use VISA, M/C, or AMEX or send check or money order + $4.95 S&H ($2.50 each add'l item) to: Books Now, 660 W. Charleston Blvd., Las Vegas, NV 89102.

Amy Wildman Longwill, *Teacher, Danville High School, Kentucky.* **Harold L. Kleinert,** *Training Director, Human Development Institute, University of Kentucky, Lexington.*

Address correspondence to Harold L. Kleinert, Human Development Institute, University of Kentucky, 126 Mineral Industries Bldg, Lexington, KY 40506-0051 (e-mail: haroldk@ihdi.uky.edu).

Authors' Note: As of this writing, Kentucky is the only state in which all students, including students with moderate and severe cognitive disabilities, are fully represented in school and district accountability indexes (Kleinert et al., 1997). Yet the 1997 Amendments to the Individuals with Disabilities Education Act (IDEA) require that all states develop alternate assessments for those students who cannot participate in general state and district educational assessments, and that these alternate assessments be in place no later than July 1, 2000.

Preparation of this article was supported, in part, by the U.S. Department of Education Office of Special Education and Rehabilitation Services (Grant No. H086J20007). However, the opinions expressed do not necessarily reflect the position or policy of the U.S. Department of Education, and no official endorsement should be inferred.

PERSPECTIVES ON TECHNOLOGY in Special Education

During the past 25 years, we have seen a dramatic evolution of technology in education: microcomputer technology, research on instructional procedures, and many new assistive devices and equipment.

A. Edward Blackhurst

My special education career began in 1960 as a teacher of adolescents with mild mental retardation in a self-contained classroom in an inner-city school. My students were between the ages of 12 and 14, and their academic achievement levels were between Grades 1 and 4. The school district supplied me with a basal reading series, and I was instructed to teach the students how to read. (This was before individualized education programs, or IEPS, were required by federal law.) Although my students needed to develop basic reading skills, these teenagers did not respond well to the "baby stuff" in the texts. I became frustrated by the lack of age-appropriate instructional materials that could be used to teach basic skills.

While casting about for resources to support my teaching, I attended a demonstration of a device called a *tachistoscope*. This was an overhead projector equipped with a camera shutter that could control the speed at which visual images, such as words and phrases, could be projected (as quickly as $1/100$ of a second). It struck me that the use of such a device might be useful in capturing and holding the attention of my students when I was teaching them how to read basic sight vocabulary words.

I arranged to to borrow a tachistoscope and designed a research study to determine whether it was useful as a supplement to reading instruction. The results of that study indicated that the tachistoscopic training was effective (Blackhurst, 1967). My interest in technology applications for students enrolled in special education programs was born.

That interest was nurtured while attending graduate school, where I had the opportunity to work with an early pioneer in programmed instruction, Robert Glaser, who coined the term "student-subject matter interface." He was interested in enhancing learning by conceptualizing devices that would make it easier for students to interact with subject matter. I became intrigued with this concept and began to speculate about potential interface devices that might be developed to address the unique needs of students with disabilities (Blackhurst, 1965).

Since those early experiences, much of my professional career has been devoted to exploring the potential that technology has for teaching students with disabilities and for preparing special education professionals to work in a variety of different roles. This article represents perspectives I have developed over the years as a participant-observer in the evolution of technology applications in special education—ways to view technology, the role technology plays in the field of special education, and some of the forces that have affected the development of technology applications (For historical and descriptive information, see Alliance for Technology Access, 1996; Baumgart, Johnson, & Helmstetter, 1990; Behrmann, 1984; Beukelman & Mirenda, 1992 Blackhurst & Hofmeister, 1980; Church & Glennen, 1992 Cook & Hussey, 1995; Flippo, Inge, & Barcus, 1995; Galvan & Scherer, 1996; Lewis, 1993; Lindsey, 1997; Male 1994; Margalit, 1990; Silverman, 1995; Taber, 1983.)

Perspectives on the Technology Continuum

To many people, the term *technology* conjures up visions of computers and other high-tech devices, both expensive and complicated. Often, such perspectives focus solely on hardware and equipment and overlook the procedures that teachers use in the classroom.

We need to view technology as a tool that can be used to solve problems in the education of their students. I like to think of solutions as a continuum—ranging from "high-tech" to "no-tech":

> **High-tech** solutions involve the use of sophisticated devices, such as computers and interactive multimedia systems.
> **Medium-tech** solutions use less complicated electronic or mechanical devices, such as videocassette players and wheelchairs.
> **Low-tech** solutions are less sophisticated aids, such as adapted spoon handles, Velcro fasteners, or raised desks that can accommodate a wheelchair.
> **No-tech** solutions require no devices or equipment. These might involve the use of systematic teaching procedures or the services of related services personnel such as physical or occupational therapists.

In making decisions about the type of technology tools or supports a particular student might require, a good approach is to start with no-tech or low-tech solutions and then work up the continuum as needed. Too often, when people make technology decisions in IEP meetings, they tend to *start* at high-tech solutions. For example, if a student has difficulty writing legibly, IEP planners may recommend providing the student with a laptop computer to take from class to class (cost: $1,500–3,000). In reality, an electronic keyboard with memory that can be downloaded into a desktop computer later in the day may be more appropriate (cost: about $300). Although the student in this example may eventually need a laptop computer, the electronic keyboard may be a better place to start.

Perspectives on Types of Technology

In 1926, Pressey developed the first "teaching machine." Was this the first example of educational technology? Not necessarily—as the congressional Commission on Instructional Technology (1970) concluded: In addition to devices and equipment, instructional technology also involves a systematic way of designing and delivering instruction.

During the past 25 years, we have seen a dramatic evolution of technology in education: microcomputer technology, research on instructional procedures, and many new assistive devices and equipment. In addition to technology productivity tools such as word processors, researchers and educators today recognize four types of technology: the technology of teaching, medical technology, instructional technology, and assistive technology (Blackhurst & Cross, 1993):

> **The technology of teaching** includes systematically designed procedures and strategies that are applied in precise ways. They typically include well-defined objectives; precise instructional procedures based on the tasks students are required to learn; small, sequenced units of instruction; a high degree of teacher activity; high levels of student involvement; liberal use of reinforcement; and careful monitoring of student performance. These technologies include direct instruction, applied behavior analysis, competency-based instruction, learning strategies, and response prompting (see, e.g., Alberto & Troutman, 1995; Carnine, Silbert, & Kameenui, 1990; Wolery, Ault, & Doyle, 1992).
> **Medical technology** continues to amaze us, with almost miraculous surgical procedures and new devices that keep people alive. For example, new technologies provide respirator assistance (oxygen supplementation, mechanical ventilation, positive airway pressure devices) and surveillance of vital signs (cardiorespiratory monitors, pulse oximeters) (Batshaw & Perret, 1992).
> **Instructional technology** includes various types of hardware and software, combined with innovative teaching methods, to accommodate learners' needs in the classroom. Such technology may include videotapes, computer-assisted instruction, or complex hypermedia programs in which computers are used to control the display of audio and visual images stored on videodisc (Blackhurst & Morse, 1996). The use of telecommunication systems, particularly the Internet (Williams, 1995) and its World Wide Web (Williams, 1996), has great promise for use in classrooms and for distance education.
> **Assistive technology** includes various services and devices designed to help people with disabilities function within the environment. Examples include communication aids, alternative computer keyboards, adaptive switches, and services such as those that might be provided by speech/language pathologists. To locate such services, educators can use computer databases such as HyperABLEDATA (Trace Center, 1996) and the Adaptive Device Locator System (Academic Software, 1996).

Creative and knowledgeable educators—or teams of educators and other professionals—often use these technologies in combination. For example, students who are unable to use their hands to operate a computer keyboard may use a voice-operated computer (assistive technology) that provides instruction from a software program that was designed to deliver spelling instruction (instructional technology) using a constant time delay response prompt fading instructional procedure (technology of teaching).

A Functional Perspective About Technology

Unfortunately, many decisions about applications of technology in special education are "device driven." As new devices appear on the market, it is not uncommon to find consumers, parents, vendors, and professionals advocate strongly for their acquisition and use with different students—often with less than satisfactory results. Instead of getting caught up in the allure of new products with intriguing features, a better perspective is to focus on problems that children have in functioning within the environment. For example, a preschooler with cerebral palsy may lack the fine muscle control that will permit her to fasten buttons so that she can get dressed independently. A boy with a visual impairment may be unable to use printed material that is being used for instruction in an English class. Another student, due to unknown cause, may be unable to solve math problems. Similarly, a child who has been in an automobile accident may have had a severe head injury that has impaired her ability to speak clearly.

In all of these cases, environmental demands have been placed on the children to perform some function that they will find difficult to execute because of a set of unique circumstances or restriction in functional capability caused by the lack of personal resources. For example, the above children lack the physical or mental capability to button, read, calculate, or speak.

Many variables, which interact in very complex ways, are involved in making decisions about the provision of special education and related services and the selection and use of technology. Figure 1 illustrates those variables and their interrelationships.

When making planning decisions, there is the need to know things such as the nature of the demands that are being placed on the child from the environment and how those demands create the requirements to perform different human functions, such as learning, walking, talking, seeing, and hearing. It is important to know how such requirements are—or are not—being met by the child and how factors such as the child's perceptions and the availability of personal resources such as intelligence, sight, hearing, and mobility can affect the responses the child can make. In addition, it is important to understand how availability of external supports, such as special education, different types of therapy, and technology can impact on the child's ability to produce functional responses to the environmental demands.

Although each exceptional child will be unique, the common challenge is to identify and apply the best possible array of special education and related services that will provide support, adjustment, or compensation for the child's functional needs or deficits. A variety of responses may be appropriate. For example, Velcro fasteners may be used to replace buttons on garments for the child having difficulty with buttoning. Braille or audio materials may be provided for the child who cannot read conventional print. The student who has difficulty calculating may require specialized, intense direct math instruction, while a computerized device that produces speech may enable the child who cannot talk to communicate. Monitoring and evaluation provide feedback about the personal changes that have occurred in order to determine whether additional modifications may be required.

The model in Figure 1 places technology in its proper perspective: as an external support. Functions that can be aided by technology include existence, communication, body support and positioning, travel and mobility, environmental adaptation, education and learning, rehabilitation, and sports, leisure, and recreation. Additional information about this functional approach and how it relates to special education and technology applications can be found elsewhere (Blackhurst & Cross, 1993; Blackhurst & Lahm, 1997).

Perspectives on Federal Initiatives

Over the years, the federal government has stimulated technology applications in special education. Federal laws and regulations have included technology mandates and funding to support a variety of technology research and development, training, and service activities.

Legislated support for technology can be traced back to Public Law 45-186 in 1879, which awarded $10,000 to the American Printing House for the Blind to produce Braille materials. Although many other laws were established to support services to people with disabilities, four acts—and their amendments—have had the greatest impact for technology applications.

Figure 1

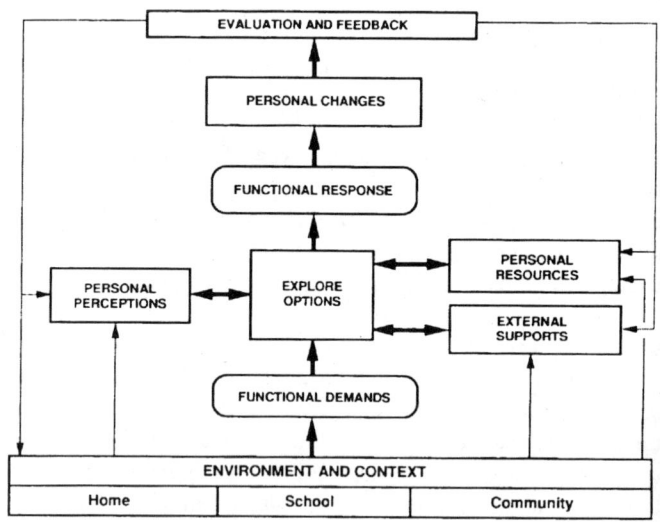

The Individuals with Disabilities Education Act (IDEA, P.L. 94-142 and its amendments) guarantees the right of all children with disabilities to a free and appropriate education in the least restrictive environment. As part of the IEP planning process, parents, teachers, and administrators are required to consider technologies that may help a child meet the IEP objectives.

P.L. 99-506 amended the Rehabilitation Act of 1973 by adding Section 508. This amendment ensures access to computers and other electronic office equipment in places of federal employment. The guidelines ensure that users with disabilities can access and use the same databases and applications programs as do other users. Users with disabilities also will be able to manipulate data and related information sources to attain the same results as other users and will have the necessary adaptations needed to communicate with others on their system.

P.L. 101-336, the Americans with Disabilities Act, broadened the definition of those who are considered to have disabilities. It also broadened the types of agencies and employers

> The technology of teaching includes systematically designed procedures and strategies that are applied in precise ways.

covered by Section 508 requirements and mandates additional protections, such as accessible public transportation systems, communication systems, and access to public buildings.

P.L. 100-407, the Technology-Related Assistance for Individuals with Disabilities Act, was signed into law in 1988. Under the auspices of that Act, a number of states are developing systems for providing a variety of technology assistance to children and adults with disabilities and their parents and guardians. The purpose of P.L. 100-407 is to provide financial assistance to the states to enable them to conduct needs assessments, identify technology resources, provide assistive technology services, and conduct public awareness programs, among others. It also provided a definition of assistive technology devices and services that was added to IDEA in one of its amendments.

In addition to these legislative actions, other federal assistance includes the funds that various government agencies have provided to support technology-related projects. The agency that has been the most active is the Division of Innovation and Development of the Office of Special Education Programs (OSEP) in the U.S. Department of Education. [See Kallas (1996) for a listing of projects that were being supported in 1996.]

U.S. schools and districts need knowledgeable staff to implement technology applications in special education. The Division of Personnel Preparation in OSEP has supported many projects to fund technology-training programs for teachers, administrators, leadership personnel, and parents.

Many of the technology advances that have occurred would not have been possible without federal support. Legislators and professionals in the executive branch of the federal government should be commended for their past support of technology initiatives and should be strongly encouraged to continue their efforts. The results of past federal initiatives have paid rich dividends to people with disabilities.

Perspectives on CEC's Role in Technology

In commemoration of CEC's 75th anniversary, we need to recognize some of the contributions that the Council has made to the growth and development of technology applications in special education. The Council's membership—along with federal funding—has supported many activities.

CEC has operated the Educational Resources Information Center (ERIC) Clearinghouse on Disabilities and Gifted Education since 1966. This Clearinghouse is responsible for reviewing and abstracting much of the world's literature on special education and related topics. In addition to contributing data for ERIC's publications and electronic database, CEC's Clearinghouse maintains its own electronic database and publishes *Exceptional Child Education Resources (ECER),* which abstracts all literature reviewed by that project. ERIC's online and CD-ROM resources contain only a sampling of ECER resources; complete listings from ECER's databases are available on CD-ROM in many libraries (Barbara Sorensen, CEC-ERIC Clearinghouse, personal communication; SilverPlatter Information, 1996). The CEC ERIC Clearinghouse also publishes mini-bibliographies in various topical areas, including technology (e.g., ERIC Mini-Bib, 1996).

From the mid-1960s through the late 1970s, the Coordinating Office for the national Instructional Materials Center Network for Handicapped Children and Youth (IMC Network) was housed at CEC. (For more information, see the September 1968 issue of *Exceptional Children.*)

This journal, *TEACHING Exceptional Children (TEC),* is a direct outgrowth of work done with the IMC Network. A committee was formed to find ways to provide practical information about teaching exceptional children. The committee developed a publication prospectus (Blackhurst, 1968), and *TEC* was born. The first issue (see above) appeared in the fall of 1968. A primary goal of *TEACHING Exceptional Children* is to help translate theory and research into effective practice (Blackhurst, 1968).

CEC was an early leader in exploring satellite technology for distance education. In 1978, broadcasts from the First World Congress on Special Education in Stirling, Scotland, were transmitted to sites in the United States, thus enabling those who were unable to travel abroad to benefit from that international conference.

The Technology and Media (TAM) Division became affiliated with CEC in 1984 and received its charter as an official division in 1989. TAM's annual conferences, special initiatives, and *Journal of Special Education Technology* are invaluable resources to both its members and professionals from related fields. TAM also monitors and responds to pending federal legislation and regulations related to technology through its political action network.

CEC has operated federally funded technology projects, such as the Special Education Technology Center (1987–1991) and Project Retool (1983–1992). Hundreds of people have attended research symposia and training programs and received resource documents from these projects.

CEC is a leader in publications on educational technology—journal articles, books, monographs, and special reports. The first book on applications of microcomputers in special education was published by CEC (Taber, 1983).

From Then to Now

When I began writing about the implications of technology for special education more than 30 years ago, it was fun specu-

> **Instead of getting caught up in the allure of new products with intriguing features, a better perspective is to focus on problems children have in functioning within the environment.**

lating about what the future might hold. Although some of the devices I speculated about eventually were developed in one form or another, I missed the mark badly on others because I did not anticipate the development of personal computers and the many marvelous applications that were developed as extensions to them.

In projecting technology developments as we move to the 21st century, we can say few things with certainty. On the high-tech side, microprocessors will continue to get smaller and faster; and telecommunication systems will be developed with greater capacity and speed. Costs of computers and related equipment will decline. Software developers will develop smarter software, and computer memory and file storage requirements will increase. Interconnectivity among classrooms and schools will improve—and people will develop products that we cannot even conceptualize today.

On the no-tech side, people will become more knowledgeable about the various technologies and their application. Educators and other team members will pay more attention to the implications of technology when planning IEPs for individual students. Technology specialists and support systems will become more available in schools; more technology in-service training programs will be provided for special education teachers and related personnel; and colleges and universities will add instruction about technology for people who are preparing for special education positions and those who are involved in providing related services.

Ingenious computer scientists, creative engineers, clever software programmers, and talented tinkerers have produced—and will continue to produce—an amazing array of low-tech to high-tech devices that can help people who have severe medical problems to stay alive and function in our society, enable people who have difficulty speaking to communicate, assist people who cannot hear to use the telephone system, assist people who have limited muscle control to operate machinery and appliances, aid people who cannot walk move from place to place, help people who cannot see listen to machines that can read for them, and provide children who have difficulty learning with effective instruction. Many applications that once seemed futuristic are already available: expert systems (Aldinger, Warger, & Eavy, 1995), virtual reality (Inman, 1996a, 1996b), robotics (Cook & Hussey, 1995), voice recognition systems (Cavalier & Ferretti, 1996), and telecommunication systems (Slaton & Lacefield, 1991), to name a few.

Many of the current technology applications in special education reflect the "state of the art." A major challenge facing us for the future is to move those applications to the point where they reflect a "state of the science." We must continue to conduct research and study the application of technology devices and services in objective ways so that we can make informed decisions about their use.

References

Academic Software, Inc. (1996). Adaptive device locator system [Computer program]. Lexington, KY: Author.

Alberto, P. A., & Troutman, A. C. (1995). *Applied behavior analysis for teachers* (4th ed.). Columbus, OH: Merrill.

Aldinger, L. E., Warger, C. L., & Eavy, P. W. (1995). Expert systems software in special education. *TEACHING Exceptional Children, 27*(2), 58–62.

Alliance for Technology Access. (1996). *Computer resources for people with disabilities: A guide to exploring today's assistive technology* (2nd ed.). Alameda, CA: Hunter House.

Batshaw, M. L., & Perret, Y. M. (1992). *Children with disabilities: A medical primer.* Baltimore: Paul H. Brookes.

Baumgart, D., Johnson, J., & Helmstetter, E. (1990). *Augmentative and alternative communication systems for persons with moderate and severe disabilities.* Baltimore: Paul H. Brookes.

Behrmann, M. (1984). *Handbook of microcomputers in special education.* San Diego, CA: College-Hill Press.

Blackhurst, A. E. (1965). Technology in special education: Some implications. *Exceptional Children, 31*, 449–456.

Blackhurst, A. E. (1967). Tachistoscopic training as a supplement to reading instruction for educable mentally retarded children. *Education and Training of the Mentally Retarded, 2*, 121–125.

Blackhurst, A. E. (1968). Dissemination: TEACHING Exceptional Children. *Exceptional Children, 35*, 315–317.

Blackhurst, A. E., & Cross, D. P. (1993). Technology in special education. In A. E. Blackhurst & W. H. Berdine (Eds.), *An introduction to special education* (3rd ed., pp. 77–103). New York: HarperCollins.

Blackhurst, A. E., & Hofmeister, A. M. (1980). Technology in special education. In L. Mann & D. Sabatino (Eds.). *Fourth review of special education* (pp. 199–228). New York: Grune and Stratton.

Blackhurst, A. E., & Lahm, E. A. (1997). Foundations of technology and exceptionality. In J. E. Lindsey (Ed.), *Technology for exceptional individuals* (3rd ed.). Austin, TX: PRO-ED.

Blackhurst, A. E., & Morse, T. E. (1996). Using anchored instruction to teach about assistive technology. *Focus on Autism and Other Developmental Disabilities, 11*, 131–141.

Carnine, D. W., Silbert, J., & Kameenui, E. J. (1990). *Direct instruction reading* (2nd ed.). Columbus, OH: Merrill.

Cavalier, A. R., & Ferretti, R. P. (1996). Talking instead of typing: Alternate access to computers via speech recognition technology. *Focus on Autism and Other Developmental Disabilities, 11*, 79–85.

Church, G., & Glennen, S. (1992). *The handbook of assistive technology.* San Diego, CA: Singular Publishing Group.

Commission on Instructional Technology. (1970). *To improve learning: A report to the President and the Congress of the United States.* Washington, DC: U.S. Government Printing Office.

Cook, A. M., & Hussey, S. M. (1995). *Assistive technologies: Principles and practice.* St. Louis, MO: Mosby.

ERIC Mini-Bib. (1996). *Readings on the use of technology for individuals with disabilities.* Reston, VA: ERIC Clearinghouse on Disabilities and Gifted Education, Council for Exceptional Children.

Flippo, K. F., Inge, K. J., & Barcus, J. M. (Eds.). (1995). *Assistive technology: A resource for school, work, and community.* Baltimore: Paul H. Brookes.

Galvan, J. C., & Scherer, M. J. (1996). *Evaluating, selecting, and using appropriate assistive technology.* Gaithersburg, MD: Aspen.

Inman, D. (1996a). A virtual reality training program for motorized wheelchair operation. In A. Kallas (Ed.), *Innovation and development in special education: Directory of current projects.* Reston, VA: ERIC Clearinghouse on Disabilities and Gifted Education, Council for Exceptional Children. (ERIC Document Reproduction Service No. ED 392 224)

Inman, D. (1996b). Science education for secondary students with severe orthopedic impairments using virtual reality. In A. Kallas (Ed.), *Innovation and development in special education: Directory of current projects.* Reston, VA: ERIC Clearinghouse on Disabilities and Gifted Education, Council for Exceptional Children. (ERIC Document Reproduction Service No. ED 392 224)

Kallas, A. (Ed.). (1996). *Innovation and development in special education: Directory of current projects.* Reston, VA: ERIC Clearinghouse on Disabilities and Gifted Education, Council for Exceptional Children. (ERIC Document Reproduction Service No. ED 392 224)

Lewis, R. B. (1993). *Special education technology.* Pacific Grove, CA: Brooke Cole Publishers.

Lindsey, J. E. (Ed.). (1997). *Technology for exceptional individuals* (3rd ed.). Austin, TX: PRO-ED.

Male, M. (1994). *Technology for inclusion: Meeting the special needs of all students* (2nd ed.). Needham Heights, MA: Allyn & Bacon.

Margalit, M. (1990). *Effective technology integration for disabled children: The family perspective.* New York: Springer-Verlag.

Silverman, F. H. (1995). *Communication for the speechless* (3rd ed.). Needham Heights, MA: Allyn & Bacon.

SilverPlatter Information. (1996). *Exceptional child education resources* [CD-ROM]. Norwood, MA: Author.

Slaton, D. B., & Lacefield, W. E. (1991). Use of an interactive telecommunications network to deliver inservice education. *Journal of Special Education Technology, 11,* 64–74.

Taber, F. M. (1983). *Microcomputers in special education: Selection and decision making process.* Reston, VA: Council for Exceptional Children. (ERIC Document Reproduction Service No. ED 228 793)

Trace Center. (1996). *HyperABLEDATA* [CO-NET CD-ROM program]. Madison: University of Wisconsin, Author.

Williams, B. (1995). *The Internet for teachers.* Foster City, CA: IDG Books Worldwide.

Williams, B. (1996). *The World Wide Web for Teachers.* Foster City, CA: IDG Books Worldwide.

Wolery, M., Ault, M. J., & Doyle, P. M. (1992). *Teaching students with moderate and severe disabilities: Use of response prompting procedures.* White Plains, NY: Longman.

A. Edward Blackhurst *(CEC Chapter #180), Professor, Department of Special Education and Rehabilitation Counseling, University of Kentucky, Lexington. Blackhurst chaired the committee that conceptualized* TEACHING Exceptional Children *and served as the Chairperson of its first Editorial Advisory Board.*

Address correspondence to the author at the University of Kentucky, Department of Special Education and Rehabilitation Counseling, 229 Taylor Education Building, Lexington, KY 40506-0001 (e-mail: blakhrst@pop.uky.edu).

Preparation of this article was supported by Grant H180U50025, Examination of the Effectiveness of a Functional Approach to the Delivery of Assistive Technology Services in Schools, from the Division of Innovation and Development, Office of Special Education Programs, U.S. Department of Education. The perspectives presented herein do not necessarily reflect the official position of the U.S. Department of Education.

Unit 9

Unit Selections

29. **"Can I Play Too?" Adapting Common Classroom Activities for Young Children with Limited Motor Abilities,** Kristyn Sheldon
30. **Listening to Parents of Children with Disabilities,** Linda Davern
31. **Accessible Web Site Design,** Stacy Peters-Walters

Key Points to Consider

❖ Can children with severe motor disabilities benefit from the same activities as their nondisabled peers in the classroom? How can this be accomplished?

❖ How can school-home partnerships assist children with disabilities?

❖ Why do browsers make it more difficult for people with orthopedic impairments to access the Web? How can Web sites be made more accessible?

 Links   www.dushkin.com/online/

28. **Association to Benefit Children (ABC)**
    http://www.a-b-c.org
29. **Introduction: Community Travel**
    http://isd.saginaw.k12.mi.us/~mobility/ctpintro.htm
30. **Resources for VE Teachers**
    http://cpt.fsu.edu/tree/ve/tofc.html

These sites are annotated on pages 4 and 5.

Orthopedic and Health Impairments

The word "handicapped" used to be applied indiscriminately to all persons who needed assistive devices (e.g., braces, canes, wheelchairs) to walk after about 2 years of age. Older dictionaries defined "handicapped" as inferior and in need of an artificial advantage. People were described as handicapped if they were encumbered by physical limitations. Today, describing a person as "handicapped" is derogatory. People who need medical assistance or assistive devices are not inferior. They are equal to other persons but have somewhat different functional abilities. The correct way to describe such a person is to say that he or she has a disability. The preferred order is person first, disability second; e.g., Tom with quadriplegia, Harry with diabetes. It is also polite to describe all of the things the person can do with the stress on abilities, not disability. Handicap is synonymous with hindrance. If a property of the environment prevents a person with an orthopedic or health impairment from functioning to the best of his or her abilities, then the environment has imposed a handicap.

Children and youth with orthopedic and health impairments can be divided into classifications of mild, moderate, and profound. Within most impairments, the same diagnosis may not produce the same degree of disability. For example, children with cerebral palsy may be mildly, moderately, or profoundly impaired. Orthopedic impairments are usually defined as those that hinder physical mobility and/or the ability to use one or more parts of the skeletomuscular system of the body. Health impairments are usually defined as those that affect stamina and predominantly one or more systems of the body: cardiovascular, respiratory, gastrointestinal, endocrine, lymphatic, urinary, reproductive, sensory, or nervous systems. Orthopedic and health impairments are not always mutually exclusive. Many times a child with an orthopedic impairment also has a concurrent or contributing health impairment, and vice versa. In addition, children with orthopedic and health impairments may also have concurrent problems (the addition of one or more other disorders such as learning disability, mental retardation, behavioral disorder, speech and language impairments, or sensory disorders).

Some children with orthopedic and health impairments have only transitory impairments; some have permanent but nonworsening impairments; and some have progressive impairments that make their education more complicated as the years pass and may even result in death before the end of the developmental/educational period.

Each of the dimensions defined in the preceding paragraphs makes educational planning for children with orthopedic and health impairments very individualistic. The reauthorized Individuals with Disabilities Education Act (IDEA) mandates a free and appropriate public school education in the least restrictive environment for all children with orthopedic and health impairments from the age of diagnosis until age 21, if needed. This may require only minimal special education, as in the cases of children with mild impairment, with only one problem, or with a transitory disability. On the other end of the spectrum, children with profound or progressively worsening disabilities may need maximal special education services over a very long period of time. Between these two poles lie the majority of children with orthopedic and health impairments. They have widely differing needs (qualitatively and quantitatively), depending on the nature of their impairments.

Orthopedic problems may have a neurological etiology (injury or dysfunction of the brain or spinal cord) or skeletomuscular etiology (injury or dysfunction of an area of the muscles or skeletal bones). Regardless of etiology, the child with an orthopedic impairment usually has a problem with mobility. A child with a mild impairment may be able to walk alone. A child with a moderate impairment may need crutches or other aids in order to walk. A child with a more profound orthopedic disability will probably be in a wheelchair.

Children with health impairments usually have to take medicine or follow a medical regimen in order to have the energy or salubrity required to attend school. The degree of impairment (mild, moderate, profound) is usually based on limitations to activity (none, some, many), duration of problem (temporary, chronic, progressive), and extent of other problems (none, some, many).

When orthopedic or health impairments are diagnosed in infancy or early childhood, an interdisciplinary team usually helps plan an individualized family service plan (IFSP) that includes working with parents, medical and/or surgical personnel, and preschool special education providers. When the orthopedic or health impairment is diagnosed in the school years, the schoolteachers collaborate with outside agencies, but more of the individualized educational planning (IEP) is in their hands. Children who have orthopedic and/or health impairments need psychological as well as academic support. Teachers need to help them in their peer interactions and encourage their friendships. Teachers should also work closely with parents and significant others in the lives of children to ensure a smooth transition toward a lifestyle that fosters independence and self-reliance.

The first article presents information about inclusive educational programming for children with orthopedic and health impairments. Kristyn Sheldon is concerned with how to adapt the classroom so that it is more user-friendly to children with limited motor abilities. She stresses the importance of highlighting the activities that are possible for children with orthopedic and health impairments and deemphasizing what they cannot do. Sheldon's suggested adaptations are very useful for reducing the number of hindrances to potential functioning and for reducing the number of handicaps that society imposes.

The next article suggests helpful ways to design the most appropriate IEP for each child with an orthopedic or health impairment. Linda Davern advises talking to parents frequently.

The last selection in this unit considers the benefits of computer technology in breaking down some of the barriers faced by students with physical disabilities. The author points out that educators may need to help students with disabilities use computers. They may need to find out whether Web sites are accessible to students with unique disabilities. They also may need to alert the Web site designers to the fact that their information is not accessible to some students, and why, and then suggest ways to overcome the barriers to use. "All Web designs should be accessible to all people," according to Stacy Peters-Walters.

Article 29

Early Childhood Special Education

"Can I Play Too?" Adapting Common Classroom Activities for Young Children with Limited Motor Abilities

Kristyn Sheldon[1,2]

This paper offers suggestions on adapting common classroom activities found in early childhood classrooms to increase participation of young children with limited motor abilities. It stresses the importance of de-emphasizing differences among children and highlighting that all children, even those with severe disabilities, can benefit from the same activities.

KEY WORDS: adapting activities; inclusion; limited motor abilities.

INTRODUCTION

Amber, eager to attend her first day of school in her new classroom, enters the room ready to play. The art easel looks like a good place to start, but she discovers she cannot reach the paint. Amber tries the dramatic play area next, but her wheelchair will not fit in the space and she accidently bumps toys and shelves everywhere. She would like to play with puzzles, but is unable to manipulate the small pieces. Amber attempts to play at the sensory table, but it is too high and her wheelchair gets in the way. Circle time is no better. There is nowhere for her to sit and she is unable to participate in the group activities.

Many children with special needs are enrolled in early childhood programs. Such enrollment is a wonderful learning opportunity for all, but it involves more than placing children together in the same program (Odom & McEvoy, 1990). Many early childhood educators are open to the inclusion of preschoolers with mild to moderate disabilities, but may be hesitant to include children with severe disabilities because they believe extensive modifications will be needed (Demchak & Drinkwater, 1992). Teachers are constantly challenged with arranging the environment to allow young children with physical impairments to participate and engage in the environment. These special challenges include increasing the amount and quality of participation for young children with limited motor abilities (Bigge, 1991).

Although there are an increasing number of children with motor difficulties integrated into early childhood classrooms, many early childhood teachers have limited experience and training in working with these children. Existing day care services and preschool settings provide natural and rich environments for early education experiences with only minor modifications or adaptations needed in daily activities to accommodate children with limited motor ability (Klein & Sheehan, 1987). This article provides suggestions on adapting common classroom activities found in early childhood classrooms to increase participation of young children with limited motor abilities.

DEFINITION OF LIMITED MOTOR ABILITY

The term, limited motor ability, is used in this article to define any movement difficulty that negatively affects a child's participation in an activity (Bigge, 1991). For example, Randy, age 4, has cerebral palsy that affects his equilibrium and ability to control his movement. Jamar, age 5, has cerebral palsy which has limited his ability to walk, run, or even sit up by himself. Kelly, a 3-year-old girl, has spina bifida and no sensation below her waist. She wears braces on her legs, uses a walker for mobility, and depends on her upper body for engaging in most activities. Sara uses a wheelchair, has only minimal use of her left arm, and needs support to sit upright in her chair. What is important to remember about children with special needs such as Randy, Jamar, and Kelly is not their physical limitations but their abilities.

Neisworth and Madle (1975) stressed the importance of de-emphasizing differences and highlighting that all children, even those with severe disabilities, can benefit from the same activities. Developmentally Appropriate Practice guidelines currently followed in early childhood classrooms are also appropriate for children with disabilities (Bredekamp, 1987). The guidelines for developmentally appropriate practice (Bredekamp, 1987) and the curriculum and assessment guidelines with NAEYC and NAECS/SDE (1991) clearly recognize the importance of individual differences and the need to adapt the curriculum to those differences (Wolery, Strain, & Baily, 1992). The guidelines are the context in which appropriate early education of children with special needs should occur; however, a program based on the guidelines alone is not likely to be sufficient for many children with special needs. Programs that use the guidelines may be good places for children with special needs to receive early education, but those programs must be adjusted to be maximally beneficial to those children (Wolery et al. 1992). Adaptations are usually needed so children with special needs, especially children with limited motor abilities, can participate.

It is not always necessary for children to participate in an activity to the same degree as children without disabilities for the activity to be enjoyed. Partial participation is a valid goal as long as meaningful participation is encouraged. The principle of partial participation states that, regardless of severity of disability, individuals can be taught to participate in [a] variety of activities to some degree, or activities can be adapted to allow participation (Baumgart, Brown, Pumpian, Nisbet, Ford, Sweet, Messina, & Schroeder, 1982). Activities and materials should be adapted or modified, and/or personal assistance strategies used. Have a child with a disability and a peer without a disability play together to allow the child with a disability to participate in the activity to the maximum extent appropriate.

SPECIAL ADAPTATIONS

In planning activities for children with limited motor ability, start with typical activities planned for all children. When special adaptations are needed, they should be designed to include other children whenever possible (Chandler, 1994). Special activities such as speech or physical therapy, if needed, should be provided in addition to, not instead of, typical program activities. In successfully integrated preschools, teachers strive to use the least intrusive, natural prompts, and contingencies needed to help children participate actively and meaningfully in the routines of the preschool (Drinkwater & Demchak, 1995). Encourage and assist the child to participate as fully as possible in activities such as circle time, art, books, sensory play, fine motor activities, dramatic play, snack, and gross motor activities. Some suggestions are provided below.

Circle Time

Circle time is a popular activity in early childhood classrooms, but certain environmental adaptations may be needed during circle to ensure that everyone can participate. Some problems children with limited motor abilities experience at circle time are difficulties in finding a place to sit, a difference in eye level from other children, and the possibility of being unable to communicate with the other children or the teacher. During circle time, children often sit on the floor or on carpet squares. This can become a problem for children in a wheelchair or children unable to sit independently on the floor. They may not be able to physically fit in the circle area or the children with limited motor abilities may not be comfortable. Remember children in a wheelchair will be at a different eye level than the rest of the group. It is important to recognize this when presenting circle time activities or reading books. Children with limited motor abilities often have communication difficulties, so adaptations must be used to ensure all children are able to communicate with the teacher and their peers.

Suggestions for Circle Time

- To facilitate the integration of children in wheelchairs have the children and teacher sit in chairs at circle time. This will allow all children's eye level[s] to [be] more similar and make children in wheelchair[s] "less different."
- Include modalities of communication other than verbal language. For example, a song board can be incorporated for all of the children to select what songs they want to sing. The board can have pictures of the songs the children sing during circle and both children with limited motor abilities and typical peers can use this board to choose a song.
- Use songs that can involve the children interacting with one another. For example, "If you're happy and you know it, hug a friend, give them five."
- Use books which talk about and include children with disabilities.
- Seat children with disabilities next to their peers to provide natural opportunities for interaction (Hanline, 1985).

Art

Children with physical disabilities have difficulties coloring and painting for many reasons. Some children with limited motor ability have problems because they cannot grasp and hold the tools or they are unable to maintain their arms and hands in the necessary angle or position to draw, color, or paint (Bigge, 1991). Others cannot reach the materials or enter the art area. A common problem for children who are nonambulatory is their inability to reach the standard art easel typically used in classrooms.

Suggestions for Art

- Provide a variety of areas and surfaces for children to paint. For example, place the paper on the floor or more easily accessible surfaces such as a window, wall, refrigerator, etc.

9 ❖ ORTHOPEDIC AND HEALTH IMPAIRMENTS

- Cut off the legs of an art easel so children can crawl to or kneel at the easel.
- Use adaptations such as velcro or yarn to fasten a paint brush to the child's hand or wrist.
- Encourage children to paint using their fingers, feet, and other body parts.
- Use edible paint for those who engage in hand mouthing. For example, paint with jello and water, marshmallow whip or pudding. Food coloring can be added with many edible painting mediums.
- Assign a buddy to be paired with a child with disabilities to encourage meaningful participation (Drinkwater & Demchak, 1995).
- Use age appropriate clothing for activities. For example, use a paint shirt as a cover-up and not a bib (Drinkwater & Demchak, 1995).

Specific Art Activity Suggestions

- *Funnel painting.* Place a large funnel made of paper over a table and allow the children to push the funnel back and forth, dripping paint out of the funnel onto a large piece of paper.
- *Record player art.* Place a piece of paper on a record player and have the children hold a crayon, pencil, or paint brush on the paper as the record player turns.
- *Swing art.* This activity allows a child with limited motor ability to color or paint a large piece of paper. The child is placed in a seater swing and a crayon or paint brush is attached to the swing. As the child is slowly pushed back and forth a drawing is created.
- *Contact paper collages.* This activity is appropriate for children with limited motor movement because they do not have to manipulate any tools, they simply drop or place items onto the sticky surface of the contact paper. A piece of contact paper is taped on a flat surface and the child is given different materials to drop onto the sticky side of the contact paper. Contact paper collages can be made with a variety of different materials such as, feathers, torn colored paper, uncooked macaroni or beans, cotton balls, etc.
- *Glue activities.* Glue activities can be challenging for children with limited hand movement and control. In order to increase the participation of children in these activities, have the children brush the glue onto the paper or materials instead of using squeeze bottles. The glue can be provided in foil pie dishes or bowls.

Sensory Play

The use of sensory play (water, sand, cornmeal, shaving cream, cotton, etc.) is a wonderful activity for young children with limited motor abilities. Many times children are unable to reach the sensory table where the items are commonly placed or are hesitant to explore a sensory activity because of the textures involved. When adaptations for this activity are implemented, children with limited motor abilities can actively participate and engage in sensory play.

Suggestions for Sensory Play

- Arrange some of the sensory items in a messy tray on the floor or use a sensory table that is wheelchair accessible.
- Place sensory items in a zip lock bag and tape it to the table or tray on the children's wheelchairs for exploration.
- Place sensory items directly on the children's tray.
- Encourage children to touch the sensory items with their feet or rub it on their arms or legs.
- Use large mirrors to increase engagement in the activity. For example, place a mirror on the table, spray shaving cream on the mirror, and allow children to explore with their fingers or toys (small cars, paint brushes, etc.).
- Encourage the children to explore the object with a variety of senses.

Specific Sensory Activity Suggestions

- *Tactile stimulation.* Provide sponges, honey, peanut butter, marshmallow fluff, mashed bananas, cotton candy, snow, whipped gelatin, etc. for children to experience various textures.
- *Visual stimulation.* Blow bubbles, play with bubble wands, or use automatic blowers for children who may have difficulty in blowing. Paint on black paper with fluorescent paint and use lights to show off the child's art.
- *Auditory stimulation.* Play music with regular classroom activity or help children make shakers with uncooked beans and macaroni.
- *Aromatic stimulation.* Let the class feel and smell cut fruit, flowers, and spices. For example, oranges, lemons, fresh flowers, herbs, spices in jars, etc.

Books

Children with limited motor abilities often have difficulty engaging in book time or playing in the book area. The books may be too difficult to manipulate, out of their reach, or not stimulating enough. Some books have very thin pages which are difficult for young children with limited motor abilities to manipulate. High and unstable book shelves are often found in an early childhood classroom. This arrangement makes it difficult for children to have access to books and the area.

Suggestions for Book Area

- Arrange shelves at different levels so the materials are accessible to everyone.
- Provide headphones and tapes so children can listen to the stories.
- Add a bookstand to hold the book for children unable to hold the book.
- Incorporate textured books (homemade or commercial) to book selection.
- Encourage the use of musical books that include individual sounds, songs, and voices.
- Provide books in several areas of the classroom, especially if the book area is in a loft.

Fine Motor

Fine motor activities are often difficult for young children with limited motor movement because many of the fine motor activities involve the manipulation of small pieces and materials. Puzzles are usually a fun activity for young children, but sometimes the pieces are too small or there are too many. Also, if the activity is done on a table top, items may slip around on the table causing difficulties for children with limited motor abilities to complete the task.

Suggestions for Fine Motor Area

- Select puzzles that have large knobs on the tops of the pieces and only three to four pieces per puzzle.
- Provide puzzles with auditory stimulation. For example, puzzles that play music when children place the puzzle piece in the correct place or take it out.
- Select musical shape sorters with auditory stimulation. For example, a song plays when the child places the correct shape into the holder.
- Try to keep the fine motor items large enough for the children to manipulate. The size can be changed as the children progress with the activity. For example, large chalk, crayons, pencils, and pegs can be used.
- Use Velcro to prevent materials from sliding around on the table or their tray. Velcro can be placed under the toy or puzzle.

Dramatic Play

Some problems young children with limited motor abilities may experience in the dramatic play area of a preschool classroom are difficulties in participating in the social games, the area may not be wheelchair accessible, and the toys may be too difficult to manipulate. Social interactions typically occur during dramatic play. However, children with limited motor abilities often also have language and communication delays which make social interactions more difficult. Also, the dramatic play area often contains many pieces of furniture which limits space and accessibility for children with limited motor abilities. If a child needs additional or different type of space modifications, they should be made only if necessary. This is so attention is not called to the child's disability and opportunities for children to move around in and accommodate to physical barriers in the natural environment are not lost (McCormick & Feeney, 1985).

Suggestions for Dramatic Play Area

- Make this section of the room accessible to children with limited motor abilities.
- Incorporate items such as hats, dishes, and utensils that are large and easy to manipulate.
- Label shelves with pictures as well as words so children do not have to be able to read to participate in clean up.
- Encourage peers to include and play with the children with limited motor ability. For example, plan integration experiences and activities for the children (Chandler, 1994).
- Allow children to use adaptive equipment on the dolls and their peers in the dramatic play area. For example, the children can explore and play with wheelchairs, walkers, and braces. Monitor this activity so equipment is not damaged (Chandler, 1994). Children can gain a sense of what equipment feels like and will likely be less fearful or anxious about the apparatus and the child who uses it.
- Create opportunities for children with motor impairments to interact with their normally developing peers. For example, provide materials and toys that promote play, engagement, and learning (Sainato & Carta, 1992).
- Structure the social dimensions of the environment to include peer and adult models.
- Facilitate proximity to responsive and imitative adults (Odom, McConnell, & McEvoy, 1992b).

Snack

Some problems children with limited motor abilities encounter during snack are cups that easily tip, bowls that slide on the table, difficulty finding a seat, communicating their needs and overall inclusion in the activity. Regular cups and bowls can cause frequent spills. Also, children with limited motor ability are sometimes unable to communicate their wants and needs.

Suggestions for Snack

- Encourage peers to help the children with limited motor ability. For example, peers can help the child communicate or eat.
- Use bowls with suctions to avoid table sliding and sipper cups to avoid spills.
- Design a job board to include jobs for all children. For example, include children with limited motor ability by allowing them to pass out the cups, napkins, or bowls at snack.
- Include all of the children at the table during snack, even if not all the children are eating.

Gym and Playground

Playground and gym time can be very difficult for children with physical impairments. Most children are running, jumping, and climbing during this time. Children with limited motor abilities may become frustrated at not being able to perform these skills. Young children with limited motor abilities may not be able to sit safely in a swing, have access to the sand box, or engage in social games.

Suggestions for Gym and Playground

- Provide scooter boards for the children to sit on. The children can either push themselves around or be pulled by a peer.
- Include a pool of balls for the children to sit in and explore.
- Encourage wagon, blanket, and sheet pulls. The child with limited motor ability can be in the wagon, blanket or sheet while the peer pulls them around.
- Provide adaptive tricycles (adaptive pedals or hand cycles) and/or roller skates.
- Make sand tables and swings accessible for everyone.

Computers and Technology

Computers and related technology can help provide the means to adapt classroom areas and activities in order to provide for children's diverse needs. Technology can provide young children with and without disabilities the opportunity for maximum participation in the social and educational environment of the early childhood setting. Young children with limited motor abilities who have difficulty communicating, playing, and/or interacting with their environment can benefit from technology in a number of ways (Brett, 1995).

Suggestions for Computer Use

- Use battery-operated toys, switches, and computer games to provide children with and without disabilities the opportunity to play together.

- Use alternative keyboards or switches with speech output for children who are nonverbal to participate in language development activities.
- Provide children with exploratory and open-ended computer programs to provide children the opportunity to play together.
- Include modifications of the standard keyboard, alternative keyboards, touch-sensitive screens, hand-held devices, switches, and voice input (Brett, 1995).

Modifications for the Standard Keyboard

- Place stickers on keys for a particular program to help children locate them more easily.
- Set a template or overlay over a keyboard so that only certain keys show.
- Place a keyguard over a standard keyboard to allow only one key to be hit at a time (Brett, 1995).

Alternative Keyboards

- Muppet Learning Keys feature large keys in alphabetical order with pictures that designate functions.
- The PowerPad is a large touch-sensitive board which can be divided into squares of various sizes. Each square can be easily programmed to generate voice and visual output.
- Condensed keyboards or minikeyboards are small enough so children with a limited range of motion can reach the keys.
- Unicorn Keyboard is a touch-sensitive membrane keyboard which has 128 squares that can be programmed to operate in several different ways, including imitation of the standard keyboard.
- A touch-sensitive screen such as Touch Window is an input device which allows children to point to their selections on the screen.
- Hand-held devices, such as the mouse and the joystick, are input devices which require less fine motor skill than a keyboard.
- Switches are on-off devices that are activated by contact or by detection of motion, sound, or light.
- Voice input allows an individual to speak commands into the computer and have the computer carry out these commands (Brett, 1995).

CONCLUSION

Teachers in typical early childhood settings need to provide an effective learning environment for children who exhibit a wide range of abilities within the context of the naturally occurring activities. Adaptations to activities can enhance opportunities for interactions and increase the quality of participation among children with limited motor ability. As part of a developmentally appropriate program, these adaptations can be integrated into the curriculum to make the preschool environment stimulating and interesting for all children.

ACKNOWLEDGMENTS

Support for this research was provided by a Leadership Training Grant (H029D10054) from the Office of Special Education and Rehabilitation Services, U.S. Department of Education.

[1]Department of Educational Services and Research, The Ohio State University, Columbus, Ohio.
[2]Correspondence should be directed to Kristyn Sheldon, Department of Educational Services and Research, 356 Arps Hall, 1945 North High Sreet, Columbus, Ohio 43210l-1172.

REFERENCES

Baumgart, D., Brown, L., Pumpian, I., Nisbet, J., Ford, A., Sweet, M., Messina, R., & Schroeder, J. (1982). Principle of partial participation and individualized adaptations in educational programs for severely handicapped students. *Journal of the Association for the Severely Handicapped, 7*(2), 17–27.

Bigge, J. L. (1991). *Teaching individuals with physical and multiple disabilities* (3rd Ed.). New York: Macmillan Publishing Company.

Bredekamp, S. (Ed) (1987). *Developmentally appropriate practice in early childhood programs serving children from birth through age 8.* Washington, D.C.: National Association for the Education of Young Children.

Brett, A. (1995). Technology in inclusive early childhood settings. *Day Care and Early Education, 10,* 8–11.

Chandler, P. A. (1994). *A place for me.* Washington, D.C.: National Association for the Education of Young Children.

Demchak, M., & Drinkwater, S. (1992). Preschoolers with severe disabilities: The case against segregation. *Topics in Early Childhood Special Education, 11*(4), 70–83.

Drinkwater, S., & Demchak, M. (1995). The preschool checklist integration of children with disabilities. *Teaching Exceptional Children, 28*(1), 4–8.

Diamond, K., Hestenes, L., & O'Conner, C. (1994). Integrating young children with disabilities in preschool: Problems and promises. *Young Children, 49*(2), 68–75.

Hanline, M. F. (1985). Integrating disabled children. *Young Children, 40*(2), 45–48.

Janney, R. E., Snell, M. E., Beers, M. K., & Raynes, M. (1995). Integrating students with moderate and severe disabilities into general education classes. *Exceptional Children, 61*(5), 425–439.

Klein, N., & Scheehan, R. (1987). Staff development. A key issue in meeting the needs of young handicapped children in day care settings. *Topics in Early Childhood Special Education, 7*(1), 13–27.

McCormick, L., & Feeney, S. (1995). Modifying and expanding activities for children with disabilities. *Young Children, 50*(4), 10–17.

Newsworth, J. T., & Madle, R. A. (1975). Normalized day care: A philosophy and approach to integrating exceptional and normal children. *Child Care Quarterly, 4,* 163–171.

Odom, S. L., & McEvoy, M. A. (1990). Mainstreaming at the preschool level: Potential barriers and tasks for the field. *Topics in Early Childhood Special Education, 10*(2), 48–61.

Odom, S. L., McConnell, S. R., & McEvoy, M. A. (1992). *Social competence of young children with disabilities: Issues and strategies for intervention.* Baltimore, MD: Paul H. Brookes.

Sainato, D. M., & Carta, J. J. (1992). Classroom influences on the development of social competence in young children with disabilities. In S. L. Odom, S. R. McConnell, & M. A. McEvoy, (Eds.) Social competence of young children with disabilities: Issues and strategies for intervention (pp. 93–109). Baltimore: Paul H. Brookes.

Snell, M. E. (1993). *Instruction of students with severe disabilities* (4th ed.). New York: Merrill/Macmillan.

Wolery, M., Holcombe, A., Venn, M., Brookfield, J., Huffman, K., Schroeder, C., Martin, C., & Flemming, L. (1993). Mainstreaming in early childhood programs: Current status and relevant issues. *Young Children, 49*(1), 78–94.

Wolery, M., & Wilbers, J. S. (1994). *Including children with special needs in early childhood programs.* Washington, D.C.: National Association for the Education of Young Children.

Wolery, M., Strain, P., & Baily, D. (1992). *Reaching potentials: Appropriate curriculum and assessment for young children.* Washington, D.C.: National Association for the Education of Young Children.

Listening to Parents of Children with Disabilities

Linda Davern

Linda Davern is an Assistant Professor, Education Department, The Sage Colleges, Troy, NY 12180.

Interviews with parents of mainstreamed children shed light on building effective school-home partnerships.

A growing number of children with disabilities are becoming members of general education classes. As someone involved in teacher preparation, I am particularly interested in what teaching teams can do to build productive alliances, or strengthen existing relationships, with the parents or caregivers of these children.

To explore this issue, I conducted a series of in-depth interviews with 15 families (21 parents) whose children were fully included in general education programs—mostly at the elementary level. Many of these children needed a great deal of support and modification to participate successfully in general classes. Overall, these parents were extremely pleased with the impact that inclusion had on their children. They also offered suggestions for improving the quality of home-school relationships.[1] The following recommendations to teaching teams come from an analysis of these parents' perspectives.

■ *Convey a clear, consistent message regarding the value of the child.* How school personnel talk about children in both formal and informal interactions early in the school year has a significant impact on the development of relationships with their families. Several parents in this study valued the ability of teachers to see different aspects of a child's personality aside from academic achievement. As Gail put it,

> For teachers to say to me, "I really like your kid," or "You know, he really has a great sense of humor"... lets me know that they really care about him as a person.

These parents also commended personnel who focused on the individual child's progress, rather than using other children as a reference for comparison. As Anna said:

> So our child's not going to be the top of her class in gym. We understand that. Just take her for who she is. Find space for her.

Members of the teaching team need to convey clear, consistent messages that they are happy to have this child in the classroom and that they hold high expectations for the child's achievement.

■ *Put yourself in the shoes of the parent.* The parents I interviewed valued the efforts of school personnel to try to understand what it is like to have a child with a disability—for example, to have to negotiate both the general and special education bureaucracies in order to gain access to classes, accommodations, and support services. Several of these parents felt that some staff did not understand their anger and frustration with educational systems. While one mother felt more strongly than others I spoke with, she expressed the sense of detachment experienced by families of children in special education:

> Parents hate special ed.... Parents hate it because the kids hate it.... They hate the isolation of it.

Parents often felt they were viewed as impatient. They wanted staff to better understand their frustration with the slow pace of school improvement efforts related to inclusive practices. School staff who attempt to understand the parent's frame of reference are less likely to assume the judgmental attitudes that can be damaging to the home-school relationship.

■ *Expand your awareness of cultural diversity.* Building an awareness of cultural diversity will strengthen school personnel's ability to teach as well as connect successfully with families. Marguerite believed that "a lot of teachers have never had... training in multiculturalism or diversity." Through effective staff development, schools can help personnel examine "the cultural base of their own belief system" in relation to children and families (Harry 1992, p. 23), and how these beliefs affect relationships.

Harry and colleagues emphasize that cultures are greatly influenced by generational status, gender, social class, education, occupational group, and other variables (1995, p. 106). Such an approach to professional development will help personnel be aware of the cultural lenses through which they make judgments about children and families.

■ *See individuals, challenge stereotypes.* A few parents felt that some teachers made assumptions about them and their parenting skills simply because their child had a disability. Doria saw some of these attitudes arising from a lack of understanding of some types of disabilities such as emotional disturbance. Marguerite felt that school personnel frequently "lumped parents together"—working from inaccurate assumptions about single parents and parents who were not of European heritage. School personnel need opportunities to explore the impulse to stereotype, and encouragement and support to challenge this tendency in themselves as well as their colleagues.

■ *Persevere in building partnerships.* While federal law requires school teams to invite parents into the planning process for their children with disabilities, the collaborative outcome envisioned by the legislation does not always materialize. Several parents thought that schools gave up too soon—that personnel were quick to dismiss parents who didn't attend meetings, and were cynical about the possibilities for change. Parents felt that building partnerships took commitment and vision over the *long* term. As one father stated, "The first year you make a decision to team with parents, maybe you're not going

> **Schools will not become proficient in building alliances with these families until general class membership, with adequate supports, is the norm for children with disabilities.**

to get all the parents... but give it a little time, nurture it along."

Parents suggested looking at how schools share information with parents, using more flexibility in setting up meeting times with them, and assisting parents in connecting with other parents who might share child care responsibilities to free one another to attend planning meetings.

■ *Demonstrate an authentic interest in the parent's goals for the child.* A first step in establishing dialogue is to connect with parents as individuals. Participants in the study commended some staff as very skilled in diminishing the psychological distance between parents and professionals. These teachers were able to create an atmosphere where parents did not feel that they had to "watch their p's and q's," as one parent put it. Staff did this through their choice of language, as well as their interaction styles. Their interest in parents' ideas felt authentic.

Parents also mentioned interactions that they viewed as evidence of an "expert syndrome." In these cases, parents felt that the attitude coming from staff was, "You couldn't possibly know what you're talking about." One parent described a critical distinction between those personnel who talk with parents as opposed to those who talk at them. Teachers can maintain their expertise as educators while fully acknowledging the information and insights held by parents. The interplay of these complementary roles can greatly enrich the outcome for students.

■ *Talk with parents about how they want to share information.* Successful collaboration requires effective ongoing communication between home and school. Some participants thought that having one school person as the primary contact would be helpful. Several parents in this study did not want their primary contact to be a special educator, for fear that this would lessen the feelings of ownership on the part of the general educator for the child's progress. Yet consistent communication with a person who really knew the child and his or her unique learning characteristics was important.

Teachers need to ask parents which school representative they would like to communicate with, how frequently, and through which means (for example, combinations of meetings, phone calls, and written communication). Moreover, parents' preferences for involvement may change over time given a variety of factors such as the child's age and the family's circumstances.

Several families found home visits by school staff very helpful. Parents felt that opportunities to visit with children in their homes might give staff insight into children's capabilities that had not been demonstrated at school.

■ *Use everyday language.* Parents often felt excluded from the planning process when professionals used unfamiliar educational terms when discussing test results, staffing patterns, and ways of organizing and identifying services. One parent referred to this practice as "blowing all that smoke." As another put it:

> What does it mean "30 minutes three times a week," "one plus one," "parallel curriculum"?... When you do that stuff you just close out the parent. As soon as

you use language that's exclusive of parents, they're gone.

It is an unfortunate irony that in order to graduate from many teacher preparation programs, preservice teachers must master a professional lexicon that ultimately creates significant barriers to being effective in their professions.

■ *Create effective forums for planning and problem solving.* Yearly review meetings, mandated by law, are held for each child with an Individualized Education Plan (IEP). During these meetings, school personnel and parents (and students at the secondary level) review assessments, make placement decisions, determine children's services, and identify individual goals. The parents I interviewed described these formal meetings as some of the most difficult interactions they experienced during the year. They used such phrases as "very intimidating" to describe them, adding that they felt at times like token participants in discussions about their children.

In contrast to these formal yearly reviews, at least six of the children involved in this study were the focus of regularly scheduled team meetings, composed of teachers, parents, related service providers, and occasionally teaching assistants. Although evaluations of these meetings varied greatly, parents indicated that, compared to the formal meetings, they felt more comfortable discussing their children in an atmosphere that recognized achievements, friendships, interesting stories, and humorous anecdotes. As one mother put it,

> **Successful collaboration requires effective ongoing communication between home and school.**

When we go to team meetings, a lot of times it *is* a celebration. That's how it feels. By George, we're doing something *right* here—it's working!

The literature offers direction for districts interested in developing their expertise in the arena of team planning for individual children (Giangreco 1996, Giangreco et al. 1993, Thousand and Villa 1992).

■ *Build long-term schoolwide plans that offer full membership to all children.* Several of the parents I interviewed had advocated extensively for a general class placement for their child. Schools will not become proficient in building alliances with these families until general class membership, with adequate supports, is the norm for children with disabilities. These findings reinforce calls from parents and others in the educational community for districts to develop long-term schoolwide plans to offer full membership to all students, not just set up programs for children in response to the requests of individual parents (Gartner and Lipsky 1987, Stainback and Stainback 1990). Teachers can actively support such restructuring (with appropriate safeguards to ensure adequate resources). Such efforts will result in inclusive settings becoming available to those children whose parents are not in a position to pursue such extensive advocacy actions.

[1]Parents' names are pseudonyms.

References

Gartner, A., and D. Lipsky. (1987). "Beyond Special Education: Toward a Quality System for all Students." *Harvard Educational Review* 57, 4: 367–395.

Giangreco, M. F. (1996). *Vermont Interdependent Services Team Approach: A Guide to Coordinating Educational Support Services.* Baltimore: Paul H. Brookes.

Giangreco, M. F., C. J. Cloninger, and V. S. Iverson. (1993). *Choosing Options and Accommodations for Children (COACH).* Baltimore: Paul H. Brookes.

Harry, B. (1992). *Cultural Diversity, Families, and the Special Education System.* New York: Teachers College Press.

Harry, B., M. Grenot-Scheyer, M. Smith-Lewis, H. Park, F. Xin, and I. Schwartz. (1995). "Developing Culturally Inclusive Services for Individuals with Severe Disabilities." *The Journal of The Association for Persons with Severe Handicaps* 20, 2: 99–109.

Stainback, S., and W. Stainback. (1990). "Inclusive Schooling." In *Support Networks for Inclusive Schooling,* edited by W. Stainback, and S. Stainback. Baltimore: Paul H. Brookes.

Thousand, J. S., and R. Villa. (1992). "Collaborative Teams: A Powerful Tool in School Restructuring." In *Restructuring for Caring and Effective Schools,* edited by R. A. Villa, J. S. Thousand, W. Stainback, and S. Stainback. Baltimore: Paul H. Brookes.

Accessible Web Site Design

Stacy Peters-Walters

The World Wide Web (WWW) is a wonderful tool for classroom use. Students can explore many virtual libraries and museums and conduct research. The WWW has the ability to bring information to everyone who has access to a computer. The Web and other telecommunications applications like e-mail can help students with disabilities in many ways. When a Web site is designed correctly, there is very little discrepancy between users with disabilities and those people temporarily without disabilities. Computers and the WWW can be a great equalizer in the classroom and in the world. Figure 1 provides information about users with disabilities who have used telecommunications applications to overcome barriers (U.S. Department of Commerce, 1994).

The Importance of Web Site Design

Many people with disabilities have difficulties accessing information over the Internet because of poor Web site designs. Many of the site designs actually create barriers for information access (Paciello, 1996). Students with visual and cognitive disabilities have the greatest barriers to overcome to gain access to information (Paciello). There is very little that users can do to change site design to accommodate their own needs. Site designers must accommodate the user. Educators who wish to create Web sites that are accessible need to follow a few simple site design rules so that all students can access information.

Figure 1

Technology Can Break Down Barriers

Reduced Barriers to Full Participation in Society
I am a C7 quadriplegic who has completed a course in desktop publishing. I have been disabled for 2 years and am very eager to get back into the work force. I have learned I'm still employable regardless of my disability. I recently learned about telecommunications and the different networks for communicating. With electronic mail, I communicate with various people from all around the world. My life has really opened up with my career change and the electronic information systems.

Reduced Barriers to Business and Employment
I am a C5 quadriplegic living in the Silicon Valley and a current intern with the Networking and Communication Department. I have been disabled for 10 years from a motor vehicle accident in 1983. I use computer telecommunications daily in numerous functions. Telecommunications has opened up a new world, allowing me to communicate via e-mail with colleges, government agencies, and organizations. The future success of telecommunications is phenomenal, especially for the disabled community. It not only allows a person unable to go out into the community to access endless amounts of information, but also permits persons with disabilities, such as myself, to eventually return to the work force (via telecommuting) and become productive citizens again.

Reduced Communication Barriers
I am 17 years old. I am an oral, profoundly hearing impaired student who is fully mainstreamed in the 12th grade. I did not really have access to e-mail until early October, when a friend of mine proposed we e-mail each other. . . . E-mail turned out to be easier than I thought, and it has been wonderful because it has enabled me to communicate with my friends from around the Atlantic Seaboard region.
   The "electronic super highway" is a boon for deaf/hearing impaired people because it enables them to communicate via the written word, which is a very effective alternate means of obtaining vital information in a relatively short period of time. It is my hope that the White House will make access to the information highway universal.

Reduced Barriers to the "Basics" in an Information Society
Rodney, a senior, has no use of his arms or legs and uses a mouth wand to operate a computer. He began using a computer at age 6, and learned to read and write in this manner.
   When asked a question, Rodney balances his wand on a box strategically placed near his terminal. "A computer," he says, "is sort of like running water. You don't know what you'd do without it."

31. Accessible Web Site Design

Table 1: HTML Coding

HTML is the programming language used to create WWW pages. HTML can be hand coded by using a word processor or created by an HTML generator. All suggestions in this article can be hand coded. Some of the suggestions can be created using an HTML generator, depending on the generator's complexity and quality.

Below are a few hand coded tags for programming in HTML. All HTML tags are placed within brackets when hand coding. Tags without the "/" are placed at the end of the text or image that is to be formatted. When hand coding, all tags are formatted using capital letters.

Tag	Placement	Function
<HTML></HTML>	These are placed at the beginning and ending of a document.	These tags tell the browser that it will be reading an HTML document.
<HEAD></HEAD>	These are placed inside the HTML tags. They surround the TITLE tags.	These tags tell the browser that this is prologue information.
<TITLE></TITLE>	These are placed before and after the text of the title.	These tags tell the browser that the text they surround is part of the title bar and not the actual page.
<BODY></BODY>	These are placed before and after the entire body text.	These tags tell the browser that everything within these tags is body text.
<P></P>	These tags surround each paragraph.	These tags tell the browser to format the text like a paragraph.
<A HREF = "url name"> </A>	These tags surround text that is to be linked to the URL named in the quotation marks.	These tags tell the browser that the text enclosed by tags is a link to the URL specified within the quotes.
<H1></H1> to <H6></H6>	These tags surround the text that the user wants to be displayed as headers.	These tags (H1, H2, H3, H4, H5, H6) tell the browser that the text they surround is a header. The text displays the text in a larger size and as bold. H1 specifies the largest while H6 specifies the smallest.
<IMG SRC = "image.gif">	These tags are placed anywhere the user wants to place an image.	These tags tell the browser to read and display the images specified within the quotes.

Web Barriers to Overcome

- Some barriers that people with *visual disabilities* face is not being able to access information because of its graphical format.
- People with *auditory problems* cannot access the information in sound files.
- People with *attention deficit disorder* can become easily distracted from the information by the use of continual animations.
- Users with *cognitive disabilities* may become lost due to poor navigation controls.
- People with *physical disabilities* face the barrier of not being able to run the browser that would give them access to the information.

- Educators can run "Bobby" (http://www.cast.org/bobby) to find out whether their site designs are accessible. "Bobby" is a Web site validator (Center for Applied Special Technology, 1997).
- Users who wish to validate their Web site with accessibility requirements type the specific URL they want validated into the form provided.
- "Bobby" goes to that URL and validates whether it meets the accessibility requirements. Images of a blue hat with the "handicapped" sign on them appear next to areas that are not accessible.
- "Bobby" also provides written reports as to what is wrong and how to fix the problem.
- "Bobby" also contains an advanced validator that validates the code for specific browser types.

If a site meets with "Bobby" specifications, the site designers are invited to use the "Bobby Approved" logo on the site (Center for Applied Special Technology, 1997).

Second, educators can help students indirectly by educating site designers about information-access barriers on the WWW and how to overcome those barriers. A barrier that people with visual disabilities face is not being able to access the information because of its graphical format. People with auditory problems cannot access the information in sound files. People with attention-deficit disorder can become easily distracted from the information by the use of continual animations. Users with cognitive disabilities may become lost due to poor navigation controls. People with physical disabilities face the barrier of not being able to run the browser that would give them access to the information.

Visual Disabilities

People with visual disabilities have difficulties accessing information published on the WWW because the Web is a highly visual medium. Web pages are designed to be visually stimulating, which can make them difficult to read. Many people with visual disabilities access information from the WWW by using screen readers or refreshable Braille displays. These machines can only access and read text. When the machine arrives at a graphic, the machine either ignores the graphic or informs the user that it is reading a graphic and has no description to read. This cuts down on

Many people with disabilities have difficulties accessing information over the Internet because of poor Web site designs.

9 ❖ ORTHOPEDIC AND HEALTH IMPAIRMENTS

the usability of the WWW because graphics are used to convey much information.

Graphics. Web site designers can alleviate the problem of interpreting graphics for people with visual disabilities by using the IMG ALT tag when creating WWW pages (see Table 1 for an illustration of this tag). This tag allows the designer to embed a text description of the image into the image source code so that a screen reader will be able to describe the picture. Example code for the IMG ALT tag is <IMG SRC = "cat.gif" ALT = ["A big black cat is perched on the windowsill looking outside at the trees blowing in the wind. It is a sunny day outside."] > The IMG SRC = "cat.gif" is telling the browser that it will be viewing the picture cat.gif. The ALT tag tells the browser that if a user is browsing the Web in text mode or through a screen reader, instead of viewing the graphic, the text should read: "Graphic: A big black cat is perched on the windowsill looking outside at the trees blowing in the wind. It is a sunny day outside."

Graphic Links. Graphics that link one page to another page can be troublesome for people with visual disabilities. Because the screen reader cannot orally "read" the graphical link, people with visual disabilities do not have a description of the link that they will be visiting. The user will have to click the link and scan the page to decide whether the information on the page is what the user was looking for. This can amount to wasted time for the user when he or she is trying to access information. To help users with visual disabilities, all graphical links should have an alternate text link beside or beneath the graphical link.

Text links should be short yet descriptive. An example of a short descriptive link is "WWW and Visual Disabilities." Text links should not be placed in horizontal lines like Home Education Sites Student Work. While the screen reader can read the links, it can make comprehension difficult. The screen reader will not pause between the links, but read the links like a sentence (Paciello, 1996). It is difficult for the person listening to decide whether the link is the home page, which contains the educational sites and student work, or three separate links.

Video Files. More and more WWW pages are embedding video files that users can access. While a user with visual disabilities can hear the audio in the movie, the user will not be able to view the video. Because much of the information in video files is accessible only by viewing the video, without ad-

Table 2

Sample Table

Student	Sue	Joe	Matt
Math Grade	A	B	C
Science Grade	C	B	A

Web Tutorials

There are many products on the market to help people build Web pages. When deciding what to purchase, educators must look at how much time and money they would like to invest in Web page development.

For those educators serious about Web page development and willing to learn how to hand code, Laura Lemay has published several informative tutorials on the different aspects of Web page design. Lemay speaks in layman's terms so that the user is not fumbling through computer jargon. Each book contains lessons for the user to try and examples for the user to view. Lemay's book Learn HTML in 14 Days covers the wide range of HTML programming that most beginners are willing to use.

While learning to hand code is beneficial for any HTML programmer, learning to hand code can be time-consuming. For those educators who do not have the time to learn hand coding, there are HTML generators. There are several types of HTML generators, most of which can be found in any software store. These programs range in price from thirty dollars to several hundred dollars. For the most part, the more a person pays for these programs, the more features the programs have.

HTML generators usually come with some type of documentation to explain how they work. There are also multitudes of books about each generator. Many of these books follow a lesson format like Lemay's books.

Other Devices to Enable People with Disabilities to Access Computers

- Dragon Dictate
- Dragon Naturally Speaking
- Microsoft "Access Pack"
- Word Prediction Software
- Mouth stick
- Switches (hand, head, mouth)
- Eyegaze
- Screen readers
- Refreshable Braille Screens
- Stickybear ABC and Talking Stickybear
- Muppet Learning Keys
- IntelliKeys
- Touch Windows

Use "Bobby" (http://www.cast.org/bobby) to find out whether your Web site designs are accessible.

aptations the user will be unable to use much of the informational content of the video. WWW designers can add a text file that gives the full transcription of the audio and a description of all visual elements in the video. Site designers can create a text file and then provide a link to it beside the link to the video.

Imagemaps. Another problem for screen readers and other adaptive devices is reading imagemaps. An imagemap is a large picture that has hot spots, or links, embedded into the image. When a user runs a cursor over the imagemap, there are certain areas, the hot spots or links, where the cursor turns into a hand and can access another page of the site. Because screen readers and other adaptive devices cannot access pictures, the person with a visual disability will not be able to access the links. The user will not be able to follow the informational links if he or she cannot access the links within imagemaps. If WWW designers want to use imagemaps for their visual appeal, designers need to make text links that correspond with the links in the imagemap and place those links beneath the imagemap.

Tables. Tables are another difficulty for screen readers and other adaptive devices to interpret. A screen reader will not read the information in each separate cell as one entity. The screen reader will read across the table from left to right. For example, a simple table like Table 2 will be difficult for the screen reader to interpret.

Rather than reading that Sue received an A in math and a C in science, the user will read: "Student Sue Joe Matt Math Grade A B C Science Grade C B A." If possible, tables should be avoided. A designer who wants to use a table should also provide an alternate, text-only page that provides the same information but not in a table format. Some designers prefer to build their entire sites using tables. Users should be notified of the table format and a text-based site needs to be provided.

Forms. Screen readers also have difficulty reading online forms. Online forms allow the user to enter information online in a guest book, request information through a form, use search engines, and register for shareware computer application. Forms should be available as a text file to download to the user's hard drive and then to be mailed either through e-mail or postal mail. All forms should list the e-mail address that the form is being sent to. Users who cannot download forms will then be able to write directly to the address.

Table 3. Keyboard Commands for Tool Bar Functions in the Microsoft Internet Explorer

Function	Keyboard Commands	Description
Access Menu Bar	F10	Open and view menus
Reload Page	F5	Reload current page
View Previous URLs	F4	View list of URLs previously visited
Help	F1	Access help menu
Stop	Esc	Stop page download
Open New Window	Ctrl + N	Open new window
Open URL	Ctrl + O	Type URL to visit
Print	Ctrl + P	Print current page
Save	Ctrl + S	Save current page
Find	Ctrl + F	Find keyword on current page
Go Back	Alt + Left Arrow	Move back a page
Go Forward	Alt + Right Arrow	Move forward a page
Next Anchor (Link)	Tab	Move to next anchor (link) and stop at end of document
Previous Anchor (Link)	Shift + Tab	Move to previous anchor and stop at beginning of document
Scroll Line Up	Up arrow key	Change view of document by one line up
Scroll Line Down	Down arrow key	Change view of document by one line down
Scroll Page Up	PageUp key	Change view of document by one height up
Scroll Page Down	PageDown key	Change view of document by one height down
Top of Page	Home key	Change view to beginning of document
Bottom of Page	End key	Change view to end of document

Colors and Backgrounds. Color and background patterns are another difficulty for people with visual disabilities. Pages with too many color combinations can be difficult to read for anyone, especially people with low vision and other visual disabilities. To decide whether the color combinations are difficult to read, designers need to view their pages in 256 shades of gray. Designers can adjust their monitors in the Control Panel to read only 256 shades of gray. While viewing the pages in gray, designers need to ask themselves whether they can read and distinguish the differences between colors on the basis of only lightness and darkness. Designers should also ask a person who has not helped to design the site to read the information on the site and to distinguish between the different shades of gray.

Another problem is the use of the color combinations of blue/yellow and red/green for text and backgrounds. People who are colorblind cannot see what is on these pages. Designers must never use these color combinations, unless they are providing an alternate site. The link to this alternate site should never be in blue, yellow, red, or green.

Background patterns can also create difficulty for people with low vision or other visual disabilities. A background that has many images on it or a pronounced texture is too decorative for the text to show well. Long pages of unbroken text are also a disadvantage for people with visual disabilities.

Unbroken Text. Long pages of unbroken text are difficult to skim for content for anybody, but especially for people with visual disabilities because it takes longer to read a passage. Long pages of text can be broken up by the use of headers (tags H1 to H6), which will help with the skimming process (see Table 1 for examples of tags used in HTML coding).

Frames. A major problem for people with visual disabilities is the use of frames. Although frames that are well designed can be visually stimulating, frames make an already small computer screen smaller. Also, frames act

> **Sites that are meant to be wonders of design should have an alternate site built specifically for accessibility.**

Table 4: Keyboard Commands for Tool Bar Functions in the Netscape Navigator

Function	Keyboard Commands	Description
Access Menu Bar	F10	Open and view menus
Reload Page	Ctrl + R	Reload current page
View Previous URLs	F4	View list of URLs previously visited
Help	F1	Access help menu
Stop	Esc	Stop page download
Open New Window	Ctrl + N	Open new window
Open URL	Ctrl + O	Type URL to visit
Print	Ctrl + P	Print current page
Save	Ctrl + S	Save current page
Find	Ctrl + F	Find keyword on current page
Increase Font	Ctrl +]	Increase font size
Decrease Font	Ctrl + [	Decrease font size
Page Source	Ctrl + U	View page source code
Page Info	Ctrl + I	View information about page
Next Anchor (Link)	Tab	Move to next anchor (link) and stop at end of document
Previous Anchor (Link)	Shift + Tab	Move to previous anchor and stop at beginning of document
Scroll Line Up	Up arrow key	Change view of document by one line up
Scroll Line Down	Down arrow key	Change view of document by one line down
Scroll Page Up	PageUp key	Change view of document by one height up
Scroll Page Down	PageDown key	Change view of document by one height down
Top of Page	Home key	Change view to beginning of document
Bottom of Page	End key	Change view of end of document

like tables for a screen reader, which causes confusion. Designers should avoid the use of frames. If frames must be used, designers need to provide an alternate site without frames.

Auditory Disabilities

Currently, people with auditory disabilities have few problems accessing information on the WWW. This is because Web design is primarily visual. More and more, however, Web designers are incorporating audio and video files into their pages. These formats pose problems for people with auditory disabilities.

Audio and video files should have full-text transcriptions of the audio. If possible, movies should be created that have a person signing the audio. The video of the person signing can either be added to the video file by using video editing software or as a separate file from the original video file. This will help the user—more than just reading the transcription—because the user can watch the movie and the signing at the same. Designers can also add closed captioning to the video.

Cognitive Disabilities

Navigating the WWW is currently very difficult; it is not an intuitive process. Not only are browsers difficult to use, but most Web page navigation is poorly designed. Site designers can make navigating a WWW page or site more intuitive by creating small menus at the top of the page for users to follow. Graphical "You Are Here" site maps can also be created using a graphics/drawing package and placed in each page.

Students who have difficulty reading will not receive much benefit from the WWW since the majority of the information is in a text format. Although it is extra work for Web designers, creating an audio file of the information on the page will alleviate the problem of long reading time or a lack of comprehension due to poor reading skills. The audio file can be designed as a downloadable option so that users who like to read text will not have to listen to the audio. Designers can add audio files by using sound recording and editing software and a computer microphone to create the files and then use an HTML generator to link the files into the site.

Long Web pages filled with unbroken text are difficult for users with cognitive disabilities to skim for information. Long pages of text can be broken up by the use of Headers (tags H1 to H6) and by graphics. Headers allow users to skim for the important parts of the document so that they will not have to read the entire document. Graphics break up the monotony of the pages and add another dimension to the user's understanding of the text.

Attention Deficit Disorder

The WWW has the ability to focus the attention of people with attention deficit disorder (ADD) by using graphics to lead the user through the information. But some Web designers create difficulties for people with ADD.

Multiple or long pages of unbroken text cannot keep people focused on the task of reading. Web designers can alleviate this problem by using descriptive headers (tags H1 to H6) to differentiate between important pieces in the document. Descriptive graphics can also be used to break up the monotony of long pages of text.

Many WWW pages are designed so that it is difficult to remain focused on an informational piece of text or graphic due to blinking text, scrolling marquees, or continual animation. This is a simple problem for Web designers to control. The designer can either not use the continual movements or can design an alternate page that does not contain the continual movements. Designers who wish to use continual movements for focusing the user's attention on one section can program the continual animations to stop after a few seconds. This will focus the user's attention to what the designer wants the user to view first, but will not become a distraction.

Physical Disabilities

Browsers make it difficult for people with limited mobility to access Web pages. Most browsers are designed for mainly mouse input. For people with limited mobility, mouses are difficult to use because they require fine motor skills of the fingers, hand, and arm.

For ease of navigation, many browsers are incorporating keyboard commands that function like mouse commands. Tables 3 and 4 list some of the keyboard commands for navigating the WWW with the Microsoft Internet Explorer and the Netscape Navigator.

Design and Accessibility

Because the WWW is a visual place where design is highly respected, many designers may want to focus more on design rather than accessibility. Sites that are meant to be wonders of design should have an alternate site built specifically for accessibility. These sites should allow users to access the alternate site or alternate pages on the first page of the site and then on every page throughout the site. For example, Page 1 of a site would contain a link to Page 1 of the alternate site. Page 2 of the graphical site would contain links to Pages 1 and 2 of the alternate site. Page 3 of the graphical site would contain links to Pages 2 and 3 of the alternate site, and so on. This enables users to move through sites at their ease, rather than at the designer's ease.

To many WWW designers, it may seem easier to create alternate text-only pages for users with disabilities. Though many users with disabilities (and users with slow modem connections) may use only the alternate pages, it is best to provide both alternate pages and the accessibility tips listed here. In this way, there will not be two standards and levels of quality for WWW design. All Web designs should be accessible to all people.

References

Center for Applied Special Technology. (1997, December 6). *Bobby* [Web site]. URL = http://www.cast.org/bobby/

Lemay, L. (1996). *Teach Yourself Web Publishing with HTML 3.2 in 14 Days* (Professional Reference Edition). [Web site]. URL = http://www.mcp.com/sansnet/

Paciello, Mike (1996; 1997, August 20). *Making the Web accessible for the blind and visually impaired* [Web site]. URL = http://www.yuri.org/webable/mp-blnax.html

Paciello, Mike (1996; 1997, August 20). *People with disabilities can't access the Web* [Web site]. URL = http://www.yuri.org/webable/mp-pwdca.html

Trace Research and Design Center. (1997, December 6). *Trace research and design* [Web site]. URL = http://www.trace.wisc.edu/

U.S. Department of Commerce, Technology Administration, National Institute of Standards and Technology. (1994; 1997, August 18). *People with disabilities and NII: Breaking down barriers, building choice* [Web site]. URL = http://www.itpolicy.gsa.gov/coca/SB_paper.htm

Stacy Peters-Walters, *Instructional Assistant, Governor's Technology for Teaching and Learning Academy, College of Education, Dakota State University, Madison, South Dakota.*

Address correspondence to the author at RR3, Box 28, Madison, SD 57042 (e-mail: peterss@triton.dsu.edu).

Unit 10

Unit Selections

32. **Meeting the Needs of Gifted Learners in the Early Childhood Classroom,** Brooke Walker, Norma Lu Hafenstein, and Linda Crow-Enslow
33. **Gifted Students Suggest Reforms for Education: Listening to Gifted Students' Ideas,** Lugene Polzella
34. **Accountability for Gifted Students,** James J. Gallagher

Key Points to Consider

❖ How can preschool teachers meet the needs of all students, including those with special gifts and talents?

❖ What ideas do gifted students have about their own education?

❖ How should gifted programs be assessed and how should schools change to meet the needs of high-ability students?

 **Links**   www.dushkin.com/online/

31. **Kenny Anthony's Gifted and Talented and General Educational Resources**
    http://www2.tsixroads.com/~kva/

These sites are annotated on pages 4 and 5.

Giftedness

Children with special gifts and talents do not qualify for special educational services under the Individuals with Disabilities Education Act (IDEA). The U.S. Omnibus Education Bill of 1987 provided modest support for gifted and talented identification and education. It required, however, that each state foot the bill for the development of special programs for children with special gifts and talents. Some states have implemented special education for the super-able. Most states have not.

Since many textbooks on exceptional children include children with special gifts and talents, and since these children are exceptional, they will be included in this volume. Instructors who deal only with the categories of disabilities covered by IDEA may simply omit coverage of this unit.

Are children with superability really at a disadvantage in our society? Do their powerful abilities and potentialities in some area (or areas) leave them bored in a regular classroom? Are they disabled by their potencies? Many professional educators, researchers, and experts in the area of creative genius argue that children with special gifts and talents are excluded from the mainstream. Their exceptionalities do, in fact, deprive them of some of the opportunities with which less exceptional children are routinely provided. Giftedness can be viewed as both a blessing and a curse. Problems of jealousy, resentment, misunderstanding, embarrassment, indignation, exasperation, and even fear are often engendered in the people who live with, work with, or get close to a child with exceptional knowledge or accomplishments.

Children and youth with special gifts and talents often test the patience of parents, teachers, peers, and even of special tutors or mentors, who are asked to help them in their areas of exceptionality. Gifted students tend to ask a lot of questions and pursue answers with still more questions. They can be incredibly persistent about gathering information about topics that interest them. They may, however, show no interest at all in learning about topics that do not. They may be very competitive in areas where they are especially skilled, competing even with teachers and other adults. They may seem arrogant about their skills, when, in their minds, they are only being honest.

Many children and youth with special gifts and talents have extraordinary sensitivity to how other people are reacting to them. As they are promoted through elementary school into middle school and high school, many such children learn to hide their accomplishments for the secondary gain of being more socially acceptable or more popular. Because they have been underchallenged and/or discouraged from achieving at their highest potentialities, many gifted high school students are underachievers. They have poor study habits as a result of not needing to study in elementary school. They are unmotivated, intensely bored, and discouraged by the educational programs available to them.

Researchers who have studied creative genius and exceptional giftedness have found that most accomplished high achievers share one similarity in their childhoods. Their parents recognized their special abilities early and found tutors or mentors who would help them develop their skills. This is true not only of mathematicians and scientists but also of world class sports players, musicians, artists, performers, writers and other producers of note.

Educational programs that refuse to find tutors or mentors, or to encourage original work, or to provide special education in the skill areas of gifted students, are selling short the future society's potential producers.

The earlier that children with special gifts and talents are recognized, the better. The sooner they are provided with enriched education, the more valuable their future contributions will become. Children from all ethnic backgrounds, and from all socioeconomic levels, and from both sexes, can have exceptional gifts and talents. One cannot predict from parents' productivity whether or not their child will have an area of special giftedness. Researchers who have reported that parents of gifted persons recognize talent early, have not, concurrently, reported that the parents had any special talents of their own. Many exceptionally gifted children come from families without creative skills or talents.

The assessment of children with special gifts and talents, especially in the early childhood years, is fraught with difficulties. Should parents nominate their own children when they see extraordinary skills developing? How objective can parents be about their child's ability as it compares to the abilities of other same-aged children? Should measures of achievement be used (e.g., recitals, performances, art, reading levels, writings)? Do all parents want their children to have special gifts or talents? The evidence suggests that, to the contrary, many parents are embarrassed by their child's extraordinary aptitudes. They would rather have their child be more like his or her peers.

The first article in this unit emphasizes the importance of enriching the education of children with special gifts and talents as soon as they are identified. The authors, Brooke Walker, Norma Lu Hafenstein, and Linda Crow-Enslow, describe the characteristics of young intellectually gifted children. They stress that preschool curriculum can consist of integrated thematic units that offer a choice of activities. Each child can work at the level that is most meaningful. Intellectually gifted children can be given in-depth studies and concept exercises that meet their high-ability needs.

Lugene Polzella, in the second article, asks "What ideas do gifted students have about their own education?" The answers given by students with special gifts and talents may come as a surprise. Most of the students surveyed wanted more work and more challenges. They like evening and weekend adventures in learning. They like pursuing their individual interests with adult mentors. They want flexible, hands-on work experiences with other people of similar intellect. And they want access to libraries, laboratories, and equipment which will enhance their learning experiences.

The last selection in this unit asks the questions, "How should gifted programs be assessed and how should schools change to meet the needs of gifted students?" James Gallagher offers several suggestions for the assessment of gifted education to assure its accountability. He also describes appropriate curriculum and instruction for gifted students. He believes we must give serious attention to educational programs for our high-ability students.

ic prowess (Nutall, Romero, & Kalesnick
Meeting the Needs of Gifted Learners in the Early Childhood Classroom

Brooke Walker,
Norma Lu Hafenstein,
and Linda Crow-Enslow

In one corner of an early childhood classroom, there is a cave constructed of brown butcher paper. Stalactites and stalagmites fabricated from iridescent cellophane hang from the roof of the cave. A model of a volcano, painted in bright colors, graces the window. The parts of the volcano are labeled: magma, lava, crater, crust, and ash. Inside the volcano are "gems" fashioned from glitter that sparkles when the sun shines through the window. Hanging from the classroom ceiling is a large model of the earth with the interior parts labeled: crust, mantle, outer core, and inner core. Stories written or dictated by the children, titled "When I Went to the Center of the Earth," decorate the walls.

Fifteen children, ages three and four, are engrossed in many different learning-center activities designed around the theme The Earth, their present integrated-thematic unit. In the block center three children build ramps to roll their rocks down. Brian exclaims as he knocks down a ramp, "An earthquake struck and broke my ramp."

In the math center Sarah separates rocks into sets of eight. Steven is adding up his rocks: "One plus four is five," he counts as he writes the answer in his equation book. In the science center Patty sorts rocks into "soft" and "hard" piles. George and Sally are weighing rocks on a scale, then graphing results with a teacher's help. In the art center two children create sand paintings while two others paint "pet rocks." In the language center Peter writes different rock words to put in his "Can Can," a small can containing slips of paper with unit words on them: earth, cave, rock, mantle, plate, volcano, fault, crust, lava, fossil, core.

True learning in early childhood occurs when children involve themselves in a variety of developmentally appropriate learning experiences presented in an interdisciplinary manner. Effective early childhood teachers continually adapt and expand these experiences to respond to the individual needs of the children in their classrooms.

The vignettes above describe activities in a classroom in which an integrated-thematic curriculum has been designed to meet the needs of young gifted children. To develop an appropriate curriculum for these children, early childhood teachers need an understanding of the characteristics that distinguish such children from their peers and ways to differentiate the curriculum to address their educational needs.

Today the concept of giftedness is expanding beyond the traditional emphasis on general academic prowess (Nutall, Romero, & Kalesnick 1992). Research with preschoolers is pinpointing capabilities that may be the building blocks of giftedness in differentiated areas such as science, art, and music (Goldsmith & Feldman 1985; Wexler-Sherman, Gardner, & Feldman 1988). Recognizing this, Nutall, Romero, and

There are many types of giftedness. A person can be musically gifted, artistically gifted, athletically gifted, and so on. This article is about intellectually gifted children.

Kalesnick (1992) propose the following definition for gifted children:

> Gifted children are those showing sustained evidence of advanced capability relative to their peers in general academic skills and/or in more specific domains (music, art, science, etc.) to the extent that they need differentiated educational programming. (p. 302)

Characteristics of young intellectually gifted children

Labeling children is not a preferred method of dealing with differences; however, it is sometimes necessary in order to provide children with appropriate educational programming. Although there are always differences among children (Barbour 1992), research has demonstrated that as a group, young gifted children possess characteristics that distinguish them from their peers in the areas of cognitive, affective, and physical development.

In their cognitive development, young gifted children may demonstrate a high level of language development, an accelerated pace of thought, the ability to generate original ideas and solutions, a sensitivity to learning, and the ability to synthesize and think abstractly (Roedell, Jackson, & Robinson 1980; Hollinger & Kosak 1985; Lewis & Michaelson 1985; Parke & Ness 1988; VanTassel-Baska 1988; Lewis & Louis 1991).

These children's attention spans and interests often differ from the norm. They are able to concentrate for comparatively long periods of time on subjects that interest them. In many cases they develop "passion" areas in which they are intensely interested (Parke & Ness 1988).

There may be discrepancies between physical and intellectual development (Roedell 1990). Motor skills, often fine-motor, lag behind cognitive and conceptual abilities (Webb & Kleine 1993). Young gifted children may see in their mind's eye what they want to draw or construct, but their motor skills do not allow them to achieve their goal (Webb 1994).

In their affective development, young gifted children often have an evaluative approach to themselves and others. They attempt to organize people and things in a search for consistency and justice. They may invent complex games and try to organize their playmates (Webb 1994).

Young gifted children are often very sensitive to their emotions and those of others (Schetky 1981). They are more aware of the world around them, of their place in it, and of the relationships between people and places, time and spaces. Their mature vocabularies and ideas and frequently uneven development make them vulnerable to social isolation if they lack interaction with children of similar abilities.

These children are still preschoolers developmentally, however, and their curriculum needs to emphasize exploration, manipulation, and play (Parke & Ness 1988). As Riley notes,

> Much of the knowledge children absorb is best acquired by exploration in the real world where they may freely, actively, construct their vision of reality, rather than be passively instructed about it. (1974, 139)

Young children learn by observing what happens when they interact with materials and people. Development of their skills is achieved through hands-on learning (Piaget & Inhelder 1969).

Developing curriculum to meet the needs of high-ability young children

While young gifted children need developmentally appropriate activities similar to those of their same-age peers, their unique characteristics dictate the need for curriculum differentiation. Children with advanced abilities require opportunities to be exposed to and use the vocabulary and concepts typically used by much older children. They need to study subjects in depth because they have

Photo courtesy of the authors

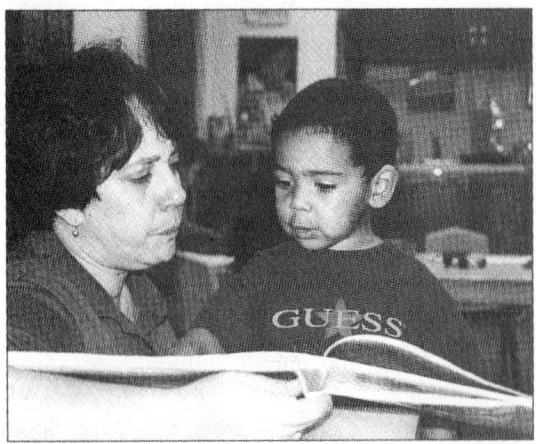
©Subjects & Predicates

unusually keen powers to make connections and perceive relationships. Curriculum should be individualized to meet their high levels of ability in particular domains.

An integrated-thematic curriculum can be adapted to meet the needs of young gifted children while also meeting the needs of the other children in the classroom. It is an enrichment tool in the highest sense. It provides children with an intellectual framework not available when studying only one content area and exposes them to many ideas not covered in traditional curricula (Van-Tassel-Baska 1988). The children described at the beginning of the article enjoy learning complex vocabulary such as magma, lava, and crust. However, their learning activities such as building a ramp with blocks or comparing soft and hard rocks are experiential and hands-on.

Providing depth

The first step in developing an integrated-thematic curriculum appropriate for young gifted children is to select an overarching theme around which to organize the year of study. The theme provides children with the opportunity to see and understand relationships while they explore concepts in depth.

For instance, teachers in our early childhood classroom example selected the theme "The Magic School Bus Explores My World and Beyond." It is based on the Magic School Bus series of books in which the children "ride" in a magic school bus through their different units of study. Month by month children explore a variety of social studies and science units that relate to the overall theme. Teachers select units that are rich in content and appeal to young children. Within each unit, all disciplines are represented in developmentally appropriate and meaningful ways.

In our example four units were chosen to express the exploration theme: The Human Body, The Earth, The World of the Imagination, and Rainforests. The units become meaningful as the children participate in creating unit-related environments in the classroom—during the rainforest unit the children made life-size replicas of plants, trees, and animals that live and grow in the rainforest.

Providing connections between the disciplines

In *Interdisciplinary Curriculum: Design and Implementation,* Jacobs (1989) writes that one disadvantage of integrated curriculum is that it can suffer from the "potpourri" approach: units may become samplings of knowledge without incorporating the different disciplines and skills to be covered. Teachers can avoid this problem by employing a web such as the one on the next page titled "Design for an In-Depth Integrated Unit."

When teachers design activities and lessons using this structure, they attend to each of the disciplines and to the connections between them. The web contains opportunities for higher-level thinking and creativity. Maker (1982) includes higher-level thinking skills as essential elements in a curriculum for high-ability children. Gifted learners also have a very high potential for creative activity and should begin developing that potential as early as possible (Clark 1997).

Guiding *inquiry questions* provide a framework for the experiences in which the children engage. These types of questions provide a focus for children's exposure to key ideas and themes within and across domains of knowledge (VanTassel-Baska 1988). For example, the guiding inquiry questions for the human body unit in The Magic School Bus Explores My World and Beyond theme include the following:

1. What are the systems in the body?
2. How do they work together?
3. How does what I do affect my body?
4. How do I care for my body?

Additionally, inquiry questions lend personal meaning to the study. In answering unit questions, children are encouraged to explore how their learning relates to them personally. The last two questions address this issue specifically: "How does what I do affect my body?" and "How do I care for my body?"

"How to Develop an In-Depth Integrated Unit" is a complete web that builds on the basic skills and disciplines, using a variety of specialized

Curriculum should always be created so that high-ability and low-ability children, children with special needs, and children with special gifts can individually find it challenging and achievable.

activities relating to the human body, the chosen unit of study.

Providing opportunities to address content at different levels

Besides providing young gifted children with occasions to explore topics in depth and make connections between disciplines, a meaningful curriculum needs to furnish children with opportunities to address content at many different levels.

Individualizing means recognizing and allowing for differences in development, understanding, approach to learning, and interests when teachers plan activities so that there is sufficient variety to meet the needs and interests of each child (Dodge & Colker 1992). In the case of young gifted children, individualizing means making sure that children are allowed to develop their abilities even though they are working at a level above what is considered age or grade appropriate.

Design for an In-Depth Integrated Unit

[Concept map with KEY CONCEPT at center, connected to: Technology, Analyze/Compare, Art/Music, Research/Inquire, Language Arts, Affective, Map/Chart/Graph, Solve Problem, Experiment, Imagine, Careers, Create, Math/Science, Produce/Write/Speak, Social Studies, Propose Plan]

1. Why is this important to learn?
2. Does this topic have sufficient depth and breadth?
3. What do I need to know and understand before beginning this unit?
4. Have I been inclusive of gender and ethnicity awareness?
5. Can this learning be applied to other areas?
6. What connections are there in the other units within the strand?
7. Are the experiences "real" in terms of problem, process, product, and audience?
8. What evaluation processes will I use?

Consider the example of Adam. When Adam entered an early childhood program at age three, he could read at a third-grade level. Participating with the class in learning to recognize the letters of the alphabet would have been frustrating to Adam and inhibiting to his development. Teachers designed an individualized reading program for Adam in which he read books appropriate for him during times when other children were learning their letters. He was allowed to write his own stories in the writing center and read them to the class.

Individualization can be accomplished in both learning-center and group activities.

Learning-center activities

Learning centers encourage both autonomy and self-control. They allow children to take responsibility for their own learning and engage in activities that interest them (Isbell 1995). Teachers can design learning centers to meet the needs of young gifted children by generating activities that challenge the children's highest level of skill and concept development. Some of the learning-center activities presented during the human body unit include

- comparing animal bones with replicas of human bones,
- dictating or writing stories that include facts about bodies,
- weighing fruits and vegetables and graphing their differences,
- using spaghetti and meatballs to do math problems,
- creating self-portraits,
- creating skeletons from Popsicle sticks, and
- counting the number of tiles needed to equal the length of the small intestine.

Learning-center activities address different levels of ability. While one child chooses to use spaghetti and meatballs to practice counting, another child may use them to add and

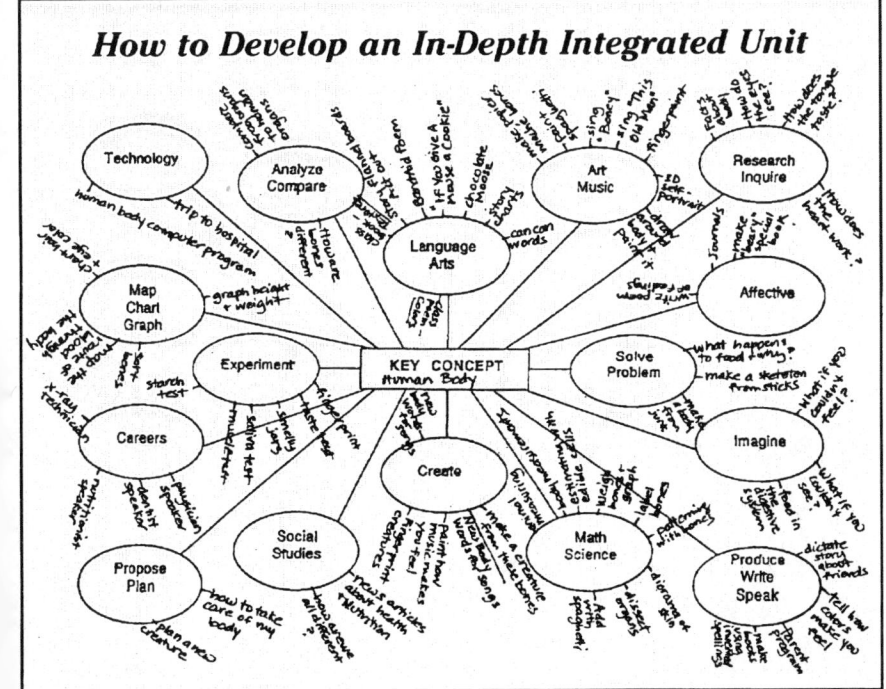

How to Develop an In-Depth Integrated Unit

> Curriculum for high-ability children should never be shallowly show-offy. Curriculum for any child should be meaningful.

subtract. Some children read their stories to a teacher or a parent volunteer, while others dictate stories. A child gifted in music might write a song to fit the unit.

While all good preschool programs include choice in activities, offering activities that address the highest level of skills of the children in the class ensures that the learning needs of all children are met.

Group activities

Group activities provide the opportunity for children to develop a classroom community and learn content that is unfamiliar to all of them. During the human body unit, the children role-played blood cells passing through the heart and lungs, sang songs about the body parts, dissected animal organs (with adult help), and acted out organ functions.

The children's interests help to guide the unit of study. If a class is particularly interested in the senses, for example, more time may be spent on this topic than on others. Guest speakers and field trips are interesting to all children and provide enrichment to the curriculum for young gifted learners.

In summary

All children have unique patterns of development, individual interests, and needs. Many gifted young children, however, share some common characteristics and needs in the cognitive, physical, and social and emotional domains. An integrated-thematic curriculum, which is appropriate for all early childhood learners, can be adapted to meet gifted children's needs by providing opportunities for in-depth study and concept development. Individualizing activities to meet children's highest level of ability will ensure that high-ability young children's educational needs are met.

©Elisabeth Nichols

References

Barbour, N. B. 1992. Early childhood gifted education: A collaborative perspective. *Journal for the Education of the Gifted* 15 (2): 145–62.

Clark, B. 1997. *Growing up gifted*. 5th ed. Upper Saddle River, NJ: Prentice Hall.

Dodge, D. T., & L. J. Colker. 1992. *The creative curriculum for early childhood*. 3d ed. Mt. Rainier, MD: Gryphon House. (ERIC Document No. ED 342 487).

Goldsmith, L. T., & D. H. Feldman. 1985. Identifying gifted children: The state of the art. *Pediatric Annals* 14 (10): 709–16.

Hollinger, C., & S. Kosak. 1985. Early identification of the gifted and talented. *Gifted Child Quarterly* 29 (4): 168–71.

Isbell, R. 1995. *The complete learning center book: An illustrated guide for 32 different learning centers*. Brooklyn, NY: Gryphon.

Jacobs, H. H. 1989. The growing need for interdisciplinary curriculum content. In *Interdisciplinary curriculum: Design and implementation,* ed. H. H. Jacobs, 13–24. Alexandria, VA: Association for Supervision and Curriculum Development.

Lewis, M., & B. Louis. 1991. Young gifted children. In *Handbook of gifted education,* eds. N. Colangelo & G. Davis, 365–81. Needham Heights, MA: Allyn & Bacon.

Lewis, M., & L. Michaelson. 1985. The gifted infant. In *The psychology of gifted children: Perspectives on development and education,* ed. J. Freeman, 35–57. New York: Wiley.

Maker, C. J. 1982. *Teaching models in the education of the gifted*. Rockville, MD: Aspen.

Nutall, E. V., I. Romero, & J. Kalesnick. 1992. *Assessing and screening preschoolers: Psychological and educational dimensions*. Needham Heights, MA: Allyn & Bacon.

Parke, B., & T. Ness. 1988. Curricular decision making for the education of young children. *Gifted Child Quarterly* 32 (1): 196–99.

Piaget, J., & B. Inhelder. 1969. *The psychology of the child*. New York: Basic.

Riley, S. S. 1974. Some reflections on the value of children's play. In *Providing the best for young children,* eds. J. McCarthy & C. R. May, 138–45. Washington, DC: NAEYC.

Roedell, W. C. 1990. *Nurturing giftedness in young children*. Report No. EDO-EC-90. Reston, VA: Council for Exceptional Children. (ERIC Document No. ED 321 492).

Roedell, W., N. Jackson, & H. Robinson. 1980. *Gifted young children*. New York: Teachers College Press.

Schetky, D. H. 1981. The emotional and social development of the gifted child. *Gifted Child Today* 4 (3): 2–4.

Webb, J. T. 1994. *Nurturing social-emotional development of gifted children*. Report No. EDO-EC-93-10. Reston, VA: Council for Exceptional Children. (ERIC Document Reproduction Service No. ED 372 554).

Webb, J. T., & P. A. Kleine. 1993. Assessing gifted and talented children. In *Testing young children,* eds. J. Culbertson & D. Willis, 383–407. Austin, TX: Pro-Ed.

Wexler-Sherman, C., H. Gardner, & D. H. Feldman. 1988. A pluralistic view of early assessment: The Project Spectrum approach. *Theory into Practice* 27 (1): 77–83.

VanTassel-Baska, J. 1988. Curriculum for the gifted: Theory, research, and practice. In *Comprehensive curriculum for gifted learners,* eds. J. VanTassel-Baska, J. Feldhusen, K. Seeley, G. Wheately, L. Silverman, & W. Foster, 1–17. Needham Heights, MA: Allyn & Bacon.

FOR FURTHER READING

Bredekamp, S., & C. Copple, eds. 1997. *Developmentally appropriate practice in early childhood programs*. Rev. ed. Washington, DC: NAEYC.

Foster, S. M. 1993. Meeting the needs of gifted and talented preschoolers. *Children Today* 22 (3): 23–30.

James, R., & L. Johnson. 1991. The preschool/primary gifted child. *Journal for the Education of the Gifted* 14 (3): 56–63.

Kitano, M. 1989. The K–3 teacher's role in recognizing and supporting young gifted children. *Young Children* 44 (3): 57–63.

Smutny, J. F., K. Veenker, & S. Veenker. 1989. *Your gifted child: How to recognize and develop the special talents in your child from birth to age seven.* New York: Ballantine.

Whitmore, J. R. 1986. *Intellectual giftedness in young children: Recognition and development.* New York: Haworth.

Wolfle, J. 1989. The gifted preschooler: Developmentally different, but still three or four years old. *Young Children* 44 (3): 41–48.

Brooke Walker, M.A., has taught at the Ricks Center for Gifted Children in Denver, Colorado, for seven years. She has made presentations on the education and development of young gifted children at state and national conferences. Her research has been published in Gifted Child Quarterly, Roeper Review, *and* Research in Middle Level Education Quarterly.

Norma Lu Hafenstein, Ph.D., is founder and director of the Ricks Center for Gifted Children. She consults throughout the country on giftedness and has works published in Gifted Child Quarterly, Roeper Review, *and* Research in Middle Level Education Quarterly.

Linda Crow-Enslow, M.A., has taught early childhood education for eight years and has presented the gifted education curriculum model used in the early childhood classrooms at state and national conferences.

Gifted Students Suggest Reforms for Education

Listening to gifted students' ideas

by Lugene Polzella

At this time of concern for basic skills, educational standards, achievement testing, and curriculum guides, there is little interest in the educational needs of brighter students. Budget cuts have made programs for the gifted in public schools practically obsolete. Still, these able students remain in the classroom, sitting in the background, bored with the slow pace, questioning their own special needs as learners, and often feeling isolated and alone. Schools today are seriously limited in their ability to meet the needs of these able children. Some teachers, on the other hand, are particularly sensitive to the unique aspects of gifted children and plan an open-ended curriculum. Often parents need to become directly involved in order to encourage experiences that match the interests and learning styles of their gifted children.

Summer programs for gifted students often provide the necessary components for them to advance in their learning and to feel good about themselves (Feldhusen & Clinkenbeard, 1982; VanTassel-Baska, Landau, & Olszewski, 1984). However, it is unfair that these students have to spend 10 months out of the year suffering in low level, single-faceted courses (Kunkel, Chapa, Patterson, & Walling, 1992) to have their educational needs met for only a few weeks in the summer (Lenz & Burruss, 1994). American public school education is free for everybody and should more accurately meet the needs of a diverse population of learners (Nielsen, 1993). Parents of brighter students should not have to pay extra for their children to get a quality education. Their regular schools must provide the intellectual stimulation they need during the traditional school year. We as educators have just as much responsibility to brighter students as to all other levels of students. When asked, the students themselves offer a wide range of suggestions for ways of enhancing their own educational experiences. It is time we start listening to the gifted students themselves and put energy toward ensuring their successes, both academic and social/emotional, in their regular schools.

Fifty returning students in grades 4–11 at the 1995 Bryn Mawr College session of the Summer Institute for the Gifted completed a survey containing three open-ended questions: Why did you return to the Summer Institute? What is your favorite area of interest—both academic and cultural? Which aspects of the program would you like to have as part of your regular school year experience?

Informal interviews were also conducted to obtain more qualitative information. Student responses that related to school improvements and reform were given emphasis, rather than the quantity of similar responses.

When asked their primary reason for returning, the most popular response was to further their education. Many students mentioned that their attendance in this program would help them "get ahead" in life. The second most popular response was that the program was fun. They most enjoyed the mixture of academic and recreational aspects. The third most popular response was that they were able to make new friends, and most notably, from among their intellectual peers. Lastly, students mentioned that this program were something productive to do in the summer. By far the most popular reasons for attending this program were academic; however, friendships, exciting dorm experiences, and the chance to be more independent were also important to this group of students.

When students were asked to indicate their favorite areas of interest, the most popular responses indicated enjoyment of the following classes: drama and theater, swimming and water games, SAT preparation, mock trials and the justice system, tennis, and several of the science classes. It seemed that the popularity of some classes and experiences related somewhat to their novelty. Many students do not attend schools with the type of facilities a college campus can afford. Tennis courts and an Olympic-size pool, a full-sized computer lab with a wide range of available software, and a full-size auditorium with a large stage, are luxuries for upper elementary, middle, and high school students. Many students mentioned they enjoyed their computer classes and use of the computer lab during free time. Clearly they enjoyed taking full advantage of the available facilities. The SAT prep courses were important to the students because of the test's mandatory requirement for college entry. Most interesting was the enthusiasm for science classes, which were challenging and offered students a hands-on approach. As one student wrote: "I like my science classes a lot because there is a lot of hands-on lab education." This is an area in particular need of improvement in the regular schools, and was clearly appreciated by these students.

When asked "Which aspects of the program they would like to have as part of their regular school year experience?" the most popular response indicated the students' enjoyment of the evening special programs and the weekend trips. Special programs of this summer program ranged from a '50s singing group, to a man pretending to be Mozart, a woman playing Harriet Tubman, a masked man who explained and cleverly modeled the uses for masks, a theater sports group, a talent show, a brain bowl, and two dances, each with themes. The weekend "get away days" ranged from the Hershey amusement park, a Renaissance Faire, river rafting on the Delaware River, a historical tour of Philadelphia, exploring museums, and several different trip choices in Washington, DC, including the Smithsonian Institute, Air and Space museum, a tour of the White House, and the Lincoln Memorial. Each of these trips offered countless opportunities for extending the imagination, knowledge, and understanding of bright young people.

The second most important aspect these students would like to see incorporated into their regular school experience was more challenging coursework in their classes. Some specifically mentioned the opportunity to take college level courses early if ready. These students were hungry for a challenge, which in turn challenged their teachers to offer more rigorous, complex, meaningful, applications to their curricula.

The third aspect mentioned by several students was more free time, and most specifically, more time between classes. One student wrote: "I liked that we had 15 minutes between our classes to relax or look over things before class." Several others mentioned that they enjoyed the "greater freedom around campus." Students often have trouble making transitions from one subject to another because regular school time is tightly structured. Their comments clearly mirrored this idea. Students need time to unwind from one course, and appreciate the chance to prepare mentally for the next.

Several other interesting responses that have a direct influence on our desire to improve regular school experiences are worth noting. Students particularly loved the chance to choose their own courses and felt they deserved that freedom during the school year. They also appreciated the support they felt from other students within the classroom environment, the excitement and love for learning generated by dedicated, young teachers, the small, low-stress classes, and finally, the emphasis on hands-on learning.

Often as administrators, parents, and teachers, we feel we know what is best for students. Unfortunately, in the public schools of today, the reality of overcrowded classes, budget cuts in staffing, programming and supplies, and frequent resulting teacher burn-out makes serving the needs of exceptionally bright children a difficult challenge. Often, we fail to ask the students about their needs. If we take the time to really listen, their requests and needs are obtainable. Clearly, the gifted students of this study have much to teach us about how we can better serve them during the regular school year. Here are some suggestions based on their ideas:

1. **Curriculum-related field trips.** On-site visits to local community areas of particular interest and intrigue spark the imaginations and create innovative ideas in our brightest students. Trips to museums, experiences in nature, and historical tours are an essential part of an enriched curriculum. Students need the exposure to the real world, and want the chance to interact with people in the field of study they are pursuing. Many such trips are inexpensive, and often only require coordination and parent volunteers.

2. **Serving individual student interests.** Sometimes the needs of a particular individual require a careful listening ear and strong advocates willing to extend themselves in providing specific growth experiences. Using community resources to help make those experiences happen is an effective way of serving our brightest. For example, taking an aeronautics enthusiast to a local airport and linking him or her with a pilot willing to explain the intricacies of flying and offering him or her a flying lesson, may make all the difference to an eager learner. Fostering the enthusiasm of excited students and matching their interests to experiences will bring learning to life for our most able students.

3. **Use of college campus facilities.** Local college campuses often provide equipment and facilities that better suit the needs and abilities of young people with advanced talents or aspirations. Weekend programs offered to the community could include these students. Arrangements for special students to attend seminars, work with trainers and coaches, and obtain acting parts in local productions are possibilities. Pairing a college student with an advanced gifted student with similar interests would afford the gifted student a learning partner and advocate. Those who are ready should attend college classes and be allowed to obtain college credit for their efforts.

4. **Flexible school policies and teacher planning.** Several other requests revolve around school policy and administrative decision-making. Students need greater freedom in their course selections and require more time between classes. A small class size initially seems unobtainable, but with effective coordination of other staff members, school volunteers, and administrators, small groups could be possible, at least for part of the class time experience. For example, if the librarian, the computer teacher, and the principal each work with a group of students from the same class, the homeroom teacher would then have a quarter of the students at a time. Such an arrangement could supplement and enrich the learning experience for the students by involving other subject area teachers. Smaller groups increase student-to-teacher and student-to-student interactions and allow more time for student response. Student-to-student interactions also increase in smaller classes. These are ways to make that "comfortable feel of small class size" happen.

Several students were impressed with the expertise of their teachers and their integrated, open-ended teaching styles. Many developed lasting friendships with their summer program teachers as a result of their willingness to involve their students directly and to listen carefully to their ideas. Teacher training in the areas of the educational needs of gifted students and curriculum integration methods are necessary for gifted students to feel comfortable with the teachers in their regular classes. Teacher sensitivity to the unique qualities and needs of gifted individuals helps create an atmosphere in which bright children feel more comfortable getting involved.

5. **Hands-on science and technology.** Emphasis on hands-on learning is of key importance in

teaching today. Students need to experience the world in both concrete and abstract ways and must have enthusiastic, capable teachers to facilitate their learning. Particularly in the sciences, students need a strong background in technology, computers, and the sciences to experience first-hand the questions or problems they wonder about. Teachers must be knowledgeable and supportive, guiding students toward inherent challenges. A flexible curriculum with direct student contribution allows for individual differences. Gifted students have an opportunity to express themselves creatively when they have a chance to play around with ideas. The result is a crucial unspoken message to the brighter students that their ideas and input are vital to the success of the curriculum.

6. **Opportunities for gifted students to spend time working together.** One of the most important aspects of the summer experience for these students was the chance to work on meaningful areas of pursuit with their intellectual peers. Often as classroom teachers we distribute the brightest students across several groups in order to have a wide range of abilities within each group. This heterogeneous grouping is often detrimental for the brighter students who often end up tutoring the slower students in the group to the group's level, or doing more than their fair share of the work. When brighter children in a class work together in one group, they have a chance to enrich their experiences and incorporate a more abstract, complex view of the curriculum presented. By sharing their work with others, gifted students are able to show the entire class a more advanced way of learning.

In middle school and high school, certain times of the year (often for a week at a time) are designated for presenting concepts and ideas from an interdisciplinary perspective. A topic or theme for the unit is chosen which incorporates several disciplines. An example might be: "Man's Influence On His Environment In Turn Causes His Change." Teachers from various classes meet to generate ideas for projects and explore new methods for creating meaning for the students. Individual disciplines are taught from this perspective as students are invited to suggest ways to explore the theme. A variety of forms of expression of their ideas are encouraged. This open-ended approach to exploring ideas helps gifted students present their ideas in a less rigid educational forum.

The Governor's Scholars Program (GSP) in Kentucky presents a superb example of this interdisciplinary style of teaching. Eleventh graders are given the opportunity to participate in "an intensive living-learning experience." During this five-week summer program, students explore a variety of disciplines, and apply their learning to the real world. Work and play become one. Students attend non-traditional classes held in unique settings at different times of the day. For example, "Some teachers remove the furniture from the rooms; some conduct class peripatetically, teaching while walking through a town at dawn; some meet their students in the dining commons or dormitory lounges" (Riegelman, Wolf, & Press, 1991, p. 7). Students elect to "major" in one of 12 disciplines, but also take courses that seem antithetical. If they choose a major in the humanities, they must also take some science and math classes. Courses are taught from an interdisciplinary perspective. Emphasis is on hands-on learning in the real world. Some examples include: "A history class studies the Civil War by becoming Civil War soldiers at a nearby battlefield—eating beans and hardtack, drilling in 100 degree heat, wearing authentic wool uniforms, and sleeping in pup tents between patrols. A biology class studies the environment by analyzing water samples from a polluted stream and researching waste treatment alternatives, later forming an active organization to lobby for environmental change. A philosophy class, after discussing the ethical implications of current medical decisions, decides to spend time in a crippled children's hospital" (Riegelman et al., pp. 7–8). This type of enriched, involving, relevant educational experience will guide our brightest students toward becoming concerned, informed experts in their chosen fields.

Students spend the majority of their educational life in their regular hometown school. In most cases, this is public school with limited funding and resources. Often teacher attention revolves around the needs of the average and special education students with frequent neglect of the brighter students. It is imperative that we as teachers and administrators take the time to include enriching, challenging, dignifying experiences for our gifted students. These experiences often are easily obtained. By listening to the suggestions of students attending a summer camp experience especially tailored to the needs of the gifted, we can create strategies designed to help make the dreams of all gifted students a reality.

References

Feldhusen, J. F., & Clinkenbeard, P. R. (1982). Summer programs for the gifted: Purdue's residential programs for high achievers. *Journal for the Education of the Gifted, 5*(3), 178–184.

Kunkel, M. A., Chapa, B., Patterson, G., & Walling, D. D. (1992). Experience of giftedness. "Eight great gripes" six years later. *Roeper Review, 15*(1), 10–14.

Lenz, K., & Burruss, J. D. (1994). Meeting affective needs through summer academic experiences. *Roeper Review, 17*(1), 51.

Nielsen, B. (1993). An attempt to make a difference: Overlooked disadvantaged gifted Appalachian children. *Roeper Review, 16*(1), 62–64.

Reigelman, M., Wolf, K., & Press, L. (1991). Creating an effective learning environment. *Gifted Child Today, 14*(3), 6–11.

VanTassel-Baska, J., Landau, M., & Olszewski, P. (1984). The benefits of summer programming for gifted students. *Journal for the Education of the Gifted, 8*(10), 73–82.

Accountability for Gifted Students

BY JAMES J. GALLAGHER

The call for a differentiated curriculum or program for gifted students raises the issues of how such changes should be made and how they should be assessed. Mr. Gallagher proffers some suggestions.

Illustration by John Berry

ONE OF the key elements of the new education reform movement is clearly accountability. Over the years, members of the general public have become distressed by what they perceive to be the excessive promises of educators who were trying to overcome the effects of larger societal problems. In addition, the public schools were given responsibility, without substantial help from other segments of the society, for tasks that had little chance of success (for example, doing away with intergenerational poverty).[1] In the wake of limited results, the public schools have been asked to document their good works and to demonstrate that their requests for resources are justified by performance.

The call for accountability does not necessarily mean we have lost our affection for or trust in our teachers. It is more in the spirit of President Reagan's slogan "Trust, but verify." We know that teachers, like other professionals, are sometimes victims of self-delusion about their own work or captives of their own self-interest. Just as we want our physicians, bankers, and politicians to be accountable, so do we want verification of the positive results that teachers claim their efforts have produced.

JAMES J. GALLAGHER is Kenan Professor of Education, Frank Porter Graham Child Development Center, University of North Carolina, Chapel Hill.

Assessment in the Education of Gifted Students

Traditional measures have rarely been helpful in assessing either gifted individuals or educational programs for gifted students. There are several reasons for the limited usefulness of instruments that are designed for average students.

1. *Ceiling effects.* Many gifted students score at the top level of the tests that are traditionally administered, often even before instruction begins. When a student scores at the 98th percentile on a test, that tells us only that he or she has mastered the content of that test; it does not inform us as to the upper limits of the student's knowledge.

2. *Content covered.* Most standardized achievement tests measure mastery of facts and low-level associations. Gifted education aims at higher levels of thinking than are measured by these instruments. Using these tests to assess gifted students is similar to trying to measure a 100-foot tower with a yardstick

3. *General measures of achievement.* The use of broad general achievement measures, such as the SAT I or exams to measure growth during specific instructional units or projects, inevitably underestimates or fails to document the gifted student's mastery and growth in these specific knowledge areas.

4. *Previous evaluation models.* Previous efforts at school evaluation have often focused on inputs to the school program (number of certified teachers, computer stations established, and so on) rather than on tangible growth or change in student knowledge, skills, motivation, or attitude.[2]

The attempt of some school administrators to take credit for the high scores that gifted students make on standardized achievement tests, statewide achievement tests, or end-of-grade tests is disingenuous at best and borders on the fraudulent. Those students would be making high scores on those tests even if they had stayed home for the entire year, a proposition now being tested by increasing numbers of parents who have resorted to home schooling after being disillusioned by what the public schools are doing—or not doing—for their children.

There is now evidence to document the relatively weak and limited attempts being made in many schools to provide educational experiences for gifted children. Many schools that claim to have "programs for gifted students" allow these students a special experience for an hour or two per week. This is what practitioners of medicine would call a "nontherapeutic dose."

One way to discover what gifted students are thinking about their education is to ask them. In one study, my colleagues and I asked gifted elementary, middle, and secondary students in nine separate school systems if they were being challenged by their current coursework.[3] More than half of the gifted students in the middle schools reported that they were not challenged by their coursework in language arts, social studies, and science. The percentages of negative replies at the elementary and secondary levels were only slightly lower.

Another study observed 46 elementary classrooms to determine whether the teachers were offering any differentiation in program content for the gifted students.[4] The researchers found very few, if any, attempts by the teachers to provide something different for the gifted students, despite these students' obvious mastery of the regular curriculum.

Appropriate Curriculum and Instruction for Gifted Students

The various textbooks in gifted education have all stressed the importance of a differentiated education—something beyond the regular curriculum.[5] There is a general call for "curriculum compacting," or finding out what parts of the curriculum the gifted students have not already mastered and teaching them that material so that they can quickly move on to other, more challenging and interesting material.[6]

The call for a differentiated curriculum or program for gifted students raises the issues of how such changes should be made and how they should be assessed. One approach is to change both the content that is presented and the thinking strategies that the student learns. Shelagh Gallagher and I have suggested four methods of content differentiation.[7]

1. *Acceleration.* The material presented to the gifted student may be drawn from the established curricula of a grade or more above the student's current level (e.g., algebra in the seventh grade).

2. *Enrichment.* The same curriculum goals are used for the entire class, but the material assigned to the gifted students is more extensive and in-depth (e.g., studying the diaries of the Lewis and Clark expedition as the class discusses westward movement).

3. *Sophistication.* The material presented to the gifted students is at a higher level of complexity—representing systems of knowledge—than that given to regular students (e.g., studying the laws of physics and their applications).

4. *Novelty.* Gifted students may study material that is not part of the regular curriculum but that holds some interest for them (e.g., the study of the stock market and its operations).

Whatever the method of content differentiation chosen by the teacher, the evaluation of these special content units would involve measuring the degree of mastery that the student has been able to attain over the special material, combined with weighing the relevance or importance of the special material chosen. For example, a study of the origins of the game of Ping-Pong or a paper titled "Waterfalls I Have Known" might not rank high on appropriateness of curriculum.

Thinking Strategies for Gifted Students

A wide variety of efforts have been made to enhance the creative and productive thinking abilities of gifted students.[8] One approach focuses on problem-finding abilities, the selection of the important problems to tackle in science or themes to address through the arts or topics to explore in language arts projects.[9] The student would be expected to show mastery of these skills through actual performance.

Ideally, these student projects would be individual in nature and so would have to be dealt with on an individual basis. Consider that one student may be doing a biographical sketch of Mozart, another conducting a research project on the pH level of acids, and a third tracking factors underlying World War II. Think how futile it would be to use the SAT or the Iowa Tests of Basic Skills as a measure of their progress and attainment!

Gifted Education for All?

If a differentiated program for gifted students involved their working with a question such as "What might have happened had Lincoln survived the assassination attempt?" many educators would respond, "Well, yes, that is an interesting problem to pose to these students." But why just these students? Shouldn't all students have the opportunity to tackle this interesting proposition? The short answer is, of course, that all students should be provided with interesting tasks that require them to use their full intellectual abilities. But it is not quite so simple.

The biggest enemy of the teacher is time, and time poses a dilemma for the teacher who would present this question to the whole class. For the gifted student who already has at his or her disposal a broad array of facts about the Civil War as well as an understanding of some of the forces at play during that historical period, it would be a manageable task to assemble an answer to this proposition. But what about the student who has only a very limited fund of information about that era and would need to learn a great deal more about the times, the cultures, and the historical facts before being ready to cope with the proposition? How much time is the teacher willing to spend on this assignment? If the answer is two weeks, then the task may well fall within the means of the gifted student while presenting an impossible challenge for the average student who has so much more collateral information to obtain. Should we then say that, if all students cannot experience this assignment, none should? What about orchestras, football teams, school plays, debate teams, and so on?

Purposes of Assessment

Accountability depends on a clear statement of purpose that can then be assessed for significance and attainment. There are two types of objectives that together make up accountability.

Management objectives. Management objectives are very important in education and are a necessary first step to achieving program objectives. For example, a management objective might be stated as "We will send 10 elementary teachers for special training in content differentiation for gifted students." This action might be a prelude to introducing "cluster grouping" at the local school level.

Program objectives. These are specific statements of expected changes that will take place in the students (or the teachers) as a result of a particular intervention. For example, the students will know something more, will be able to use new skills, or will have an enhanced motivation for school as a result of services provided.

Once the management objectives have been accomplished, the program objectives of students' mastering more difficult content can be tested. Sometimes the link between management objectives and program objectives gets lost, and we find educators celebrating the attainment of a management objective as if it were the true objective. We celebrate the hiring of new staff, or the attainment of a grant, or the reorganization of a department as though it were the goal instead of just a necessary first step to ensuring student achievement. We must have both types of objectives in the evaluation plan, but to be meaningful the management objectives must be linked to program objectives.

Evaluation Practices for Program Objectives

The essence of differentiated curricula and special programming for academically or intellectually gifted students is that they are expected to create a change in the student—presumably, an improvement. To determine that a program has been effective, we must have evidence that change in the student has taken place in one or more of the following domains.

Knowledge. The student demonstrates the mastery of bodies of knowledge that he or she had previously not mastered (e.g., discusses Newton's laws or explains the structure of a sonnet).

Skills. The student demonstrates the mastery of new skills and new competencies (e.g., designs and executes a scientific experiment or produces a sonnet).

Attitude. The student manifests a change in attitude toward studies, peers, content fields, and self (e.g., tolerates different styles of music, dress, or thinking or sustains interest despite temporary setbacks).

Motivation. The student shows an increased motivation for learning and for education (e.g., volunteers for a special project or improves school attendance).

If we cannot demonstrate change in one or more of these four broad arenas, then we will have a difficult time justifying the effort and resources required to support programs for these special students. However, it is not always easy to demonstrate these changes since the available instruments may not be the appropriate tools to measure specific interventions. Some indicators beyond tests are needed to show student gains. There are a variety of additional sources of documentation.

Products. The ultimate demonstration of knowledge or skills is their use in producing some entity, whether a poem, painting, experiment, or class presentation. (Portfolio assessment is one of the recent efforts to use products for evaluative purposes.)

Processes. The demonstration of new skills can be accomplished by having a student move through a complex process successfully and in systematic fashion (e.g., designing a scientific experiment and carrying it to completion or demonstrating the ability to use a procedure for conflict resolution and peer mediation).

Problem finding. The ability to discern the significant question to pose or artistic design to produce from a variety of circumstances or options (e.g., determining the essential issues to attack in dealing with world hunger).

Problem solving. The ability to take a well-structured problem (e.g., Given that Joe displays the following symptoms, what condition might he have?) and apply the appropriate heuristics to it in order to reach a solution.

Another source of information for evaluation is to ask the student and the teacher directly for their reactions to the tasks and problems they have been assigned.[10] Allowing students and teachers to provide open-ended responses to questions about the level of interest, challenge, and difficulty of the differentiated services being offered can yield interesting information on the strengths and shortcomings of those services. Since one of the goals of formative evaluation is the progressive improvement of the differentiated services, such information can be highly useful. Questions such as the following can yield instructive responses.

• What were the most important ideas that you learned from this project?

- Were the activities interesting and challenging or mainly routine?
- Do you now have some new skills that will improve your ability to do such tasks better in the future? Describe them.
- Would you like to do some other activities like this later on? Such as?
- What was the hardest part of this project or problem to do?

While some tests have been deliberately constructed to measure complex thought processes, all such measures have technical limitations of one sort or another.[11] The tendency in recent times has been to try and measure complex thinking processes as they are used in the instructional program. The use of portfolios to collect and judge products of student assignments and the use of performance testing and other forms of authentic testing come closer to effectively evaluating gifted students' output.[12]

We must face the fact that if we wish to have qualitative excellence in curricular differentiation, then we must design qualitative procedures to properly assess the programs.

A Last Word

The various fields that deal with the education of exceptional children have led to many advances for education in general. Our ways of thinking about intelligence and creativity have been enriched by data gathered both from children with special talents and from children with mental retardation. Our skills and interest in educational diagnosis have been furthered by our attention to children with learning disabilities, and our understanding of behavioral problems and how they can be handled has been enlarged through our concern with children with emotional disturbances. It is not too much to hope that serious attention to educational programs for gifted students will give us a more profound grasp of the proper scope and depth of educational evaluation through the process of accountability.

---

1. Edward Zigler, Sharon L. Kagan, and Nancy Hall, eds., *Children, Families, and Government* (New York: Cambridge University Press, 1996).

2. Carolyn Callahan and Michael Caldwell, *A Practitioner's Guide to Evaluating Programs for the Gifted* (Washington, D.C.: National Association for Gifted Children, 1995).

3. James Gallagher, Christine Harradine, and Mary Ruth Coleman, "Challenge or Boredom? Gifted Students on Their Learning," *Roeper Review*, vol. 19, 1997, pp. 132–36.

4. Karen Westberg et al., "The Classroom Practices Observation Study," *Journal for the Education of the Gifted*, vol. 16, 1993, pp. 120–46.

5. Barbara Clark, *Growing Up Gifted* (Upper Saddle River, N.J.: Prentice-Hall, 1997); and Nicholas Colangelo and Gary Davis, eds., *Handbook of Gifted Education* (Boston: Allyn and Bacon, 1997).

6. Joseph Renzulli, Linda Smith, and Sally Reis, "Curriculum Compacting: An Essential Strategy for Working with Gifted Students," *Elementary School Journal*, vol. 82, 1982, pp. 26–33.

7. James Gallagher and Shelagh Gallagher, *Teaching the Gifted Child* (Boston: Allyn and Bacon, 1994.)

8. Teresa Amabile, *The Social Psychology of Creativity* (New York: Springer-Verlag, 1983); Mihaly Csikszentmihalyi and Jack W. Getzels, "Creativity and Problem Finding," in Frank Farley and Ronald Neperud, eds., *The Foundations of Aesthetics, Art, and Art Education* (New York: Praeger, 1988), pp. 91–106; and Beth Hennessey, "Teaching for Creative Development: A Psychological Approach," in Colangelo and Davis, pp. 282–91.

9. Howard Barrows, *The Tutorial Process* (Carbondale: School of Medicine, Southern Illinois University, 1988); and William Stepien and Shelagh Gallagher, "Problem-Based Learning: Authentic as It Gets," *Educational Leadership*, April 1993, pp. 25–28.

10. James Borland, "Evaluating Gifted Programs," in Colangelo and Davis, pp. 253–66.

11. Callahan and Caldwell, op. cit.

12. Grant Wiggins, "Creating Tests Worth Taking," *Educational Leadership*, May 1992, pp. 26–33.

Unit 11

Unit Selections

35. **Making Comprehensive Inclusion of Special Needs Students Work in a Middle School,** Paul D. Deering
36. **Competitions and Exceptional Children: A Great Combination,** Tracy L. Riley and Frances A. Karnes
37. **School-to-Work: A Model for Learning a Living,** Michael Hartoonian and Richard Van Scotter

Key Points to Consider

❖ What services are needed to make the transition from primary to middle school work?

❖ How do competitions for students with disabilities assist with transitional planning?

❖ Why should students with disabilities have transition services that focus on self-development and citizenship as well as on employment?

www.dushkin.com/online/

32. **National Transition Alliance (NTA) Home Page**
   http://www.dssc.org/nta/index.html

These sites are annotated on pages 4 and 5.

Transition

In 1990 an amendment to the Individuals with Disabilities Education Act (IDEA) extended special educational services to students from the completion of their public school education through age 21. This extension of services is to prepare students with disabilities to make a successful transition from the dependent status of student to a more independent status as community member and participant in the world of work.

The commencement of transitional services has been slow. The first step is to plan for an appropriate transition plan for each unique student. Many teachers, special educators, vocational counselors, and employment mentors (job coaches) are not sure what kind of vocational preparation should be given in the public schools, or when. Should children with disabilities start planning for their futures in elementary school, in middle school, in high school, throughout their education, or just before they finish school? Should there be a trade-off between academic education and vocational education for these students? Should each student's vocational preparation be planned to meet the kind of needs and abilities of the individual, with no general rules about the wheres and whens of transitional services?

These and other questions about implementation of transitional services for children with exceptionalities abound. The U.S. government defined transitional services as outcome-oriented, coordinated activities designed to move students with disabilities from school to post-school activities such as college, vocational training, integrated employment, supported employment, adult education, adult services, independent living, and community participation. Choices are not either/or, but rather multiple: to help students with disabilities move from school to successful adulthood. While some students may only be able to achieve partial independence and supported employment, others may achieve professional degrees and complete self-sufficiency.

The reauthorized IDEA stipulates that every student have an individualized transition plan (ITP) added to his or her individualized education plan (IEP) by age 16. This mandate defines the upper limit for beginning transition planning, but not the lower boundary. Transition planning may begin in elementary school.

The transition from student to employee in the work world usually receives a great deal of attention. The transitions from child living at home to adult living away from parents, and from noncommunity participant to full participant in community activities, should also be supported in an ITP.

The transition to the world of work may take the form of supported employment (mobile work crew, clustered or enclave placement, on-site training and supervision by a job coach, group providing a specific service product) or of sheltered employment (in a workshop). Many students with disabilities can make a transition from school to competitive employment. If they will eventually work side by side with nondisabled coworkers, they may need transitional services such as assertiveness training, conflict resolution, negotiating skills, and personal empowerment counseling.

The transition to independent living requires careful planning, with goals and objectives as detailed as those for the transition to employment. Independent living may range from complete autonomy in a home or apartment, to partial autonomy with a spouse or roommate, to residence with a live-in aide or a part-time aide, to residence in a group home. Just a few years ago, adults with disabilities were expected to live in institutions or with parents, siblings, or extended family members. This is no longer considered appropriate. Each individual with a disability should be encouraged to be as autonomous as possible in adulthood. Self-sufficiency is enhanced by providing education in life skills such as meal preparation and cleanup, home deliveries (for example, mail) and delivery pickups (for example, trash), using money and paying bills, making household repairs, and following home safety precautions.

The transition from noncommunity participant to fully participating member of society requires ITP modifications quite different from IEP academic goals. Students with exceptional conditions may need more than the usual amount of assistance in learning to drive a car or to use public transportation. They need to know how to read maps and schedules. They need to be able to assert their right to vote in secret (for instance, ballots in braille or computerized for their software), and to marry, divorce, reproduce, sue, defend themselves, or even run for public office. They should know social conventions (greetings, conversation skills, manners), grooming fashions, and clothing styles. They deserve to have the same access to health settings, religious locales, social activities, and information services (telephone, television, computer networks) as do persons without disabilities. Much is still left to be done to ensure a better life for adults with disabilities.

The first article included in this unit on transition offers insights into the collaborative efforts required of administrators, staff, regular and special education teachers, and the student body when a child with special needs transfers into a middle school. It reports the findings of a 2-year research project on transition. It identifies key issues that must be faced, addresses school policies and practices that can enhance or detract from a smooth transition, and discusses the dangers of resegregation of children with special needs. The author, Paul Deering, argues that all of the adults involved in making inclusion work in a middle school need to keep an eye on the broader, long-term picture of inclusive education for children with disabilities. Scaffolding students' academic and social goals will help everyone reap the full benefits of cooperation, friendship, and tolerance in our society in the future.

In the second article in unit 11, Tracy Riley and Frances Karnes extol the virtues of competitions for children with exceptionalities. Many competitions can be introductions to lifelong interests. Transition planning is enhanced by students' excitement and involvement with outside activities. The authors provide many addresses for contact information about activities and competitions appropriate for children with disabilities.

Three interrelated goals for transition planning—self-development, citizenship, and employment—are the focus of the last article in this unit. Michael Hartoonian and Richard Van Scotter argue that students should be educated with an eye toward "learning a living," not just earning a living.

Making Comprehensive Inclusion of Special Needs Students Work in a Middle School

Paul D. Deering

More and more middle level schools are taking on the challenge of an inclusion approach to educating their special needs students (Bergen, 1993; Rothenberg, 1995). Inclusion, also known as mainstreaming, places students who have special educational needs in regular classrooms with peers who have no such identified needs. This is in contrast to the traditional self-contained approach in which special needs students are grouped together in separate rooms with special education teachers for all or most of the school day. The shift to an inclusion approach presents middle level schools with complex challenges as they attempt to shift the locations and methods for meeting all their students' needs. This article offers insights from a two-year study that may help schools to identify key issues, policies, and practices in serving the needs and bringing forth the talents of all of their on-site educational constituents—special needs and mainstream students, special education and mainstream teachers, administrators, and staff.

The widespread shift to inclusion was prompted by Public Law 94-142, the Education of the Handicapped Act of 1975, and its more recent updates (P.L. 99-457 of 1986; P.L. 101-476 of 1992). Based on the premise that mandating separate educational contexts for special needs students is inherently unequal, these laws require that special needs students be educated "in the least restrictive environment possible," in other words, in regular educational contexts with non-special needs students (Kellough & Kellough, 1996). Special educational needs defined by these acts may include any combination and degree of the following: autism, hearing impairment, mental impairment, orthopedic impairment, health impairment, emotional disturbance, learning disability, speech impairment, and visual impairment. Other special educational needs identified and served by many schools include giftedness and limited English proficiency. Inclusion of a particular child can range from partial, encompassing some fraction of the school day, to full—the entire school day. This is generally determined jointly by special education and mainstream teachers, counselors, and the child's parents (Kellough & Kellough, 1996).

Inclusion is especially important to middle schools as it is in concert with their fundamental embracing of diversity (e.g., National Middle School Association, 1995; Stevenson, 1997). The kinds and degree of physical, emotional, and academic diversity among students in the various special education categories are often not that different from what is found in the mainstream young adolescent population, so it makes sense for all-inclusive educational contexts to be the norm. Furthermore, all young adolescents need to broaden social horizons as part of their development of identity and social skills. Inclusion can support this development by providing students opportunities to interact with others different from themselves and to see others who are just as "different" as they are.

While middle school educators may wish to move from a self-contained special education approach to an inclusion model, it is no simple task. The shift to inclusion profoundly affects both teachers and students, not only in classrooms, but throughout the school environment. All of a sudden, persons who are not used to interacting with one another find themselves face-to-face on a regular basis.

Paul D. Deering teaches at the University of Hawaii at Manoa.

Mainstream teachers and special program teachers who have never worked with each other, much less each other's students, are often called upon to collaborate closely. Similarly, special needs and mainstream students who have minimal contact with one another find themselves in the same classrooms and social settings (Bradley & Fisher, 1995). Thus, inclusion of special needs students implies more than a policy decision, it entails a profound shift in the ways people view themselves, their actions and their peers in and around school. By examining one school's efforts with this process, we can learn about some of its challenges and promise.

A Study of Inclusion

I spent two years studying school culture at "Banner Middle School" (a pseudonym, by agreement with the participants). One of the focuses of my study was Banner's approach to inclusion of its special needs students who were from the following categories: developmentally disabled (DD); emotionally-behaviorally disabled (EBD); English as a second language (ESL); gifted and talented (GT); learning disabled (LD); multiple handicapped (MH); and severe learning handicapped (SLH). Banner is located in a large Western metropolitan area in the United States. Its 750 students were approximately equally distributed between Caucasians and Latinos, almost all of whom were from lower-middle class and low-income families.

I used ethnographic methods in this study, including participant and non-participant observation, formal and informal interviews, surveying the physical environment, and collecting artifacts (Bogdan & Biklen, 1992; Erickson, 1996). I observed more than 300 class sessions and school-related events in classrooms, the cafeteria, the school grounds, and the neighborhood. In my data analysis, I searched for patterns and recurring themes, then built tentative assertions to explain them. I focused on the interplay between policies and practices, and between local contexts, such as classrooms, and broader ones, such as the school grounds. As I developed tentative assertions I would return to the field to confirm, disconfirm, or alter them, often checking them directly with participants (Goetz & LeCompte, 1984).

The issues discussed in this article deal primarily with social relations in the classrooms and school relative to the inclusion process. Although academic learning is not the primary focus, it is explored in terms of students' access to learning opportunities, since access is strongly affected by the social structures constructed in classrooms and throughout schools (Heath, 1983; McDermott, 1977). For example, it is widely accepted that teacher-directed recitation where students compete to get called on, places students with limited English proficiency and other special needs at a disadvantage; they simply cannot respond quickly enough to compete with their mainstream peers (Kellough & Kellough, 1996; Mehan, 1979). By contrast, cooperative or collaborative learning approaches are widely recommended for heterogeneous learning contexts as they offer students more equal access to discussions (Johnson & Johnson, 1987; Slavin, 1983).

Insights into Comprehensive Inclusion

Comprehensive inclusion denotes that all students—special needs and mainstream—are consistently provided with positive opportunities for social and academic development. This means that all students have equal access to successfully participating in meaningful social and academic interactions with a variety of peers. Comprehensive inclusion necessitates two conditions—coordination and scaffolding. Each is explained with examples below. Briefly, coordination exists when policies and practices within and between the levels of the classroom and the school are in concert with each other, and not at odds—that is, they consistently support inclusion. Scaffolding entails providing "just enough" assistance for a learner to succeed at a task (Vygotsky, 1978). In the context of inclusion, scaffolding is evidenced in classroom and institutional policies that help students successfully bridge the gulf between special needs and mainstream to establish positive social and academic relations.

Comprehensive inclusion is a multi-level process requiring coordination of institutional policies and classroom practices to address students' social and academic interactions.

Actions of school participants must be in concert at the school and classroom levels in order for there to be comprehensive inclusion of special needs students. Coordination of policies and practices across these levels is necessary to ensure that students are able and encouraged to interact with each other in ways that include all. By contrast, lack of coordination can undermine the best intentions of both educators and students. The examples provided illustrate the need for a comprehensive approach to inclusion.

School Level

An inclusion policy is a good start, but only a start.

An institutional policy of inclusion is a good first step at fully including special needs students in the academic and social life of a school. It provides the opportunity for intergroup contact to take place and for positive relations to develop between special program and mainstream students.

Banner's *School Vision* called for inclusion of its special needs students, and all spent at least a substantial portion of their school day in heterogeneous classrooms. The more profoundly handicapped students, those in the DD, MH, and SLH programs, were in mainstream classes for about one-third of their day while the GT students were mainstreamed for all but a two-hour, weekly pull-out program. All the compensatory (non-GT) special needs students met in resource rooms with specially certified teachers for one or more class periods per day, and were usually accompanied by support staff when in mainstream classes.

The potential of intergroup contact to spontaneously spark new friendships was illustrated at Banner by Freddie and Joe, two boys with cerebral palsy. Freddie walked with a pronounced limp and drooled, and Joe was confined to a support wheelchair. They could easily have been objects of ridicule among their status-conscious peers, but instead, both boys were incredibly popular. Wherever they went, boys and girls called out greetings, waved, and came over to talk with them. Neither boy was ever harassed or teased by anyone—and how many young adolescents can say *that*?

> **The shift to inclusion profoundly affects both teachers and students, not only in classrooms, but throughout the school environment.**

The inclusion policy clearly benefited Freddie, Joe, and their able-bodied peers, judging from all of their smiles and laughter. However, it appeared that these boys enjoyed special status because of the severity of their disabilities. Their less dramatically disabled peers did not enjoy the same kind of celebrity status and, in fact, were often excluded from classroom and social groups. Thus, an inclusion policy can start the process of broadening students' social relations, but is insufficient by itself to promote comprehensive inclusion. At least some special education students' needs will not be addressed by merely placing them out in the mainstream; they and their mainstream peers require scaffolding in order to succeed together socially.

Mainstream and special program students need scaffolding in order to develop positive social and academic relationships with each other.

Middle level students have difficulty transcending the boundaries of their group identities, whether defined by gender, special program, ethnicity, or other factors (Eder & Parker, 1987; VanHoose & Strahan, 1988). This social difficulty is especially profound for the "more different" special needs students, such as those in DD, ESL, MH, and SLH programs. As noted, these students are not as different or "special" as Freddie and Joe, yet they are not as "normal" as those in GT or LD programs so they have a harder time blending in with their mainstream peers.

As an example of this phenomenon, Banner's DD, MH, and SLH students ate lunch at a table by themselves in the cafeteria, assisted by their adult aides. Meanwhile, the ESL students sat in an isolated group at another table. Only rarely did anyone from either group interact with the hundreds of other non-special program students surrounding them. This was especially ironic for the ESL students since so many of their peers were bilingual. For lack of social scaffolding, each group of special program students remained an island in a sea of mainstream peers.

One way in which Banner was beginning to scaffold student interactions across the special program-mainstream gulf was through peer tutoring. In this program, mainstream student volunteers helped special needs students with their school work, both in the special education resource rooms and in mainstream classrooms. The program became so much a part of the school life during the course of the study that it was almost a rarity to enter a classroom and not see it occurring. The social benefits of peer tutoring were evident in the non-classroom settings such as the cafeteria and school dances. It became increasingly common to see tutors and tutees laughing and talking together in these settings, thanks to the scaffolding that their working relationship had provided.

Peer tutoring can thus provide an accessible, meaningful structure to scaffold the development of both academic *and* social relationships among participants. At the same time, peer tutors provide modeling for their other mainstream peers that interaction with special program students can be non-threatening and even rewarding. The comments of Nina, a seventh grade peer tutor underscore the importance of this modeling, "When I'm around the mentally retarded kids or the slow learners I feel good, 'cause I like to help them. Sometimes mean kids make fun of them."

Other schools with which I have worked have scaffolded lunch room social relations with exploratory activities such as homeroom-based intramurals and participatory careers presentations. Others have "buddy programs" where an established student helps a newcomer or special needs student to get acquainted with the school and peers. Regardless of how it is done, some form of social scaffolding can help students to overcome their shyness and cliqueishness to form relationships across the special education barrier.

Classroom Practice

Teachers must examine their practices in light of the bigger picture of comprehensive inclusion.

Comprehensive inclusion requires that teachers take a broad, school-wide view of their roles. They must consider more than the academic and in-class impact of their practices. They must examine the effects of students' social relations. In addition, they must consider the degree to which their practices support comprehensive inclusion rather than undermining it, as illustrated in the following examples.

Heterogeneous group learning can support inclusion.

Numerous studies have confirmed the effectiveness of cooperative and collaborative group learning approaches for promoting positive intergroup relations among students and stimulating impressive academic gains (see reviews by Johnson, Johnson, Maruyama, 1983; Slavin, 1983, 1990). However, group learning is no panacea for comprehensive inclusion, nor for any other educational aims. *How* it is done is just as important as if.

PHOTO BY DOUG MARTIN

Working in heterogeneous groups can provide an excellent opportunity for building meaningful relationships between special program and mainstream students, as well as for academic learning. This was apparent in many Banner classrooms. Those in which students built positive relationships via group work and other activities were characterized by a spirit of warmth and collaboration. In these contexts, there was a high degree of positive interaction between the special program and mainstream students in their peer work groups. Ideas and materials flowed so freely that it was often difficult to tell who was in which program. Discussion, laughter, and excitement permeated these classrooms, and students often left them talking enthusiastically with group mates from across the special education divide. A nerdy boy in the LD program who had lots of problems with persecution by peers described his work group mates as, "Nice, they're polite. They don't bully people around. They know stuff and tell you how to do it."

Teachers in the classrooms have confirmed where group work "clicked" did not simply focus on "warm fuzzies." They were also quite demanding regarding behavior and effort. They clearly communicated high academic expectations, both verbally and in writing. In addition, they quickly intervened in a firm but low-key manner when student behavior got out of line. In other words, they were nice *and* tough. Students appreciated having high behavioral expectations as expressed by Bobby, a seventh grader in the LD/EBD program:

> I like working in groups, but sometimes they play around and I want to get done. Sometimes I play around too, but I'm trying to pass! I like it with Mr. Moc. People work because he's got a loud voice.

Interestingly, these teachers also made sparing use of formal cooperative learning structures, only occasionally drawing upon the approaches of Kagan (1989) and the Johnsons (1987). Usually the teachers just instructed students to "work together," sometimes with some modeling or discussion of appropriate ways to interact. Perhaps most importantly, the learning tasks were active, varied, and challenging so that collaboration was useful and even *necessary*. Composing and illustrating myths, researching and building Native American villages, and finding examples and making collages of advertising propaganda drew rigorously upon multiple intelligences (Gardner & Hatch, 1989) so that all students' weaknesses and strengths were exposed. Thus, the special program students often provided the artwork or the breakthrough idea that eluded their mainstream peers. Several students described quite sophisticated and egalitarian outlooks on the processes of working in heterogeneous groups:

> You can ask your group if you don't understand. If you get stuck on a question they'll tell you more about the question and you figure it out from their information . . . not just give you the answer. (Steven, 7th grader, LD program)

> They can give to you and you give to them . . . maybe I don't know about mountains so I ask someone who knows about them. They could explain about them, and I could tell them about Mexico. It helps when you explain stuff 'cause you learn how to get along with others. (Mike, 7th grader, GT program)

The teachers in these classrooms provided several crucial forms of scaffolding for the building of positive social and academic relations between and among their special needs and mainstream students. In addition to the opportunity for face-to-face contact in heterogeneous groups, they provided scaffolding for meaningful interactions in the form of clear, high, social, and academic expectations, and interesting, multi-dimensional tasks that motivated and required the participation of all members.

Competition undermines inclusion—"I don't mind the special ed kids except when we're in a competition" (seventh grade boy).

Numerous studies have criticized overt classroom competition for sorting students into winners and losers (Goldman & McDermott, 1987; Johnson & Johnson, 1987; Kohn, 1986; Sapon-Shevin, 1994). Those on the social and academic margins, such as special education and minority students, are especially susceptible to being made consistent losers in competitive school environments. The findings of this study add still more evidence to the case against overt classroom competition. The only class at Banner in which mainstream students staunchly resisted working in groups with special program peers was one in which the teacher used a team competition approach to cooperative learning. Based on Slavin's (1990) methods, the approach required students to calculate group members' grade averages to determine improvement points. The points were to be tallied for team competitions for pizza parties. A couple [of] problems emerged with this cooperative learning approach. For one, the accounting procedures were so complex that few students ever figured how to calculate improvement points properly. Thus, they never saw how low-achieving teammates could contribute improvement points as readily as high-achievers. As a result, mainstream and GT students resisted working in groups with other special program students. The competition heightened this resistance, as Nick, a GT student, explained:

> It's fun when you're in a group when people are willing to work and know how. When I'm in a group where people don't know how or don't care and we're in a competition, it gets frustrating. Usually we know, so we'll get in a group with real intelligent kids.

Students like Nick frequently dealt with these concerns by taking over group materials while special program students looked on passively or engaged in disruption.

It may be that clarification of the accounting procedures would have gotten this cooperative learning program operating more smoothly. This might then have helped the mainstream students to view their special program peers more positively. Nevertheless, the team-versus-team competition added an extra level of tension that short-circuited students' ability to focus on anything but the contest and the pizza. Thus, it seems reasonable to conclude from this and the many prior studies that explicit classroom competition should be viewed very skeptically in an inclusion environment.

Be wary of resegregation

There are myriad ways in which inclusion can be undermined. While a school-level inclusion policy can place special needs students into the mainstream they can all too readily be resegregated within teams and classrooms. Ironically, the rationales for such practices can make perfectly good sense on some levels while appearing ill-advised on others. Coordination of philosophy, policies, and practices within and across contexts can help to avoid resegregation.

Banner educators wrestled with resegregation of special program students in several ways. For example, the seventh grade was divided into two teams, one of which had all of the DD, EBD, GT, LD, and SLH students and the other all of the ESL students. This decision had the unfortunate effect of concentrating Latino students in the latter team, creating what one teacher called, a "brown track/white track" effect. In addition, this division made the former team into this "special ed" team in the eyes and words of students. The rationale for this arrangement was that it would cut down on the running around demanded of the special program teachers, thus allowing them to focus more of their energy on their students. Unfortunately, this worthwhile goal came with the cost of making both the minority and special education students more concentrated and identifiable. The school addressed this problem the following year, opting to maximize inclusion with a more random distribution of students even though this was not as convenient for the teachers.

The seventh grade "special ed" team grappled with other resegregation issues as well. The teachers placed all of the GT, LD, and EBD students into a single class for all of the core subjects, reasoning that this would make it easier to challenge the GT students and would minimize the running around by the LD/EBD resource teacher. In math class, the teachers went one step further by placing the GT students on one side of the room and the other special program students on the other. Not surprisingly, this heightened teachers' and students' awareness of special program identities. One boy in the LD program illustrated this by referring to the "smart half of the room and the not-so-smart half." They found it too hard to plan and teach with the schizophrenic class distribution and also found that the EBD students were reinforcing each others' undesired behavior. After one grading period the team dispersed all of the special needs students across their four classes. The teachers subsequently found it easier to maintain appropriate behavior with the EBD students and

> **Comprehensive inclusion means that all students have equal access to successfully participating in meaningful social and academic interactions with a variety of peers.**

found no big drawback to the resource teacher's covering more ground with the dispersed placement approach.

Resegregation of special needs students can also occur during group work. For example, when Banner students chose their own groups, they invariably chose others from the same special program and gender, although they showed no ethnic preferences. In addition, some teachers assigned special program students to work together in their own groups. For example, one kept the ESL students in a separate group with their translator during both direct instruction and group work. This may have been useful during direct instruction for translation, but it was unnecessary during group work with so many bilingual students present. This in-class segregation cost the ESL students several important social and academic opportunities: (a) interactive, discourse-based learning of mathematics (Webb, 1989); (b) active use of English in a meaningful context (McGroarty, 1989); and (c) building of intergroup friendships (Johnson & Johnson, 1987).

I should clarify that I am not advancing an argument that cooperative groups should always be heterogeneous. Work by Webb (1982, 1989) and Palincsar and Brown (1984) strongly suggests that homogeneous groups can sometimes be highly beneficial for student learning. Nonetheless, it is abundantly clear from this and much prior work that student work groups should not *always* be homogeneous, as this eliminates the face-to-face interaction necessary for the development of intergroup friendships (Johnson & Johnson, 1987). Still more, consistent homogeneous grouping reinforces the social and academic divisions among students rather than bridging them.

It is apparent that resegregation of special needs students can occur inadvertently as a by-product of well-intentioned decisions. This illustrates the complexity of balancing inclusion goals with other important priorities, and by extension, the need for coordination of inclusion practices and policies at all levels of the school. The concentration of certain special needs students in one or the other of the seventh grade teams conflicted with the school's broader goal of fully including special needs students in the social and academic life of the school. So too did the in-class grouping of LD and EBD students and of ESL students. Prior research (Johnson, Johnson, Maruyama, 1983; Slavin, 1983, 1990) suggests that these students' isolation in the cafeteria and other school contexts could have been reduced if they had had more regular classroom opportunities to interact with non-special program peers. A coordinated, whole-school approach to inclusion, a comprehensive approach, could help ensure such opportunities at all levels of the school.

Inclusion benefits everyone.

One of the clearest conclusions to be drawn from this study is that the "special" students are not the only beneficiaries of an inclusion program. *All* students and educators can benefit from the broader, richer social interactions that inclusion can provide. Again, this is especially important for young adolescents as it addresses their developmental need to socialize with a wide variety of others (National Middle School Association, 1995; Stevenson, 1997). Banner Middle School was a far richer community for having the various special needs students, first of all, in the building and, secondly, out among their peers. Having seen the school's promising, trial-and-error struggles with inclusion, it is hard to imagine going back to "quarantining" the special needs students in self-contained classrooms.

The benefits to mainstream students from interacting with peers such as Freddie, Joe, and others in the special programs can scarcely be overestimated. Instead of reacting with fear or rejection toward disabled peers, they were learning to reach out to them. Mike, the GT student quoted earlier, had his eyes opened by working in heterogeneous groups to the potential for *all* other students to contribute unique and important ideas. No "curriculum" can promote such learning the way experience can.

Peer-tutoring similarly benefits all participants, not just the targeted special needs students. Tutors develop broader social relations just as their tutees do. They also gain a well-founded sense of accomplishment as well as compassion. Nikki, a seventh grader described her experiences with peer tutoring as follows: "Things come easier for me, and having a sister, I can understand how it is. So I like to help kids. I don't really get anything out of it except when a kid does better. That feels good." The gains in self-esteem can be especially dramatic for peer tutors who are themselves in special programs. Banner teachers found students in the EBD program to be exceptionally patient and compassionate tutors for their peers in the DD and SLH programs. This gave the EBD students a much-needed opportunity to be needed and appreciated by someone. Their special program teacher noted that this boost in self-esteem carried over outside the tutoring sessions in much calmer demeanor for her student tutors.

Inclusion belongs to everyone.

Students need help in bridging the longstanding social gulf that has separated "special program" and "mainstream," regardless of which side they are on. They need educators to provide scaffolding that will help them to interact in meaningful ways with peers from across programs. By bridging the social gap, students and educators will be taking a giant step toward closing the academic gap between "special" and "mainstream" education. When all students have equal access to the social and academic benefits of widespread interaction in school, all will be better served.

Such a goal, comprehensive inclusion, requires that all of a middle school's participants take ownership of the process at both classroom and institutional levels. Simply "doing one's job" in the classroom and ignoring the institutional level of policy and scheduling is not enough. Leaving students' social relations in non-classroom contexts to take care of themselves is not enough. In order for comprehensive inclusion to occur, classroom practices and institutional policies must be coordinated to consistently work for inclusion, rather than against it.

Comprehensive inclusion requires that middle level educators use "bifocal lenses" to see both the immediate and broader implications of their practices. Only then, will classroom and institutional practices be coordinated to consistently scaffold the academic and social functioning of special needs and mainstream students. Only then will all of us—students and educators, special program and mainstream—reap the full benefits of inclusion.

References

Bergen, D. (1993). Teaching strategies: Facilitating friendship development in inclusion classrooms. *Childhood Education, 69*, 234–36.

Bogdan, R. C., & Biklen, S. K. (1992). *Qualitative research for education.* Boston: Allyn & Bacon.

Bradley, D. F., & Fisher, J. F. (1995). The inclusion process: Role changes at the middle level. *Middle School Journal, 26*(3), 13–19.

Eder, D., & Parker, S. (1987). The cultural production and reproduction of gender: The effect of extracurricular activities on peer-group culture. *Sociology of Education, 60*, 200–213.

Erickson, F. (1986). Qualitative methods in research on teaching. In M. Wittrock (Ed.), *Handbook of research on teaching* (3rd ed.) (pp. 119–161). New York: Macmillan.

Gardner, H., & Hatch, T. (1989). Multiple intelligences go to school: Educational implications of the theory of multiple intelligences. *Educational Researcher, 18*(8), 410.

Goetz, J. P., & LeCompte, M. L. (1984). *Ethnography and qualitative design in educational research.* Orlando, FL: Academic Press.

Goldman, S. V., & McDermott, R. (1987). The culture of competition in American schools. In G. D. Spindler (Ed.), *Education and cultural process: Anthropological approaches* (2nd ed.) (pp. 282–300). Prospect Hts., IL: Waveland Press.

Heath, S. B. (1983). *Ways with words: Language, life, and work in communities and classrooms.* Cambridge: Cambridge University Press.

Johnson, D. W., & Johnson, R. T. (1987). *Learning together and alone: Cooperative, competitive and individualistic learning* (2nd ed.). Englewood Cliffs, NJ: Prentice Hall.

Johnson, D. W., Johnson, R. T., & Maruyama, G. (1983). Interdependence and interpersonal attraction among heterogeneous and homogeneous individuals: A theoretical formulation and a meta-analysis of the research. *Review of Educational Research, 53*, 5–54.

Kagan, S. (1989). *Cooperative learning: Resources for teachers.* San Juan Capistrano, CA: Resources for Teachers.

Kellough, R. D., & Kellough, N. G. (1996). *Middle school teaching: A guide to methods and resources.* Englewood Cliffs, NJ: Prentice-Hall.

Kohn, A. (1986). *No contest: The case against competition.* Boston: Houghton Mifflin.

McDermott, R. P. (1977). Social relations as contexts for learning in school. *Harvard Educational Review, 47*, 198–213.

Mehan, H. (1979). *Learning lessons: Social organization in the classroom.* Cambridge, MA: Harvard University Press.

McGroarty, M. (1989). The benefits of cooperative learning arrangements in second language instruction. *National Association of Bilingual Education Journal, 13*, 127–143.

National Middle School Association. (1995). *This we believe: Developmentally responsive middle level schools.* Columbus, OH: Author.

Palincsar, A. S., & Brown, A. L. (1984). Reciprocal teaching of comprehension-fostering and comprehension-monitoring activities. *Cognition and Instruction, 1*, 117–175.

Rothenberg, D. (1995). Inclusion in the middle school: An update. *Middle School Journal, 27*(1), 56–58.

Sapon-Shevin, M. (1994). Cooperative learning and middle schools: What would it take to really do it right? *Theory into Practice, 33*(3), 183–190.

Slavin, R. E. (1983). *Cooperative learning.* New York: Longman.

Slavin, R. E. (1990). *Cooperative learning: Theory, research, and practice.* Boston: Allyn & Bacon.

Stevenson, C. (1997). *Teaching ten to fourteen year olds* (2nd ed.). New York: Longman.

Van Hoose, J., & Strahan, D. (1988). *Young adolescent development and school practices: Promoting harmony.* Columbus, OH: National Middle School Association.

Vygotsky, L. S. (1978). *Mind in society development of higher psychological processes.* M. Cole, V. John-Steiner, S. Scribner, & E. Souberman (Eds). Cambridge, MA: Harvard University Press.

Webb, N. M. (1982). Group composition, group interaction, and achievement in cooperative small groups. *Journal of Educational Psychology, 74*, 475–484.

Webb, N. M. (1989). Peer interaction and learning in small groups. *International Journal of Educational Research, 13*, 21–40.

The author wishes to thank the students, educators, and families of Banner Middle School and the Industry community for welcoming him among them. Thanks also to Margaret A. Eisenhart, Michael S. Meloth, Evelyn Jacob and the C.U. College of Education Anthropology Group for helping develop this research.

Competitions and Exceptional Children

A Great Combination

Tracy L. Riley
Frances A. Karnes

The Special Olympics oath is . . . *Let me win. But if I cannot win, let me be brave in the attempt.*

In education today, competition and cooperation sometimes seem to be mutually exclusive terms—particularly considering children with disabilities. How can students with disabilities possibly compete in a field that also includes gifted children and other children without disabilities? As we note in this article, Special Olympics comes immediately to mind, as well as Very Special Arts. But there are a host of other competitions that are not only inclusive, but fun, educational, and rewarding to children.

Many competitions offer opportunities for authentic performance assessments—as well as introductions to lifelong interests (see box, "Benefits of Competitions").

Preparing for Competitions

For successful participation in competitions, students must be prepared. As teachers, we can help guide that preparation by teaching students skills such as planning, organization, and time management. Here are some basic steps in preparing students for involvement in competitions:

- Skill and content inventory.
- Planning and preparing a timeline.
- Assessing and gathering information.
- Seeking sponsorship.
- Acquiring knowledge and skills.
- Practice, practice, practice.
- Evaluation.

Each student may want to develop his or her own preparation checklist or use the one designed by Karnes and Riley (1996). Safris (1996) further suggested the importance of maintaining high levels of motivation, developing self-reliance, practicing without overpracticing, and criticizing and praising effectively. Students who are well prepared will be more willing to participate in future competitions.

> Help prepare students for competitions by teaching them skills such as planning, organization, and time management.

Preparing students for success also means addressing some of the problems they may face as participants in competitions. Students may experience feelings such as anxiety, disappointment, intimidation, and uncertainty as they present their entries for judging and eventually awarding. Discussing openly the real possibility of these feelings and teaching some strategies for coping before, during, and following the competition may help alleviate any anxieties—or prevent them. Students may keep a competitions journal, as suggested by Karnes and Riley (1996), in which they reflect on their experiences and prepare for future ones. A competitions club or discussion group within the school may also be helpful in discussing these issues.

"Special" Competitions

Perhaps the most well-known competitions for children with disabilities are **Special Olympics** and **Very Special Arts.** As the names indicate, the former one is devoted to a wide range of athletic events; the latter focuses on the visual and performing arts. Both competitions have local to international events. The intent of both is to provide educational and rehabilitative benefits to those with special needs.

Contact Information
Special Olympics International
1325 G Street, N.W., Suite 500
Washington, DC 20005
Website: www.specialolympics.org
Very Special Arts International
1300 Connecticut Avenue, N.W.
Suite 700
Washington, DC 20036

There are many more opportunities in the arts, academics, leadership, and service learning.

The Arts

Art is an area enjoyed by students of all ages, and competitions abound! Here is a sampler, but remember that there are many more.

- For those students with a keen interest in horses, check out **The American Morgan Horse Association for Youth Photo Contest.** This contest provides students, ages 18 and under, an opportunity to demonstrate their creative abilities through photography. Taking photos of horses sounds like a great adventure! Contact the sponsor in early fall for the guidelines.

Contact Information
AMHAY Photo Contest
American Morgan Horse Association
P.O. Box 960
Shelbourne, VT 05482-0960

- The **Two-Dimensional Art Contest** is open for all students in Grades 1–12. Students submit original pieces of art (excluding photography and sculpture). The purpose is to identify, encourage, and reward promising art students who compete for $55,000 in scholarship awards each year. For students with disabilities, as well as gifted students, desiring to pursue an arts curriculum at the postsecondary level, this competition may provide the funds to help achieve that goal. For the specifics, write the sponsor in the fall of the year.

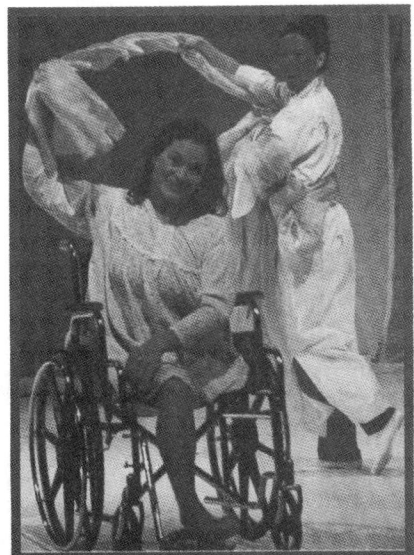

Very Special Arts produces plays that depict the lives of people with disabilities.

36. Competitions and Exceptional Children

Contact Information
Frances Hood Scholarship Fund
P.O. Box 597346
Chicago, IL 60659-7346

- Another contest open to all students in secondary school is the **Young Playwrights Program** sponsored by the Very Special Arts. Scripts are selected that reflect the needs and rights of people with disabilities and that heighten public awareness and understanding. The theme, setting, and characters are the writer's choice. Five to 10 scripts are selected by a panel of members associated with the sponsoring organization. A group of award-winning directors and playwriters then select one or two of the plays to be performed at the John F. Kennedy Center for the Performing Arts in Washington, D.C. A teacher's guide and related materials are available by writing to the Very Special Arts (address given previously).

Service Learning and Leadership

Exceptional children and youth make contributions to their communities every day of the year. Here are several competitions that encourage service and leadership.

- One competition designed specifically to recognize youths, 14 years of age or under, for outstanding service, is **The Kids' Hall of Fame.** A description of 25–100 words on the nominee and how he or she made a difference to his or her own life, family, school, community, state, nation, or world is all that is needed. Take a few minutes and nominate one of your exceptional students!

Contact Information
Pizza Hut Kids' Hall of Fame
P.O. Box 428
Wichita, KS 67201

- Another group wanting to honor students for their outstanding service to their communities is **A Pledge and A Promise Environmental Awards.** The program has been designed to recognize the outstanding efforts of school groups in the areas of environmental awareness and action. The awards are given for the steps school groups take toward protecting the planet. The participants may apply by grade level in five categories: K–5, 6–8, 9–12, and university. Groups wanting to apply can do so by submitting the environmental projects they have completed or works in progress. This competition would be a great tool for encouraging a group of students—both with and without disabilities—to work together as a team. Note: The sponsor advises that it

Duracell sponsors scholarship competitions where students design and build working devices powered by Duracell batteries.

is critical that applications be completed accurately and that projects are both creative and student-driven.

Contact Information
Sea World
Education Department
7007 Sea World Drive
Orlando, FL 32821

Academics

Toys are fun for all children. Toys can also be educational, can boost creativity and problem-solving skills, and can even teach math and science.

> The purpose of one competition is to allow students the opportunity to put their hands-on science skills to a competitive test.

- Students in Grades 4–6 can make toys better as participants in the **Super Science Blue's Annual Toy Tester Contest.** Participants may work in teams of five. The purpose is to allow students the opportunity to put their hands-on science skills to a competitive test. Boys and girls take a simple toy of the sponsor's design and improve its performance. A Super Folder, which includes the guidelines, comes with each set of *Super Science Blue's* November/December issue. Science toys and books are given for winning student teams, and catalog gift certificates are awarded to their teachers. Your students will like getting involved in this event!

Contact Information
Super Science Blue
Scholastic
555 Broadway
New York, NY 10012-3999

- Are your students creative—and do they like to invent? If the answer is yes, then get them involved in the **Duracell/National Science Teachers Association (NSTA) Scholarship Competitions.** Students in grades 9–12 have the opportunity to design and build working devices powered by Duracell batteries. The boys and girls submit ideas for their inventions, with descriptions, wiring/schematic plans, and a photograph. The top 100 finalists are notified to send the actual device for judging. The first-place award is $20,000, and the other prizes are also great!

Contact Information
Duracell/NSTA Scholarship Competition
1840 Wilson Boulevard
Arlington, VA 22201-3000

- Another competition in the same vein is the **Young Games Inventors Contest,** which provides students an opportunity to apply their creativity in inventing a board game, including rules and game board. Judges look for a fun game and creative ideas. This sounds exciting for all exceptional children and youth!

Contact Information
U.S. Kids
Box 567
Indianapolis, IN 46202

- Math competitions add up to fun and learning for all. **The Continental Mathematics League** has been established to enhance students' mathematical problem-solving skills and is open to all students in Grades 2–12. There are five meets held each year, with five questions per meet. Medals and certificates are awarded to winners.

Contact Information
Continental Mathematics League
Box 2196
St. James, NY 11780

This is just a sampling of the many competitions in which exceptional children can participate. The wide variety of competitions available for young people ensures that each child will find one that matches his or her special strengths and interests. You can find more competitions by looking in magazines, surfing the Internet, and checking out the school or local library.

After students select and participate in competitions, the game's not over. There's plenty more to do!

> Preparing students for success also means addressing anxieties and frustrations they may face as participants in competitions.

Evaluation and Assessment

Upon completion of a competition, encourage your students to evaluate their participation. This evaluation should move the student in the direction of further self-enhancement. Students may enjoy designing their own evaluation rating scale or use the one developed by Karnes and Riley (1996). Items such as planning, organization, time management, attitude, appearance, and interac-

36. Competitions and Exceptional Children

Benefits of Competitions

Enhancing Learning Skills. Development of potential is just one of the many benefits of participation in competitions. A range of social and learning skills can also be cultivated. Academically, students can further develop their skills across content areas, including mathematics, science, history, and language arts. Communication can be enhanced as students begin to focus on writing and speaking. Students become more adept in presentation as they develop visual tools, musical products, plays, speeches, and an array of other products required for competitions. These are but a few of the learning skills developed through participation in competitions.

Integrating and Individualizing Curriculum. Competitions allow us, as teachers, the opportunity to integrate visual arts, music, theatrics, physical activities, and the like into instruction. Student involvement in competitions also promotes individualization of teaching and learning activities. As students select competitions based on their personal strengths and interests, it is only natural for teachers to also focus their attention on individuals.

Developing Social Skills. Socially, children involved in competitions are given opportunities to interact with peers, either as team members or in competition settings. Working as a member of a team requires cooperation, planning, leadership, and communication. Meeting new friends is an obvious outcome of being involved in local, regional, and perhaps national events. Talking to judges and sponsors also enhances children's abilities to interact with adults who share common interests, either personally or professionally.

Focusing on Goals and Achievement. Setting and meeting goals can be both motivational and rewarding for students of all ability levels. Learning to focus on the milestones to achievement will help each child learn to celebrate his or her successes. Feelings of self-worth and confidence can be increased through involvement in competitions. They expose students to new ways of gaining independence. Students also develop emotional maturity as they learn to win and lose gracefully.

Developing Lifelong Interests and Skills. Competitions also facilitate the development of lifelong leisure activities as students are encouraged to try new things. Painting, writing, singing, designing, and acting are but a handful of the modes of participation offered by involvement in competitions. Although some of these skills are purely academic, others may be considered leisure or recreation. These are also talents that society values. By showcasing their abilities, students are integrated into the mainstream of society.

---

tion with others are identified as some of the dimensions for evaluation.

Students may also decide to start a competitions file. This can be organized by individuals or as a group project. Through the file, students can recommend competitions, highlight the positive and negative aspects of their own involvement, and give advice to their peers who might consider giving it a try.

Other means of sharing their experiences might be designing a competitions newsletter or organizing a competitions club. Be sure that *all* students are recognized for their participation—not just the competition winners. All students who take the first step, joining in, are winners!

Strengths—Not Weaknesses

Competitions and exceptional children form a partnership that accentuates individual abilities and strengths. And isn't this what we want for all children? Competitions and exceptional children make a great combination.

References

Karnes, F. A., & Riley, T. L. (1996). *Competitions: Maximizing your abilities.* Waco, TX: Prufrock Press.*

Safris, R. (1996). *The winning edge: Tips for creative problem-solving.* Parsippany, NJ: Good Apple. [ERIC Document Reproduction Service No. ED 397 988]

Books Now

* To order the marked by an asterisk (*), please call 24 hrs/365 days: 1-800-BOOKS-NOW (266-5766) or (801) 261-1187; or visit them on the Web at http://www.BooksNow.com/TeachingExceptional. htm. Use VISA, M/C, or AMEX, or send check or money order + $4.95 S&H ($2.50 each add'l item) to: Books Now, Suite 125, 448 East 6400 South, Salt Lake City, UT 84107.

Tracy L. Riley, *Senior Lecturer, Department of Learning and Teaching, Massey University, Palmerston North, New Zealand.* **Frances A. Karnes** *(CEC Mississippi Federation), Professor, Department of Special Education, and Director, The Center of Gifted Studies. The University of Southern Mississippi, Hattiesburg.*

Address correspondence to Frances A. Karnes, The Center of Gifted Studies, The University of Southern Mississippi, Box 8207, Hattiesburg, MS 39406-8207 (e-mail: Karnesfa@aol.com).]

School-to-Work

A Model for Learning a Living

BY MICHAEL HARTOONIAN AND RICHARD VAN SCOTTER

Individuals embark on the path toward learning (a living) by embracing active scholarship, citizenship, and artisanship—all three together. We cannot distinguish where one characteristic ends and another begins, Messrs. Hartoonian and Van Scotter maintain.

> I know of no safe depository of the ultimate powers of the society but with the people themselves; and if we think them not enlightened enough to exercise their control with a wholesome discretion, the remedy is not to take power from the people, but to inform their discretion through instruction.
> —Thomas Jefferson[1]

THE FUNDAMENTAL purpose of education in any society is to maintain the cultural heritage and to improve both society and the individual. Thus the nature of schooling and the form it takes are defined within the context of a particular society. In the United States education serves to promote the interrelated goals of self-development, citizenship, and employment.

The Role of Education In a Democratic Republic

Our democratic republic is built on the idea of "enlightened citizens." Such individuals are aware of their cultural heritage and possess a working knowledge of the economic, political, and social conditions that make up our human ecosystem. For example, they understand the concepts of the basic rule of law, legal limits to freedom, and majority rule with minority rights. They also realize that, in addition to being a legal document, the U.S. Constitution serves as a symbol of the story of America that provides its citizens with meaning and a moral light. They themselves display, and expect in others, such characteristics as fairness, cooperation, integrity, responsibility, and the performance of high-quality work.

Without a conscious effort by society to teach and learn these cultural and civic virtues, a democratic capitalistic republic will not long endure. Thus this nation's first priority and public policy goal must be to ensure our republic's survival as a free nation by developing in the minds and hearts of its students the qualities of good scholars, citizens, and workers.

Education's Response To Global Markets

The dynamics of economic cycles affect virtually every aspect of society, and education is no exception. Similarly, the U.S. domestic economy is embedded within the tides and currents of the global economic ocean. In fact, to speak of a domestic economy today is outmoded. Economic activity is essentially global; we all inhabit one economic world. As a result, education must address both broader and higher standards.

As global markets ebb and flow, business and government leaders have applied pressure to American schools to help maintain and expand the international economic competitiveness of the U.S. This relationship between markets and education is a theme that dates back more than 100 years, to the time when the United States became a minor and then a major player in the global economic network. In the closing decades of the 19th century, authorities criticized schools as the United States continued to lose market share to the Germans in the machine tool industry. Then, in the 1930s, educators were told that, if schools had better educated students for employment, we might have avoided the Great Depression. Needless to say, reasonable and discerning observers understood that government policy and corporate practices had much more to do with these economic conditions than did school curriculum.

With the end of World War II and the beginning of the Cold War, critics led by Vice Admiral Hyman Rickover demanded that schools help keep the U.S. militarily ahead of the Soviet Union. Rickover argued that "education is even more important than atomic power in the Navy."[2] Rickover blamed professional educators for creating an anti-intellectual atmosphere in schools and claimed that schools were the weakest link in America's overall defense strategy. When the Soviets put Sputnik I into space in 1957, a shocked nation, influenced largely by business and government officials, demanded that schools develop stronger science and mathe-

MICHAEL HARTOONIAN *is a professor of education and liberal studies in the Graduate School, Hamline University, St. Paul, Minn.* RICHARD VAN SCOTTER *is vice president of education policy, marketing, and evaluation with Junior Achievement, Colorado Springs, Colo.*

matics programs. In the late 1950s and early 1960s educators embarked on, and the public endorsed, major curriculum reform efforts, believing that the nation's schools were using outdated learning materials. And in the wake of the economic recession of the late 1950s, assessment of schooling was linked to the performance of the economy.

In the early 1970s another recession, fueled by the oil embargo of 1973, ushered in a call for "back to basics." Again, this simplistic reaction to a complex economic issue failed to address the essential philosophical principles that underlie our democratic capitalist system and failed to acknowledge the merits of citizenship, scholarship, and artisanship.

A decade later, coinciding with another recession and stiff competition in global markets, particularly from the Japanese, the National Commission on Excellence in Education issued *A Nation at Risk,* a report that brutally detailed the poor quality of American schools.[3] The influence of business leaders and their education agendas since then testifies to the continued strength of the belief in the link between schools and the economy. Yet the purposes of education in America have always been much broader than preparing efficient workers and serving the goal of economic competitiveness—as important as these objectives are. In fact, we can't nurture a high-quality work force in the absence of informed, responsible, and ethical citizens.

Our nation benefits immensely from the legacy of Thomas Jefferson and from that of Adam Smith, who gave us the simple yet profound precept that free markets cannot function unless they are grounded in ethics.[4] And most of the reports on school reform in recent years, including *A Nation at Risk,* acknowledge the broader purposes of schooling. As the members of the National Commission on Excellence in Education wrote, "Our concern . . . goes well beyond matters such as industry and commerce. It also includes the intellectual, moral, and spiritual strengths of our people which knit together the very fabric of our society."[5] However, this type of message receives little attention from the media. As a result, the public—including many educators—is reluctant to build school programs around the intellectual, moral, and spiritual strengths of our traditions, opting instead for the quick fix of skills training.

School-to-Work Issues

As an organization, agency, or school system explores the challenge of developing a new secondary program grounded in school-to-work opportunities, it will need to address underlying cultural issues. In addition, any sound school-to-work model must create smooth pathways from learning in schools to learning in the workplace.

But any school-to-work effort, despite good intentions and hard work, will be disappointing if participants take what communications and media expert Neil Postman calls "a rearview mirror" approach to reform. Fundamental change in schools, classrooms, and students won't occur if we drive into the 21st century looking into the rearview mirror—attempting to do what apparently worked a decade or even a generation ago.

First, we need to recognize that the school can be a place both where students learn and where they carry on productive work. In turn, the workplace ought not to be just a business where people develop products, provide services, and collect a paycheck, but one in which they continuously learn, grow, and create. Such environments would be fertile ground for genuine school-based learning and work-based learning, two educational components that are called for in the School-to-Work Opportunities Act of 1994.

This is the message that management reformers such as Peter Senge and the late W. Edwards Deming (father of Total Quality Management) have persuasively put forward in recent years. To use Senge's language, the healthy, productive business or school is a "learning organization." Likewise, Theodore Sizer, founder of the Coalition of Essential Schools, proposes an engaging, productive learning environment that features students as workers and teachers as coaches.

Second, we must be aware that preparing young people for the workplace is like "shooting at a moving target." By this we mean that concentrating just on job skills and career opportunities will leave us off the mark 20, 10, or even five years from now. Willard Daggett, director of the International Center for Leadership in Education, points out, "As the waves of technological change break faster and faster, the technologies we teach today may be outdated by the time students graduate. Furthermore, using technology to do a better job of teaching the old curriculum misses the point of first addressing whether that curriculum is still appropriate."[6]

Next, our culture emphasizes what we possess and what we do. It falls short in building character, in helping people to understand who they are. Good school-based learning and good work-based learning both can help us to develop this third dimension, thereby fostering the growth of psychologically healthy workers and people, enriching the learning place, and enhancing our lives.

John Gardner explained, "A society that scorns excellence in plumbing because it is a humble activity and tolerates mediocrity in philosophy because it is an exalted activity will have both bad plumbing and [bad] philosophy. Neither its pipes nor [its] theories will hold water."

Finally, it is dangerous and disingenuous for schools to promise high-paying jobs to young people. We corrupt students when we use extrinsic motivation. Furthermore, neither the U.S. nor any industrialized nation can promise high-paying, high-skilled jobs to all its able workers. It should surprise no one that an increasingly service-oriented U.S. economy requires people with a range of job skills and includes a significant proportion of humble, low-paying jobs.

As researchers at the Sandia National Laboratories found, U.S. schools are supplying future workers whose levels of schooling are strikingly consistent with the requirements of employers. "The education system," they report, "turns out in today's youth roughly 26% as college graduates, an additional 60% with 12 to 15 years of schooling, and the final 14% with less than a high school diploma."[7] The researchers add that these percentages correlate with the findings in both the Hudson Institute's report on near-term work-force requirements, *Workforce 2000,* and the report by the Commission on the Skills of the American Workforce, *America's Choice: High Skills or Low Wages!*

The culture we inhabit plays a powerful role in fostering an egocentric, narcissistic, materialistic, and individualistic vision rather than a common one. And schools collaborate in this spurious mission when they stress such things as normative grading, standardized tests, college tracks, and an assortment of honors. But without a common vision, we are not likely to have a healthy community. The purpose of schooling is not to help people to be *better off,* but to be *better*—better scholars, citizens, and workers.

A New School-to-Work Model

People in the work force and those preparing to enter the work force will require three distinct but interrelated attributes or qualities: scholarship, citizenship, and artisanship. This triad serves as a model to prepare a productive and enlightened work force and could guide the development of school-to-work programs.

Scholarship. This characteristic involves learning by doing and the ability to apply knowledge. Proponents of school-to-work plans, particularly those in industry, stress that students need to be prepared with essential academic, problem-solving, and interpersonal skills for the "Age of Electronic Communications." (Curiously, some policy makers refer to the high-tech era of instant communications as the "Information Age." This is misleading. The Information Age began when the printing press was invented in the 15th century.)

As an example of the kinds of skills being sought by industry, the BellSouth Corporation's definition of core academic skills includes the ability to

- understand and interpret written information;
- locate data to answer questions;
- apply mathematical methods to multistep problems;
- listen to, interpret, and respond to verbal messages; and
- organize ideas and speak in a concise, accurate manner.[8]

No doubt, the most fundamental core academic skill is the ability to communicate thoughts, information, and opinions in writing, using clear, concise style and sound grammar. The late Ernest Boyer expressed this idea nicely when he said, "Clear writing leads to clear thinking; clear thinking is the basis for clear writing. Perhaps more than any other form of communication, writing holds us responsible for our words and makes us more thoughtful human beings."[9]

In turn, problem-solving skills include the ability to

- organize and plan multiple tasks;
- generate new ideas, display imagination, and apply ideas to new situations;
- make decisions that account for obstacles and choose among best alternatives; and
- analyze problems and devise plans of action.[10]

In effect, this means that students should be able to think, write, and communicate with the clarity, conciseness, variety, complexity, and richness that are appropriate for high-quality work. Likewise, students should develop habits of mind that include curiosity, speculation, thoughtfulness, and imagination. Unfortunately, as Sizer notes, most students, including many so-called high achievers, fall short. "Many are lively, well-intentioned, and adept at cranking out acceptable test scores," he explains, "but they are without habits of serious thought, respectful skepticism, and curiosity about much of what lies beyond their immediate lives."[11]

In the ideal environment, learning becomes a shared responsibility between teacher and student. Rather than serve as providers of information, teachers stimulate and coach students, ultimately holding them responsible for their own learning. Likewise, teaching becomes a sophisticated form of learning. In the process, young people acquire skills and attitudes—including a love of learning—that will sustain lifelong learning. We are not likely to inculcate such attitudes unless students are involved in projects, simulations, role playing, demonstrations, internships, and other hands-on activities.

Citizenship. What employers desire—and our economy needs—are people who bring to the workplace a strong work ethic, characterized by dependability and perseverance. We also call for civilized and virtuous behavior. In fact, the literature from employers on school-to-work preparation increasingly stresses the importance of personal characteristics in the workplace. Behaviors that employers expect of their employees including being at work each day, on time; accepting responsibility for one's own actions and decisions; demonstrating understanding, friendliness, adaptability, and concern for others; working with minimal supervision; displaying integrity and honesty; and showing a willingness to take risks and to learn new things.[12]

In a recent survey of human resource executives in the Minneapolis-St. Paul area, conducted by Northwestern Mutual Life Insurance Company, respondents cited shortcomings in personal characteristics as the greatest deficiency that recent high school graduates bring to the workplace. New workers, they said, tend to be undependable; they lack commitment, a strong work ethic, experience in the business world, and a good attitude. In addition, cooperative behavior and teamwork are becoming increasingly important in the workplace. Business knows that students need more than knowledge and skills to contribute substantially in the workplace. They must also exhibit civility.

Alongside the intellectual skills espoused by business, most employers believe that interpersonal skills are essential for workers. Again, if the BellSouth Corporation represents the sentiments of other employers, they would have schools prepare young people to understand the needs of others (customers), to participate cooperatively as team members, to perform at high levels, to negotiate agreements and mediate differences, and to work with others from diverse cultural backgrounds.[13] Needless to say, these specifications from employers reinforce the efforts many schools are making to implement such strategies as cooperative learning; the use of projects, demonstrations, and simulations; and authentic assessments.

The Sandia researchers corroborated these views in their study of skill requirements for the work force. They found from investigations by the Commission on the Skills of the American Workforce that only 5% of employers feel that education and skill requirements are increasing significantly. Likewise, only 15% of the employers surveyed said that they had difficulty finding skilled workers, and such shortages generally occur in chronically underpaid occupations. Finally, when businesses complain about workers' "skills," they are generally referring to lack of a work ethic and poor social skills.[14]

Ours is a political economy in which civic virtues, economic behavior, and government policy are intertwined. A recent National Youth Survey conducted by the Gallup Organization for Junior Achievement revealed that young people have little confidence in most U.S. institutions. While secondary school students indicated modest confidence in religious institutions and public schools, they appeared soundly disenchanted with big business, the media, and the federal government.[15] No doubt, their views reflect those of the general public. As Robert Bellah and his associates explain, "Individualistic Americans fear that institutions impinge on their freedom.... Yet, if this is our only conception of institutions, we have a very impoverished idea of our common life."[16]

Artisanship. Producing high-quality goods and services requires that everyone take immense pride in being a craftsperson or artisan, regardless of one's trade or profession. Artisanship, both in school and on the job, taps a person's gifts and talents, reveals what one is very good at, commands deep involvement in and respect for work, and gives one's work meaning. With opportunities to do high-quality work, learning and working become inseparable.

Craftsmanship was the basis of the tech schools that every major U.S. city established in the early 1990s. The emphasis these schools placed on "learning by doing" paralleled the practices of such educational organizations as Junior Achievement, which initiated its Company Program in 1919. Through study and work, students in these schools and programs practiced a craft and learned much about themselves.

Within the past two decades Junior Achievement has been at the vanguard of developing K–12 school programs that involve students in hands-on learning.

When Vince Lombardi, the legendary football coach, was asked what distinguished his Green Bay Packers from other teams, he replied, "Love." His players, he elaborated, had a deep love for one another and for their craft. As Coach Lombardi explained, the Packers never lost a game, they just ran out of time on a few occasions, and they always performed to the best of their ability.

Not surprisingly, young people today do not appear to be learning that the route to fulfillment and happiness is paved with moderation and meaningful work. Instead, distracted by the abundance pervasively displayed in society, they place importance on acquiring material goods and prestige. The Junior Achievement-Gallup youth survey revealed that most young people expect to have a professional or managerial career; fewer than 10% say that their chosen vocation will be in the services or skilled crafts. Virtually all those surveyed (99%) expect to be "as well off" as or "better off" than their parents. The other 1% "don't know." Likewise, young people view higher education as the key to professional and financial rewards—82% plan to enter a college or university. Only small numbers of those surveyed desire to enter work training (4%), seek a job immediately (6%), or enter the armed forces (4%). In reality, closer to 50% of U.S. high school graduates will attend college, with approximately one-half of those students eventually receiving a bachelor's degree.[17]

From another perspective, this optimism and naiveté suggest that young people are crying out to be prepared for what many of them view as a mysterious world of work. Increasingly over the past generation, this work has taken place in large private and governmental organizations operating within the steel-and-glass towers of the urban skylines.

As school programs and curricula incorporate characteristics of this scholarship/citizenship/artisanship triad, we have the opportunity to demystify the modern corporate environment. In turn, the school would come to look and feel much like a creative, productive, humming, and learning workplace. Likewise, a healthy workplace can look much like a school—a good school. In short, this is a schoolplace-to-workplace model in which students develop not only worthy habits of mind and of hand but also habits of the heart.

Implications for School-to-Work Programs

The pedagogical ideas underlying the "School-to-Work: Learning a Living" model and embodied in the scholarship/citizenship/artisanship triad can lead to a variety of program components suitable for the sciences, technology, English and communication, the humanities, and other curricula. Here are six components or units that might be integrated into a high school program designed to help students understand the political/economic system of the U.S. and the world of business:

- studying the history of the political and economic thought of democratic capitalism,
- exploring democratic and ethical behavior in business by interviewing corporate CEOs,
- evaluating personal characteristics and career opportunities,
- looking at economic trends and policy making,
- examining philosophical issues related to politics and the economy, and
- acquiring firsthand knowledge of businesses through internships and mentorships.

History of political and economic thought. One unit of study in a high school program would survey ideas from political economists and intellectual statespeople who helped shape our democratic capitalist system. The roots of democratic capitalism might be traced to ancient Greece and the works of Plato and Aristotle. From there the story could move to the Middle Ages—specifically, to the 12th and 13th centuries—to tell the role that Christianity played in political and economic thought, largely through the intellectual work of St. Thomas Aquinas.

The historical trail of our democratic capitalist heritage would highlight the contributions of such "worldly philosophers" as Thomas Jefferson and Adam Smith, while illustrating the enlightened views of Robert Owen and John Stuart Mill regarding a moral economy and workplace. It could also contrast the practices of the democratic capitalist James J. Hill with those of the mercantilist Jay Gould. This path could extend to contemporary thinkers, including Milton Friedman and John Kenneth Galbraith. This historical unit would be designed to reveal fundamental principles that have come to define the U.S. economy today. In addition it would provide a valuable background to the issues that the students will consider in the program's philosophical unit.

Democratic and ethical behavior. High school students being prepared for the working world would conduct interviews with current and retired CEOs of major corporations. These business leaders would be selected because of their trailblazing efforts to promote economic democracy in their firms or to set standards of ethical behavior, or both. Among the questions that might be explored during these interviews would be the following:

- Does ethical behavior enhance or erode profits, and why?
- In what ways can modern companies give workers a stronger voice in management practices and workplace policies?
- Does a firm need a mission statement that addresses democratic and ethical responsibility?
- How can employees and employers continue to learn on the job?
- In what ways does this personal growth help the company, if it does?
- What is the proper relationship between a firm and the community?

Personal characteristics and career opportunities. Students would take part in a variety of classroom activities designed to help them understand their personal learning styles, gifts, talents, and vocational strengths. Some activities would be conducted individually, but many would involve working together and sharing insights with classmates. The aim of these experiences would be to help students find their authentic selves and discover what intrinsically motivates them to display vigor in work and play. In addition, this component would help students understand the cultural forces that encourage them to be consumption-oriented, outer-directed, and distracted from engaging in that which is good for self and society.

Social and economic trend data. In this component, students would work with economic, social, and demographic data that reveal national and global trends. These analyses could help students perceive the nature of the emerging local, regional, national, and global society they are inheriting. Likewise, the data would help them have as clear a view as possible into the living, learning, and working places that lie ahead in the coming century. Students would learn how these data can be used to make personal decisions and public policy. In the process, they would examine such questions as, How should U.S. population trends be used to devise policies on immigration, economic development, workplace diversity, government spending, and taxation? And what relationship exists between national and international trends and personal decisions about careers, location of work, and living?

Philosophical issues. Informed and responsible citizens must be capable of addressing fundamental questions if we are to maintain a healthy democratic capitalist system. The following questions are examples of topics that could be discussed.

- What is the proper relationship between one's private (economic) life and one's public (civic) life?
- What is the relationship between socioeconomic status and forms of government?
- What is the relationship between the health of institutions and the well-being of citizens?
- What is the importance of embracing inclusiveness and abandoning separateness in our organizations, communities, and nation?
- What degree of responsibility does the individual have for the community, and what degree of responsibility does the community have for the individual?

Business internships and mentorships. The indifference many young people today display toward business, politics, and various economic values that older generations tend to cherish probably stems from both bewilderment and a moral inner voice. Young people seem to have acquired a conscientiousness, compassion, creativity, and idealism—fostered by a musical and visual subculture—that their elders don't appreciate. In turn, the world of large organizations and institutions that adults understand and in which they feel comfortable appears abstract to young people.

Providing internships and matching students with mentors can intimately engage young people in the modern workplace and help clarify this mysterious world for them. In addition, being deeply involved in the workplace helps young people identify their genuine vocational talents and desires and prepares them for productive and rewarding careers.

In his extensive research into human learning, Harvard psychologist Howard Gardner has demonstrated how ill-suited traditional school materials and practices are to our natural ways of learning. By the time children enter school at age 5, Gardner maintains, they have developed theories that help them make sense of their social and physical worlds. However, "these understandings are often immature, misleading, or fundamentally misconceived." The learning that takes place in schools, including colleges, does little to divest students of the misconceptions they possess about science, of their mechanical approach to mathematics, of the problems they have with economics, and of the stereotypes and simplifications they carry about history, literature, and the arts. Until we become "disciplinary experts" (or skilled persons), a stage of knowing that for many applies only to their vocation and is reached well after their school years, we do not have an accurate understanding of the world.[18]

In contrast to the accepted approach to education, Gardner submits that the best path to genuine understanding for young children is through children's museums. For older children, it is through apprenticeships. We would add that the various curriculum applications described here—including internships, mentorships, and apprenticeships—can lead to deeper and more meaningful understanding of the disciplines.

Finally, Mortimer Adler reminds us that "all genuine learning is active, not passive. It involves the use of the mind, not just memory. It is the process of discovery, in which the student is the main agent, not the teacher."[19] Adler took care to clarify what is meant by active learning, while reminding us of a lesson that John Dewey had imparted. In so doing, he also described how learners acquire expertise, craftsmanship, and artisanship.

> What John Dewey had in mind was not exclusively physical doing or even social doing—engagement in practical projects of one kind or another. The most important kind of doing, as far as learning is concerned, is intellectual or mental doing. In other words, one can learn to read or write well only by reading and writing.... To learn how to do any of these things well, one must not only engage in doing them, but one must be guided in doing them by someone more expert in doing them than oneself.[20]

Likewise, individuals embark on the path toward learning (a living) by embracing active scholarship, citizenship, and artisanship—all three together. We cannot distinguish where one characteristic ends and another begins. Dewey might well agree that this approach would be the best preparation for living and, because of it, the best preparation for the world of employment.

1. Thomas Jefferson, "Letters to William Charles Jarvis," in Paul L. Ford, ed., *The Writings of Thomas Jefferson* (New York: Putnam's, 1892–99), vol. 10, p. 161.
2. Edward R. Murrow, Foreword to Hyman G. Rickover, *Education and Freedom* (New York: Dutton, 1959), pp. 5–7.
3. National Commission on Excellence in Education, *A Nation at Risk: The Imperative for Educational Reform* (Washington, D.C.: U.S. Department of Education, 1983).
4. Adam Smith, *Theory of Moral Sentiments* (1759; reprint, New York: A. M. Kelley, 1966).
5. National Commission on Excellence in Education, p. 7.
6. Willard R. Daggett, "Everything New Looks Old Again," *Vocational Education Journal*, September 1994, p. 26.
7. C. C. Carson, R. M. Huelskamp, and T. D. Woodall, "Perspectives on Education in America: An Annotated Briefing," *Journal of Educational Research*, May/June 1993, pp. 293–94.
8. *Hook-up: Job Skills for the Information Age* (a booklet produced by BellSouth in cooperation with the U.S. Department of Education, Southern Regional Education Board, and Georgia Department of Education), p. 3. Copies of *Hook-up* can be obtained free of charge by phoning 800/631–1586.
9. Ernest L. Boyer, *High School: A Report on Secondary Education in America* (New York: Harper & Row, 1983), p. 57.
10. *Hook-up*, p. 3.
11. Theodore R. Sizer, *Horace's School: Redesigning the American High School* (Boston: Houghton Mifflin, 1992), p. 1.
12. *Hook-up*, p. 12.
13. Ibid., p. 3.
14. Carson, Huelskamp, and Woodall, p. 294.
15. Richard Van Scotter, "What Young People Think About School and Society," *Educational Leadership*, November 1994, pp. 72–73.
16. Robert N. Bellah et al., *The Good Society* (New York: Alfred A. Knopf, 1991), p. 10.
17. Van Scotter, p. 75.
18. Howard Gardner, *The Unschooled Mind: How Children Think and How Schools Should Teach* (New York: Basic Books, 1991), pp. 6–11.
19. Mortimer Adler, *The Paideia Proposal: An Educational Manifesto* (New York: Macmillan, 1982), p. 50.
20. Ibid., p. 52.

Index

A

ABLEDATA, 101
Adler, Mortimer, 224
adult-child interactions, 115
agitation, behavior management and reducing, 136-136
aide services, 20
Alternate Portfolio, peer tutoring and, 163-164, 166
American Sign Language (ASL), 150-151, 153
Americans with Disabilities Act, 164, 170
anhedonia, 120
appetite fluctuation, in students who may be depressed, 120
art, and children with limited motor abilities, 177-178
assessment: active, 20; performance-based, 20
assistive technology devices, 100-101
attention deficit disorder (ADD), 9, 57, 63-64, 67-68, 188
autism, 107, 132

B

Baratta-Lorton, Mary, 147
baseline forms. *See* autism
behavior, targeted by self-regulation, 127
behavioral analysis and interventions, 107
blind or visually disabled, 140, 142
block scheduling, 162
"Bobby," 185
body composition. *See* Wellness Programming
books, adapting classrooms for children with limited motor abilities and, 178
Braille reading, 141
brain injuries, 117

C

cardiorespiratory endurance. *See* Wellness Programming
camcorder. *See* videotaped self-modeling
chromosomal disorder, 112
circle time, adapting for children with limited motor abilities and, 177
citizenship, role of educational system and, 222, 223
classroom transition skills, 131
classroom-based training, 159-160
cluster grouping, of gifted/talented students, 201
Cognitive Credit Card (CCC), 76-80; benefits of, 76; facilitating the completion of long-division questions, 78; history of, 79
collaboration at school, 146; home and, 147; planning and, 106; programmatic barriers and, 108; teaching methods and, 107
collages, 178

community-based instruction (CBI), 165-166
comprehensive inclusion, of special needs students in middle schools, 208-215
comprehensive services for children with disabilities, 38
computer technology: adapting for children with limited motor abilities and, 179-180; Web site design and, 184-189
consultation, 20
contact paper collages, 178
cooperative learning, inclusion and, 19, 21
Cornett, Orin, 144
co-teaching, 20-21
Council for Exceptional Children, 106
counseling services, 31
cued monitoring. *See* self-regulation
cued speech, 143-144
cultural appropriateness, developmentally appropriate practice and, 37
cultural diversity, listening to parents of children with disabilities by teachers and, 181-182
culturally and linguistically diverse (CLD) students, distinguishing language disorders in, 88-91

D

Danville, Kentucky, High School (DHS), peer tutoring at, 162-167
deaf children, multimedia stories for, 149-153
DEAR (Drop Everything and Read) program, 145, 147
delayed facial expressions, shown in infants with Down Syndrome, 114
depression, signs of, 120-123
depressive disorders, 120-122
desensitization process, 119
"Design for an In-Depth Integrated Unit," 194-195
developmentally appropriate practices, 36-50
Dewey, John, 224
"diagnostic pie," 88-89, 91
differentiated curriculum, 203
diffusion, of confrontations, and behavior management, 134-137
direct training. *See* Teaching-Skills Training Program
Division of Innovation and Development of the Office of Special Education Programs (OSEP), 171
Down, John Langdon, 112
Down Syndrome (DS), 9, 52, 112, 114-116; congenital condition of, 112; hypotonia or low muscle tone in, 113; Trisomy 21 form of, 112
dramatic play, adapting for children with limited motor abilities, 179

E

early intervention, and hypotonia, 113
early intervention program, 82
early literacy programs, 83-84
economic thought, teaching of, 223-224
Edinburgh Longitudinal Study of Early Learning in Infants and Young Children, 113
Education for All Handicapped Children Act, 140
education reform movement, 202
educational interpreters, distinguishing language differences from language disorders and, 90
educational reform, suggestions of gifted/talented students for, 198-201
Educational Resources Information Center (ERIC), 171
electronic communication device, 100
Elementary and Secondary Education Act, 57
emotional disorders. *See* learning disabilities
Exceptional Child Education Resources (ECER), 171
exceptional children competitions, 216-219
"expert syndrome," 182

F

facilitator, of communication, 143
field trips, 200
fine motor activities, adapting classrooms for children with limited motor abilities and, 178-179
flexibility. *See* Wellness Programming
focal brain damage. *See* learning disabilities
forms, accessible Web site design and, 187
frames, accessible Web site design and, 187-188
funnel painting, 178

G

Gardner, Howard, 224
Gardner, John, 220
gifted students, 202-205; and educational reform, 198-201
girls, learning disabilities and, 62
Glaser, Robert, 168
glue activities, 178
Governor's Scholars Program (GSP), in Kentucky, 201
graduation rates, dropout rates of students with LD, 81; students with learning disabilities and, 81
grammar, language development and, 95
graphics, accessible Web site design and, 186
graphing, self-recording data, 128

grief counseling, and reaching out to students after traumatic events, 31–32
gym, adapting for children with limited motor abilities and, 179

H

hands-on learning: educational reform and, 200–201; children's skills developed by, 193; hearing-impaired children, inclusion and, 42, 143–148; multimedia stories for, 149–153
helping component, 24
high school heroes, 28
High School-Taught Elementary Program (Hi-Step), 28

I

identification rates, 61
image maps, accessible Web site design and, 187
Impact Improv, 26–28, 30–32
impact program, 23–25
inclusion, 8–10, 22, 34, 41, 43, 106, 108, 147, 181, 208–210, 214; benefits and challenges of, 20; comprehensive, of special needs students in middle schools, 208–215; guidelines for teaching and, 16–18; for models of, 19–22; steps for moving from philosophy to practice in, 36–50; students with different types of disabilities and, 41–43
individual appropriateness, developmentally appropriate practices and, 37
Individualized Education Plan (IEP), 19, 22, 100–102, 106–109, 118, 132, 141, 168–169, 172, 183; collaborative planning and, 106, 108–110
Individuals with Disabilities Education Act (IDEA), 8–10, 12, 36, 57, 67, 106, 121, 132, 162, 170
innovative peer tutoring program, 162–166, 211, 214
instructional technology, 169
integrated-thematic curriculum, 194, 196
intelligence quotient (IQ), 59, 63–64, 93, 118; scores, 117
interaction, between children with Down Syndrome and their mothers, 114
Interagency Committee on Learning Disabilities (ICLD), 63
internships, 224
interpreters. See educational interpreters
interval observation. See self-regulation

J

"joint attention," 115

K

Kentucky Education Reform Act of 1990 (KERA), 163
Kentucky's mandatory assessment and accountability system, 163, 167
keyboards, adapting classrooms for children with limited motor abilities and, 180

L

language, definition of, 88–89
language development, techniques for stimulating, in at-risk children, 92–99
language differences, distinguishing language disorders from, in linguistically and culturally diverse classrooms, 88–91
language games, language development and, 94
language interaction techniques, for stimulating language development in at-risk children, 92–99
language-learning disability, 91
LCD students. See linguistically and culturally diverse students
learning disabilities, 56–61, 63–64, 67–71, 81, 117; attention deficit disorder and, 63–66; defining, 56–58; defusing confrontations and, 134–137; discrepancy standard for, 56–57, 59, 64; interventions for, 69–70; outcomes for, 71–72; prevalence of, 58–59, 61–63; research on, 63–67
learning environment, affected by Down Syndrome children with lower expectations of, 112
learning strategy deficits, conditions to recognize by, 77
least restrictive environment (LRE), 8–10, 19
limited instructional time, 130
limited motor ability, adapting classrooms and, 176–180, 188
limited pullout services, 21–22
linguistically and culturally diverse (LCD) students, 88–89; distinguishing language differences from language disorders among, 88–91
links, accessible Web site design and, 186
Listening In (Newkirk), 146
literacy and dropout prevention, 83
literacy portfolios, 152
low performance, and Down Syndrome children with low expectations, 112

M

Magic School Bus books, the, 194
mathematics, learning disabilities in, 69
mental health community, 122
mental retardation, 100, 113, 117, 120–122, 168
mentorships, 224
Mexican-American deaf children, multimedia stories and, 149–153
mild mental retardation, 122
multimedia stories, for deaf children, 149–153
multimedia technology, 149–153
Muppet Learning Keys, 180
muscular fitness. See Wellness Programming

N

Nation at Risk, A, 22
National Association for the Education of Young Children (NAEYC), 36–37, 39, 177; developmentally appropriate practice and, 36–37, 39–40
National Commission on Excellence in Education, 22
National Institute of Child Health and Human Development (NICHD), 63–66
neurological damage, 117
neuropsychological evaluations, 118
Newkirk, Thomas, 146
North Kansas City High School (NKCHS), 23; guidelines for students to heal, 31–32

O

Oberti v. Board of Education of the Borough of Clementon School District, 9
"on-task" data, 127–128
open-ended curriculum, 198

P

paraeducators, 156, 158–159, 161
parent panel, 12–15; and approach to parental/educator collaboration, 12
parents, language development and, 96–97; of children with learning disabilities, 181–183
partial paralysis, 199
participation component, 24
peer mediators, 26
peer tutoring, 162–167, 214
Peers Always Listen (PAL), 28
performance-based assessment, 20
"phonic ear," 143
phonological awareness, 62, 66, 69–70, 84
physical fitness programs. See Wellness Programming
physical handicaps, and mild to profound levels of retardation, 117
physical transitions, 119
physically disabled, Web site design for, 188
play, language development and, 94–95

playground time, adapting for children with limited motor abilities and, 179
Postman, Neil, 220
PowerPad, 180
Practical and Academic Transitions to High School (PATHS), 29–30
prereferral interventions, behavior management plans and, 126
preschool program. See Teaching-Skills Training Program
Present Level of Performance (PLP), 108
problem-solving skills, 222
profound hearing loss, 143–144, 147
pronunciation, language development and, 95
psychoeducational methods of intervention, 113–114
psychological assessment, 121; disorders and, 120; services and, 122
psychological counseling, 121
Public Law 45–186, 170
Public Law 94–142, 19, 170, 208
Public Law 99–506, 170
Public Law 100–407, 171
Public Law 101–336, 170
Public Law 105–17, 12
pullout services, limitations and, 21–22

R

reading, learning disabilities and, 56–75
recall, language development and word, 97
recess, adapting for children with limited motor abilities and, 179
recognition, language development and word, 97
record player art, 178
reforms for education, 198–201
Rehabilitation Act of 1973, 170
reinforcement. See paraeducators
resegregation, inclusion and, 213–214
resources, for early literacy, 84
Rickover, Hyman, 220–221
role-play, language and social behavior and, 131

S

safe-school training program, 23
School-to-Work Opportunities Act of 1994, 221
School Resource Officer, 30–31
self-regulation: benefits and, 129; potential of, 129; steps for using, 127; techniques of, 126–128

sensory play, adapting classrooms for children with limited motor abilities and, 178
severe disabilities, 156, 158–159, 161–162, 167
sign language videos, 153
sleeping habits, and mentally retarded students, 120
sleeping patterns, 121
snack time, adapting for children with limited motor abilities and, 179
social skills deficits. See learning disabilities
special education, 100, 102, 100, 162, 166, 168, 170, 208, 213; expenses of, 142; itinerant teacher of, 142; schools and, 140–141; services of, 126; systems and, 117; teachers of, 134, 156
Special Olympics. See exceptional children competitions
staff training programs, 157
state's assessment system, 163
Student Aptitude Test (SAT), 94
student assistance program, 24
Students Against Destructive Decisions (SADD), 27–28
Students Against Violence Everywhere (SAVE), 24, 26, 29–30, 32
swing art, 178

T

tables, accessible Web site design and, 187
tachistoscopes, 168
teachers: and detecting inappropriate behavior of students, 121; guidelines for including students with disabilities and, 16–18; listening to parents and, 181–183; team teaching and, 16–17, 20–21
Teaching and Reaching Youth (TRY), 29
Teaching Exceptional Children (TEC) journal, 171
Teaching Research Early Childhood Program, 36, 39
teaching technology, 156
Teaching-Skills Training Program (TSTP), 156–161
team teaching, 20
technological devices, for children with disabilities, 102, 169
Technology and Media (TAM) Division, of CEC, 171
Technology-Related Assistance for Individuals with Disabilities Act, 171
Test of Standard Written English (TSWE), 94
therapy, types of, 122

toolbook software. See multimedia technology
touch-sensitive screens, for children with limited motor abilities, 180
Tourette's Syndrome, 9
toys, mobility training, 180; language development and, 94
training programs, 172
transition planning, 108
transitional program, 118
tutors. See peer tutoring

U

Unicorn Keyboard, 180

V

Very Special Arts. See exceptional children competitions
video files, accessible Web site design and, 186–187
videotaped self-modeling (VSM), 131–132; interventions and, 132; production of behavior changes due to exposure of, 130; technology needed for, 130; training purposes of, 132
visually disabled. See blind or visually disabled
visually-impaired students: inclusion of, 42; Web site design for accessibility and, 185–188

W

Web site design, factors in accessibility, 184–189
Web sites for visually disabled, 184–189; for self-regulating student behavior, 127
Web tutorials, 186
Wellness Programming in Early Childhood Education, 44–48
word recall: language development and, 97; recognition and language development and, 97
workforce, educational system and preparedness for, 220–221
World Wide Web. See multimedia technology
writing, work skills of, 220; learning disabilities and, 69

Z

zone of proximal development (ZPD), 113

AE Article Review Form

We encourage you to photocopy and use this page as a tool to assess how the articles in **Annual Editions** expand on the information in your textbook. By reflecting on the articles you will gain enhanced text information. You can also access this useful form on a product's book support Web site at **http://www.dushkin.com/online/**.

NAME: _____ DATE: _____

TITLE AND NUMBER OF ARTICLE:
_____

BRIEFLY STATE THE MAIN IDEA OF THIS ARTICLE:
_____

LIST THREE IMPORTANT FACTS THAT THE AUTHOR USES TO SUPPORT THE MAIN IDEA:

_____

WHAT INFORMATION OR IDEAS DISCUSSED IN THIS ARTICLE ARE ALSO DISCUSSED IN YOUR TEXTBOOK OR OTHER READINGS THAT YOU HAVE DONE? LIST THE TEXTBOOK CHAPTERS AND PAGE NUMBERS:

_____

LIST ANY EXAMPLES OF BIAS OR FAULTY REASONING THAT YOU FOUND IN THE ARTICLE:

_____

LIST ANY NEW TERMS/CONCEPTS THAT WERE DISCUSSED IN THE ARTICLE, AND WRITE A SHORT DEFINITION:

ANNUAL EDITIONS revisions depend on two major opinion sources: one is our Advisory Board, listed in the front of this volume, which works with us in scanning the thousands of articles published in the public press each year; the other is you—the person actually using the book. Please help us and the users of the next edition by completing the prepaid article rating form on this page and returning it to us. Thank you for your help!

ANNUAL EDITIONS: Educating Exceptional Children 00/01

ARTICLE RATING FORM

Here is an opportunity for you to have direct input into the next revision of this volume. We would like you to rate each of the 37 articles listed below, using the following scale:

1. **Excellent: should definitely be retained**
2. **Above average: should probably be retained**
3. **Below average: should probably be deleted**
4. **Poor: should definitely be deleted**

Your ratings will play a vital part in the next revision. So please mail this prepaid form to us just as soon as you complete it. Thanks for your help!

We Want Your Advice

RATING / **ARTICLE**

1. Inclusion of Children with Disabilities: Seeking the Appropriate Balance
2. The Parent Panel: Supporting Children with Special Needs
3. What Do I Do Now? A Teacher's Guide to Including Students with Disabilities
4. Four Inclusion Models That Work
5. Promoting a Safe School Environment through a Schoolwide Wellness Program
6. From Philosophy to Practice in Inclusive Early Childhood Programs
7. Together Is Better: Specific Tips on How to Include Children with Various Types of Disabilities
8. Wellness Programming for Preschoolers with Disabilities
9. Is Everyone Included? Using Children's Literature to Facilitate the Understanding of Disabilities
10. Learning Disabilities
11. Cognitive Credit Cards: Acquiring Learning Strategies
12. Dropout Prevention: A Case for Enhanced Early Literacy Efforts
13. Distinguishing Language Differences from Language Disorders in Linguistically and Culturally Diverse Students
14. Language Interaction Techniques for Stimulating the Development of At Risk Children in Infant and Preschool Day Care
15. Family and Cultural Alert! Considerations in Assistive Technology Assessment
16. Collaborative Planning for Inclusion of a Student with Developmental Disabilities
17. Children with Down Syndrome: Implications for Adult-Child Interactions in Inclusive Settings

RATING / **ARTICLE**

18. Getting the Student with Head Injuries Back in School: Strategies for the Classroom
19. Identifying Depression in Students with Mental Retardation
20. Teaching Students to Regulate Their Own Behavior
21. "Look! I'm on TV!" Using Videotaped Self-Modeling to Change Behavior
22. How to Defuse Defiance, Threats, Challenges, Confrontations . . .
23. Schools for the Visually Disabled: Dinosaurs or Mainstays?
24. A Child with Severe Hearing Loss Joins Our Learning Community
25. Multimedia Stories for Deaf Children
26. Training Basic Teaching Skills to Paraeducators of Students with Severe Disabilities
27. The Unexpected Benefits of High School Peer Tutoring
28. Perspectives on Technology in Special Education
29. "Can I Play Too?" Adapting Common Classroom Activities for Young Children with Limited Motor Abilities
30. Listening to Parents of Children with Disabilities
31. Accessible Web Site Design
32. Meeting the Needs of Gifted Learners in the Early Childhood Classroom
33. Gifted Students Suggest Reforms for Education: Listening to Gifted Students' Ideas
34. Accountability for Gifted Students
35. Making Comprehensive Inclusion of Special Needs Students Work in a Middle School
36. Competitions and Exceptional Children: A Great Combination
37. School-to-Work: A Model for Learning a Living

(Continued on next page)

ST. JOSEPH'S COLLEGE CALLAHAN LIBRARY

3 1960 01500 85

ITIONS: EDUCATING EXCEPTIONAL CHILDREN 00/01

BUSINESS REPLY MAIL
FIRST-CLASS MAIL PERMIT NO. 84 GUILFORD CT

POSTAGE WILL BE PAID BY ADDRESSEE

Dushkin/McGraw-Hill
Sluice Dock
Guilford, CT 06437-9989

NO POSTAGE
NECESSARY
IF MAILED
IN THE
UNITED STATES

```
LC 4031 .E385

Annual Editions
Educating Exceptional
Children 00/01
```

ABOUT YOU

Name   Date

Are you a teacher? ☐   A student? ☐
Your school's name

Department

Address   City   State   Zip

School telephone #

YOUR COMMENTS ARE IMPORTANT TO US!

Please fill in the following information:
For which course did you use this book?

Did you use a text with this *ANNUAL EDITION*? ☐ yes ☐ no
What was the title of the text?

What are your general reactions to the *Annual Editions* concept?

Have you read any particular articles recently that you think should be included in the next edition?

Are there any articles you feel should be replaced in the next edition? Why?

Are there any World Wide Web sites you feel should be included in the next edition? Please annotate.

May we contact you for editorial input? ☐ yes ☐ no
May we quote your comments? ☐ yes ☐ no